APPAREL QUALITY

A GUIDE TO EVALUATING SEWN PRODUCTS

D0932722

FAIRCHILD BOOKS

APPAREL QUALITY

A GUIDE TO EVALUATING SEWN PRODUCTS

JANACE E. BUBONIA, PH.D.
TEXAS CHRISTIAN UNIVERSITY

FAIRCHILD BOOKS
An imprint of Bloomsbury Publishing Inc.

Fairchild Books
An imprint of Bloomsbury Publishing Inc.

1385 Broadway   50 Bedford Square
New York   London
NY 10018   WC1B 3DP
USA   UK

www.bloomsbury.com

Library of Congress Cataloging-in-Publication Data
Bubonia, Janace E.
Apparel quality : a guide to evaluating sewn products / Janace E. Bubonia.
pages cm

Summary: "This user-friendly guide to evaluating apparel quality presents the roles of product designers, manufacturers, merchandisers, testing laboratories, and retailers from product inception through the sale of goods, to ensure quality products that meet customer expectations. Bubonia provides an overview of apparel production, with emphasis on quality characteristics and cues, consumer influences and motivations impacting purchasing decisions, and the relationship of apparel manufacturing and production processes, cost, price point and the quality level of an apparel product. A key aspect of the book is the focus on both U.S. and international standards and regulations required for apparel analysis, performance, labeling requirements and safety regulations. Heavily illustrated with images of stitch and seam types plus photos of their uses in actual garments, students will have the tools needed to skillfully evaluate and critique quality elements in apparel and textile products"— Provided by publisher.

ISBN 978-1-60901-512-1 (paperback)

1. Clothing trade—Quality control. 2. Textile fabrics—Quality control. 3. Clothing and dress. I. Title.
TT497.B83 2014
338.4'7687—dc23
2014000212

Typeset by Precision Graphic Services, Inc.
Text design by Alicia Freile, Tango Media
Cover Design by Eleanor Rose
Cover Art Credit © Trunk Archive
Technical Illustrations by Q2A Media Services Private Limited
Printed and bound in China

CONTENTS

EXTENDED CONTENTS

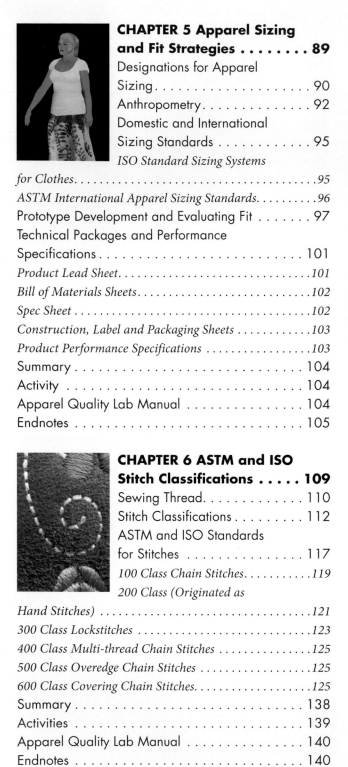

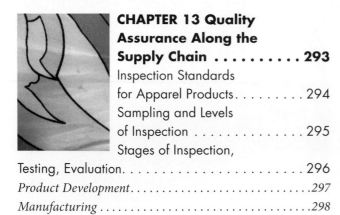

LIST OF INDUSTRY SCENARIOS

LIST OF TABLES

PREFACE

Apparel Quality: A Guide to Evaluating Sewn Products offers a comprehensive approach to assessing quality. This book includes methods for integrating quality into the design and development stages of apparel products, including considerations for materials selection, assembly and finishing, as well as methods for evaluating finished sewn products. This text was written to provide students, educators, and young professionals with a user-friendly resource that offers an international perspective on apparel quality. It is appropriate for intermediate-level students in courses that cover the assessment and evaluation of apparel quality, such as Apparel Analysis and Apparel Evaluation. It is appropriate for classes composed solely of lectures, that contain a lab component that focuses on the visual analysis of actual garments, or provide a testing-lab environment for materials and garments to be both visually analyzed and tested using industry standards. This book is meant to provide a comprehensive approach to quality that allows course instructors to tailor the scope of quality analysis that is appropriate for the course they teach.

Key Features

Engages students in critical thinking through the evaluation of apparel products in terms of industry procedures, standards, and expectations.

- Discusses current domestic and international sizing standards and classification systems, including ASTM and ISO.
- Includes robust international labeling information for the United States, Canada, EU, and Japan.

Emphasizes product value for the consumer through the relationship between price point and quality of materials, construction techniques, performance attributes, and functionality for the intended end use.

- Coverage and images of fabric and garment construction details such as darts and seams, gathers, pleats and tucks, closures, hem finishes, and more.
- Follows the production cycle and provides an overview of the organization structure of the global apparel industry

Enhances student learning with effective pedagogical tools and engaging visuals.

- Chapter objectives, key terms, and summaries to guide readers through chapters.
- Hands-on activities integrated into each chapter to help reinforce the concepts discussed and engage critical thinking skills.
- Industry Scenarios woven throughout the book to challenge the reader with case studies replicating real world situations such as the Lululemon recall.
- Full-color book contains more than 450 photos and illustrations to visually demonstrate and strengthen the understanding of concepts covered in each chapter.
- Companion Student Lab Manual (sold separately) offers tested lab projects and activities.

Organization

Chapters are presented in a logical progression, from quality and the consumer, to raw materials selection, design development, manufacturing, labeling and safety regulations, visual assessment, testing and inspection, to the distribution of finished goods.

Chapter 1 provides a brief overview of apparel quality in relation to the consumer. Quality characteristics and cues are presented and the factors that contribute to consumer expectations and quality perceptions, both pre and post purchase are discussed. An introduction to the major global and national organizations developing standards for apparel products is provided to underscore the important roles they play to help promote and facilitate fair trade, and to specify methods for safe and efficient development, manufacturing, and distribution of apparel products in today's global market.

In Chapter 2, the basic design elements and principles are presented, and images are used to reinforce the understanding of how they are integrated into the design development of apparel products to create aesthetically pleasing garments and to shape and enhance fit. This chapter also allows students to gain an understanding of how color is communicated and managed, from initial selection through to the end product.

Chapter 3 provides a review of raw materials, from fibers, yarns, fabric construction, colorants, and finishes, to trims and surface embellishments, to support materials and shaping devices used to create the overall aesthetic appeal, function, and fit of an apparel item. This chapter is intended to review the information covered in basic textiles courses. Students will be introduced to performance attributes, the importance of compatibility of materials selection, and how these factors can impact the quality of the finished sewn product. An industry scenario 3.1 School uniform product development is provided to engage the reader's critical thinking skills with a real world situation.

Chapter 4 focuses on garment shaping and construction methods for achieving fit. Visual examples are provided throughout the chapter to assist the reader in making the visual connection regarding the identification of specific shaping and assembly methods. Factors that contribute to the quality, function, and design are emphasized in relation to the ease of physically putting a garment on the body and taking it off.

Chapter 5 provides an overview of apparel sizing, prototype development, and ways for evaluating fit of apparel products. Apparel size designations are defined as well as the variances found within a size across brands in the marketplace. Vanity and manity sizing are both discussed in relation to the confusion they cause consumers when selecting garments to fit their body. International and national size studies used for gathering anthropometric data are also highlighted in relation to size standards.

Chapter 6 focuses on stitching used for apparel product assembly. Thread construction and sizing are discussed to provide an understanding for selection in regard to performance, fabrication, and end product use. Both ASTM and ISO standards for stitch classifications are featured. Illustrations and photographs of over 20 of the most commonly used stitches found in garments (showing both the face and back views) are included to reinforce the understanding and aid in visual recognition and identification of the standards accepted and utilized throughout the world. Images of sewing equipment are also featured to provide the reader with an understanding of the variety of sewing equipment used for apparel construction to form the stitches within each category.

Chapter 7 provides an overview of seams and the importance of selection and application within apparel products. Both ASTM and ISO seam classifications are discussed to provide the reader with an international perspective of the standards accepted and used around the world. Illustrations and photographs of over 30 of the most commonly selected ASTM and ISO seams are featured (showing both the face and back views) to help students identify seam designations and common locations for application within apparel products. ASTM and ISO seam designations are categorized differently, unlike the stitch classes. In an effort to help the reader make the connection between the seam types across classifications within each of these standards, each commonly used

ISO seam is cross referenced with ASTM. In addition, this chapter features stitchless seam technologies and the common methods for application and equipment used.

In Chapter 8, sourcing of factories for mass-produced apparel products is discussed in relation to quality. Apparel production processed and assembly operations and productions systems provide students with an understanding of how goods are prepared, assembled, and finished in a manufacturing facility. An industry scenario 8.1 Sustainability and environmental impact of manufacturing apparel is provided to challenge the reader knowledge with a real world situation.

Labeling and safety regulations for the major consumer markets are discussed in Chapters 9 and 10. Because products are manufactured and shipped for sale in countries around the world, it is important for students to be introduced to the regulations requiring compliance in order for products to legally enter into commerce. These chapters cover both the compulsory and voluntary regulations for manufacturing apparel products. These chapters introduce the reader to the regulations and nuances for the major consumer markets in an effort to provide a global perspective. Three industry scenarios 9.1 Disclosure of country of origin on luxury coats, 9.2 Fiber content labeling for fur trimmed parkas, and 10.1 Flammability recall of children's sleepwear provide a means for the reader to assimilate the knowledge gained in real-world situations.

Chapters 11 and 12 focus on testing of materials and sewn products as a means for analyzing material characteristics, appearance, and performance. Methods of refurbishment are discussed to provide students with a basic understanding of cleaning methods and the substances used for soil and stain removal. Two industry scenarios 11.1 Active wear customer complaints, and 12.1 Dress damaged when drycleaned are used in these chapters to reinforce concepts and engage the reader with real-world situations. In an effort to provide a comprehensive approach to the evaluation of apparel product quality, a discussion of testing as a means of assessment is included. During my career as a lab technician and later as an evaluator in the children's division of JC Penney's Research and Technology Laboratory, it is my belief that quality of sewn products cannot solely be assessed through visual inspection. There must be some level of discussion about testing and the role it plays in the development and verification of quality and compliance with industry standards.

Lastly, in Chapter 13, inspection of apparel products is discussed across the stages of product development, manufacturing, and retail. The types of defects found during inspection, inclusive of material and garment defects, that can arise during piece goods production, cutting, fusing, assembly, and finishing are all discussed in this chapter. Images of over 40 defects are included to help students better understand and visually identify common flaws found in sewn apparel products. All defects are located within this chapter for ease of reference and because they are part of the inspection processes that occur during development through point of sale. Defects will be cross-referenced from other chapters. A real-world Industry Scenario 13.1 Radioactive belts recalled is also provided to challenge the reader's critical thinking skills.

The book also provides an extensive glossary as well as an appendix with a chart for converting U.S. customary units to metric units.

Student Lab Manual

Designed for courses that emphasize textile testing and offer a laboratory component, the Apparel Quality Lab Manual (978-1-62892-457-2, sold separately) is broken into ten chapters that include: Overview of Laboratory Testing and Safety; Utilizing Standard Specifications to Evaluate Results from Appearance and Performance Testing; Measuring Garments to Determine Variance between Brand Sizing and Sizing Standards; and Inspection of Raw Materials and Sewn

Products. Each project included in the manual offers instructions for the lab activities and worksheets on which students can log their results.

Instructor's Resources

■ The Instructor's Guide includes sample syllabi, in-class activities, project sheets, and test bank for quizzes and exams with answer keys. The Guide also corresponds to the student's lab manual and includes assignments for testing and evaluating materials and garments, project sheets for comparison, sample worksheets showing how data should be recorded, sample forms showing how specimens should be mounted after testing, and templates for cutting specimens.

■ The PowerPoint presentation provides a basis for lecture and discussion, and reproduces over 485 images from the text.

ACKNOWLEDGEMENTS

I would like to convey my sincere appreciation to everyone who helped make this book a reality. Thank you to everyone at Fairchild Books for your tireless hours and support, including: Priscilla McGeehon, Publisher; Amanda Breccia, Acquisitions Editor; Amy Butler, Development Editor; Edie Weinberg, Art Development Editor; Ken Cavanagh, Photo Researcher; and Charlotte Frost, Production Editor.

Thank you to the following reviewers, selected by Fairchild Books, for your valuable comments: Ronald M. "Reece" Allen, Ph.D., East Carolina University; Bruce A. Cameron, Ph.D., University of Wyoming; Joyce Chan, The Hong Kong Polytechnic University; Maureen Cohen, Johnson & Wales University; Tricia Edwards, Fashion Institute of Design and Merchandising; Ermine Ercan, Ph.D., Buffalo State College (State University of New York); Tatyana Grant, University of North Texas; Rebecca Greer, Stephen F. Austin State University; Jan Haynes, Delta State University; Diane Morton Limbaugh, Oklahoma State University; Evelyn Pappas, Savannah College of Art and Design; Erin D. Parrish, Ph.D., East Carolina University; Elisabeth Reed, Illinois State University; Diana Saiki, Ph.D., Ball State University; KallieRae Sebwe, The Art Institutes International Minnesota; Natalie Swindell, The Art Institute of Indianapolis; Louise Wallace, Fashion Institute of Design and Merchandising.

To companies, industry professionals, institutions, and organizations, thank you for your willingness to provide images to reinforce the understanding of apparel quality concepts, materials, equipment, and the various aspects that go into developing quality sewn products for today's global market.

To the Dean of the College of Fine Arts and the faculty and staff in the Department of Interior Design and Merchandising, thank you for your encouragement and support during the preparation of this book.

Last but certainly not least, thank you to my loved ones and close friends for your inspiring words, unwavering support, patience, and endless encouragement during the development of this book.

APPAREL QUALITY LAB MANUAL

Apparel Quality Lab Manual is a companion resource to compliment *Apparel Quality: A Guide to Evaluating Sewn Products,* by providing hands-on projects and activities that enhance learning and engage student's critical thinking skills, through simulating methods used for analyzing quality in today's fashion industry. There are lab components that correspond with every chapter, except Chapter 8 Sourcing and Mass Production of Sewn Products. The activities found at the end of this chapter adequately reinforce the concepts presented in the text. *Apparel Quality Lab Manual* identifies the main text chapter(s) that corresponds with the lab manual in the beginning of every chapter.

Activities and projects have been developed to reinforce the chapter contents and lecture material covered in this book, therefore allowing for greater understanding, and better recognition of quality issues that arise with apparel production and end use. Through these activities students will actively participate in determining the quality level of apparel products and gain a better understanding of the causes for product failure and customer dissatisfaction. They will also learn how product development and manufacturing decisions influence the quality of end products.

The *Apparel Quality Lab* manual includes activities for analyzing products, testing and evaluating materials and garments, project sheets for product comparison testing, worksheets to record data, directions for mounting specimens after testing, templates for cutting specimens, and inspection forms for evaluating product defects. The lab manual is presented in a user-friendly format that is easy to read and understand. Perforated pages allow students to tear out completed worksheets.

It is important to note that not all programs have equipment for textile testing; therefore the manual includes both product analysis labs and visual inspection as well as testing activities to enhance learning to meet the needs of both types of classroom and laboratory environments. Some programs have testing labs complete with testing equipment while others do not. Therefore, based on the availability of equipment, instructors can determine which project components and lab activities their students will complete. The lab activities and projects are designed to meet the needs of courses focused on visual inspection as well as those that conduct physical testing. *Apparel Quality Lab Manual* can also be utilized as a standalone resource to supplement a course with hands-on relevant activities.

Lab Activity 8.1: GARMENT SAFETY REGULATIONS AND COMPLIANCE

Evaluate each of the garments listed here and answer the questions regarding safety compliance. Use Table 8.1 to help you complete this worksheet.

Your Name

Name(s) of Teammate(s)

Children's Sweatshirt with Hood	
Available in sizes 2T to 6x 100% cotton Made in Cambodia Pullover fleece sweatshirt with drawstring hood and pouch pocket	 Illustration by Janace Bubonia
This garment will be shipped to retail stores in the United States, European Union, Canada, and Japan. Are there any safety regulations to be concerned with for the countries listed? ☐Yes ☐No If yes, list the safety concern(s)?	

CORRELATION BETWEEN BOOK AND LAB MANUAL CHAPTERS AND ACTIVITIES

The following table shows the *Apparel Quality Lab Manual* chapters and activities and their corresponding chapters from this text.

Text Chapter	Lab Manual Chapter	Lab Activities
1	1	1.1 Customer Expectation Survey for Jeans 1.2 Quality Cues Comparison 1.3 Product Selection 1.4 Comparison Project Customer Expectation Survey
2	2	2.1 Analysis of Aesthetic and Design Details of Woven Garments in Relation to Design Elements and Principles across Price Categories 2.2 Comparison Project Product Analysis of Aesthetic and Design Details in Relation to Design Elements and Principles of Competing Brands 2.3 Farnsworth Munsell 100 Hue Test
3, 11	3	3.1 Raw Materials Classification 3.2 Specimen Templates and Sampling Plan 3.3 Characterization Testing on Piece Goods 3.4 Characterization Testing on Comparison Project Garment 3.5 Wear Testing Comparison Project Garments
4	4	4.1 Garment Analysis of Construction Details across Price Classifications 4.2 Comparison Project Garment Analysis of Construction Details across Competing Brands 4.3 Comparison Project Garment Evaluation of Appearance and Color Change after Laundering
5	5	5.1 Comparison Project Garment Analysis of Size and Fit
6, 7	6	6.1 Comparison Project Garment Identification of Stitches and Seams 6.2 Comparison Project Garment Thread Consumption Calculations
9	7	7.1 Comparison Project Garment Label Compliance 7.2 Garment Care
10	8	8.1 Garment Safety Regulations and Compliance
11, 12	9	9.1 Test Methods for Evaluating Selected Garments 9.2 Piece Goods Appearance and Performance Testing 9.3 Comparison Garment Appearance and Performance Testing 9.4 Comparison Project Garment Results and Performance Specifications
13	10	10.1 Inspection of Randomly Selected Garments 10.2 Comparison Project Garment Inspection 10.3 Comparison Garment Customer Satisfaction Survey

APPAREL QUALITY

A GUIDE TO
EVALUATING
SEWN
PRODUCTS

Overview of Apparel Quality and the Consumer

CHAPTER ONE

Objectives:

- Define quality and understand its basic elements
- Examine factors that impact consumer perceptions and expectations of apparel products before and after purchase
- Identify the major organizations developing standards for apparel performance
- Understand how apparel quality is measured

Armand V. Feigenbaum, creator of the total quality control concept and former president of the American Society for Quality (ASQ), stated ". . . control must start with the design of the product and end only when the product has been placed in the hands of the customer who remains satisfied . . . the first principle to recognize is *that quality is everybody's job*."[1]

There are many different approaches to defining quality. David Garvin, author of *Managing Quality*, stated "If quality is to be managed, it must first be understood".[2] The *Merriam-Webster Dictionary* defines **quality** as "degree of excellence; superiority in kind; inherent feature."[3] The American Society for Quality (ASQ) defines quality as "a subjective term for which each person or sector has its own definition. In technical usage, quality can have two meanings: 1. the characteristics of a product or service that bear on its ability to satisfy stated or implied needs; 2. a product or service free of deficiencies."[4]

Quality, as it relates to physical product, can be explained based on three distinct approaches:

product-defined, manufacturer-defined, and user-defined. **Product-defined quality** focuses on the physical features and attributes that are measureable. The inherent physical features of an apparel item help determine the overall level of quality. For example, when designers or product developers create a line, they must consider all of the various physical aspects of the apparel item that will influence the quality of the finished product when making selection for materials and component parts, methods of assembly, seam construction, and finishing. These selections are based on the brand's established quality level, performance expectations of the consumer, and targeted price point for each of the products in the line. From a buyer's perspective, the quality level of the physical products they purchase must be appropriately matched to the retail stores, ecommerce sites, catalogues, or shopping networks in which they will be sold. The quality of a product is defined by its physical structure and elements in this approach.

The **manufacturer-defined quality** approach is concentrated on meeting specifications for conformance to production standards and is based on the concept that consumers are interested in purchasing quality products they can rely on. From a manufacturer's perspective, they must comply with materials, component parts, methods of assembly, construction, finishing, and packing specifications provided by product developers or designers. Some of the specifications can be government regulations that must be met and are communicated through garment specification packets. It is the manufacturer's responsibility to ensure the products they make conform to production standards and specifications so the target customer will be satisfied with their purchase.

Individual customers' needs and wants in relation to their personal preferences for desired product attributes and value determine the **user-defined quality** approach. Value is important to the user in terms of appropriateness and fitness or performance of the product in relation to cost and purchase price.[5] For example, when a customer is making a purchase decision, there are certain criteria the product must meet in regard to aesthetics, performance, and function. From a retailer's perspective, the products they sell need to be selected with the customers' needs and wants in mind to ensure they will keep coming back.

ELEMENTS OF QUALITY

Quality is composed of five elements and can be divided into the following basic categories: performance, durability, serviceability, conformance, and aesthetics. These basic elements are often interrelated, which can cause problems when one aspect of a product is improved—it can negatively impact another aspect. For example, wrinkling is a common problem with cotton trousers. If the customer desires a garment that does not require the maintenance of ironing yet a crisp aesthetic appearance during wear, a wrinkle-free finish can be applied during manufacturing. Although the finish will improve the aesthetic appearance of the garment, it weakens the strength of the fibers and causes the material to tear more easily than it would without the finish. In these instances, understanding quality expectations from the consumer's point of view assists product developers and manufacturers when determining which compromises are best in relation to their products and competitors offerings.

Performance

The first element of quality, **performance**, encompasses the functional aspects and features of a garment for its intended use. This component utilizes a combination of product-defined and user-defined perspectives for determining quality. A garment's performance can be measured based on its physical attributes; however, individual consumer preferences, interests, and use may provide different perspectives in relation to performance and how it equates to quality in their mind. Garment **features** are the physical characteristics or special components that enhance and support product performance such as fibers, yarns and material structure, seam construction, and fabric finishes. Features are directly linked to product performance.

Durability

The element of quality that indicates a product's ability to resist physical and mechanical deterioration and function for its intended use over a specified period of time is **durability**. In other words, the useful life of the product, which can be explained as the length of use before it becomes physically damaged and the consumer chooses to replace the item rather than repair it. This component of quality becomes more important as the individual uses the garment and refurbishes (cleans and restores appearance) it. Durability is based on product-defined and user-defined approaches to quality.

Serviceability

A product's **serviceability** relates to its ease of care, ability to retain its shape and appearance, and cost of **maintenance** (care and repair). With wear and refurbishment, the appearance and comfort of a garment can change. The method and cost for caring for an apparel product can impact whether a consumer purchases a garment or not because it can add to the cost of the garment. An example of this is a garment that requires drycleaning as the method of care. Some customers will make purchasing decisions based on the care instructions found on the garment's care label to determine the maintenance it will require. All methods of care for apparel items require some additional cost to the consumer, whether it is cleaned at home (cost includes water, detergent, bleach, fabric softener, stain remover, and electricity or gas) or it is sent to a professional laundry or drycleaner. Serviceability relies on the user-defined approach to quality.

Conformance

The fourth element of quality, **conformance**, indicates the degree to which the design and performance of a product meets established standards. Product specifications should conform to standards established by the designer/product developer and the manufacturer and can also require meeting government regulations. All manufactured apparel products have specifications. **Material specifications** provide performance expectations required for all materials that will be used to complete a garment style. The styling details, design features, and characteristics of an apparel item in relation to aesthetic appeal are known as **design specifications**. **Product specifications** provide standards for intrinsic components (essential parts of the physical product) of a completed product such as size and fit, garment assembly, finishing, labeling, packaging, and performance. Conformance to specified standards for materials and garment components and the design and assembly of the product are important to achieving the desired quality level and performance of the finished garment. Conformance utilizes the manufacturing-based approach when defining quality and is measured objectively rather than on individual consumer preferences. When durability or conformance elements are improved, the other is typically enhanced, therefore increasing the quality performance of a product. For example, a pair of leggings made of jersey knit fabric must withstand the wearer pulling the garment on and off the body. If the fabric does not conform to established standards for durability and strength, it will not perform at the intended level. One of the problems that can result is a hole in the garment caused by the wearer's finger puncturing the fabric when dressing. Therefore, when the durability of the garment is improved and complies with minimum specification standards, the product will perform better during normal use and care.

Aesthetics

The last element, aesthetics, relies on the user-based approach to quality. **Aesthetics** of a garment engage the senses and include the appearance, comfort, sound, and smell. This element is highly subjective and relies on personal preferences and judgment.

A goal of designers and product developers is to create apparel products that incorporate specific product attributes that are matched to consumer preferences for particular products.

QUALITY CHARACTERISTICS AND CUES

Apparel manufacturers and retailers strive to provide their customers with the products they want, at the targeted price points and desired quality levels. Quality in apparel product development and manufacturing is based on meeting standards and specifications to make sure products conform to designated requirements and are appropriate for the intended end use. Factors that help determine quality level include garment styling, sizing and fit, fabric, component materials, findings, and trims, workmanship, and precision of assembly. Product quality is an important aspect of manufactured goods and is contingent upon the basic elements of aesthetic design, performance of materials, the durability and reliability of construction for the intended use, and maintenance or care. These internal garment features help determine quality in addition to other external influences that can be categorized into primary and secondary quality cues.

Primary Quality Indicators/Intrinsic Quality Cues

Primary quality indicators, also known as intrinsic attributes, include those that are part of the physical structure of the product. Consumers observe the physical features, performance characteristics, and product benefits when making determinations about quality. These are all part of **intrinsic quality cues**, also known as **tangible attributes** which can be assessed using one's senses such as sight, touch, sound, and smell. The primary quality features can be further categorized as physical attributes, performance features, and product benefits. A product's intrinsic qualities cannot be altered without physically changing it.

Physical attributes include the design of the product, the materials used, and how the product is constructed and finished. Raw materials such as fibers, yarns, fabric construction, dyes and surface designs, findings and trim components, and finish can all be indicators of quality. The overall style and construction details for assembling the garment also influence product quality. The aesthetic appeal and positioning of fitting details such as darts, tucks, seams, gathers, and pleats affect the physical character of an apparel item. These physical attributes play a part in the aesthetic and functional performance of a garment. For example, a series of darts or tucks are used to shape the garment around the contours of the body to improve the fit and functional performance. Additionally, the placement of these darts or tucks adds visual interest to the styling of the garment as part of the aesthetic performance. **Performance features** dictate the garment's primary functional characteristics, which include comfort, usefulness, and benefits for the consumer and are composed of both aesthetic and functional characteristics.

Aesthetic characteristics include the overall attractiveness of the materials, styling, and design of the garment for its intended use. The garment must also maintain its shape and appearance after cleaning (refurbishment). The **functional characteristics** directly relate to the garment's ability to perform as it is intended with relation to fit, durability, effectiveness, and ease of care. **Product benefits** result from the right combination of physical attributes and performance features that are desired by consumers to meet their needs and expectations.

Secondary Quality Indicators/Extrinsic Quality Cues

Secondary quality indicators, also known as extrinsic attributes, include those that add to a consumer's perception of quality although they may not reflect reality. Extrinsic attributes are external to the product and not part of the physical makeup but are used by consumers as indicators of quality level. **Extrinsic**

quality cues include price, image and reputation of the brand and retailer, country of origin, advertising and marketing, and visual presentation. These cues are implied and do not always directly correlate to a product's quality level; they are based on perception rather than fact. The primary contributors to quality perception are price and reputation.

Apparel products are available in the marketplace under a variety of brands and at different price points. **Retail price** is the amount designated by the retailer to be paid by the consumer in exchange for a product or service. **Price point classification** refers to the range of prices, lowest to highest, upon which competitive products are offered in the marketplace. Within the designated price classifications of budget, moderate, better, bridge, and designer the quality of merchandise can differ greatly among brands. A brand represents the reputation of a product or company that is conveyed through brand image, wordmark, logo, product design, quality, marketing and promotion, distribution of goods, and customer service. Brand reputation can provide competitive advantage and be perceived as a significant quality indicator. Consumers often equate price with quality—the higher the price the higher the quality. This is not always an accurate indicator. Products should be distinctive in quality level of fabrics and findings, construction techniques, and details for the consumer to discern obvious distinctions between the price classifications.

Apparel product styling and design ranges from basic to fashion forward (contemporary) apparel items that are offered at all price points and quality levels. **Budget** is the lowest price category for mass-produced apparel products, geared toward a wide range of market segments. Mass market appeal, value-driven products, and low prices distinguish apparel brands and retailers within this price category. The **moderate** price point includes average prices for mass-produced apparel products geared toward meeting the needs of middle-income families and individuals. Broad appeal, value, and quality in relation to price are important factors for selection. Above-average prices for mass-produced apparel products are found within the **better** price range with the consumer expectation of better quality fabrics and more advanced construction details. The **contemporary** price classification is similar to better priced goods but is slightly higher. This category offers very fashion-forward, trendy apparel items for the junior and misses size ranges. **Bridge** includes mass-produced apparel products priced between the better and designer price categories with the customer perception and expectation of high-quality fabrics and elements of designer apparel at a price point lower than designer products. **Designer** is the highest price category for mass-produced apparel products with the customer expectation of exclusive design, high-quality fabrics, and construction details for a narrowly defined niche target market.

CONSUMER QUALITY PERCEPTIONS AND EXPECTATIONS

In 1956 Armand Feigenbaum stated, "While delivery and other factors may sell a product the first time, it is usually quality which keeps the product sold and which keeps the customer coming back a second and third time".[6] This is still true today. Quality leads to customer satisfaction; therefore, it is important for product developers, manufacturers, and retailers to understand what elements of quality consumers seek in the products they purchase. There are many factors that influence customer expectations and perceptions of product quality.

Influences and Motivators

Understanding one's target market helps product developers, manufacturers, and retailers provide apparel products that meet the needs and expectations of their customers. **Target market research** provides valuable demographic and lifestyle data for both existing and potential customers within specific market segments that are used to develop more narrowly defined customer profiles. **Demographic** data is statistical information about a population that includes age, gender, income, education, geographic area, family size, housing type, nationality/ethnicity/race, marital status, occupation, spending patterns, and religious affiliations. Demographic data can be obtained from census studies conducted by national governments in developed countries. Census data has its limitations in that these studies are conducted in various countries around the world once every 10 years. Vital statistics registries can provide limited information such as births, deaths, marital status, and geographic location. The Consumer Price Index (CPI) provides monthly and yearly data regarding spending patterns of consumers within a country. The Harmonized Indexes of Consumer Prices (HICP) includes the same type of information as CPI; however, it is used to compare countries within Europe. Table 1.1 provides a list of countries/regions that are compared in the International Consumer Price Indexes by index type. The CPI and HICP monitor the changes in prices of selected consumer goods from different product categories to measure inflation or deflation rates.[7,8] These indexes are used by governments to monitor consumer spending. There are also marketing firms around the globe that specialize in providing demographic data specific to a company's needs.

Although demographic data is very important, lifestyle data must also be considered in order to more accurately determine the needs and wants, as well as expectations of a defined target market. **Lifestyle data** (also known as psychographics) includes the social and psychological factors that motivate consumers to buy such as life stage, reference groups/peers, social class, personality, attitudes and values, generation group, and cultural preferences based on ethnic or cultural influences. Lifestyle data is gathered by manufacturers and retailers primarily through surveys and focus groups. The combination of demographic and lifestyle data provides a wealth of information about the target market of a brand or retailer. This information is used to develop, promote, and sell apparel products that possess the

Table 1.1 List of Countries by Consumer Price Index Type

Country/Region	Index Type
Austria	CPI & HICP
Belgium	CPI & HICP
Brazil	CPI
Canada	CPI
Chile	CPI
China	CPI
Czech Republic	CPI & HIPC
Denmark	CPI & HIPC
Estonia	CPI & HIPC
Finland	CPI & HIPC
France	CPI & HIPC
Germany	CPI & HIPC
Great Britain	CPI & HIPC
Greece	CPI & HIPC
Hungary	CPI & HIPC
Iceland	CPI & HIPC
India	CPI
Indonesia	CPI
Ireland	CPI & HIPC
Israel	CPI
Italy	CPI & HIPC
Japan	CPI
Luxembourg	CPI & HIPC
Mexico	CPI
Norway	CPI
Poland	CPI & HIPC
Portugal	CPI & HIPC
Russia	CPI
Slovakia	CPI & HIPC
Slovenia	CPI & HIPC
South Africa	CPI
South Korea	CPI
Spain	CPI & HIPC
Sweden	CPI & HIPC
Switzerland	CPI
The Netherlands	CPI & HIPC
Turkey	CPI & HIPC
United States	CPI

Note: CPI = Consumer price index; HICP = Harmonized indexes of consumer prices (used to compare inflation rates between European countries).
Sources: http://www.bls.gov/fls/intl_consumer_prices.pdf

characteristics and features customers are seeking at the expected quality levels and prices.

Product Value

Consumers have many choices when it comes to purchasing apparel products, and they are seeking product value. **Product value** is based on the customer's perception of quality for the price paid; therefore, value is a subjective term that varies from individual to individual. When consumers make purchasing decisions, they consider the intrinsic features such as the initial appearance and overall aesthetic of the garment, its perceived comfort and functionality for its intended use, how to care for the item, and safety inferences. The primary extrinsic features that also play a role in purchase decisions are price and brand. Ultimately, price is a major driving factor for purchasing decisions. Price can influence a consumer's perception of quality. Quality level can be linked to price point; however, not all higher-priced items are high quality, just as not all lower-priced items are low quality. **Perceived quality** is the consumer's opinion of the level of superiority of a product based on brand reputation, value, and the ability of the product to meet the expectations of the wearer. Consumers' perception is based on both tangible and intangible aspects of a product. Brand name, country of origin, packaging, advertising, and social media communicates cues that become part of a consumer's perception of quality whether they are factual or not.

The actual value of an apparel item cannot be determined at the point of purchase; it is only realized when the customer has come to the end of the useful life of the product. "Every textile product has a 'life expectancy' according to its intended purpose, material content, and rate of change in fashion or style. . . . Beyond the point of 'life expectancy'; however, an article may retain a degree of usefulness. It, therefore, has some value for as long as it remains useful" to the customer.[9] The International Fair Claims Guide for Consumer Textile Products, which contains a list of apparel items and their life expectancy, was developed by the Drycleaning Institute of Australia Ltd., Federal Bureau of Consumer Affairs, International Fabricare Institute, Neighborhood Cleaners Association, Guild of Cleaners & Launderers, School of Textiles, and private and government consumer organizations. This guide was approved as an American National Standard in 1988.[10] See Table 1.2 for the textile life expectancy rate in years for men's, women's, and children's apparel products.

Cost per wear is another way to determine the value of a product. **Cost per wear** is determined by dividing the purchase price of a garment by the number of times it has been worn. For example, if a customer purchased two pairs of jeans, pair A cost $79.99 and pair B cost $130.00. The customer wore pair A 14 times and wore pair B 27 times. Which pair is the better value based on cost per wear? Pair A $79.99 ÷ 14 = $5.71 cost per wear. Pair B $130.00 ÷ 27 = $4.81 cost per wear. Pair B is a better value because the customer wore the item more and although the purchase price was higher, the cost per wear is lower than pair A. It is vital for product designers and manufacturers to understand the value and quality level consumers are looking for in relation to the price they are willing to pay.

MEASURING PRODUCT QUALITY

In today's global marketplace apparel manufacturers and retailers are trying to balance costs while maintaining quality expectations of consumers. As the cost of raw materials and labor continues to rise, manufacturers are seeking ways to cut costs and overall product quality can be compromised if they are not careful. **Quality assurance** is the method for managing and controlling the processes for development and manufacturing of apparel to ensure product quality and compliance with safety regulations. **Quality control** is the process for ensuring specified standards for quality are maintained through continual testing at different phases of production, performing frequent inspections, and ensuring proper use of equipment

Table 1.2 Textile Life Expectancy in Years for Apparel Products

	Men's and Women's Apparel Items				
Apparel Item	Description or Fiber Content	Life Expectancy in Years	Apparel Item	Description or Fiber Content	Life Expectancy in Years
Bathing Suit		2	Rainwear & Windbreakers	Film & plastic coated	2
Blouses (Dress & Sports)	White cotton	3		Fabric	3
	Colored cotton, silk, & synthetic	2		Rubber & plastic	3
Coats, Jackets, & Blazers	Cloth (dress and sport)	4	Scarves		2
	Pile fabrics	3	Shirts	Plain	2
	Fur	10		Wool or silk	2
	Imitation fur	3		Casual cotton blend	3
	Leather & suede	5		Leather	5
	Imitation suede	3		Suede	4
	Wool	4		Other	2
	Cotton & blends	3	Ski Jackets	Fabric	3
	Plastics	2		Quilted fabric	2
	Flocked or coated	2		Rubber & plastic	2
Denim Apparel	Jackets	3	Skirts	Wool	4
	Jeans or skirts	2		Cotton	2
	Bleached or stonewashed	3		Leather	5
Dresses	Casual	1		Other	2
	Fancy	2	Suits	Summer weight	3
	Evening	3		Winter weight wool	4
	High fashion	2		Wool or wool blends	3
	Suede	3		Cotton & synthetic	2
	Imitation suede	3		Wash suits	2
	Leather	4		Imitation suede	2
Dressing Gowns	Wool	3	Trousers, Slacks, & Shorts	Wool or wool blends	4
	Lightweight fabrics	1		Cotton blends	2
	Quilted & heavy fabrics	3		Leather	5
	Silk	2		Suede	3
	Other	2		Fur	5
Formal Wear		5	Underwear	Socks	1
Jumpers & Cardigans	Wool	4		Foundation garments	1
	Wool blends	3		Underpants	1
	Synthetics	3		Lingerie	2
Neckties		1	Vests	Leather, suede or fur	5
Plastics Apparel		2		Other	2
			Work Uniforms		1
	Children's Apparel Items				
Coats & Baby Sets		2	Suits		2
Dresses		2	Play Clothes		1

Note: Taken from the International Fair Claims Guide for Consumer Textile Products.
Source: Drycleaning Institute of Australia, Ltd. 2010. International Fair Claims Guide for Consumer Textiles Products, http://www.drycleanersweb.com.au /complaint/, 23

Figure 1.1 Quality control apparel inspector
Toronto Star via Getty Images

and established procedures (see Figure 1.1). Preventative measures such as monitoring and inspection of product quality, and testing throughout the development and manufacturing of apparel products ensure compliance with quality control standards and safety regulations. In turn, these measures reduce defects, returns, and customer complaints and can prevent product recalls. **Inspection** includes the evaluation of factories in relation to capacity and quality control, function, and appearance of materials and components, random selection of production garments to identify defects and deviations from contracted specifications to ensure that quality standards are being met. Product testing and inspection lead to better quality garments and higher customer satisfaction, which in return stimulate repeat sales.

Standards for Apparel Performance

Product quality is measured by **standards**, which are technical documents developed and established within the consensus of international, national, federal organizations and agencies, consortiums, or individual companies. These documents provide methods for producing repeatable results to increase product quality and safety. "Standards ensure desirable characteristics of products and services such as quality, environmental friendliness, safety, reliability, efficiency and interchangeability—and at an economical cost."[11] Industry standards are developed by international and national trade associations or industry organizations. Government standards are a little different. They can be developed by government agencies or through the private sector, which are then adopted as government standards. Some companies develop standards that are used internally for maintaining specific quality levels and are typically more rigorous than those developed for industry or government. There are also smaller groups or consortiums with similar interests and goals that will utilize the resources of the group to develop standards that they would not have the means to create on their own.

There are mandatory/regulatory standards and voluntary standards. **Mandatory/regulatory standards** are those that are part of required laws or regulations that are enforced by government. **Voluntary standards** are not enforceable but are often utilized to maintain quality standards that are developed by retailers, manufacturers, importers, government agencies, and consumers through consensus among all parties. See Chapters 9 and 10 for further discussion.

Standards include test methods and specifications. **Test methods** are procedures for conducting and gathering test results for identification, measurement, and evaluation purposes. After testing is conducted the results must be examined against **specifications**, a set of established requirements for determining whether the material or product satisfies quality standards related to performance criteria, safety, or physical, mechanical, or chemical properties.

Organizations Developing Standards for Textile and Apparel Performance

There are many organizations around the world that develop standards for a multitude of industries at the national and international levels. The prominent organizations providing standards for the textile and apparel industry will be discussed in this section.

The largest organization for developing and publishing standards worldwide is the **ISO (International Organization for Standardization)**, established in 1947 in Geneva, Switzerland (see Figure 1.2). This international organization is a nongovernmental body composed of members of the national standards institutes from 162 countries around the world.[12,13]

Figure 1.2 ISO
Courtesy of ISO

ISO publishes more than 19,500 consensus standards that are highly specific to a material, product, or process to provide conformity assessment.[14] ISO defines **conformity assessment** as "checking whether products, services, materials, processes, systems, and personnel measure up to the requirements of standards, regulations or other specifications."[15] The ISO technical committee responsible for Textiles Standards is TC 38. This committee was founded in 1947 and oversees 109 published standards today.[16] In addition, ISO provides "generic management system standards" ISO 9001 (a quality management system), and ISO 14001 (an environmental management system). These generic management systems can be implemented by any type of organization.[17]

ASTM International (formerly known as the American Society of Testing and Materials) was founded in 1898 by chemists and engineers from the Pennsylvania Railroad (see Figure 1.3). This international organization publishes roughly 12,500 voluntary standards that are developed through consensus by technical experts from around the globe.[18] ASTM International publishes 82 volumes that are divided into 16 sections that are highly specific to materials, products, and processes within various industries. Section 7, volumes 07.01 and 07.02 includes 364 standards for textiles.[19]

Established in 1921, **AATCC (American Association of Textile Chemists and Colorists)** is internationally recognized for its development of standard

Figure 1.3 ASTM
Courtesy of ASTM

Figure 1.4 AATCC
Courtesy of AATCC

Association of Textile, Apparel & Materials Professionals

test methods (see Figure 1.4). It publishes nearly 130 voluntary test methods and evaluation procedures in the *Technical Manual of the American Association of Textile Chemists and Colorists* annually that are developed through consensus by technical experts.[20,21] AATCC test methods cover colorfastness, dyeing properties, biological properties, identification and analysis, physical properties, and evaluation procedures related to textiles. The **Technical Advisory Group (TAG)** represents the United States (U.S.) in all ISO/TC 38 Textile Committee actions. TAG is jointly administered by ASTM International's D13 Textile Committee and AATCC.[22]

ANSI (American National Standards Institute) is a private non-profit organization founded in 1918 by five engineering societies and three government agencies that administrators and coordinators

Figure 1.5 ANSI
Courtesy of ANSI

the voluntary standardization system in the U.S. (see Figure 1.5).[23] They are the "voice of the U.S. standards and conformity system . . ." with a mission "to enhance both the global competitiveness of U.S. business and the quality of life by promoting and facilitating voluntary consensus standards and conformity assessment systems, and safeguarding their integrity".[24] ANSI is the U.S. accreditation body for ISO 9000 and ISO 14000 management systems and promotes the development of U.S. standards by certifying organizations developing standards.

Founded in 1901, **BSI (British Standards Institution)** is the **National Standards Body (NSB)** of the United Kingdom (UK; see Figure 1.6).[25] BSI has 34,000 standards across a broad spectrum of industries developed by technical experts through consensus. They currently develop and publish 1,800 standards annually. They also act as the accrediting body for ISO 9001 and ISO 14001, which originated as British Standards. BSI represents the UK as the National Standards Body for ISO/TC 38 Textile Committee actions and European standards (EU) through participation in the European Committee for Standardization (CEN). [26]

CEN (European Committee for Standardization) is an international non-profit organization established in 1975 in Brussels, Belgium. They

Figure 1.6 BSI
Courtesy of BSI

develop voluntary European standards (ENs) based on consensus of technical experts in 33 member countries. These ENs also serve as the national standards used in each of the member countries. CEN "is the only recognized European organization according to Directive 98/34/EC for the planning, drafting, and adoption of European Standards with the exception of electrotechnology (CENELEC) and telecommunication (ETSI)."[27,28] The European member countries are represented by CEN in all ISO TC/38 Textile Committee actions. The Consumer Products sector within CEN oversees more than 300 standards for textiles and textile products.[29]

In 1990, **CNIS (China National Institute of Standardization)** was established as a non-profit organization affiliated with the General Administration of Quality Supervision and Inspection and Quarantine of the People's Republic of China. CNIS "serves as the Secretariat of the National Technical Committee of Standardization Theories and Methods Standardization and the liaison office for promotion and implementation of ISO."[30] It supports and develops standards and policies in accordance with international standards to be implemented by the government within China as well as represents China in all ISO/TC 38 Textile Committee activities.[31]

In 1945, the Minister of Trade and Industry approved the formation of **JSA (Japanese Standards Association)**, which was the result of a merger between Dai Nihon Arial Technology Association and the Japan Management Association. The main goal of this association is to "educate the public regarding the standardization and unification of industrial standards, and thereby to contribute to the improvement of technology and the enhancement of production efficiency".[32,33] JSA publishes the **Japanese Industrial Standards (JIS)**. The Japanese Industrial Standards Committee (JISC) was established within the Ministry of the Economy, Trade, and Industry, and develops standards for a variety of industries including textiles and apparel.[34] "JISC is set up to conduct deliberations on the adoption and revision of JIS [Japanese Industrial Standards]."[35] Members

of the Japan Textile Evaluation Technology Council are assigned by JISC to represent Japan in ISO/TC 38 Textile Committee actions. In addition, JISC serves as the secretariat of ISO/TC 38.[36]

SCC (Standards Council of Canada) was established in 1970 as a result of the federal government's review of standards activity within Canada (see Figure 1.7).[37] The SCC administers the **National Standards System (NSS)**, which works with committees of technical experts to develop voluntary standards and adapt international standards for use in Canada. Standards development organizations, companies, laboratories, and inspection groups as well as quality management and environmental management systems are accredited by the SCC. Canada is represented by the SCC as the National Standards Body for ISO/TC 38 Textile Committee actions.[38]

There are international organizations developing voluntary standards based on the consensus of technical experts specifically for the nonwovens industry. **INDA (Association of the Nonwoven Fabrics Industry)** was founded in 1968 as a non-profit organization under the name International Nonwovens and Disposables Association. The name was changed in 1976, but the acronym INDA continues to be used today (see Figure 1.8). After just three years in existence

Figure 1.7 SCC
© SCC Standards Council of Canada

Figure 1.8 INDA
© INDA® is a registered trademark of INDA

and significant growth of the nonwovens industry, it became evident that one organization could not meet the needs of the global community, and **EDANA (European Disposables and Nonwovens Association)** was established in 1971.[39] This non-profit organization primarily serves the nonwovens industries in Europe, the Middle East, and Africa.[40] *Standard Test Methods for the Nonwovens Industry* is a publication produced through the joint efforts of INDA and EDANA. For additional information on organizations developing standards for textiles and apparel performance, see Table 1.3.

Through the development of standards, these organizations help promote and facilitate fair trade among countries, specify methods for safe and efficient development, manufacturing, and distribution of goods, and provide a basis for conformity assessment across governmental, private, and public sectors

Compliance Roles

When products are developed quality must be considered just as carefully as the design. Armand Feigenbaum defines total quality control as "an effective system for integrating the quality development,

quality-maintenance, and quality-improvement efforts of the various groups in an organization so as to enable marketing, engineering, production, and service at the most economical levels which allow for full customer satisfaction".[41]

$$\text{Control (design + material + product + process)} \div$$
$$\text{Costs (inspection + rejects)} \times \text{Customer satisfaction}$$
$$= \text{Total Quality Control}[42]$$

Quality starts at the inception of the product. Designers, manufacturers, testing labs, and retailers all play an important role in maintaining product quality through compliance. **Compliance** is the ability of a material, finding, or apparel product to conform to established standards and specifications to meet customer expectations that lead to satisfaction.

Designers and retail product developers have an important role when it comes to quality compliance. They must understand how to select the appropriate raw materials to provide the desired aesthetic and product performance for the garment's intended end use. Designers are responsible for the aesthetic and functional characteristics of apparel products including the styling, sizing, comfort and fit, selection of fabric, component materials and findings, and providing specifications for assembly. They must ensure that the materials and prototype garments conform to quality specifications prior to production.

Sourcing production in the factories that can manufacture apparel products at the desired price and quality level is very important. Manufacturers are responsible for complying with the specifications for assembly and finishing. Inspection and testing at various stages of production of materials and apparel products helps maintain quality and detect any defects and compliance problems that need to be addressed before distribution.

In light of the Bangladesh factory collapse in 2013 and the media coverage of apparel sweatshops over the years, there is growing consumer concern over where their garments are made. Apparel brands and retailers are listening and making a concerted effort to provide this information. "The Sustainable Apparel

Table 1.3 Organizations Developing Standards for Textiles and Apparel Performance

Organization	Website	Country Base
World Federation for Standards		
ISO	www.iso.org	Switzerland
National Standards Organizations		
ASTM International	www.astm.org	United States
AATCC	www.aatcc.org	United States
ANSI	www.ansi.org	United States
BSI	www.bsigroup.com	United Kingdom
CEN	www.cen.eu	Belgium
CNIS	http://en.cnis.gov.cn/	China
JISC	www.jisc.go.jp/eng/	Japan
SCC	www.scc.ca/	Canada
EDANA	www.edana.org	Belgium
INDA	www.inda.org	United States

Coalition was founded by a group of sustainability leaders from global apparel and footwear companies."[43] Their mission is to "lead the industry toward a shared vision of sustainability built upon a common approach for measuring and evaluating apparel and footwear product sustainability performance that will spotlight priorities for action and opportunities for technological innovation."[43] This coalition created the Higg Index for companies to evaluate both the environmental and social performance of their brand(s). Many companies such as Gap, JCPenney, Nike, Target, and Walmart are already participating in measuring the labor and social environment conditions of the establishments producing their apparel overseas.[44] This movement toward transparency in manufacturing has only just begun.

SUMMARY

In this chapter the basic elements of quality were introduced along with the factors that impact consumers' perceptions and expectations of apparel products, before and after purchase. It is important to understand what quality is and how it is evaluated as well as the relationship between customer expectations and perception of quality. These factors are very important to brands when developing, producing, and distributing products. Methods for measuring sewn products through quality control, inspection, performance standards, and compliance are all important aspects when evaluating quality, which play a role in customer satisfaction. The major organizations developing and publishing industry test methods, and standards used for evaluating apparel products were introduced to provide a better understanding of their scope and importance. The coming chapters will expand upon the concepts presented here.

ACTIVITIES

1. Select three garments from the following list, and record the aesthetic and performance characteristics that would be expected for each apparel item.

   Casual dress
   Evening gown
   Foundation garment
   Pajamas
   Rain coat
   Ski jacket
   Swimsuit
   Sweater
   Tailored suit
   Yoga pant

2. Select two garments from your wardrobe that represent two different price ranges (budget, moderate, better, contemporary, bridge, designer). Create a list of intrinsic and extrinsic cues that convey quality to you for each of the items. Briefly explain which garment in your opinion is better quality based on the intrinsic and extrinsic cues noted.

3. Calculate cost per wear for three similar garments (i.e., three T-shirts, three pairs of jeans, three pairs of athletic shorts, and so on) from your wardrobe that were purchased about the same time to determine which garment is the best value based on cost per wear. Begin by designating each garment as A, B, or C. Complete garment descriptions for each item that include:

   - Garment letter and item
   - Purchase price
   - Brand
   - Color
   - Fiber content
   - Care instructions
   - Country of origin
   - Store purchased
   - Month/year purchased

   Which garment do you believe is the better value for the price and why? Calculate the cost per wear for each of the three garments using the following formula:

   $$\text{Purchase price} \div \text{number of times garment was worn} = \text{Cost per wear}$$

   After you have calculated the cost per wear indicate, determine which garment is the better value from a cost per wear perspective. Were you surprised at the results? Explain why or why not.

4. Select a garment from your wardrobe. Analyze the garment from the standpoints of the designer/product developer, manufacturer, retailer, and consumer. Make a chart to compare how each entity would analyze the quality of the apparel item selected. Think about the product-define, manufacturer-defined, and user-define approaches to quality. List the approach(es) used for each. Now consider the elements of quality (i.e., performance, durability, serviceability, conformance, and aesthetics). Using the categories for the elements of quality, list how each of the various stages of development through to the end-user would evaluate and measure quality of the selected product.

APPAREL QUALITY LAB MANUAL

Please refer to Lab Activity 1.1 Customer Expectation Survey for Jeans; Lab Activity 1.2 Quality Cues Comparison; Lab Activity 1.3 Product Selection; and Lab Activity 1.4 Comparison Project Customer Expectation Survey in the *Apparel Quality Lab Manual.*

ENDNOTES

1. Armand V. Feigenbaum. (November 1956). "Total Quality Control." *Harvard Business Review*, 34, no. 6: ISSN 0017-8012, 94, 98.

2. David Garvin. *Managing Quality: The Strategic and Competitive Edge.* (New York: The Free Press 1988).

3. *Merriam-Webster On-Line Dictionary.* (2012). http://www.merriam-webster.com/dictionary/quality?show=0&t=1330740285.

4. American Society for Quality. (2012). *Quality Glossary.* Accessed February 26, 2012, http://asq.org/glossary/q.html.

5. David Garvin. *Managing Quality: The Strategic and Competitive Edge.* (New York: The Free Press 1988), 43–46.

6. Armand V. Feigenbaum. (November 1956). "Total Quality Control." *Harvard Business Review*, 34, no. 6: ISSN 0017-8012, 101.

7. Triami Media BV, and Home Finance. "Inflation Summary of Current International Inflation Figures." Accessed March 5, 2012, http://www.global-rates.com/economic-indicators/inflation/inflation.aspx.

8. Bureau of Labor and Statistics. (2010). *International Indexes of Consumer Prices Annual Report.* Accessed June 27, 2014,http://www.bls.gov/fls/intl_consumer_prices.pdf

9. Drycleaning Institute of Australia, Ltd. (2010). International Fair Claims Guide for Consumer Textiles Products. Accessed June 27, 2014, http://www.drycleanersweb.com.au/sites/default/files/user-content/resources/file/fair_claims_guide_0.pdf

10. Drycleaning Institute of Australia, Ltd. (2010). International Fair Claims Guide for Consumer Textiles Products. Accessed June 27, 2014, http://www.drycleanersweb.com.au/sites/default/files/user-content/resources/file/fair_claims_guide_0.pdf

11. International Organization for Standardization. (2011). "Discover ISO: Why Standards Matter." Accessed March 11, 2012, http://www.iso.org/iso/about/discover-iso_why-standards-matter.htm.

12. International Organization for Standardization. (2011). "About ISO." Accessed June 27, 2014, http://www.iso.org/iso/home/about.htm

13. International Organization for Standardization. (2014) "Who We Are". Accessed June 27, 2014, http://www.iso.org/iso/home/about.htm

14. International Organization for Standardization. (2014) "Standards: How to Find a Standard". Accessed June 27, 2014, http://www.iso.org/iso/home/standards.htm

15. International Organization for Standardization. (2005). "ISO and Conformity Assessment." Accessed March 11, 2012, http://www.iso.org/iso/casco_2005.pdf. p. 1.

16. International Organization for Standardization. (2011). "TC 38 Textiles." Accessed March 16, 2012, http://www.iso.org/iso/iso_technical_committee?commid=48148.

17. International Organization for Standardization. (2010) "Publicizing Your ISO 9001:2008 or ISO 14001: 2004 Certification". Accessed June 27, 2014, http://www.iso.org/iso/publicizing_iso9001_iso14001_certification_2010.pdf

18. ASTM International. (2011). *Annual Book of ASTM Standards 2011: Section Seven Textiles*, Vol. 07.01. West Conshohocken: ASTM International, iii.

19. ASTM International. (2012). "Committee D13 on Textiles." Accessed March 16, 2012, http://www.astm.org/COMMIT/COMMITTEE/D13.htm.

20. American Textile Chemist and Colorist. (2011). "About AATCC." Accessed March 16, 2012, http://www.aatcc.org/about/index.htm.

21. American Association of Textile Chemists and Colorists. (2011). *2011 Technical Manual of the American Association of Textile Chemists and Colorists*, Vol. 86. Research Triangle Park: American Textile Chemist and Colorist.

22. American Association of Textile Chemists and Colorists. (2011). "ISO Involvement." Accessed March 16, 2012, http://www.aatcc.org/testing/iso/index.htm.

23. American National Standards Institute. "Introduction to ANSI." Accessed March 17, 2012, http://www.ansi.org/about_ansi /introduction/introduction.aspx?menuid=1.

24. American National Standards Institute. "About ANSI Overview." Accessed March 17, 2012, http://www.ansi.org/about_ansi/overview /overview.aspx?menuid=1.

25. British Standards Institution. (2012). "About BSI Group." Accessed March 17, 2012, http://www .bsigroup.com/en/about-bsi/.

26. British Standards Institution. (2012). "About BSI Standards." Accessed March 17, 2012, http://www.bsigroup.com/en/Standards-and -Publications/About-BSI-British-Standards/.

27. British Standards Institution. (2012). "BSI British Standards' Role as the UK's National Standards Body." Accessed March 17, 2012, http://www .bsigroup.com/en/Standards-and-Publications /About-BSI-British-Standards/Our-role-as-an -NSB/.

28. European Committee for Standardization. (2009). "About us." Accessed March 17, 2012, "http://www.cen.eu/cen/AboutUs/Pages/default .aspx#.

29. European Committee for Standardization. (2009). "Work Programme." Accessed March 17, 2012, http://www.cen.eu/cen/Sectors/Sectors /Consumer%20products/Pages/Workprogramme .aspx#.

30. China National Institute of Standardization. (2014). "About CNIS". Accessed June 27, 2014, http://en.cnis.gov.cn/bzygk/kyly/

31. China National Institute of Standardization. (2014). "About CNIS". Accessed June 27, 2014, http://en.cnis.gov.cn/bzygk/kyly/

32. Japanese Standards Association. (2013). "History and Organization." Accessed March 22, 2013, http://www.jsa.or.jp/eng/about/about.asp.

33. Japanese Standards Association. (2013). "The Primary Activities of JSA." Accessed March 22, 2013, http://www.jsa.or.jp/eng/about/about02 .asp.

34. Japanese Industrial Standards Committee. "Publication of JIS." Accessed August 7, 2013, http://www.jisc.go.jp/eng/pj/index.html.

35. Japanese Industrial Standards Committee. "About JISC." Accessed August 7, 2013, https:// www.jisc.go.jp/eng/jisc/index_e.html.

36. Japanese Industrial Standards Committee. "Home page." Accessed August 7, 2013, https:// www.jisc.go.jp/eng/.

37. Standards Council of Canada. (2011). "History of SSC." Accessed March 17, 2012, http://www.scc .ca/en/about-scc/history.

38. Standards Council of Canada. (2011). "National Standards System (NSS)." Accessed March 17, 2012, http://www.scc.ca/en/national_standards _system.

39. Association of the Nonwoven Fabrics Industry. (2010). "History of INDA." Accessed March 17, 2012, http://www.inda.org/about-inda/history/

40. EDANA. (2008). "At a Glance." Accessed March 17, 2012, http://www.edana.org/content/default .asp?PageID=55.

41. Armand Feigenbaum. *Total Quality Management* (New York: McGraw-Hill, Inc. 1991). Third edition, revised. 6.

42. Armand V. Feigenbaum. (November 1956). "Total Quality Control." *Harvard Business Review*, 34, no. 6: ISSN 0017-8012, 93.

43. Marc Davis. (May 21, 2013). "Retailers Come Clean as Info Released on How and Where Products are Made." *Sourcing Journal*. Accessed September 7, 2013, https://www .sourcingjournalonline.com/retailers-come- clean-as-info-released-on-how-and-where- products-are-made/

44. Sustainable Apparel Coalition. (2012). "Scope." Accessed September 7, 2013, http://www .apparelcoalition.org/overview/.

CHAPTER TWO

Integrating Quality into the Development of Apparel Products

Objectives:

- To present key considerations when developing an apparel product line
- To explain the design development process for apparel
- To define basic design elements and principles
- To understand color management from initial design through to the end product

Design is a key ingredient to creating quality saleable garments that consumers want to buy. Geoffrey Beene stated, "Design is a revelation to me. It's like taking something that is not alive and giving it form, shape, substance, and life."[1] Incorporating quality features and components into the design and construction of the product lead to customer satisfaction. The aesthetic appearance is very important because it is what initially draws a customer to a garment.

AESTHETICS AND DESIGN DEVELOPMENT DETAILS

Charles Eames once said, "Design is a plan for arranging elements in such a way as to best accomplish a particular purpose."[2] Design elements and principles are key aspects of effective apparel designs. When product developers create a line they must first consider the purpose for the line or product. Questions they must consider include:

- What are the aesthetic attributes the target market is looking for in this apparel item?
- What are the performance attributes the target market is expecting from this apparel item?
- What level of durability is the customer expecting from this apparel item?
- What are the garment's maintenance requirements? Is the customer willing to pay for drycleaning costs over the life of the item?
- What level of quality is the consumer expecting?
- How much is the customer willing to pay?

Design Development

Research is the first step in the process of developing a mass-produced apparel line. Tracking economic trends, cultural and social trends, technology advances, and political influences impacting consumer behavior and spending provide factors that must be considered when developing product. The types of research investigated include environmental, product, and consumer. **Environmental trend research**, also known as **market and global trends research**, is conducted to determine factors impacting consumer spending that businesses cannot control. Variables such as the state of the global, national, and local economies where products are produced and sold are investigated and evaluated to track events that have occurred over the past 12 months to provide insight for projections for the coming year(s). **Target market research (consumer**

Table 2.1 Demographic and Lifestyle Data

Demographic Data	Lifestyle Data
Age	Life Stage
Gender	Reference Groups
Income	Social Class
Education	Personality
Religious Affiliations	Attitudes and Values
Family Size	Generational Group
Housing Type	Behavior
Ethnicity	Cultural Distinctions*
Marital Status	
Occupation	
Geographic Location	
Spending Patterns	

Note: *Cultural distinctions are preferences based on ethnic or cultural influences.

trend research) is vital for designers to understand who their customer is and factors that motivate them to buy or refrain from purchasing. This research is gathered and analyzed based on demographic and lifestyle data. See Table 2.1 for demographic and lifestyle data. **Product market research** provides information regarding general market trends through exploring innovative products being developed or introduced, competing products, and trend forecasts to provide insight for ways to improve existing products or to provide new opportunities in the marketplace for expanding business.

When the research phase is completed, designers begin developing the concept for the line to provide inspirational direction for the season's theme. Important colors, fabrics, silhouettes, and design details are selected for inclusion in the line. **Design details** create visual interest within the silhouette through style lines or design features such as collars, cuffs, closures, necklines, pockets, sleeves, trimmings, or yokes. Design ideation begins with the designer exploring ideas for product line solutions by creating styles, selecting color palettes and fabrics, and sourcing materials. Modifications to styles are made based on line concept, fit, functionality, cost, production limitations, and the merchandise plan. This is when the product line is selected.

During the design development process patterns are made for each garment selected for inclusion in the line. Patternmakers start with a **block**, which is a tag board or digital pattern that follows the natural contours of the body or dress form developed to brand specifications for a sample or given size. A block is used to develop first patterns of new designs or modifications of existing styles of bodices, skirts, dresses, pants, and sleeves. The initial pattern developed for a design that includes seam and hem allowances is called a **first pattern**. As the design is modified a **working pattern** is created. When the style and fit are tested and perfected, a **production pattern** is developed to include seam allowances, perforations, notches, grain lines, and pattern identifications. **Grading** is the next stage in the process that entails adjusting the pattern by increasing and decreasing the measurements of the pieces to create all sizes within the range offered for the style. Some luxury brands do not grade their patterns but rather create production patterns for each size offered. When this is done the fit is very good and all of the garment components are properly proportioned for each size. Although the cost is higher, the fit of the garment is greatly enhanced. Fit and construction details include quality cues for the customer.

Color, Texture, and Pattern

Color is powerful and can influence whether a product sells or not. It can also impact the visual quality of a garment before and after purchase and refurbishment. The color of every component of a garment is critical to quality perception. If the fabric, trim, and thread are all supposed to match but each is slightly different in color than another, the designer or product developer, manufacturer, buyer, retailer, and customer will interpret this as poor quality.

Color is created through the absorption and reflectance of light. Human eyes contain light receptors that communicate messages to the brain and interpret these light waves in the electromagnetic spectrum as color. There are seven color classifications in the visual spectrum: red, orange, yellow, green, blue, indigo, and violet. Each color classification has a visual wavelength that can be divided into hue, value, and saturation. The purest form of a color that is associated with its wavelength is known as **hue**. Tints, midtones, and shade variations of a color indicate its **value** or luminance. **Saturation** is the intensity of the color in terms of its sharpness or dullness.

The fashion industry, among others, uses **trend forecasting services** to provide seasonal color direction based on data gathered through market research on consumer preferences, lifestyle changes, social, political, and cultural influences, as well as stimuli from various traditional and social media outlets. Trend forecasters specify seasonal color palettes using standardized color matching systems. Pantone, Munsell, and SCOTDIC are color matching systems used to specify and control color throughout the development and manufacturing processes. These **color standards** help designers and product developers communicate accurate specifications for dye formulations to provide color requirements for mills and converters in order to precisely match the desired hues for production of fibers, yarns, fabrics, threads, trims, and findings for apparel products.

Color is one of the most difficult quality elements of a textile product to manage. **Color management** starts with the designer's accurate communication of color and ends when the product is in the marketplace. The process for assessing color throughout the different stages of design development and production is known as **color evaluation**. The color matching process begins when color standards are sent to mills or converters to create dyed or printed fabric samples called **lab dips** (dyed fabrics) or **strike-offs** (printed fabrics). Lab dips can be physical samples or digital representations of the color and fabric that are evaluated visually on a computer screen or in person under various lighting conditions to ensure consistent color. The lab dips are evaluated against the color standard to determine if they match. Instruments such as **colorimeters** and **spectrophotometers** provide a numeric representation of a color by digitally measuring the percentage of light reflected at each wavelength along the visual spectrum, known as **spectral data**. See Figure 2.1 for examples of spectometers. When a material registers the same or near-identical spectral data as the color standard, it is considered a **color match** and is approved. One of the problems that can occur with color that must be carefully monitored is **metamerism**. This is when colors match under certain lighting conditions and not in others. An example is when a customer purchases a red sweater set and brings it home to find the shell does not match the cardigan in incandescent lighting but did match under the fluorescent lighting used in the retail store. Metamerism is a quality problem that can be avoided if color is managed and evaluated throughout the design and production processes (see Figure 2.2).

Color production standards are those hues that have been approved and are reproducible for color consistency during manufacturing of fibers, yarns, fabrics, threads, trims, and findings and through garment assembly. The challenge of reproducing a specific color across a variety of different **substrates** (fibers and materials) calls for different

(a)

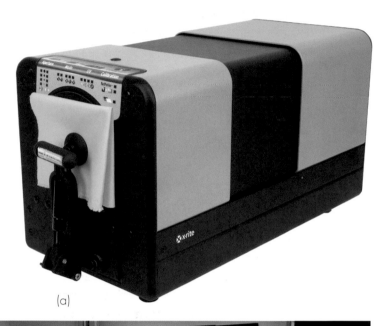

(b)

Figure 2.1 (a) Portable spectrophotometer. (b) Bench spectrophotometer.
Courtesy X-Rite, Inc.

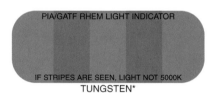

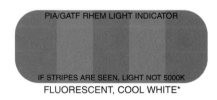

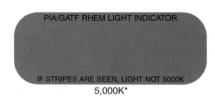

* SIMULATED

Figure 2.2 Metamerism effects on textile materials
RHEM Light Indicator, courtesy of Printing Industries of America

chemical formulations to arrive at the same color. These formulations are known as **color specifications**, which contain the requirements for matching color standards and the dye or pigment formulations for reproduction on specified materials to match the color standards. The **Colour Index** is an international online publication by the Society of Dyers and Colourists (SDC) and the American Association of Textile Chemists and Colorists (AATCC) that provides the chemical formulations for dyes and pigments (colorants).[3]

Pattern and texture add visual interest to textile products. **Texture** influences the aesthetic appearance of the surface contour of a material and can impact how it feels to the touch as well as how a garment hangs. Designers select fabrics based on the desired appearance, hand, and drape, among other specifications. Weaving, knitting, and felting processes provide texture to fabrics through the intrinsic characteristics of the selected fibers, yarns, fabric construction, finish, and weight. Texture can also be conveyed through printing on the surface of the material (see Table 2.2). Surface texture can also influence the appearance of the fabric's color by the way light is reflected off the surface. For example, the reflection or absorption of light is impacted by the direction which a velvet fabric is cut. When a garment is cut for the nap to lie down, the light reflects off the surface and makes the color appear lighter; but when the garment is cut with the nap brushed up, the light is absorbed by the textured surface and the color appears richer and can provide the perception of a better quality garment.

The application of mechanical or chemical finishes to fabrics can also alter the aesthetic and physical texture, drape, and hand of the garment. Examples of these fabric finishes include calendaring, flocking, fulling, mercerizing, napping and sueding, plisse, shearing, softening, stiffening, and washing (see Table 2.3).

Pattern, a repetitive design that adds aesthetic appeal to garments, can be created through weaving, knitting, and felting processes to provide design interest to fabrics through the intrinsic characteristics of the selected fibers, yarns, and fabric construction.

Examples of pattern constructed as part of the woven structure include fabrics such as basket weave, pique, jacquard, faille, yarn-dyed stripes, plaids, brocade, and dobby weaves. Patterns that are created through knitted structures include fabrics such as rib, cable, lace, yarn-dyed Fair Isle, and intarsia. Texture can also be created by printing on the surface of the garment or fabric to provide a more economical way of creating visual interest. Patterned fabrics can repeat or be **engineered prints** that do not repeat within a garment section and are created to fit specific dimensions. Fabric prints can create the illusion of texture or alter the visual perception of proportion within a garment. See Figure 2.3 for examples of pattern and texture.

Proportion, Balance, and Emphasis

The design and appearance of a garment is determined in part by its proportion and balance. Garments are comprised of various component parts. The way in which these elements are arranged impacts the aesthetic appeal and overall visual appearance of an apparel item on the wearer. **Proportion** refers to the position and scale of one garment portion in relation to another. The harmonious interrelationships among silhouette, design details, style lines, and fabric grain define the proportion within a given design. Proportion of a garment can produce an illusion and alter the visual perception of height, weight, and place emphasis on a certain part of the body to add design interest. The **golden ratio**, also known as **divine proportion**, is an irrational mathematical constant equal to approximately 1.618. The golden ratio can be traced back to ancient Greece in 500 BC when they "recognized this 'dividing' or 'sectioning' property and described it generally as 'the division of a line into extreme and mean ratio.'"[4] This golden ratio provided the most aesthetically pleasing proportion of sides of a rectangle and has since been applied by many artists, architects, and designers. The natural proportion of the human figure lends itself well for applying divine proportion for clothing design. See Figure 2.4 for examples of proportion.

Table 2.2 Texture Created Through Structure, Yarns, Fibers, and Surface Design

Woven Textures

Knitted Textures

Felted Textures

Texture Prints

Photos courtesy of Janace Bubonia

Table 2.3 Textile Finishes that Alter the Appearance and Texture of Fabrics

Finish Name	Process	Effect
Calendering	Mechanical	Embossing Glazed appearance (low-high sheen) Moiré effect
Flocking	Mechanical	Patterned surface Suede or velvety texture
Fulling	Mechanical	Felting Improves hand, softness, and thickness
Mercerizing	Chemical	Luster Improves drape, hand, and strength
Napping and Sueding	Mechanical	Brushed surface Improves hand, insulation, and softness
Plisse	Chemical	Puckered surface
Shearing	Mechanical	Trimmed surface fibers Consistency and uniformity
Softening	Chemical & Mechanical	Improves drape and hand
Stiffening	Chemical	Improves crispness and stiffness
Washing	Chemical & Mechanical	Distressed, faded, worn appearance Improves softness

Balance is defined as equilibrium or stability. In relation to apparel design, balance refers to the vertical symmetry of a garment when divided down the center front and center back. There are two types of balance—symmetric and asymmetric. **Symmetric**, also known as **formal balance**, is well proportioned; this means that each side of the garment when divided vertically down the middle appears identical or as a mirror image of the other side. **Asymmetric**, or **informal balance**, does not look the same on each side. The visual weight is not distributed evenly when the garment is divided down the center front or center back of a garment. See Figure 2.5 for balance used in garment designs.

Figure 2.3 Engineered prints
Images courtesy of [TC]² NC USA www.tc2.com

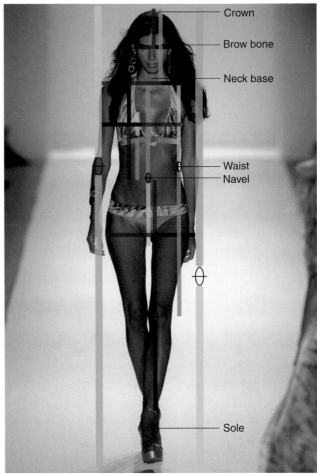

Crown

Brow bone

Neck base

Waist
Navel

Sole

Figure 2.4 Divine proportion. Bottom row: Divine proportion shown in the Valentino Fall 2011 collection
WWD/Giovanni Giannoni

(a)

(b)

(c)

(d)

(e)

(f)

Figure 2.5 (a) and (b) Asymmetric balance in designs by Alexandre Vauthier and (c) Yuna Yang. (d)–(f) Symmetric balance in designs by Alexander Wang, Raf Simons, and General Idea

Designers need to carefully plan where the focal point or **emphasis** of a garment will be. When a person looks at a garment, the emphasis is where the eye travels to first. The focal point of a garment is very intentional. The **rule of thirds** is a composition guideline used by visual artists and designers. Use of this rule gives designers the ability to integrate design elements within a garment in an effort to intentionally control where the viewer's eyes are drawn and what they see. Application of the rule of thirds produces asymmetric designs that create more visual interest within the garment. The movement of the viewer's eye through each part of the garment is known as **rhythm** and can be controlled through lines created by seams, darts, and other design details.

The human eye will follow the line until it is intersected by another line or element, where it may pause while the viewer interprets what he or she sees before moving on to the next portion of the garment. Design details can also be placed in a section of the garment that is void of seams, darts, or other elements to create focal interest to draw the attention of the viewer. When all of the design elements of a garment work together to create a unified overall pleasing aesthetic, **harmony** is achieved (see Figure 2.6).

Silhouettes and Garment Styles

The outline or overall shape created by a garment is the **silhouette**. The interior portion of a silhouette is made up of shapes that define the garment's details to

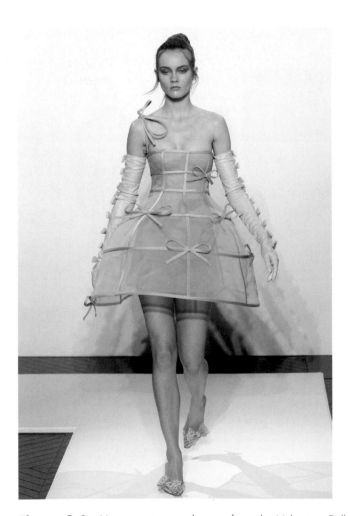 

Figure 2.6 Harmony in two designs from the Valentino Fall 2010 haute couture show
WWD/Giovanni Giannoni

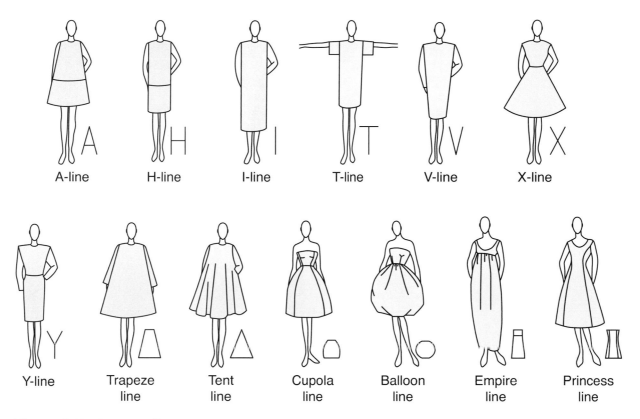

Figure 2.7 Garment silhouettes
Illustration by Q2A Media Services Private Limited

add visual interest, provide fit, and designate proportion and symmetry. There are a variety of silhouettes that have been developed through the ages. Some silhouettes were named after specific time periods, some after letters because the form they create is similar to that of the letter they are named after, while others were named for the specific shapes they create. See Figure 2.7 for illustrations of garment silhouettes. **Line** is used to create silhouette as well as the shapes formed within the garment. Designers use structural details such as darts, seams, tucks, pleats, gathering, stitching, linear trims, and piecing to create design interest and provide fit through the use of line within a garment. Line can also be created through texture and pattern. The direction of line with a garment creates visual interest and can also create the visual perception or illusion of height or weight. Vertical lines denote height and can create a slenderizing

effect while horizontal lines can add visual weight and shorten the appearance of the figure. A sense of motion and youthfulness is created through the use of diagonal or curved lines that add interest due to the asymmetric balance they create. Additional characteristics of line such as length, boldness, consistency, continuity, and repetition all add different levels of interest and impact to a garment design. See Figure 2.8 for ways line is used in garment design.

Design elements and principles discussed in this chapter provide a means for designers to effectively create aesthetically pleasing garments that will appeal to customers and lead to purchases. Lack of knowledge and understanding of how these elements and principles are applied to the design process can result in poor design, unflattering proportions, competing garment features, and lead to customer dissatisfaction and the perception of poor quality.

(a)

(b)

(c)

(d)

(e)

(f)

Figure 2.8 Line. (a) Valentino Resort 2012; (b) Norma Kamali Resort 2012; (c) and (d) Salvatore Ferragamo Resort 2012; (e) Tadashi Shoji Spring 2013; (f) BCBG Max Azria Spring 2013
(a)–(d) and (f) WWD/John Aquino; (e) WWD/Thomas Iannaccone

SUMMARY

In this chapter the process used for designing and developing an apparel line is presented in the logical order in which it occurs in the fashion industry. Key consideration for the development of salable apparel products are touched upon. The importance of research as the starting point of the design process is vital. Researching trends that impact consumer spending allows a designer to knowing who the target consumer is and what motivates them to buy. Reviewing and selecting fashion trends appropriate for the brand, customer, and season are equally important to ensure the customer will understand the trends and be comfortable purchasing and wearing garments that reflect these trends. Additionally, knowing about new products that will be introduced into the marketplace as well as understanding what the competition is offering is critical to a designer's awareness of products in the marketplace that will compete with the line he or she is developing. An overview of the design elements and principles is presented along with discussion of how they are used to create aesthetically pleasing salable products consumers want to buy. Color management and methods for effectively communicating color are discussed as they are utilized throughout the design and manufacturing stages.

ACTIVITIES

1. Find two garments within your wardrobe that contain good use of the design elements and principles outlined in this chapter. Document each garment through photos, and label each element and principle. Briefly explain how each element and principle is used to create harmony and an overall aesthetically pleasing garment.

2. Find one garment within your wardrobe that could use improvement in the application of the design elements and principles to improve the styling. Document the garment through photos and label each element and principle. Briefly explain how you would change the design of the garment by modifying the design elements and principles to create a more aesthetically pleasing garment. Sketch your version of the garment.

APPAREL QUALITY LAB MANUAL

Please refer to Lab Activity 2.1 Analysis of Aesthetic and Design Details of Woven Garments in Relation to Design Elements and Principles across Price Categories; Lab Activity 2.2 Comparison Project Product Analysis of Aesthetic and Design Details in Relation to Design Elements and Principles of Competing Brands, and 2.3 Farnsworth Munsell 100 Hue Test in the *Apparel Quality Lab Manual*.

ENDNOTES

1. Geoffrey Beene. BrainyQuote.com. Xplore Inc. (2012). Accessed March 22, 2012, http://www.brainyQuote.com/quotes/authors/g/geoffrey_beene.html.

2. Charles Eames. BrainyQuote.com. Xplore Inc. (2012). Accessed March 22, 2012, http://www.brainyQuote.com/quotes/authors/c/charles_eames.html.

3. Society of Dyers and Colourists and American Textile Chemists and Colorists. (2014). *Colour Index*. Accessed June 27, 2014, http://www.sdc.org.uk/technical-services/colour-index/.

4. *Encyclopedia Britannica Online*. "golden ratio." Accessed May 11, 2012, http://www.britannica.com/EBchecked/topic/237728/golden-ratio.

Raw Materials Selection and Performance

CHAPTER THREE

Objectives:

- To review fiber types, yarn construction, fabric structures, colorants, and finishes
- To understand fabric characteristics in relation to performance and selection

- To introduce performance attributes and compatibility in relation to component materials such as support fabrics, shaping devices, findings, trim, and surface embellishments
- To understand why materials selection impacts quality

Materials selection for apparel items has a significant impact on the function, performance and quality of the finished product. Fibers, yarns, and unfinished fabrics created by mills for use in apparel products are known as **raw materials**. Animal skins, including fur and leather, are additional materials that can be used in apparel manufacturing. Designers, product developers, and buyers need to understand the fundamentals of textile science so they can make good choices when creating or buying apparel.

The fiber content, yarn construction, fabric count, weight, color, and finish all have direct bearing on the quality and performance of the product. In addition, component materials selected for the garment must be compatible so quality is not compromised. For example, if fabric is selected for swimwear, it must be colorfast to rubbing, water, sun, and perspiration, and retain its shape when wet, dry, and after repeated cleanings. It must also have the ability to dry quickly and have some level of abrasion resistance to avoid

Table 3.1 Textile Science Resources
Industry Resources
ASTM International. *Online Standards 2014: D7641-10 Standard Guide for Textile Fibers*, 1–13.
ASTM International. *Online Standards 2014: D123-13a Standard Terminology Relating to Textiles*, 1–68.
ASTM International. *Annual Book of Standards 2014: D4849-13 Standard Terminology Related to Yarns and Fibers*, 1–11.
Academic Resources
Allen C. Cohen and Ingrid Johnson. *J.J. Pizzuto's Fabric Science*, 10th Edition. (New York: Fairchild Books 2011).
Virginia Hecken Elsasser. *Textiles: Concepts and Principles*, 3rd Edition. (New York: Fairchild Books 2010).
Sara J. Kadolph. *Textiles: Basics.* (Boston: Pearson 2013).
Sara J. Kadolph. *Textiles*, 11th Edition. (Upper Saddle River: Prentice Hall 2010).
Mary Humphries. *Fabric Reference*, 4th Edition. (Upper Saddle River: Prentice Hall 2009).
Mary Humphries. *Fabric Glossary*, 4th Edition. (Upper Saddle River: Prentice Hall 2009).

pilling. Other component materials and findings such as lining fabric, bra cups, hooks, sliders, thread, and elastic must all be compatible with use and care procedures for the end product. Failure of any of these will result in consumer dissatisfaction. In the case of active wear, material that wicks moisture away from the skin is more desirable than fabric that absorbs moisture and retains it against the body. The intent of this chapter is to provide a brief review of basic textiles in relation to selection, performance, and quality. For additional resources having more in-depth coverage of textile science, refer to Table 3.1.

FABRICS

Fabric is a substrate composed of fiber and yarns that have been woven, knitted, or chemically, thermally, or mechanically bonded. Materials are an important indicator of quality of apparel items and account for a significant portion of the cost of a garment. Materials used in apparel construction are evaluated throughout the design and production processes. Textile inspection, testing, and analysis during the fabric selection phase allow for a better understanding of specification requirements and if the materials selected will meet the standards and expectations for the design and for the customer. Suppliers have the opportunity to correct problems prior to the purchase of production yardage and assembly during manufacturing. Prototype and production samples are tested for performance and appearance to ensure the product will meet designated specifications and safety regulations. These samples are analyzed to verify consistency of the material's performance once in garment form. Fabrics are inspected when they are received into the factory before any spreading and cutting begins. When production starts, garments are again inspected along the assembly and finishing processes to ensure quality is maintained. Companies will also pull merchandise from the warehouse or retail floor and send it for additional testing to ensure quality is consistent throughout the process. See Chapter 13 for inspection procedures and common defects found in fabrics and garments.

Fibers

A **fiber** is the smallest unit within the structure of a textile fabric having a minimum length-to-width/diameter ratio of 100 to 1.[1] Fibers can be composed of cellulose (plant based), protein (animal based), or manufactured from an organic or inorganic base (synthetic chemicals). Cellulose fibers are derived from the cell walls of seeds, leaves, stems, or bast (inner fibrous bark from stems or leaves of dicotyledonous plants). Natural animal hair, feathers and down, and silk are the sources for protein fibers. Manufactured synthetic fibers result from the chemical binding of monomers to create inorganic polymer chain structures that are extruded as filament fibers. Manufactured fibers can also be formed by synthesizing organic chemical compounds or polymers derived from modified cellulose fibers, which are also extruded into filament fibers. See Table 3.2 for generic fibers listed by type and source. The length of the fibers can vary as well. **Staple** fibers are short and

Table 3.2 Generic Fiber Names and Types

Naturally Occurring Fibers	
Cellulose Fibers	**Plant Source**
Cotton	Seed
Flax	Bast fiber (soft)
Hemp	Leaf fiber (hard)
Jute	Bast fiber (soft)
Ramie	Bast fiber
Sisal	Bast fiber (soft)
Protein Fibers	**Animal Source**
Alpaca	Llama glama
Angora	Rabbit
Camel hair	Camel
Cashmere	Cashmere goat
Down	Waterfowl
Horsehair	Horse
Llama	Llama glama
Mohair	Angora goat
Silk	Silk worm
Vicuna	Llama vicugna
Wool	Sheep

Chemically Derived and Modified Fibers		
Modified or Regenerated Compounds from Natural Polymer Base (organic)	**Manufactured Fibers from Synthetic Polymer Base (inorganic)**	
Acetate [*Cellulose*] (MC)	Acrylic	Olefin [*Polypropylene*]
Triacetate [*Cellulose*] (MC)	Anidex	Lastol
Azlon (RP)	Aramid	PBI
PLA (RP)	Elastoester [*Elastomultiester*]	Polyester
Rayon [*Viscose*] (RC)	Fluoropolymer	Elasterell-p
Bamboo (RC)	Melamin	Saran
Lyocell (RC)	Metallic [*Metal Fibre*]	Spandex [*Elastane*]
Modal (RC)	Modacrylic	Sulfar
Viscose (RC)	Novoloid	Vinal or polyvinyl alcohol (PVA) [*Vinylal*]
Rubber [*Elastodiene*] (RP)	Nylon [*Polyamide*]	Vinyon [*Chlorofiber*]
	Nytril	

Note: ISO equivalent terms for generic manufactured fibers when different from the US Federal Trade Commission's Code of Federal Regulations are indicated in italicized letters surrounded by brackets.
(MC)=Modified Cellulose
(RC)=Regenerated Cellulose
(RP)=Regenerated Protein

Sources: ASTM International. *Annual Book of Standards 2011: D123-09 Standard Terminology Relating to Textiles, Section Seven Textiles*, Vol. 07.01. West Conshohocken: ASTM International, 9-80;
ASTM International. *Annual Book of Standards 2011: D7641-10 Standard Guide for Textile Fibers, Section Seven Textiles*, Vol. 07.02. West Conshohocken: ASTM International, 966-978;
United States Nation Archives and Records Administration. *Electronic Code of Federal Regulations (CFR) Title 16, Section 303.7*, accessed July 7, 2012, http://ecfr.gpoaccess.gov/cgi/t/text/text-idx?c=ecfr&sid=c6aad664cb967360b4df5d102040b413&rgn=div5&view=text&node=16:1.0.1.3.27&id no=16#16:1.0.1.3.27.0.12.7

range in length from ⅜ inch (5 mm) to 19.5 inches (500 mm). All natural fibers are staple fibers with the exception of silk. **Filament** fibers are long fibers that can be cut into staple lengths ranging from 1 inch (2.5 mm) to 8 inches (203 mm) known as **tow**, or they can be left in one continuous strand. The only natural filament fiber is silk, which is typically 1,600 yards (1,463 meters) in length but can vary depending upon the fineness of the silk.[2,3,4] See Figure 3.1 for illustrations of staple and filament fibers. The shape and surface texture of manufactured fibers is created during the extrusion process. The size, cross-sectional shape, and texture along the fiber strand are formed by the spinneret used, which is selected based on the aesthetic and performance properties desired.

The characteristics and performance properties of fibers are important to know when developing apparel products. Fiber selection should be carefully based on the attributes of the fiber, suitability for use, and performance requirements of the end product. Fiber performance properties relate directly to the elements of quality that were defined in Chapter 1 as performance, durability, serviceability, conformance, and aesthetics. Fiber performance impacts the overall functional aspects of a garment in relation to end use.

The key aspects of fiber performance include aesthetics and comfort, durability and serviceability, and conformance (see Table 3.3). Aesthetic and comfort

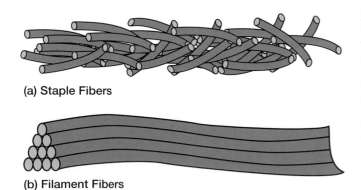

(a) Staple Fibers

(b) Filament Fibers

Figure 3.1 Staple and filament fibers
Courtesy of Fairchild Books

fiber properties focus on the appearance and palpable aspects fibers offer such as the surface texture, luster and density; the way in which the fabric hangs or drapes on the body; and the thermal retention, absorbency, and resiliency. A consumer's perception of aesthetics is based upon their visual and tactile experiences as they relate to the specific product attributes for the end use of the product. Comfort is an important aspect of this perception because most consumers are not willing to continue to wear a garment if it is not physically comfortable. The durability of fibers and serviceability directly affect a garment's ability to resist physical and mechanical deterioration due to wear and refurbishment, which can impact the functionality of the product for its intended use. Factors include the degree to which a fiber can resist abrasion, bending, flexing, stretching, and pulling, and retain its shape and size during wear and refurbishment. A consumer's perception of durability and serviceability is based upon their expectations, use, and care of the product in relation to the price paid. Consumers want to purchase apparel items that will function for their intended use and be easily maintained and cared for. Conformance of fibers is critical to the design and performance of a garment and whether it meets the standards established for the product. Safety of the wearer is part of conformance, because specifications and standards must be met for production, distribution, and sale of apparel goods to prevent harm to the wearer, whether it is a flammability or a toxicity concern. The fiber content of the yarns comprising the fabrics used for apparel production is important to the selection and performance of the end product. The rules for listing fiber content on a garment label will be discussed in Chapter 9. The pros and cons of fiber properties must be carefully weighed. When one property is enhanced it can often negatively impact another. For example, a designer is creating a women's lightweight sweater made of wool, and it must be blended with another fiber to reduce the cost. Acrylic is often blended with wool in budget and moderate priced apparel. The addition of the

Table 3.3 Performance Properties of Fibers Commonly Used in Apparel

		Aesthetics & Comfort			
Fiber	Thermal Retention	Absorption	Resilience	Density	Hand
Acetate	Poor	Fair	Poor	Medium	Excellent
Acrylic	Excellent	Poor	Good	Low	Good
Cotton	Poor	Good	Poor	High	Good
Flax	Poor	Excellent	Poor	High	Fair
Rayon	Poor	Excellent	Poor	Medium	Good
Polyester	Excellent	Poor	Good	Medium	Fair
Nylon	Good	Fair	Excellent	Low	Fair
Silk	Fair	Excellent	Fair	Low	Excellent
Spandex	Fair	Poor	Excellent	Low	Poor
Wool	Excellent	Excellent	Excellent	Medium	Good
		Durability and Serviceability			
Fiber	Abrasion Resistance	Strength	Elongation	Recovery	
Acetate	Poor	Poor	Medium	Low	
Acrylic	Fair	Fair	High	Medium	
Cotton	Good	Good	Low	Low	
Flax	Fair	Excellent	Low	Low	
Rayon	Fair	Fair	Low	Medium	
Polyester	Excellent	Excellent	Low	Low	
Nylon	Excellent	Excellent	Low	Medium	
Silk	Fair	Good	Medium	Medium	
Spandex	Good	Poor	High	High	
Wool	Fair	Poor	Medium	High	
		Conformance			
Fiber	Flammability	Odor	Type of Ash		
Acetate	Burns and melts	Vinegar	Dark hard bead		
Acrylic	Burns and melts	Bitter, fishy, acrid	Black hard bead		
Cotton	Burns	Burning paper	Gray soft ash		
Flax	Burns	Burning paper	Gray soft ash		
Rayon	Burns	Burning paper	Gray soft ash		
Polyester	Burns and melts	Sweet chemical	Black hard bead		
Nylon	Burns and melts	Celery	Tan or dark hard bead		
Silk	Burns	Burning hair	Black crisp ash		
Spandex	Burns and melts	Chemical	Black soft ash		
Wool	Burns	Burning hair	Black crisp ash		

Sources: Allen C. Cohen and Ingrid Johnson. *J.J. Pizzuto's Fabric Science*, 10th Edition (New York: Fairchild Books 2011), 25, 31, 36, 43, 52; Sara J. Kadolph. *Textiles*, 11th Edition (Upper Saddle River: Prentice Hall 2010), 28, 30–31, 35

acrylic fibers provides strength and elongation properties to the garment; however, the addition of acrylic fibers will reduce the garment's absorption and resiliency properties, causing the garment to retain wrinkles more easily and reduce the ability for the garment to breathe. A garment's ability to breathe refers to its properties that allow moisture (such as perspiration) to be absorbed and released away from the skin during wear. It is up to the designer to determine which properties are most important to the product's aesthetics, function, performance, and serviceability for the useful life of the product.

Yarns

After the fibers are prepared, they are spun or twisted into yarns. A **singles yarn** can be made from one continuous filament, one strand of filament fibers, or by twisting staple fibers together to form a spun yarn. **Ply yarns** consist of two or more yarns twisted, wrapped, entangled, or chemically bound together (see Figure 3.2). Ply yarns typically provide more strength to the fabric. Yarns can have twist applied in the Z or S direction. When held vertically, **Z-twist** yarns have a spiral of diagonal lines that extend from the upper right to the lower left creating the same direction of line as the middle of the letter Z. When a Z-twist yarn is held vertically between the index finger and thumb of the left hand and rolled in the direction to the right it will cause the yarn to untwist (see Figure 3.3). The spiral of **S-twist** yarns extend from the upper left to the lower right, duplicating the same line direction as the middle of the letter S. When an S-twist yarn is held vertically between the index finger and thumb

(a) Singles Yarn

(b) Ply Yarn

Figure 3.2 Singles and ply yarn
Courtesy of Fairchild Books

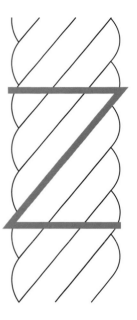

Figure 3.3 Z-Twist yarn
Courtesy of Fairchild Books

Figure 3.4 S-Twist yarn
Courtesy of Fairchild Books

of the left hand and rolled in the direction to the left, it will cause the yarn to untwist (see Figure 3.4). The direction of twist does not impact the quality of a yarn or the finished fabric; however, the amount of twist applied to a yarn, known as **turns per inch (tpi), turns per meter (tpm)**, or **turns per centimeter (tpcm)**, does. The amount of yarn twist affects appearance and performance of the fabric. Yarns with higher twist are more durable, possess greater strength, and have increased resistance to abrasion because there are fewer loose fiber ends on the surface. A smoother appearance and more lustrous surface are common characteristics of yarns possessing higher twist. Increasing the twist of the yarn does impact cost so the pros and cons must be weighed in relation to performance and quality standards as well as consumer expectations.

Fabric Construction

The structure of the fabric is dependent upon the method for making fiber or yarn into cloth and includes the method of construction, count, thickness, and weight. **Fabric construction** describes the structure of the material. Methods for producing fabrics include weaving or knitting of yarns or chemical bonding, mechanical entanglement or thermal fusion of fibers. Each of these methods have variations that provide different aesthetic appearances, variances in durability, functionality, and performance features depending upon the desired requirements for the finished garment.

Fabrics can be woven on looms with **harnesses**, which are frames that hold the **heddles** (needle like wires) that are threaded with warp yarns. The harnesses are raised and lowered to accommodate movement of the filling yarn passing back and forth to weave the fabric with each pass. Woven materials are created by interlacing warp and filling yarns at 90-degree angles to each other. The weave structure of the material is determined by the order in which the yarns are interlaced with each other.

The basic weave structures used for apparel fabrics include plain, twill, and satin weaves (see Figure 3.5). **Plain weave** fabrics are created using two harnesses with a shuttle carrying the filling yarns passing over and under the warp yarns, alternating with each row. **Balanced plain weave** fabrics are constructed of warp and filling yarns, having the same size, type, and number of yarns in both the warp and filling directions. **Unbalanced plain weave** happens when the number of warp yarns differs from the filling yarns in size, type, and amount. This type of plain weave structure can have a ribbed texture. Another basic weave structure is twill. A **twill weave** is formed using three or more harnesses, whereas the shuttle carrying the filling yarn crosses over two or more warp yarns, then passes under one or more yarns, creating a diagonal line in the right or left direction as subsequent rows are woven. When the diagonal line extends from the lower left to the upper right, it is called **right-hand twill**. **Left-hand twill** is indicated by a diagonal line that extends from the lower right to the upper left. Like plain weaves, twill weave structures can be balanced with the same number of yarns passing over and under in the warp and filling directions, which are referred to as **even twill**. **Uneven twill** fabrics are unbalanced because they have more warp yarns on the face (known as **warp-faced twill**) or more warp yarns on the back (known as **weft-faced twill**). The last basic weave used for apparel fabrics is the **satin weave**. The satin weave can be described as a variation of an exceptionally unbalanced twill weave structure that uses anywhere from 5 to 12 harnesses. In a satin weave, a yarn passes over four or more yarns before passing under one yarn. The yarns "float" over the surface. **Warp-faced satin** has warp yarns that float on the surface before passing under one filling yarn. **Weft-faced satin** has filling yarns floating on the surface before passing under a warp yarn.

Advanced or specialized weave structures that are more expensive to produce include dobby, double cloth, jacquard, and pile. (See Table 3.4 for fabrics specified by weave type.) **Dobby weave** fabrics have a geometric patterned structure created during the weaving process. **Jacquard weaves** have a figured pattern or motif structure that adds pattern to the structure of the fabric. **Pile weave** structures have an additional set of yarns (warp or filling) that are woven into the base and appear as loops on the surface of the fabric. These loops can remain intact or be cut. **Double cloth** is created by weaving two fabrics on the same loom where the two layers are interlocked by another set of yarns that is interlaced to attach the layers together.

Fabrics can also be knitted by interlocking loops together through stitches that are formed by needles. The **knit** structure depends on the direction in which the loops are formed. The two types of knit structures include weft and warp knits (see Figure 3.6; for fabrics specified by knit type see Table 3.5). In knitted fabrics, **wales** are the vertical rows of stitches or loops that run in the lengthwise direction, and **courses** are the rows of stitches or loops that run horizontally in the crosswise direction of the fabric. **Gauge** indicates the number of wales per inch or per 25 mm in a knitted fabric, the fineness of the knit, the number of needles per inch used in a machine to create knit fabrics, and the size of the stitch. The four types of stitches found in knitted materials include knit or plain stitch, purl or

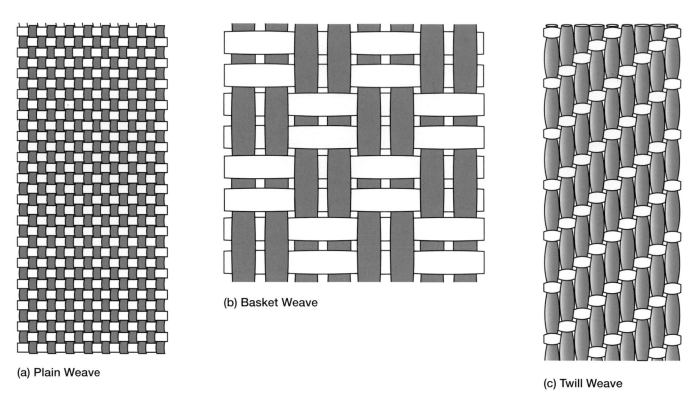

(b) Basket Weave

(a) Plain Weave

(c) Twill Weave

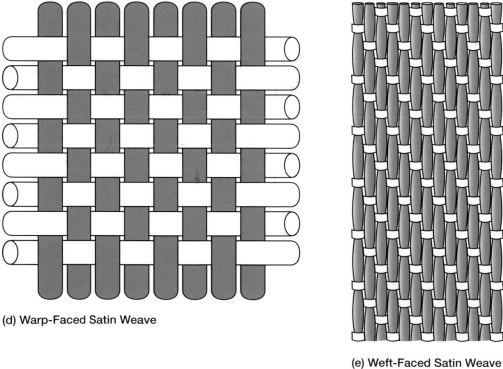

(d) Warp-Faced Satin Weave

(e) Weft-Faced Satin Weave

Figure 3.5 Basic weave structures used for apparel fabrics

Table 3.4 Fabric Names by Weave Structure

Plain Weave Structure Fabrics				
Batiste	Bengaline	Broadcloth	Burlap	Calico
Canvas	Challis	Chambray	Cheesecloth	Chiffon
Chintz	Crepe	Crepe de chine	Crinoline	Dotted Swiss
Duck	Faille	Flannel (can also be constructed with a twill weave)	Gauze	Georgette
Gingham	Hopsack (basket weave variation of plain weave)	Madras	Moiré	Monks cloth (basket weave variation of plain weave)
Muslin	Organdy	Organza	Ottoman	Oxford cloth (basket weave variation of plain weave)
Percale	Plissé	Pongee	Ripstop	Sailcloth
Shantung	Sheeting	Taffeta	Toile	Voile

Twill Weave Structure Fabrics				
Cavalry twill	Chino	Denim	Drill	Flannel (can also be constructed with a plain weave)
Gabardine	Herringbone	Hounds tooth	Serge	Sharkskin
Surah	Whipcord			

Satin Weave Structure Fabrics				
Antique satin	Brushed-back satin	Charmeuse	Crepe-back satin	Duchess satin
Peau de soie	Sateen	Slipper satin		

Dobby Weave Structure Fabrics				
Birdseye	Huckaback	Pique (can also be constructed using a jacquard weave)	Shirting madras	Waffle cloth

Double Cloth Weave Structure Fabrics				
Double cloth	Kersey	Matelassé	Melton	Velvet

Jacquard Weave Structure Fabrics				
Brocade	Brocatelle	Damask	Piques (can also be constructed using a dobby weave)	Tapestry

Pile Weave Structure Fabrics				
Corduroy	Terrycloth	Velveteen		

Source: Janace Bubonia. *Fashion Production Terms and Processes,* (New York: Fairchild Books, 2012)

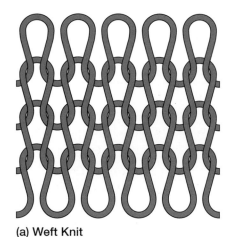

(a) Weft Knit

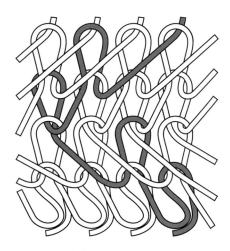

(b) Warp Knit

Figure 3.6 Knit structures
Courtesy of Fairchild Books

Table 3.5 Fabric Names by Knit Structure	
Weft Knit Structure Fabrics	Warp Knit Structure Fabrics
Balbridgan	Bobbinet
Bourrelet	Crochet
Cable knit	Filet
Double Knit	Gossamer
Faux fur	Illustion
Fleece (weft-insertion)	Intarsia
French terry (weft-insertion)	Lace
Interlock	Mali (warp-insertion)
Jacquard jersey	Malimo (warp-insertion)
Jersey knit	Mesh
Knit terry	Milanease
Lacoste	Point d' esprit
Lisle	Pointelle
Matte jersey	Polar fleece
Pile jersey	Power net
Piqué	Raschel knit
Pont di Rome	Simplex
Purl knit	Thermal knit
Rib knit	Tricot knit
Velour	Tulle

Source: Janace Bubonia. *Fashion Production Terms and Processes,* (New York: Fairchild Books, 2012)

reverse knit stitch, missed stitch, and the tuck stitch. The types of stitches and configurations provide many variations for pattern designs. Knit fabric can be produced as flat goods or in a tube for cut and sew production of garments.

Fabrics constructed as fiber web structures rather than with yarns are classified as **nonwovens**. Fibers are produced into fabrics through mechanical entanglement, chemical bonding agents, or by fusing thermoplastic fibers together with heat. Nonwoven fabrics include composite and felt. These fabrics can be produced with or without a fusible coating and can be used to add shape or support as interlining materials for apparel products through thermal bonding or stitching the layer into the garment.

Colorant and Finish

Color attracts consumers to purchase products; therefore, the ability of a fiber and fabric to retain its color is essential. Colorants and finishes are additional variables that influence quality and performance. **Colorants** are the dyes, pigments, and optical brighteners used to apply color to fibers, yarns, fabrics, and garments. **Dyes** are complex water soluble organic molecules comprised of two parts. One is the chromophore, which provides the color portion, and the second component is the auxochrome that delivers solubility and bonding capabilities. Most dyes are absorbed into the fibers and do not require a binding agent (mordant) to assist the material in holding the dye. Not all dyes can be accepted by all fibers, so dye formulations must be carefully matched with the fiber content in order to reduce colorfastness problems that can arise. **Pigments** are also used for adding color to fibers and materials but are very different than dyes. Pigments are not water soluble and require binding agents to adhere color because they stay on the surface and do not penetrate the fiber. Pigments in darker shades can cause stiffness to fabrics, negatively affecting the hand and drape of the finished garment. Color can also be imparted during the formation of manufactured fibers through solution dyeing (dope dyeing). During this process pigment is added to the liquid solution prior to extrusion into fibers. Colorless compounds that add brightness to white fabrics are known as **optical brighteners**, **fluorescent dyes**, or **whiteners**. Fabrics treated with optical brighteners glow when exposed to ultraviolet fluorescent light sources (black light). Brighteners provide fabrics with the appearance of intense white. When fabrics possessing whiteners are compared to those without them, the untreated white fabrics appear dull and can look a bit yellowed. Most consumers desire bright white rather than a yellowish-white when it comes to their clothing, because it provides a cleaner, fresher appearance. For colorants, price classifications, and characteristics see Table 3.6.

Colorants can also be applied through textile printing with the same types of dyes and pigments discussed. Textile printing colorant applications include dry prints, wet prints, and digital prints. **Dry prints** utilize dry pigment that is adhered to the substrate (base material) by a resin binder that must be heat cured. Flatbed and rotary screen printing methods are used to apply dry prints. **Wet prints** utilize liquid dyes that are made into a paste with thickening agents and printed onto the fabric, which requires aging (steaming), washing, and rinsing to remove the thickening agents. Flatbed and rotary screen printing methods

can be used to apply both dry and wet prints. **Digital prints** can be created with either disperse dyes or pigment inkjet inks and are applied to the substrate by a digital inkjet printer. The viscosity of the colorant impacts the level of processing required after printing. Binding agents are necessary for high-viscosity pigments, whereas low viscosity inks do not require them but do need additional processing after printing (see Table 3.7). The cost and quality of printing varies with the method of application and the type of pigment or dye used. 3D printing is different than traditional methods of printing textiles, because the product is printed in layers using synthetic material to form/mold the finished textile product. 3D printing used for modeling is now being used to create garments such as Iris van Herpen's 3-D printed shoes from Fall 2013 couture (See Figure 3.7). The most economical/low cost choices for printing include digital printing for sample yardage or for low-volume yardage, sublimation printing for customized short runs, or rotary screen printing for high-volume production yardage. The setup required for rotary screen printing and sampling is expensive; however, when high-volume yardage is printed it becomes very economical. Printing choices with average costs include digital printing for low-to-moderate yardage and flatbed screen printing for moderate-to-high volume yardage. The cost for setup and sampling for flatbed screen printing is average. The most expensive printing choices with the highest cost include digital printing, and sublimation printing for high-volume production yardage and low-volume yardage using rotary screen printing or 3D printing for sampling or finished products. The setup and sampling required for rotary screen printing is expensive.

Textile finishes are applied to fabrics to change their properties in an effort to produce a desired effect for the end product. The physical appearance of the fabric can be changed by using **dry finishes**, which are applied using mechanical means. The application of chemicals in the form of a liquid or foam that requires drying or curing is used to change physical performance characteristics of the fabric.

Table 3.6 Colorants, Price Ranges, and Characteristics

Dye Class & Price	Fibers Classification	Color Characteristics
Acid dyes (Anionic) $$	Protein based fibers: silk, cashmere, wool Manufactured fibers: acrylic and nylon	Wide color range Bright hues
Azoic dyes (Developed) (Naphthol) $$$	Cellulose based fibers: cotton, linen, raime, hemp	Good colors range Bright hues Deep rich color
Basic dyes (Cationic) $$$$	Manufactured fibers: acrylic, modacrylic, nylon, polyester	Complete color range Intense brilliant hues Some fluorescent
Direct dyes $	Cellulose based fibers: cotton, linen, raime, hemp Modified cellulose fibers: rayon	Wide color range Light, medium and dull shades Require mordant to affix dye to fiber
Disperse dyes $$$	Modified cellulose fibers: acetate, triacetate Manufactured fibers: acrylic, modacrylic, nylon, polyester	Good colors range except for Dark and black hues
Reactive dyes $$$$$	Cellulose based fibers: cotton, cotton blends Protein based fibers: silk, wool Manufactured fibers: nylon	Wide color range Bright hues linen
Sulfur dyes $	Cellulose based fibers: Cotton	Good muted color range Black
Vat dyes $$$$	Cellulose based fibers: Cotton, linen Modified cellulose fibers: rayon	Limited range of dull colors
Pigments $$	All fibers	Limited range of dull colors Fluorescent colors Require mordant to affix pigment
Optical Brighteners (Whiteners) $	Cellulose based fibers: Cotton Protein based fibers: silk, wool Manufactured fibers: All synthetic fibers	Make whites brighter

Notes: $ = Economical/low cost
$$ = Low to average cost
$$$ = Average cost
$$$$ = Above average cost
$$$$$ = Expensive/high cost
Sources: C. Leonard, Dye Classes: The basics. *AATCC Review Magazine for Textile Professionals,* 2007, *Vol. 7(9), 28.*
Celanese Acetate, LLC, 2009. *Complete Textile Glossary.* Retrieved July 15, 2012, http://www.celanese.com;
Allen C. Cohen and Ingrid Johnson. *J.J. Pizzuto's Fabric Science,* 10th Edition (New York: Fairchild Books, 2011);
Mary Humphries, *Fabric Science* (New Jersey: Pearson Prentice Hall, 2009)

Table 3.7 Colorant Colorfastness Performance and Application

Colorant	Crocking	Light	Refurbishment (DC) Drycleaning (L) Laundering
Acid dyes (Anionic)	Good	Good	(DC) Excellent, (L) Poor
Azoic dyes (Developed) (Naphthol)	Poor on darks hues	Excellent	(L) Good to excellent
Basic dyes (Cationic)	Excellent	Good	(L) Excellent
Direct dyes	Good on dry fabric Poor on wet fabric	Fair	(L) Poor to good
Disperse dyes	Good on dry fabric Poor on wet fabric	Fair to good	(DC) Excellent (L) Excellent on polyester (L) Good on acrylic, modacrylic, & nylon (L) Poor on acetate
Reactive dyes	Poor to good	Excellent	(L) Excellent
Sulfur dyes	Poor to good	Good to excellent	(L) Excellent
Vat dyes	Good	Excellent	(L) Excellent
Pigments	Poor to fair	Excellent	(L) Fair to good on light to medium hues (L) Poor to fair on dark hues
Optical Brighteners (Whiteners)	Excellent	Good to excellent	(L) Good
Colorant Application	**Crocking**	**Light**	**Refurbishment (L) Laundering**
Dry Prints (Pigment prints)	Poor	Good	(L) Good
Wet Prints	Good	Good	(L) Good
Digital Prints	Good	Good	(L) Good

Notes: Crocking – Color rub-off due to loose surface dye or pigment.
Light – Sunlight or artificial light source.
Sources: C. Leonard. "Dye Classes: The Basics." *AATCC Review Magazine for Textile Professionals*, vol. 7, no. 9 (2007);
Celanese Acetate, LLC., 2009. *Complete Textile Glossary*. Retrieved July 15, 2012, http://www.celanese.com;
Allen C. Cohen and Ingrid Johnson. *J.J. Pizzuto's Fabric Science*, 10th Edition (New York: Fairchild Books, 2011);
Mary Humphries, *Fabric Science* (New Jersey: Pearson Prentice Hall, 2009);
Kerry Maguire King, Genevieve Garland, Lujuanna Pagan, & Jack Nienke. "Moving Digital Printing Forward." *AATCC Review Magazine for Textile Professionals*, vol. 9, no. 2 (2009)

Aesthetic finishes are selected to change the appearance, hand, or drape of a material whereas functional finishes are used to enhance the performance characteristics of a material. (For aesthetic and functional finishes and their effects, see Table 3.8.) The longevity of finishes ranges from permanent to temporary. Permanent finishes include calendering (when applied to synthetic fibers and the rollers are hot), fulling, mercerizing, napping and sueding, plissé, shearing, stiffening (when acid is used), washing, and waterproofing. These finishes are not impacted by refurbishment and remain intact for the life of the garment. Durable finishes are weakened each time the garment is cleaned, and eventually the finish will have virtually worn off. These finishes include antimicrobial, antiseptic, antibacterial, calendering (when used on natural fibers or on synthetic fibers when the rollers are cool), durable press (wrinkle-free), flame-resistance, insect control, soil release, and stain- and water-repellant finishes. Semi-durable finishes are virtually removed after several cleanings; however, some can be renewed when drycleaned or laundered. Antistatic (treated fiber), crease-resistant, flame-resistant, and softening finishes are considered semi-durable. Temporary finishes are removed after just one cleaning. These finishes include antistatic (treated fabric), calendering, softening, and stiffening (starch). The type of finish applied and its permanency level impacts the cost and can impact the consumer's perception of quality as the finish wears off.

SUPPORT MATERIALS AND SHAPING DEVICES

Garments can have many components that add to the aesthetic appeal as well as the functional performance. The shell fabric (outer fabric) of which the garment is constructed is the first element the customer sees. However, there are a variety of other materials known as **findings** that are used to construct an apparel item, such as support materials and shaping devices that add function to the garment. Decorative elements include trims and surface embellishments. **Support materials** are integral parts of the construction of many garments and are comprised of separate plies of fabrics that reinforce portions of a garment and can allow for various silhouettes to be achieved. Areas such as necklines, armholes, waistbands, and plackets with buttonholes are vulnerable to stretching and require support materials for stabilization. These materials are also used for providing additional stiffness to maintain the shape of collars and cuffs made from lightweight or soft fabrics that would otherwise collapse without additional stabilization. Additionally, support materials can provide a clean finish to the inside of garments and even provide thermal qualities. When these materials are selected for inclusion in a garment, designers need

Figure 3.7 3D Printed Garments
WWD/Giovanni Giannoni

Table 3.8 Aesthetic and Functional Finishes and Their Effects on Fabrics

Aesthetic Finishes	
Type of Finish	Desired Outcomes from Applying Finish
Calendaring	Embossed surface Glazed appearance Moiré effect Low level sheen to high gloss
Flocking	All over or patterned surface texture similar to suede or velvet
Fulling	Better hand, drape, density, thickness, and softness Smooth surface texture
Mercerizing	Improved hand, drape Improved luster Increased strength Increased affinity for penetration of dyes
Napping & Sueding	Improved hand and softness Brushed or raised fiber surface Enhanced insulation properties
Plissé	Puckered surface texture
Shearing	Consistent, uniform fiber lengths on fabric surface
Softening	Improved hand, drape, and softness
Stiffening	Increased crispness Added stiffness or rigidity
Washing	Improved softness Distressed appearance
Functional Finishes	
Type of Finish	Desired Outcomes from Applying Finish
Antimicrobial, Antiseptic, or Antibacterial	Inhibit growth of bacteria, fungus, mold, mildew Control the spread of germs and disease Protect against damage/decay, odor, and insects
Antistatic	Eliminate static buildup by attracting moisture
Crease-Resistant	Reduce wrinkling during wear
Durable Press (wrinkle-free)	Resist or remove wrinkles
Flame-Resistant	To slow the ignition of fabrics when it comes in contact with a flame Reduce the speed in which a fabric will burn
Insect Control	Repel insects Make fibers unpalatable for insects or larva that eat certain types of fabric
Shrinkage Control	Regulate shrinkage
Soil Release	Facilitate soil release during cleaning
Stain or Water Repellant	Resist stains or water
Waterproof	Prevent penetration of water

A product developer for a major moderately priced childrenswear brand is designing school uniforms for girls' sizes 4–6x and 7–16 that will be offered in navy blue and tan. The skirts and jumpers are designed to have pleats to add fullness. Both garments are unlined. The fabric selected must be comfortable to the wearer, durable to withstand frequent use, and easy to care for. The customer expects the garments to last for the entire school year. The items will be produced in China and sold at a retail price of $14.99 for the skirt and $18.99 for the jumper. The designer has selected a chino fabric with twill weave construction.

- What fiber content would be best for these school uniforms?
- What appearance and performance properties are important for the designer to consider when selecting fiber content and fabric construction for these uniforms?
- How will the fiber content choice affect the care and maintenance required for these apparel items?
- What findings are required for these uniforms, and where will they be incorporated into the garments?

---

to consider the compatibility of the support materials with the shell fabric, type and style of garment, end use, fabric weight, surface textures, finish, and care method. Support materials include linings, fusible and sewn-in interlinings, tapes, stays, and elastic. It is critical for support materials to be compatible with the care and be appropriate for the end use of the garment. **Shaping devices** also provide structured support for garments. Designers must consider the overall aesthetic of the apparel item, the fit, the style and type of garment, and its intended use and performance requirements. They must also consider which support devices are best suited to the garment in relation to care to ensure compatibility. Shaping devices include shoulder pads, sleeve heads, sleeve puffs, bra cups, lingerie underwire and lingerie separating wire, boning, and collar stays. Support materials and devices must be carefully specified with strict tolerances for shrinkage and growth, appearance retention, resistance to abrasion, and colorfastness to a

variety of sources to maintain compatibility with the shell fabric(s) comprising the garment. These component materials and structures are often inside the garment and can be hidden where the consumer cannot readily see them; however, they can greatly impact the overall appearance and performance.

TRIM AND SURFACE EMBELLISHMENTS

Fashion trends often influence the use of decorative elements that are added to a garment and can enhance its appearance and quality. **Trim** is often added when a designer wants to embellish a garment with decorative linear materials. Trim can be attached to the surface of the garment or inserted and sewn into a seam to enhance the design. Braid, cording, fringe, lace, passementerie, piping (cordedge), and ribbon are all forms of trim. Another alternative to enhance the aesthetic appearance of a garment is with **surface embellishments**. Applique, beads, embossing, embroidery, foiling, rhinestones, screen printing, sequins, flocking, and trapunto are categorized as surface embellishments. Both trim and surface embellishments can add a focal point or emphasis to a particular garment portion and can be used to add dimension. There are a variety of materials within each of these categories ranging from casual to dressy that are offered at all price points and quality levels. When selecting trim and surface embellishments for use in apparel items, product developers must consider the following: garment style and end use, cost, availability and production timeline, quality level of materials, and compatibility of care methods and performance properties for intended use in relation to the shell fabric for the garment. A consumer's

perception of quality can be dramatically altered when a garment is refurbished and problems arise with the compatibility of the findings and shell fabric. Problems can include differences in shrinkage that cause puckering, dyes that bleed (could be intended for dryclean only care but were used on a garment intended for laundering and machine drying), color loss, or deterioration due to drycleaning solutions, and delamination due to incompatible care methods. Findings should enhance the garment's appearance and aesthetic appeal and not hinder functionality and performance properties while maintaining a consistent quality level with the rest of the item. When inexpensive trims or embellishments are selected and paired with a higher-quality garment, the customer may notice immediately whereas other times it may take refurbishment and wear of the item before the customer notices these undesirable differences.

SUMMARY

This chapter reviewed fiber types, yarn construction, fabric structures, colorants, and finishes to provide an understanding of fabric characteristics as they relate to product performance. Raw materials selection and the factors that influence the quality of apparel items are important to know when developing, manufacturing, and selling merchandise. Fabric properties and characteristics influence designers' selection of materials for use in apparel items and can impact the customer's purchase and satisfaction level with the finished product. Compatibility of garment components and performance attributes were also discussed in relation to quality.

ACTIVITIES

1. Select and dissect five yarn samples, and answer the following questions for each. Does the yarn have S-twist or Z-twist? Is the yarn a singles or ply construction? If ply, specify how many and the direction of twist for each ply. Is the yarn comprised of staple, filament, or a blend of these fibers?

2. Activity should be performed in a testing lab. Select five yarns, and burn a portion of each to assess the fiber content. Indicate if it burns or burns and melts, if it is self-extinguishing when removed from the flame, and the type of ash and odor observed. Mount all samples next to the information for each of the five specimens.

3. Evaluate a tailored jacket, and document the support materials and devices and their contributions to the garment.

4. Find two similar garments from two different price classifications (budget, moderate, better, bridge, designer) to compare. Begin by documenting the garment style selected, price categories, and price points for each garment. Document fiber content, fabric structure, comment on color and finish (aesthetic appeal, texture, hand, drape, additional properties offered), list the support materials and/or devices, trim, and surface embellishments if applicable. Compare the quality of the garments based on this information.

APPAREL QUALITY LAB MANUAL

Please refer to Lab Activity 3.1 Raw Materials Classification, Lab Activity 3.2 Specimen Templates and Sampling Plan; Lab Activity 3.3 Characterization Testing on Piece Goods; Lab Activity 3.4 Characterization Testing on Comparison Project Garment; and Lab Activity 3.5 Wear Testing Comparison Project Garments in the *Apparel Quality Lab Manual.*

ENDNOTES

1. ASTM International. *Online Standards 2014: D12313a9 Standard Terminology Relating to Textiles.* Accessed March 20, 2014, http://myastm2.astm.org/DOWNLOAD /D123.1593794-1.pdf.

2. Celanese Acetate, LLC (2009). *Complete Textile Glossary.* Retrieved June 30, 2012, http://www .celanese.com/de/index-a/fa_index/textile _glossary_filament-acetate.htm.

3. Mary Humphries (2009). *Fabric Science.* Upper Saddle River, NJ: Pearson/Prentice Hall, pp. 27–43.

4. Allen C. Cohen and Ingrid Johnson (2011). *J.J. Pizzuto's Fabric Science*, 10th edition. New York: Fairchild Books, p. 21.

Garment Construction Details

CHAPTER FOUR

Objectives:

- To examine garment shaping methods to achieve fit
- To provide an overview of commonly selected openings, facings, closures, and hem finishes used for mass produced apparel

- To understand the importance of closure selection for apparel items and ease of donning and doffing

The aesthetic appearance is what initially draws a customer to a garment but it is the fit and construction that typically leads them to purchase. Fit is such a critical factor when designing apparel for any target market. There are many different ways for designers to fit a garment to the body that can also enhance the appearance and styling of the end product.

59

FIT AND CONSTRUCTION DETAILS

When it comes to purchasing apparel, consumers look for garments that are flattering on their figure. The way a garment fits is just as important as the styling of the design. **Fit** is the relationship between the body and the size and styling of a garment. A properly fitting garment should provide a smooth appearance that is free of wrinkling, bulging, or sagging and should effectively function for its intended use to provide comfort for the wearer. A poorly fitting garment can make any design undesirable. Key fit considerations for developing apparel products include ease, fabric grain, darts and seams, manipulation of fabric through other construction details, and overall aesthetic appearance of how the garment hangs.

Ease

A key fit consideration is **ease**. This is the amount of fabric allowed in a garment design to accommodate body movement; garment dimensions minus body dimensions equals ease. This variance between the measurements of the finished product and the body measurements for the intended size varies with fashion trends as silhouettes and styles change from season to season. **Functional ease,** also known as **wearing ease**, is the appropriate amount of fullness added to a garment to allow for adequate movement of the body. When a garment does not possess enough ease it will fit tighter to the body and can restrict movement, therefore impacting the size of the garment. It is important for companies to have consistent sizing and allow for the appropriate amount of ease during the design development, patternmaking, and grading portions of the product development process to avoid problems during production because consumers perceive this inconsistency in size and restrictiveness as poor quality. If a consumer selects a larger size, the garment does not always provide proper fit and cannot always compensate for lack of ease. Too much ease can sometimes be corrected through altering the garment; however, this increases

the cost of the garment, and some consumers may not be willing to go to the additional expense in an effort to make the garment fit properly. Ease can also be used to create style and aesthetic appeal. **Design ease** or **style ease** integrates functional ease plus any additional fullness necessary to achieve a desired silhouette or design.

Fabric Grain

The overall fit, appearance, and quality of an apparel item can be affected by the direction of the fabric's grain. The direction in which fabric is cut can impact how the finished garment hangs. The three types of grainlines found in knitted and woven fabrics are straight grain, cross-grain, and bias grain. **Straight grain** runs in the warp direction in woven fabrics and the wale direction of knitted materials (parallel to the fabric's selvedge); it provides the most stability because the warp yarns are stronger than the weft. In garments cut on the straight grain of the fabric, the warp runs vertically from head to toe, providing a crisp appearance. Garments cut on straight grain are most common in the marketplace. **Cross-grain** runs in the filling direction of woven fabrics and the course direction of knitted fabrics, which is perpendicular to the selvedge. When a garment is cut on the cross-grain of the fabric it is typically to make use of a border print at the hemline of a garment. Board prints run parallel to the selvedge of the fabric so the hem of the garment makes use of the border that runs along the edge of the fabric. To achieve a body skimming effect, garments can be cut on the bias. **Bias grain** runs diagonally across a fabric. **True bias** runs at a 45-degree angle from the intersection of straight and cross-grains. Designers use bias grain to provide stretch in woven fabrics. It also allows for better fabric drape against the natural curves of the body to enhance the fit of the finished garment. See Figures 4.1a–c for grain illustrated on fabric and 4.1d–i for use of fabric grain in apparel.

While bias-cut woven fabrics do provide stretch, garments constructed of knitted fabrics do not require the same level of shaping methods as woven or felted garments. Low-stretch knits require some shaping

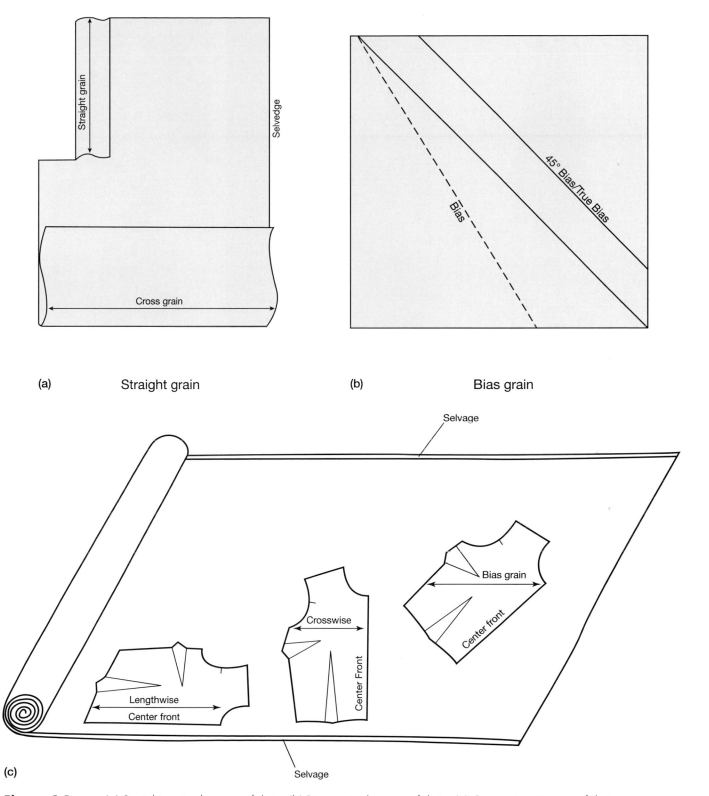

Figure 4.1a–c (a) Straight grain shown on fabric; (b) Bias grain shown on fabric; (c) Garment patterns on fabric. Grainlines on pattern pieces show how they would be cut on fabric.
(a)–(c) Courtesy of Fairchild Books

(d)

(e)

(f)

(g)

(h)

(i)

Figure 4.1d–i (d) and (e) Straight grain in garments by Chado Ralph Rucci and Raf Simons; (f) and (g) Cross grain in garments—both by Giambattista Valli; (h) and (i) Bias grain in garments by Yuna Yang and Raf Simons

to contour portions of the body while high-power knits simply stretch to fit the shape of the body. This stretch is what allows garments constructed with knit fabrics to fit a wider range of sizes. Garment styles that require a close fit such as leotards, swimwear, and active wear are constructed out of knit fabrics because they stretch and move with the body, therefore providing greater comfort and functionality.

Alignment of the fabric's yarns determines whether it is on-grain or off-grain. Fabric that is **on-grain** has warp and filling yarns that meet at right angles at the points of intersection. **Off-grain** fabrics have skewed yarns, meaning the warp and filling yarns do not meet at right angles at the intersecting points. Garments cut from off-grain fabrics are of poor quality because they do not hang properly and often appear twisted. The fabric does not have to be off-grain to cause the same problem during garment production. Occasionally during the cutting process garments will be cut off-grain, causing the same torque effect in the finished product. This torque cannot be corrected by pressing or any other means and is further emphasized when the garment is refurbished. The placements of the garment's seams are compromised by the twisting of the off-grain fabric, which is often uncomfortable and an annoyance to the wearer. The grain of the fabric can impact the overall quality of the garment and whether the consumer is satisfied with their purchase or not. This potential problem can be avoided through careful fabric inspection, production pattern and marker development, and monitoring fabric spreading and cutting. See Figure 4.2 for on-grain and off-grain fabrics. Refer to Chapter 13 for off-grain fabric and garment defects.

Darts and Seams

Garments are created by taking two-dimensional fabrics and implementing shaping strategies to contour the material around the body, a three-dimensional form. The process of designing the fit of an apparel item begins with careful consideration and selection of shaping methods. **Shaping methods (shaping**

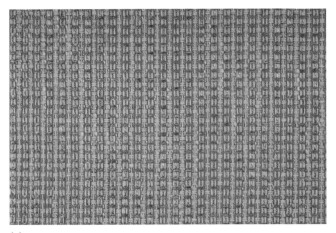

(a)

(b)

Figure 4.2 Examples of on-grain (a) and off-grain (b) fabrics
(a) Golbay/Shutterstock; (b) Ragnarock/Shutterstock

strategies) include darts and dart equivalents. When the pattern block is modified to develop a new style, the type, placement, and number of the shaping methods determine how the garment will fit. Seams are also required to assemble the style and can add aesthetic detail to the garment. The silhouette and fit of a garment are determined by the shaping methods used. Darts and dart equivalents are important shaping elements that help determine how a garment fits and can add design interest. **Darts** are utilized to take up excess fabric in areas where the garment needs to be shaped around body contours. The excess fabric is folded back on itself at the fullest point and converges to a diminishing point, creating a triangular shape in an effort to fit the natural contours of the body. The significant body contour areas where darts are frequently used in garments for shaping include the bust, waist, hips, and shoulders. There are a variety of sizes, shapes, and lengths of which darts can take the form when fitting around body contours. The length and depth of the dart are dependent upon the volume of the fabric that needs to be taken up to fit the body contour. Although darts are triangular in shape, the contour of the dart legs can vary depending upon the type of curve it is shaping. **Straight darts** (also commonly known as single-pointed darts) are typically used to remove excess fabric at the bust, elbow, hip, neck, shoulder, and the waist areas to improve fit. The **French dart** creates a diagonal design line that originates from the side seam at any point between the hipline to two inches above the waist and tapers to the bustline. This dart provides fit between the hip or waist and the bust area. **Concave darts** curve toward the body and provide a means for fitting the midriff area of a garment from the bustline to the waist. When fabric needs to contour around areas of the body that curve outward such as the abdomen, bust, and hips **convex darts** are used. A **double-ended dart** (also called double-pointed darts or fish-eye darts) may utilize straight, concave, or convex converging pattern lines. This type of dart originates at the apex level and extends to the hip level and contours fabric to the curves of the body from the bust through the waist to the hip. Double-ended darts are used to fit

one-piece dresses, coats, and long jackets at the waistline. Darts can range from basic fit elements to decorative design details. The size, length and number of darts used to fit a body contour impacts how the garment fits. Major body curves require larger darts whereas minor curves can be accommodated with narrow darts. A single dart does not provide as much fit as the combination of two or three darts to shape a body contour; however, every dart added to a garment increases the production cost. In budget-priced apparel, single darts are typically used to shape individual body contours to reduce the cost, but the fit of the garment is often compromised.

The types of darts that create visual interest to a garment are decorative darts, French darts, dart slashes, flange darts, and dart tucks. **Decorative darts** are formed on the exterior of the garment to offer a design detail by emphasizing a style line while meeting the function of fit. These can be stitched with contrasting thread to further emphasize the visual effect. Additional dart variations that integrate other shaping methods include dart slashes, flange darts, and dart tucks. The **dart slash** incorporates fullness that is gathered into one leg of the dart in an effort to shape the garment around the bust, shoulder, or hip and can also be used to add fullness to a sleeve. **Dart tucks** and **flange darts** are similar in that they are both released at one end to provide ease. The flange dart has a pleat that is formed by folding the fabric back on itself; then it is stitched down a specified length and released at the opposite end to provide design interest as well as a means for fitting the contours of the body. Dart tucks are created by folding the fabric back on itself and then stitching it to a designated length with the remaining fabric released on the outside or inside of the garment, depending upon the desired effect. See Figure 4.3 for dart variations.

Another way to fit a garment to body contours is through seams as dart equivalents. A **dart equivalent** integrates the dart into the shaped seam. **Seams** are formed when two or more pieces of fabric are sewn together to conform to a desired style. Like darts, seams can be straight or shaped. **Straight seams** are not considered dart equivalents because they are not

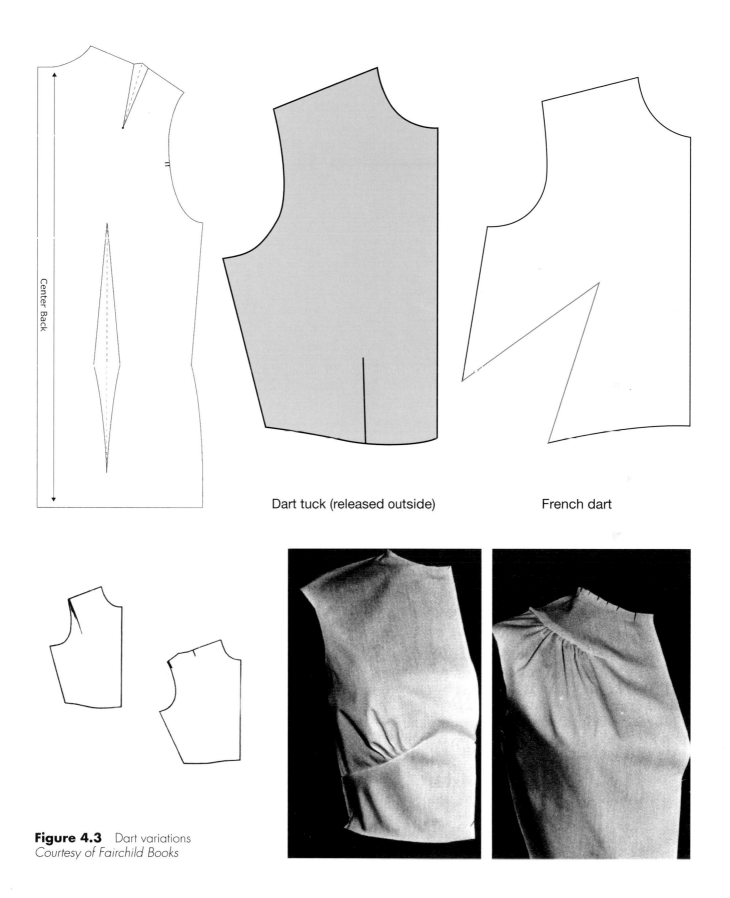

Center Back

Dart tuck (released outside)   French dart

Figure 4.3 Dart variations
Courtesy of Fairchild Books

shaping around a body contour in an effort to aid in the fit of a garment. On the other hand, **shaped seams** are dart equivalents that are used to take up excess fabric and provide a smoother appearance, better fit and cleaner garment lines than the use of multiple darts. The type of seam, placement, and size control whether alternations can be made to a garment or not. There are several different types of shaped seams that can be used. When a seam line intersects with the bust apex and extends to the shoulder or armhole it is referred to as a **princess line seam**. This type of vertical seam provides better fit and a cleaner visual aesthetic than darts. **Side panels** can be used in lieu of side seams to provide subtle fit and shape to coats, jackets, tops, and pull overs. **Gores** are another type of vertical panel that are seamed together to provide fit and add design interest to dresses and skirts. Gores typically taper to the waist to fit the contours of the body and gradually flare out at the hem to add fullness. Four-gore, six-gore, and eight-gore are the most common styles used in apparel.

A **yoke** is another type of dart equivalent that utilizes a horizontal panel to shape a garment at the seams where it is joined. Common placements for yokes include the shoulder blade area of shirts or jackets, the waist of skirts, trousers, pants, and jeans, and midriff sections of dresses or gowns. When **split yokes** are used, the fit of the garment can dramatically improve because there is a seam at the center of the yoke which provides another area in which to shape and contour. Some manufacturers will use split yokes in garments to improve fabric utilization when creating the marker for cutting, whereas the yoke may not serve any fitting purpose. However, if a garment needs to be altered, a split yoke can provide more options to improve the fit of the garment for the customer.

Fullness can also be integrated into a garment design through the use of a **godet**. This triangular or rounded panel can be inserted and sewn into a seam or slashed area to provide fullness and can also create visual interest through the use of a contrasting fabric color or texture. The point or rounded portion of the godet must be securely stitched to avoid a hole

from forming in the garment. Godets are often used to provide fullness to coats, capes, dresses, gowns, lingerie, pants, skirts, sleeves, and tops. **Gussets** are diamond-shaped insets of fabric that are stitched into garment areas to provide fullness and ease of movement. They are used in some fitted sleeve styles and the crotch area of pants, thermal underwear, intimate apparel, and active wear garments. Gussets can be cut in one, two, or four pieces. When stitched together these pieces shape the seam to fit the contour of the body. Some garments require a gusset to provide ease of movement and eliminate strain at high stress areas of garments. The addition of a gusset increases the cost of the garment and requires skilled labor to properly match and construct it. See Figure 4.4 for shaped seams and dart equivalent variations used in garments.

The number of darts and seams, as well as their complexity, directly impacts the fit and the quality of the garment. Typically, the higher the price point, the more complex the shaping and construction techniques, therefore providing better fit to the target consumer. Seam and stitch types used for garment assembly will be discussed in Chapters 5 and 6 to provide more information regarding stitch and seam selection in relation to quality level.

Gathers, Pleats, and Tucks

Shaping and fitting can also be added to the design of the garment through the integration of gathers, pleats, and tucks, also known as dart equivalents. Fullness allows for ease of body movement and can be controlled through the design and structure of these style details. Manipulation of fabric can also provide a means for fitting the body. **Gathers** allow for excess fabric to be taken up while providing a less-structured means for fit. Gathers add fullness to the garment for ease of movement while providing comfort for the wearer. Gathering, also known as shirring, provides even distribution of fullness in a garment and is created by drawing in one or more parallel rows of machine-gathering stitches. If elastic is used to gather the fabric, the garment is typically more forgiving and can provide fit for

Shaped Seams and Dart Equivalents

4-GORE A-LINE

6-GORE WITH GATHERS

10-GORE TRUMPET FLARE

Figure 4.4 (a) Princess line seams; (b) Side panel; (c) Gores; (d)–(i) Yokes; (j) Split yoke; (k) Godets; (l) and (m) Gussets

(a)–(c) Courtesy of Fairchild Books; (d)–(m) Illustrations by Q2A Media Services Private Limited

a wider size range such as extra small, small, medium, large, or extra large sizes that accommodate a variety of numeric sizes within each. For example, a misses yoga pant offered in extra small can provide appropriate fit for the numeric sizes 0–2, a small can fit sizes 4–6, a medium can fit sizes 8–10, a large can fit sizes 12–14, and an extra large can fit sizes 16–18. Gathers can be used to add design details and interest to a garment. Ruching, a form of gathering, creates a decorative detail to designated portions of apparel items by controlling predetermined fullness that is gathered and released to correspond to a parallel seam in a repeating pattern. This technique provides soft, draped folds between the gathered portions of the garment. See Figure 4.5 for gathering variations.

Pleats are created by folding the fabric back on itself along the grainline (with exception of sunburst pleats—these have radiating lines) to provide design interest as well as a means for fitting the contours of the body. There are many different types of pleats that provide different looks. Pleats can be designed as dimension or flat depending upon the desired effect. **Dimensional pleats** are set permanently into a pattern of creased ridges. Common types of dimensional pleats used in apparel include accordion, crystal, and sunburst. **Accordion pleats** are designed in a series of evenly spaced folds creating raised and recessed areas that are permanently heat set. Garments designed with this style pleating typically require the fabric panels be cut and hemmed prior to setting the pleats. If fabric is already pleated, cutting the pleating at the side seams may cause the fabric to not lay properly and can be a sign of poor quality. **Crystal pleats** are formed in the same way as accordion pleats, but the folds are narrowly spaced and the garment panels can be either hemmed prior to pleating or after. When hemming is completed after pleating, a ruffled effect is created. This type of pleat is often used for tubular and straight silhouettes. If a radiating pleat is desired **sunburst pleats** are selected. Again, like all dimensional pleats, sunburst pleats are permanently heat set. The garment panels must be cut prior to pleating to achieve the desired effect. The narrow portion of the pleating is commonly positioned around the

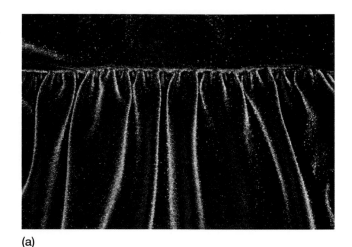

(a)

(b)

Figure 4.5 Gathering variations. (a) Gathering; (b) Ruching
Courtesy of Fairchild Books

shoulder or waistline to create a full silhouette without adding additional bulk at the waistline.

Flat pleats are folded and can be creased, stitched to a specified length, or left unpressed and can appear as a single pleat, in groups, or in an evenly spaced series. Common types of flat pleats used in apparel include knife, box, inverted, kick, and side. When pleats are formed by doubling the fabric back on itself, creating a series of folds in one direction, they are referred to as **knife pleats**. This style of pleat is typically used to add fullness to blouses, bodices, and skirts. **Box pleats** are created by two evenly spaced folds of material that are doubled over to face away from each other to add fullness to skirts, blouses, bodices, and below yokes at the shoulders and hips. **Inverted pleats**, similar to box pleats, have two folds of fabric that are doubled over but meet at a central point on the face of the garment to provide additional circumference ease to skirts, dresses, and the back of coats and jackets. **Kick pleats** are made from inverted or side pleats that are released at knee level. Garments designed to be narrow and fit closely to the body may utilize kick pleats to provide walking ease. If ease is not accounted for in the design, the customer's movement can be restricted, causing undue stress at the seams of the garment and may cause the fabric to tear or the seam to break. **Side pleats** are contoured to the body and lay all in one direction. This type of pleating allows for more movement ease and can be used to add fullness to the garment while contouring body curves. See Figure 4.6 for pleat variations.

Tucks are similar to pleats in the way they hold and shape fullness and in the way they are formed. Tucks are created by folding the fabric back on itself along the grainline and can be completely stitched down or stitched to a designated length with the remaining fabric released. There are several types of tucks found in garments, including pin tucks, spaced tucks, blind tucks, piped tucks, scalloped tucks, cross tucks, and release tucks. **Pin tucks** are created through a narrow single fold or a series of fine parallel folds that are evenly spaced in a group and stitched down from seamline to seamline or within a garment section. **Spaced tucks** are created the same way; however, the folds are wider and designed with the same amount of space between each fold. Tucks designed to have the fold meet at the stitch line of the next tuck are known as **blind tucks**. Piping can also be inserted into a tuck to draw emphasis to it. These are known as **piped tucks**. Another way to design tucks to add decorative detail and accentuate an area is with **scalloped tucks**. These shell-shaped tucks are formed by drawing in the folded edge at evenly spaced intervals and catching it at the stitch line to create a repeating scalloped edge. **Cross tucks**, which are more labor intensive, create a grid effect. A series of parallel and perpendicular folds are created and stitched down to

create this effect. **Release tucks**, like pin tucks are created through a single fold or a series of parallel folds stitched down for a designated length but are then released to direct fullness to a particular area of a garment. Tucks can enhance the look and fit of a garment but can increase the cost due to increased labor. When a garment is cut from fabric that is off-grain and tucks are planned into the design, they will never lie flat without creases. This is a sign of poor quality. The customer may not notice the fabric is off-grain at the time of purchase, but when the garment is cleaned and pressed it will become very obvious. The fabric of the tucks will be skewed and when pressed, small fold lines will show where they should not.

The complexity and number of darts, dart equivalents, and seams used in the design and construction of a garment directly relate to the consumer's perception of quality and appropriateness/suitability of fit. The more shaping elements employed to aid in the fit of a garment, the more the cost increases. The designer needs to understand the consumer and what they are willing to pay in exchange for better fit or a more complex design. See Figure 4.7 for tuck variations.

Full-Fashioned and Knit-and-Wear

Shaping methods can also be integrated into the garment panels as they are knitted. **Full-fashioned** means that two-dimensional pre-shaped garment pieces are produced by flatbed knitting machines and emerge ready to be assembled. Minimal seaming is required to assemble the product. Trim components are attached through **linking** or **looping**. During this process each stitch along the garment panel must be matched with each stitch along the edge of the trim in order to join them. Full fashioned garments are more expensive to produce, provide better fit, and are of a higher quality than cut and sewn knit garments. **Knit-and-wear** (or seamless) garments are available within each price classification and vary in design and styling complexity. However, the greater the complexity of styling and fit will typically yield a higher-quality garment that retails for a higher price. Three-dimensional pre-shaped garments are knitted

Pleat Variations

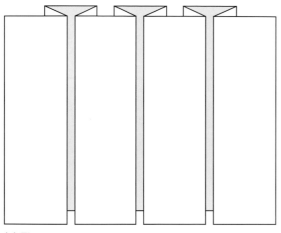
(a) Flat pleats

(b) Dimensional pleats

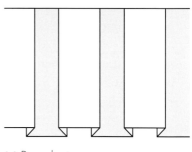
(c) Accordion pleats

(g) Box pleats

(d) Crystal pleats

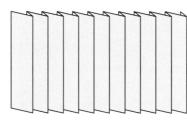
(f) Knife pleats

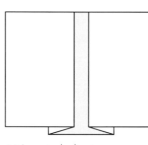
(h) Inverted pleats

(i) Kick pleats

(e) Sunburst pleats

Figure 4.6 (a) Flat pleats; (b) Dimensional pleats; (c) Accordion pleats; (d) Crystal pleats; (e) Sunburst pleats; (f) Knife pleats; (g) Box pleats; (h) Inverted pleats; (i) Kick pleats; (j) Side pleats
(a)–(b) and (j) Courtesy of Fairchild Books
(c)–(i) Illustrations by Q2A Media Services Private Limited

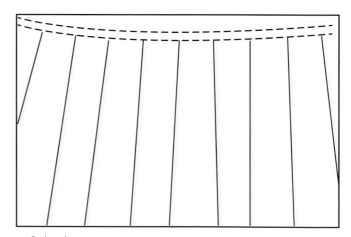
(j) Side pleats

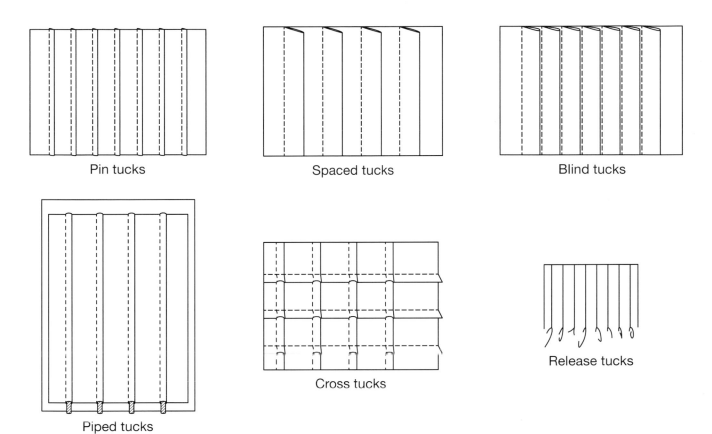

Pin tucks

Spaced tucks

Blind tucks

Piped tucks

Cross tucks

Release tucks

Figure 4.7 Tuck variations
Illustrations by Q2A Media Services Private Limited

to fit the shape of the body and may only require minimal operations for finishing, if any. This process eliminates pre-production and assembly operations such as cutting, sewing, and linking. Knit-and-wear garments emerge from the knitting machine ready to wear. See Figure 4.8 for full-fashioned and knit-and-wear examples.

Openings, Facings, and Closures

The ease of putting a garment on and taking it off (**donning and doffing**) is directly related to the openings and closures selected by the designer. These elements impact garment fit, comfort, functionality, and price. **Garment openings** allow access for the body when dressing and can be secured closed with a variety of different types of closures. **Closures** are used to secure garment openings and can be decorative as well as functional depending upon the desired effect. The style of opening and closure a designer selects depends on the design of the garment, the intended use, purpose and method of application, and fabric selected.

A **facing** is used to finish the edge of a garment opening and to control the fit when any portion of the edge is cut on the bias. Facings are created to contour the outer edge or portion of the garment area that needs to be controlled and finished at the opening. **Shaped facings** require a separate piece of material ranging from 1½ to 2 inches (3.8 cm to 5.08 cm) in width that is stitched to the outer edge of the garment opening and folded back to provide a clean finished look and hide the raw edges. In the case of a cowl neck, an **extended facing** is shaped and cut as part of the shell garment and is folded back inside the garment to provide a soft draped edge. **Bias facings** can be used in lieu of a shaped facing to finish a garment opening. This facing style typically utilizes a narrow ½-inch (1.27 cm)-wide strip of fabric that is cut on the bias and stitched along the raw edge and turned inside the garment and stitched again to conceal all the raw edges. Bias facings provide a clean finish and do not add additional bulk to the garment. They are also the most cost-effective facing option

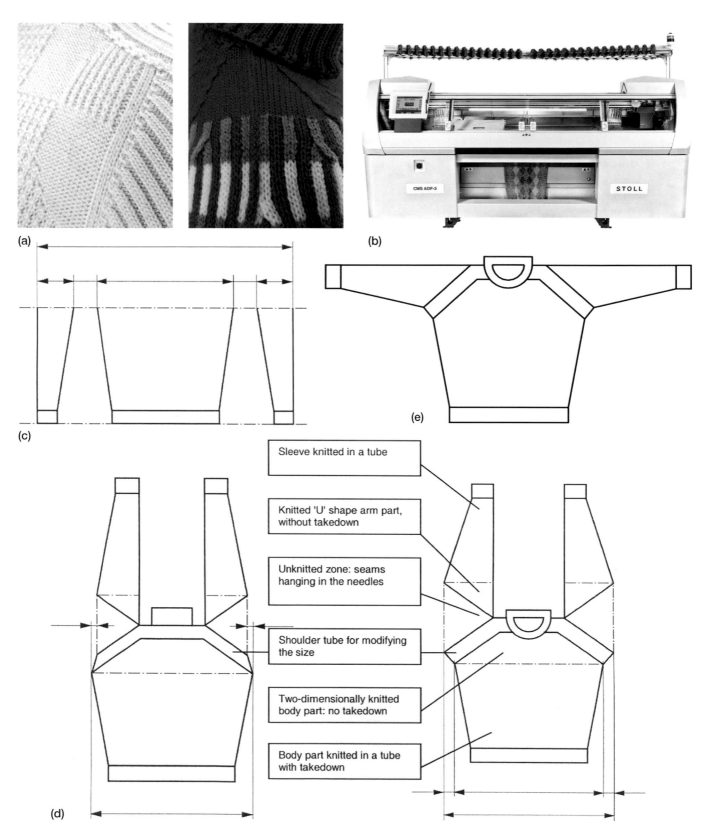

(a)

(b)

(c)

(e)

(d)

Sleeve knitted in a tube

Knitted 'U' shape arm part, without takedown

Unknitted zone: seams hanging in the needles

Shoulder tube for modifying the size

Two-dimensionally knitted body part: no takedown

Body part knitted in a tube with takedown

Figure 4.8 (a) Full-fashioned; (b)–(e) Knit-and-wear
Courtesy of H. Stoll GmbH & Co KG

because they do not require interlining material for stabilization, and they use less fabric. The two facing styles used in garments are separate and all-in-one. Individual facings are known as **separate facings** because they finish one edge of a garment area such as a neckline, armhole, vent, slit, or hem. **All-in-one facings**, also known as **combination facings**, group garment areas together into one facing. This type of facing is often used to finish a neckline and armhole all in one piece or a vent and hem all in one piece. If facings are cut too narrowly they can stick out of the garment opening and provide a very undesirable look and convey poor quality to the consumer. See Figure 4.9 for a visual comparison of separate facings and all-in-one facing.

Plackets allow for ease of dressing while providing a finish to the opening of a garment area. They are openings that have a facing or can be slits or vents that have been finished at the edge with a binding, band, or hem. Plackets can be integrated into the design of blouses, shirts, tops, skirts, dresses, coats, jackets, pants, and sleeves. These finished openings are planned extensions that can be designed without a fastener or to have closures such as buttons, snaps, zippers, hooks and eyes, or ties. A **band placket** has two finished strips of fabric that create a lapped closure and can be seen from the face of the garment. This style of placket can be used to emphasize the neckline, hemline, or sleeves of dresses, shirts, pants, and shorts. **Bound plackets** are formed by two bindings that cover the raw edges of the garment and do not produce an overlap. Bound plackets can be closed with a zipper, buttons and loops, hooks and eyes, or ties. A **continuous lap placket** is similar to the bound placket in that the edges are finished with a binding, but only one uninterrupted binding is used. This type of placket is commonly used for fitted sleeve, cuff, neckline, and hem openings to provide room for the head, hands, or feet to pass through. **Faced-slashed plackets** provide a clean finish to garment areas that have a vent where a seam is not planned. In this instance the garment edges merely meet; they do not overlap. Faced-slashed openings are commonly used for slits, vents, necklines, and sleeves that will be left open or those that will be fastened with buttons and

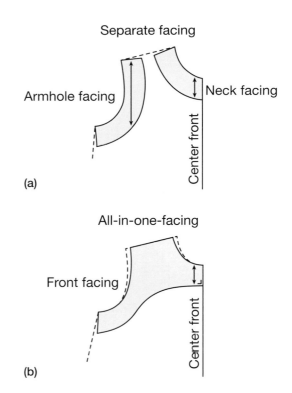

Figure 4.9 Visual comparison of separate facings and all-in-one facing. (a) Separate facing; (b) All-in-one-facing *Illustrations by Q2A Media Services Private Limited*

loops, hooks and eyes, or ties. This type of placket must be carefully secured at the rounded or pointed end of the opening to avoid a hole from forming. A **hemmed-edge placket** is commonly used for cuff openings in garments with bulky or loosely woven fabrics due to its low cost and simple construction. To create this type of placket the horizontal section of a hemmed garment is positioned between the ends of an applied band to finish the raw edges. When the cuff or band is closed, a small pleat is formed to allow for a close fit when secured while allowing ease for movement. **Tailored plackets** are more expensive to produce because they require more fabric and are more labor intensive to construct but they provide a higher quality finish. This flat-finished style placket is strong because it is formed when two unequal lengths of fabric are stitched to enclose the raw edges of the opening. The narrower strip of fabric is hidden below the wider strip that shows on the face of the garment when the placket is closed. See Figure 4.10 for placket variations. A buttonhole and button that appear in

Placket Variations

Figure 4.10 (a) Band placket; (b) Bound placket; (c) Continuous plackets; (d) Faced placket; (e) Hemmed edge placket; (f) Tailored placket
(a)–(e) Courtesy of Janace Bubonia; (f) Courtesy of Pam Howard

the sleeve placket used to secure the opening and prevent gaping is known as a **gauntlet button**, and is commonly used on better quality-dress shirts (see Figure 4.11). This adds to the cost of the garment but offers a higher quality finish and increases the functionality and fit of the garment.

Zipper applications allow garments to open and close and are selected based on the design of the garment, targeted price point, and quality level. A **center zipper insertion**, also known as a **slot zipper**, is constructed by folding back the seam edges of the opening and abutting them over the center of the zipper

(a)

(b)

Figure 4.11 Tailored sleeve plackets. (a) Tailored placket; (b) Tailored sleeve placket with gauntlet button *(a) © Viacheslav Krisanov | Dreamstime.com; (b) © Ivan Montero/Alamy*

chain and where they are stitched to the zipper tape. In poor-quality garments the zipper chain can sometimes be seen through the center front opening where the two sides meet. Some garment designs require an **exposed zipper insertion** where the teeth and part of the zipper tape are shown on the face of the garment to provide a decorative detail. Ornamental zippers with large teeth, contrasting colors, or even rhinestones can be used as a focal point in garment design. The pull portion of the zipper can also be decorative. Decorative zippers and tabs increase the cost of the garment but are typically the point of interest that persuades the customer to purchase the item. Sometimes a designer does not want the zipper to detract from the styling of the garment so an **invisible zipper insertion** is used, because it conceals the chain when it is closed. Invisible zippers applications can be used in fitted sleeves and the back or side seam of dresses, skirts, pants, and trousers. When invisible zippers are not applied properly the zipper tape can show or the zipper can be difficult to open and close. Both of these situations are indications of poor quality and are undesirable to the consumer. When constructing a **lap zipper insertion** one bottom-folded seam edge of the garment section is stitched along the zipper tape while the other garment section is folded and stitched to form a tuck that hides the zipper from view. This method can be used for side openings of dresses, skirts, pants, and sleeves, and for center front or center back openings of garments. The lap zipper insertion is typically found in budget- and moderate-priced garments when an invisible zipper is not used. **Fly-front concealed zipper applications** also have a lap that is formed when one side of the zipper is stitched to a facing that extends slightly beyond the garment closure. This extended portion hides the other half of the zipper. These are commonly used for closures on coats, jackets, rain, and snow gear. It is not uncommon to see other fasteners used in conjunction with the zipper for additional security. A **trouser fly zipper insertion** is commonly selected for trousers, jeans, and shorts. This zipper insertion technique utilizes a facing that is stitched to the zipper and extends beyond the center to hide the other side of the zipper that is secured to an underlay. Trouser flies constructed using this technique are more expensive to produce and, when properly constructed, can offer a higher-quality application than side or back zipper insertions. See Figure 4.12 for zipper insertion applications.

Waistband openings are used to fit garments to the waistline and to secure them in the proper position. They also serve the purpose of finishing the edge of the opening. There are a variety of waistband treatments for this style of garment opening. The most basic style is the **straight waistband**, which is a band that sits at the natural waistline and can be seamed at the top edge or folded over and stitched to the top edge of the waistline area of the garment. When the waistband does not contain a self-fabric

Zipper Insertion Applications

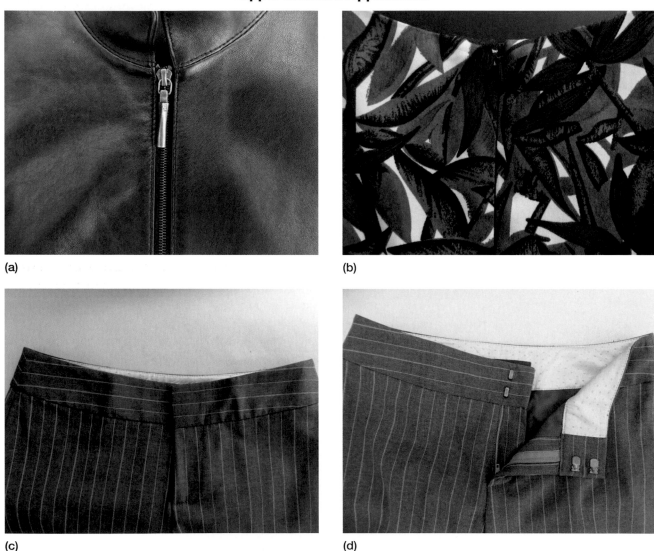

(a)

(b)

(c)

(d)

Figure 4.12 (a) Center zipper insertion (slot zipper): exposed zipper; (b) Center zipper insertion (slot zipper): invisible zipper; (c) and (d) Lap zipper insertion: trouser fly zipper
(a), (c) and (d) Courtesy of Fairchild Books; (b) Courtesy of Janace Bubonia

facing, elastic or ribbon can be used. Ribbon can eliminate additional bulk when heavy materials are used for the garment. It can also provide body and stability to sheer and loosely woven fabrics that require additional support. Elastic can also be used to back a straight waistband in knit garments to provide a non-roll option that is more compatible with the elasticity of the shell fabric. The straight waistband can be used to accommodate closure openings at the center back, center front, and side seam. It can also be planned with an extension for openings with a lap. The **contoured waistband** is selected for garments with dropped or raised waistlines because it is shaped to fit the contours of the body. Additionally, a facing shaped to match the contours of the outer waistband is required. The **bias faced waistline**, which does not contain a band at all, is designed for garments that do not have a waistband. This waistline treatment utilizes a bias cut facing that is contoured to the garment's waistline and produces a flatter, cleaner finish so as not to detract from the rest of the garment. The waistband finish that adds additional support to tailored trousers and is an indication of a higher-quality garment is the **trouser waistband**, also referred to as the **curtain waistband**. This treatment is more labor intensive and expensive because it requires a commercially prepared reinforced bias strip that is constructed with an additional bias strip designed to hang below the waistline seam and attaches along the upper edge of the waistband to support the self-fabric face. The lower edge of the waistband is not stitched closed. The trouser waistband provides a very aesthetically pleasing finish to the garment. A hook and bar are often selected in conjunction with a button to add additional security to the closure. Some waistband curtain is constructed with rows of rubber yarn or embossed or printed silicone adhered to the inner waistband material to produce a non-slip surface. This treatment is found in some waistbands of tailored garments to hold tucked-in shirts and blouses in place.

Elasticized waistlines and **stretch waistbands** provide the most ease when dressing and are one of the most economical methods for finishing the waistline opening in a knit or woven garment. The elastic can be applied directly to the waistline edge or to the waistband through means of a casing. A **casing** can be a made by folding over the edge of the garment or by a separate strip of material that is applied to hold the elastic or a drawstring to cinch in garment fullness to fit the designated body area such as a neckline, sleeve, waistline, leg opening, or hem. A drawstring allows the wearer to control the garment circumference for comfort and fit. In higher-priced apparel items, an additional ⅛-inch (3.2 mm) header is added to the top of the casing to provide stabilization for the elastic and to finish the edge. Vertical stitches can also be added through the side seams of the casing to help secure and stabilize the elastic to prevent rolling. When elastic rolls in the waistline casing it is a sign of poor quality and is often unsightly and uncomfortable for the wearer. Casings can also be applied solely to the inside or just the outside of a garment through a separate strip of fabric, bias tape, or ribbon that is stitched to only one side of the garment. When applied to only the outside of a garment it is used to emphasize a design element. Casings applied only to the inside of the garment can be used to contour curved areas of the body or to eliminate bulk when heavier fabrics are used. Casings can contain elastic or a drawstring. See Figure 4.13 for waistband and waistline treatments.

There is a wide variety of closures that can be selected to secure a garment opening. The most common closure is the button. A **button** can be made in the form of a disk, a knot, or other three-dimensional shape. Variations of button dimensions include flat, dome, half-ball, and full-ball. Buttons are available in a wide range of sizes and materials. See Table 4.1 for button sizes. They can be made from natural materials such as bone, horn, leather, wood, shell, and tagua (a nut), or man-made materials such as glass, melamine, metal (brass, steel, stainless steel, or metal alloy), nylon, plastic, polyester, synthetic rubber, and urea formaldehyde.[1] The material of the button plays a role in selection. If a button must be durable, the synthetic materials will be better choices. Shell buttons can provide a nice design detail but can chip or

(a)

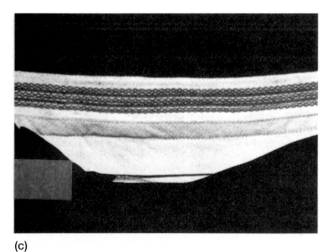

(b)

(c)

Figure 4.13 Waistband and waistline treatments in garments. (a) Contoured waistband; (b) Trouser waistband; (c) Non-slip backed waistband
(a) and (b) Courtesy of Janace Bubonia; (c) Courtesy of Fairchild Books

Table 4.1 Button Sizes	
Ligne Number	Button Diameter
14L	⁵⁄₁₆ (8 mm)
16L	³⁄₈ inch (9.5 mm)
18L	⁷⁄₁₆ inch (11 mm)
20L	½ inch (12 mm)
22L	⁹⁄₁₆ inch (14 mm)
24 L	⁵⁄₈ inch (15 mm)
27 L	¹⁰⁄₁₆ inch (17 mm)
28L	¹¹⁄₁₆ inch (18 mm)
30L	¾ inch (19 mm)
32L	¹³⁄₁₆ inch (20 mm)
36L	⅞ inch (22 mm)
40L	1 inch (25 mm)
44L	1⅛ inches (27 mm)
54L	1⅜ inches (34 mm)
72L	1¾ inches (44 mm)

Note: Ligne is the unit of measurement that is used to indicate the diameter of a button. 1 ligne = 0.025 inch (0.635mm).
Sources: Janace E. Bubonia, *Apparel Production Terms and Processes*, (New York: Fairchild Books 2012)

break when the garment is drycleaned or commercially cleaned and pressed. Men's dress shirts are often sent to commercial laundering establishments for cleaning. A common problem customers experience is the buttons cracking or breaking due to the high temperature and pressure from the pressing equipment. The three classifications of buttons are sew-through, shank, and tack. **Sew-through buttons**, commonly called "eyed" buttons, have two or four holes for use in stitching it to the garment with thread. They can be sewn flat against the fabric, or a thread shank can be created to elevate the button. **Shank buttons** have a protrusion on the underside containing a loop or hole made from metal or plastic so it can be attached to the garment. The shank allows for the point of attachment to be concealed from the face of the garment. Designers select shank buttons when they do not want the point of attachment to be visible and detract from the appearance of the garment and when heavy, bulky fabrics are used. A button shank provides the proper amount of space needed to accommodate the thickness of the fabric ply and allows the button to rest on top of the buttonhole rather than distorting the surface of the garment. **Tack buttons** are made of metal and are cast with a shank that is attached to the garment with a single or double prong tack that is inserted through the back of the garment into the cap of the button. This type of button is selected for use in garments made with sturdy fabrics such as denim. Tack buttons are available with a fixed top or one that swivels to eliminate some of the strain of inserting it through the buttonhole. See Figure 4.14 for button classifications.

For a button to serve as a closure it must have a buttonhole or loop in which to pass through. A **buttonhole** is an opening that must be large enough to accommodate a button passing through it, and it must remain secured. The buttonhole portion of the closure is constructed in the garment section that overlaps. The most common orientation for a buttonhole in garment construction is horizontal. Vertical buttonholes are used when a garment is designed with a hidden closure or with a narrow placket. It can also be selected for use in some knit garments where a horizontal orientation may cause distortion to the garment during wear. The size of the buttonhole must be appropriately scaled for the selected button size and style it is to accommodate. When a buttonhole is too small it adds stress to the area, which can cause the stitching to break. When too much ease is allowed in the buttonhole or it is not properly stabilized, the fabric can stretch and cause the button to slide out of the buttonhole. These examples of problems with buttonholes can be easily remedied if properly constructed with quality in mind.

Buttonhole classifications include straight, bound, and slot, each having its own style variations. A buttonhole that is formed by a series of zigzag stitches in a rectangular formation is referred to as a **straight buttonhole**. The stitching can vary in density and be secured at both ends with bar tacks or with one end bar tacked and the other end rounded in an eye formation. The latter is a better quality buttonhole because the stitches are more densely packed and it is designed to accommodate the shank portion of a button to avoid any distortion when the garment is buttoned. See Figure 4.15 for a comparison of the two straight buttonhole variations.

Bound buttonholes, also known as **welt bound buttonholes**, are constructed with separate strips of fabric used to form the lips where the button will pass through. This style of buttonhole is very functional and provides decorative detail when contrasting fabric is used. Bound buttonholes provide a higher-quality finish than straight buttonholes and are more

(a)   (b)   (c)

Figure 4.14 Button classifications. (a) Sew though buttons; (b) Shank buttons; (c) Tack buttons
Courtesy of Janace Bubonia

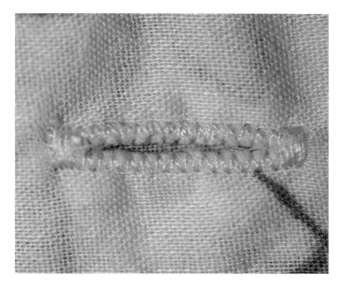

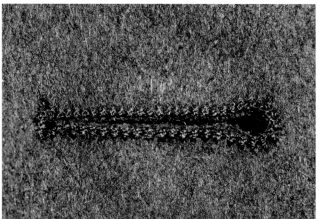

Figure 4.15 Straight buttonhole variations
Courtesy of Fairchild Books

expensive to produce because they require more fabric and are more labor intensive. **Slot buttonholes** are formed in a finished opening of a seam to provide a clean appearance and not detract from the garment's design. See Figure 4.16 for a comparison of bound and slot buttonhole styles.

When a buttonhole is not desired or cannot be accommodated in the garment's design, a loop can also be used. **Button loops** can be made from fabric, a chain of thread, braid, or cord and are sewn into the folded garment edge or seam. The loop allows for the closure to extend beyond the edge of the garment and can be used on center or lapped applications. Decorative detail can be added to the garment when the loops are made of a contrasting material. The loop ends must be securely stitched into the seam to prevent them from pulling out during dressing or wear. When this occurs it is a sign of poor quality and the customer will be dissatisfied.

The second most common closure is the zipper. A **zipper** is a device with interlocking metal or molded plastic teeth or coils that can be opened or closed through the use of its slider and pull tab. A variety of materials can be used to manufacture zippers such as aluminum, brass, copper, nickel, nylon, polyester, or zinc.[2,3] Aluminum zippers are very economical but typically do not slide easily because the metal is too soft, can become sharp along the edges of the teeth after time, and should not be used in any garment

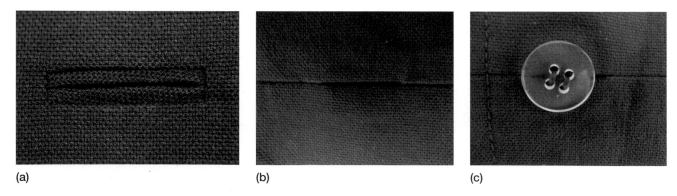

(a) (b) (c)

Figure 4.16 Bound and slot buttonhole styles. (a) Bound buttonhole; (b) and (c) Slot buttonhole
Courtesy of Fairchild Books

area that comes in direct contact with the skin or in children's apparel. Nickel is another material that can pose a safety hazard to people who have an allergy to this type of metal. Some countries will not allow any nickel to be used in apparel products (see Chapter 9 for more information regarding safety regulations and guidelines for wearing apparel). The material, style, and size of the zipper depend upon the design of the garment, durability required, placement, and visibility. Decorative zippers can be used as a focal point in a garment design. See Figure 4.17 for the component parts of a zipper.

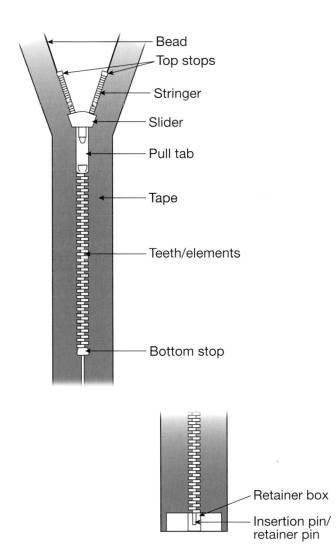

Figure 4.17 Component parts of a zipper
Courtesy of Fairchild Books

A variety of other commonly used closures in apparel construction include snaps, hooks and eyes or bars, and ties. **Snap** fasteners make dressing easy and can be used in a similar manner as a button by attaching two garment parts together. Snap varieties include sewn-in, no-sewn (utilizes a prong back similar to a tack button to secure it to the fabric), and snap tape. The surface of the snap cap can be plain or decorative, depending upon the desired effect. A **hook** is a metal fastener that can be paired with an **eye** or **bar** to secure a garment closed. Bars are typically used to secure lapped closures whereas eyes are often used to close abutted edges. The hook and eye closure performs best when there is a slight amount of tension at the point of closure. If the opening has too much ease the hooks and eyes can disengage and cause the garment to open unexpectedly. These are available as sew-on, no-sew (prong back used for attachment), or mounted on tape that is stitched into the seam or onto the surface of the garment. Lingerie hooks can be made from metal or plastic and the open portion of the hook attaches by sliding through a fabric loop. **Ties**, similar to drawstrings, are used to fasten or control fullness in a garment area and are secured by tying pairs of fabric strips together. See Figure 4.18 for these common closures.

Hem Finishes

A **hem** is used to finish the bottom edge of a garment as well as sleeves (those that do not contain cuffs) to provide stability and a clean finish at the garment's edge. The designated line along which the hem is to be folded, faced, or finished is known as the **hemline**. There are many different types of hem constructions that can be used in apparel items. Basic hem finishes commonly used in mass produced apparel include blind and book, double-folded, overedge, and rolled. **Blind hems** are stitched with a series of interlocking loop stitches, known as blind stitches, which are not visible on the face of the garment. These hems can contain a raw edge that is folded under and stitched, or that is covered with seam tape and stitched to finish the edge without it being visible from the face of

Other common closures

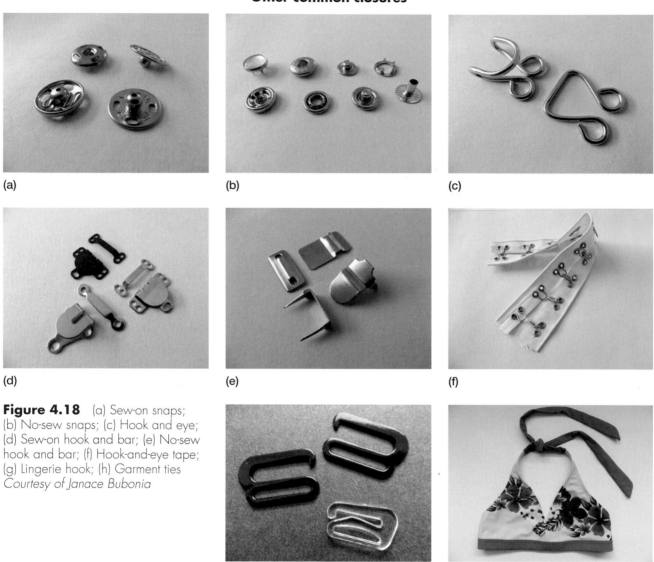

Figure 4.18 (a) Sew-on snaps; (b) No-sew snaps; (c) Hook and eye; (d) Sew-on hook and bar; (e) No-sew hook and bar; (f) Hook-and-eye tape; (g) Lingerie hook; (h) Garment ties
Courtesy of Janace Bubonia

the garment. These styles are very popular for hemming tailored trousers, skirts, and shorts. **Double-folded hems**, as their name states, are folded two full hem depths and stitched in place to help stabilize garments made from lightweight fabrics or add durability to rugged apparel items. Double-folded hems are found in many types of apparel items. When stitching is used to cover the unturned raw edges of the fabric on sleeves or the bottom edge of a garment, it is known as an **overedge hem**. This particular hem style does not add any bulk to the hemmed areas of the garment and the interlocking thread loops of the stitching formation prevent the raw edges from raveling. When a garment made of knitted fabric—such as a top or dress—is stretched along the hemline as the hem is stitched, a lettuce edge is created as the overedge hem is formed. The lettuce edge finish gives the hemline a wavy or curly appearance that is both functional and decorative. For garments made of sheer or lightweight fabrics, the **rolled hem** is a popular choice because it is very narrow. This hem style is typically ⅛ inch (0.2 mm) in depth and is formed when the layer of material is fed through an attachment that rolls the raw edges and folds them under while the hem is stitched. Rolled hems are commonly found on sheer blouses and gowns made of lightweight fabrics. See Figure 4.19 for Basic Hem Finishes Used in Mass Produced Apparel.

Common decorative hem styles used in mass produced apparel items include band, bound, and faced. **Band hems** are often used to add contrast to dresses, shorts, and tops, through color or texture at the bottom and sleeve edges of a garment. A strip of material is applied to the garment edge to conceal the raw edges and add a clean finish. Another style is the **bound hem**, which utilizes a bias strip of material to conceal the raw edges. Bound hems are sometimes referred to as a **welt finished edge** or **Hong Kong finish**. Bound hems can add contrast in color, pattern, or texture and are commonly used on sleeveless

Basic hem finishes used in mass produced apparel

Figure 4.19 (a) and (b) Blind hems; (c) and (d) Double-folded hems; (e) and (f) Over-edge hems; (g) and (h) Rolled hems
Courtesy of Janace Bubonia

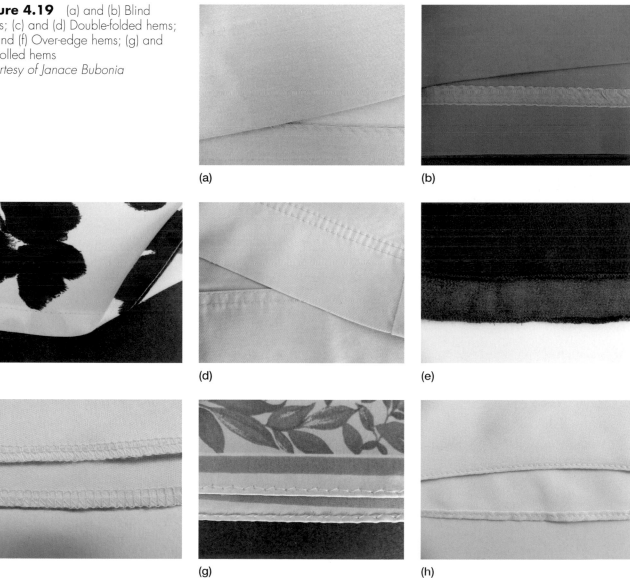

(a)

(b)

(c)

(d)

(e)

(f)

(g)

(h)

Decorative hem finishes used in mass produced apparel

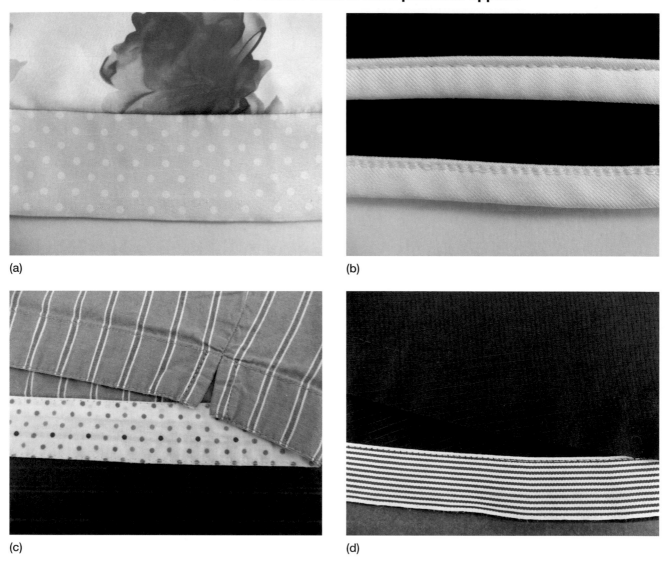

(a)

(b)

(c)

(d)

Figure 4.20 (a) Band hem; (b) Bound hem; (c) and (d) Faced hems
Courtesy of Janace Bubonia

garments and bottom edges of skirts or dresses where decorative detail is desired. Another way to add subtle contrast is with a **faced hem**. This style of hem is typically constructed along a shaped edge but can also be created on a straight edge. It is constructed using a facing made from a separate piece of fabric of the same color or contrasting in color or pattern to add a design detail. The hem facing is stitched to conceal the raw edges as well as provide additional support to maintain the desired shape at the hemline. See Figure 4.20 for Decorative Hem Finishes used in Mass Produced Apparel.

SUMMARY

In this chapter, garment construction details and methods for achieving fit of apparel items are discussed. The many options for shaping garments to contour the body while maintaining the appropriate amount of functional ease and aesthetic appeal provide many options for designers. Closure selection is equally important because it impacts the ability of the wearer to easily put a garment on and take it off. Consumers desire garments that are aesthetically pleasing, provide fit, comfort, sufficient ease for movement, and are fashion relevant. Not all consumers seek the latest fashion trends, but most desire to be dressed in apparel items that are current and consistent with goods available in the marketplace. When designers are selecting the style of openings, closures, and hem finishes that will be used for production, they must carefully consider the style of the garment, the materials that will be used, the functionality for intended use, care, and compatibility of all component materials. They must also consider their target market and the price, quality, and value expected from the customer when they purchase an apparel item.

ACTIVITIES

1. Find two garments within your wardrobe that contain good use of the design elements and principles outlined in this chapter. Document each garment through photos, and label each element and principle. Briefly explain how each element and principle is used to create harmony and an overall aesthetically pleasing garment.

2. Look through your wardrobe and document the top three shaping methods, garment openings, and closures found. Make sure to document each using the appropriate name.

3. Select three similar garments (for example, dress, trouser, jacket, and so on) from different price categories (budget, moderate, better, bridge, designer), and complete a table containing the comparison of the following: fabric and fiber content, shaping methods used (be specific), garment openings, closures, and hem finishes. Include a description of the garment style selected, pictures of each garment, the price category, and price point for each of the garments and the brands selected.

APPAREL QUALITY LAB MANUAL

Please refer to Lab Activity 4.1 Garment Analysis of Construction Details across Price Classifications; Lab Activity 4.2 Comparison Project Garment Analysis of Construction Details across Competing Brands; and Lab Activity 4.3 Comparison Project Garment Evaluation of Appearance and Color Change after Laundering in the *Apparel Quality Lab Manual.*

ENDNOTES

1. M & J Trimming (2012). *Buttons.* Accessed June 17, 2012, http://www.mjtrim.com/buttons.html.
2. YKK USA Co. (2012). *Types of Zippers.* Accessed June 17, 2012, http://www.ykk-usa.com /metalzipper.html.
3. Lenzip Manufacturing Corporation (2012). *Zipper Materials.* Accessed June 17, 2012, http://www.lenzip.com/materials/default.aspx.

Apparel Sizing and Fit Strategies

CHAPTER FIVE

Objectives:

- To identify methods for gathering body measurement data that is used for determining sizing standards for apparel
- To have an awareness of established domestic and international voluntary standards for apparel sizing

- To examine prototype development and means for evaluating fit
- To understand contents of technical packages and specifications for apparel and their importance in ensuring the production of garments at the desired quality level

Purchasing apparel is a challenge for many consumers when it comes to finding garments that fit properly. Some consumers have come to terms with the fact that apparel purchases will be followed by a visit to a tailor which ultimately drives up the cost of the garment. Although international and domestic standards for sizing apparel exist, brands do not have to conform to these and often establish their own set of measurements that relate to the size designations they offer. As fashion brands expand into new markets, the issue of sizing is further compounded. There can be quite a variance in body measurements of consumers worldwide—even within a continent such as Asia or North America—that can ultimately affect sizing and the way garments fit different body types and measurement configurations.

DESIGNATIONS FOR APPAREL SIZING

Size designations for apparel products delineate a body size, which is indicated by a letter code or number on a garment label to assist consumers with purchases. **Letter code sizing** typically encompasses two to three numeric sizes and is reported as one or more letters. A common range for letter code sizing is XXS (extra, extra small), XS (extra small), S (small), M (medium), L (large), XL (extra large), XXL (extra, extra large), or XXXL (triple extra large). The number of sizes offered in the range will depend upon the brand. Letter code sizing is used for casual garments that contain additional ease and do not require a precise fit.

Numeric sizing is based off of specific body measurements or product dimensions. Body or product dimensions are reported in inches or centimeters and typically relate to one or more key (primary and secondary) measurements such as the waist and length dimensions (for example, 34W 32L). In the case of women's apparel in the United States, numerals used to designate sizing, such as misses 00, 0, 2, 4, 6, 8, 10, 12, 14, 16, 18, and 20, may vary from brand to brand as to the specific body or product dimensions used for the same size. The range of sizes will also depend upon the brand. See Table 5.1 for U.S. designations for sizing by gender, height, and age. ASTM International designates two primary body shapes—straight and curvy (see Figure 5.1 for ASTM female body shapes). For example, a size 8 pair of trousers from Brand A has a waist measurement of 28 inches, a hip measurement of 39 inches, and an inseam measurement of 34 inches. Brand B measures 29.5 inches at the waist, 40 inches at the hip, and 34 inches in the length, but both are labeled as size 8. Each brand using this method of sizing designates the body or product dimensions they use to determine each size in the range. The increasing challenge for customers purchasing apparel products (whether shopping online or in stores) is that a size 8 garment in one brand typically does not fit the same as a size 8 of another brand.

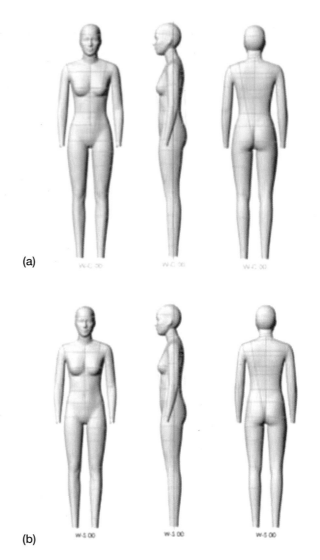

(a)

(b)

Figure 5.1 ASTM body shape designations. (a) Curvy; (b) Straight
Courtesy of ASTM

Vanity sizing has caused further confusion when companies adjust their sizes to boost customers' self-esteem or appeal to their egos by labeling garments as smaller sizes than their measured dimensions. People may find they like one brand more than another because they can wear a "smaller" size. For example, a brand labels a garment a size 6 when the dimensions of the garment are closer to a size 8 or 10, so the customer has a positive feeling about the brand because they can wear a "smaller" size. The

Table 5.1 Current U.S. Size Classifications by Gender, Height, and Age

Size Classification	Age	Height	Common Size Range
Infants	preemie to 24 months		Preemie, newborn, 3 mos to 24 mos
	(preemie)	up to17.5 in 4 (4.5 cm)	
	(newborn)	18.5 in to 20.5 in (46.99 cm to 52.07 cm)	
	(3 mos to 24 mos)	22.5 in to 35.5 in (57.15 cm to 90.17 cm)	
Toddlers	1½ to 3	35 in to 38 in (89.04 cm to 96.67 cm)	2 to 4
Children's	4–7	41 in to 49.5 in (104.30 cm to 125.93 cm)	4 to 7
Children's Slim	4–7	41 in to 49.5 in (104.30 cm to 125.93 cm)	4S to 7S
Children's Husky (Boys)	4–7	41 in to 49 in (104.03 cm to 124.46 cm)	4H to 7H
Children's Plus (Girl's)	5–7	41 in to 50.5 in (104.30 cm to 128.47 cm)	4P to 7P
Juniors	Young Adult	65 in (165.1 cm)	0 to 19 (odd numbers only)
Misses	Adult	65.5 in (163.37 cm)	00 to 20 (even numbers only)
Misses Petite	Adult	62.5 in (158.75 cm) and under	00P to 20P (even numbers only)
Misses Tall	Adult	68 in (172.7 cm) and over	00T to 20T (even numbers only)
Women's Plus	Adult	66 in (167.6 cm)	14W to 32W (even numbers only)
Women's Petite	Adult	64 in (162.5 cm) and under	14WP to 32WP (even numbers only)
Women's Tall	Adults	68 in (172.7 cm) and over	14WPT to 32WPT (even numbers only)
Maternity	Adults	63.25 in (160.66 cm) to 68.5 in (173.99 cm)	2 to 22 (even numbers only)
Boys	8–15	55.5 in to 69 in (132.29 cm to 175.54 cm)	8R to 20R (even sizes only)
Boys' Slim	8 to 15½	52 in to 69.15 in (132.29 cm to 175.54 cm)	8S to 14S
Boys' Husky	8 to 15	51.5 in to 68 in (130.81 cm to 172.72 cm)	8H to 20H
Young Men's	Young Adult	66 in to 72 in (167.64 cm to 182.88 cm)	27 to 32
Men's Short	35 and older	67 in (170.18 cm)	34S to 52S
Men's Regular	35 and older	70 in (177.80 cm)	34R to 52R
Men's Tall	35 and older	74 in (187.96 cm)	34T to 52T

Note: The following ASTM standards were used to compile this chart: ASTM D4910, D5585, D5586-D5586M, D6192, D6240/D6240M, D6458, D6829, D6860/D6860M, D6960, D7197, D7878/D7878M

garments may indeed be close in dimensions to the next size up; however, the psychology behind labeling a garment as a smaller size seems appealing to many individuals. Vanity sizing has been prevalent in the women's wear industry but has crept into men's wear in the United States and the UK. When men shop for pants, they are sized with a waist circumference dimension and an inseam length that extends from the crotch to the hem. Because men's pants are sized in inches or centimeters there is the expectation that the size measurements are accurate, and that pants marked with the size 34 waist and 32 length will measure the same as the stated dimensions. It has been found in the United States and in the UK that while the length dimensions in apparel items for men's wear remain accurate and consistent in length, the waist measurements are generously sized above the measured dimensions stated on the label. In 2010, Abram Sauer, a writer for *The Esquire Style Blog,* conducted an investigation to find out how accurate size labels were. He measured seven different brands of men's trousers from U.S. retailers that were labeled as size 36. Sauer found that the waist measurements varied between 37 inches to 41 inches, and not one of the seven pairs marked as size 36 measured 36 inches in the waist circumference.[1] In a similar study conducted in the UK in 2011 by *The Sunday Telegraph,* 50 pairs of men's pants from a variety of brands sold in 10 retail stores were measured to determine the level of accuracy of waist circumference in relation to the labeled size. Findings from the UK study were consistent with the United States. "Overall, 28 out of 50 garments checked were found to be larger than on the label: Seven were at least one and a half inches bigger; among those was a pair of Levi's 501 jeans, a fashion bulwark [staple], which was 32.5 inches and not 31 as advertised".[2] Richard Cope, chief trend analyst at the marketing research group Mintel, found that "the number of men who report their best-fit size varying from store to store has doubled" between the years 2005 and 2011.[2] **Manity sizing** is a term that has been coined to refer to vanity sizing used in the menswear industry.[1,3] The National Retail Federation stated that "sizing variations are a big contributor

to the $194 billion in clothing purchases returned in 2010, or more than 8 percent of all clothing purchases" in the United States.[4] Men are becoming more frustrated when shopping new brands because they typically do not like to try garments on prior to purchase, which results in increased returns. In an effort to assist designers and manufacturers trying to navigate sizing and fit of apparel products, voluntary standards have been established to provide some standardization for apparel products.

ANTHROPOMETRY

Systems for sizing ready-to-wear apparel are based on measurement data gathered from surveying civilian populations to determine correlations in shape and sizing of human bodies. **Anthropometric data** contains measurements gathered through researching body dimensions, examining sizes, and body shapes in an effort to make comparisons to determine variations and commonalities in sizing, to create greater standardization and better fit for apparel items. Demographic data is also utilized in conjunction with anthropometry to provide additional information regarding the consumer. Although anthropometry has existed since the 1870s, it was not fully recognized until the late 1940s and 1950s. Since the middle of the 20th century, this data has been gathered by measuring individuals using measuring tapes, spreading calipers, sliding compasses, and weight scales.[5,6,7,8]

In the United States, body-size standards were developed in the later part of the 1940s by committees composed of professionals in the fashion industry representing textile mills, manufacturers, designers, and retailers. These committees were overseen by the Department of Commerce, and body dimensions and measurement data for these voluntary size standards were provided by the Department of Agriculture.[9] Manual measurement techniques provided variances in accuracy of body measurements. On January 20, 1983, the U.S. Department of Commerce withdrew its Voluntary Product Standards and ASTM took over the development of standards for apparel sizing.[9]

Development of body scanning technologies during the latter part of the 20th century allowed for implementation of this equipment to be utilized for gathering anthropometric data with increased accuracy.[8,10] (See Figure 5.2 for body scanning technology.) Ashdown, Loker, and Rucker, researchers of a 3D body scanning technologies project funded by the National Textile Center, stated, "One of the greatest challenges facing apparel companies today is to provide quality fit to a broadly defined target market. Two issues have limited the resolution of this problem:

- Lack of data on fit characteristics of garments for different body sizes
- Lack of current anthropometric data to describe the civilian population".[11]

Three-dimensional scanning technologies are now being used around the globe to gather updated information regarding human shapes and sizing information. [TC]^2 (Textile Clothing Technology Corp.) made a 3D body measurement system commercially available in 1998 and has continued to introduce advanced body scanning technologies. In 2001 their 3D body scanner was chosen to be used in SizeUK.[10] [TC]^2 has completed an anthropometric study known as SizeUSA, which compiled measurement data gathered by means of 3D scanning technology for over 10,000 men and women representing 12 different locations throughout the United States.[12,13] Additional sizing survey research utilizing this technology has been completed or is currently in process in the Netherlands, Italy, the United Kingdom, Mexico, Canada, France, Germany, China, South Korea, and Thailand. Designers and manufacturers can purchase these surveys to develop better sizing options that reflect the body dimensions and shapes of today's consumers around the globe in an effort to offer customers better-fitting apparel items and accessories.[13,14]

According to *The Wall Street Journal*, "Many retailers say between 20 percent to 40 percent of their online sales are returned (the percent varies widely among retailers and spikes during promotions), and fit is the No. 1 reason."[15] Finding a garment that fits properly can be a challenge when purchasing online or in a store. In the past some retailers have introduced body scanning with little success.[16] Today, however, body scanning technology has become more sophisticated with greater accuracy and is becoming more available for consumers in malls, retail stores, and at home. This technology allows people to have their bodies scanned, and suggestions for brands and styles that will fit their figures are making shopping easier. Me-Ality, Bodymetrics, and Upcloud are competing to provide consumers with body scanning capabilities to find apparel items that fit their body size and shape. Me-Ality allows the customer to step inside the body scanning machine fully clothed and within 15 seconds a wand passes around the body two times to measure the moisture on the skin using low power radio waves to map figure dimensions. As the body is scanned, over 200,000 points of measurement are mapped and matched to product recommendations that customers can use to find the brands that will fit them the best.[17] Bodymetrics uses scanning pods that require the person to remove all of their clothes except for their undergarments to obtain an accurate body scan. Sixteen Xbox Kinect gaming systems are positioned within the pod and utilize infrared cameras to acquire 200 body measurements to map the figure. A 3D model of the customer's body is created and matched to product recommendations that will provide the best fit. Bodymetrics also has an iPhone app that customers can download so they can take their sizing information and brand recommendations with them.[18] Bodymetrics has plans to offer customers the opportunity to scan their bodies with a Kinect device using an Xbox gaming system in the privacy of their home. Me-Ality and Bodymetrics require the user to remove their shoes and any jewelry items before their bodies are scanned. UpCloud allows consumers to scan their bodies using a webcam and image processing technology which can be uploaded to registered brand websites to help customers find products that will fit their body shape and size.[16] There are also companies such as Acustom, IM-Label, and Brooks Brothers that are using digital tailoring (body scanning technology) in place of the

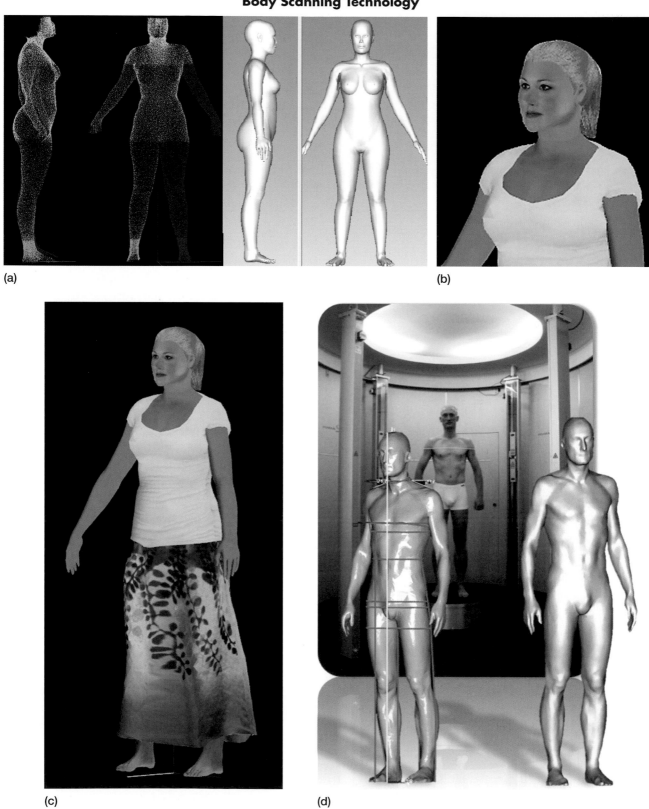

Figure 5.2

(a)–(c) Images courtesy of [TC]^2, NC US. www.tc2.com; (d) Courtesy of Human Solutions

traditional measuring tape to gather body dimensions for customized apparel that is constructed using mass production techniques. Body scanning technology is becoming more available in Canada, the United States, Europe, and Asia, is projected to see significant application and expansion over the next several years, and has the potential to revolutionize the way people shop for clothing. Although there are still some problems with accuracy, the technology is steadily improving.

DOMESTIC AND INTERNATIONAL SIZING STANDARDS

Voluntary sizing standards have been developed by organizations around the globe to provide designers and manufacturers with anthropometric body measurements that reflect current populations. International and domestic standards bodies provide size designations for body dimensions/measurements, shape, height, and weight data for men, women, and children. This data can be used for modifying size ranges and developing garment patterns to provide target customers with better fitting garments to increase quality and satisfaction while reducing sizing confusion. The caveat to voluntary sizing standards is that these are not enforceable by government. So although efforts to improve the sizing of apparel are being made, brands may choose not to conform to these standards, and customers are left with garments that do not fit as well as they could. This is a dilemma for manufacturers because they do not want to lose customers who are loyal to their brand because of the way the apparel items fit. Manufacturers are also hesitant to expand their offerings beyond their traditional fit range to offer a wider variety of sizes based on both body dimensions and shape because it would increase affiliated costs.[4] For example, Brand A and Brand B offer black bootcut jeans in misses sizes 0–14. Brand A offers each size in the range in either straight or curvy styles to provide better fit to meet the needs of customers' different body shapes. Brand

A has to produce 16 style/size combinations whereas Brand B will only produce 8.

The process for classifying apparel sizes is known as a **sizing system**. Depending upon the standardization body, sizing systems include body measurements by gender and age categories and can also be designated by garment type. Within a sizing system primary and secondary dimensions are of particular importance. The **primary dimension** is utilized for defining the size of an apparel item as it relates to a body measurement, which is reported in inches or centimeters. The **secondary dimension** is used when an additional ancillary measurement is necessary for distinguishing garment size which can be indicated in inches, centimeters, or in pounds or kilograms when body mass is a critical factor.[19,20] For example, for a man's pair of pants, the primary dimension would be the waist measurement and the secondary dimension the inseam length. ISO and ASTM International publish sizing standards for global use. In addition, the following standards organizations also publish standards for more limited use: JIS (Japanese foreign standard), EN (European standard), BS EN (British standard), DIN EN (German foreign standard represented in European CEN), and SS EN (Swedish standard represented in European CEN). These standards contain tables of body measurements for men, women, and children. **Design ease** and **functional ease** required for fitting are added to the body measurements specified by size and garment type in these tables. The intent is to standardize size labels for apparel products to improve the fit of garments and reduce consumer confusion and frustration with size inconsistencies among brands.

ISO Standard Sizing Systems for Clothes

ISO has published a technical report—*ISO/TR 10652 Standard sizing systems for clothes*—to assist in the creation or modification of garment sizing for international use in infants', men's and boys', and women's and girls' mass-produced apparel products.[20] This report contains specifications for taking body measurements, including both text descriptions and illustrations of human forms to visually show where the measurement is taken on the body. Body dimensions are not included in this technical report; these are found in individual ISO standards for size designations for clothes categorized by infants, men's and boy's or women's and girls', then by garment type (see Table 5.2 ISO standards for size designations of garments). According to ISO, it is important for the "establishment of a size designation system that indicates (in simple, direct and meaningful manner) the body size of the man or boy [or woman or girl] that a garment is intended to fit" in an effort to provide consumers with garments that fit.[21,22]

ISO has developed a standard for defining body measurements that provides instructions for taking dimensions used for all types of apparel products and all ages and genders.[23] This standard is *ISO 8559 Garment construction and anthropometric surveys – body dimensions*. Precise written procedures accompanied by illustrated human forms show where measurements should be taken. The standard is intended for use in preparing for anthropometric surveys and for developing production patterns and dimension specifications for garments. There is also a standard for designating body size on garment labels and *ISO 3635 Size designation of clothes – Definitions of body*

Table 5.2 ISO Standards for Size Designations of Garments

Standard Number	Size Designation of Clothes
ISO 3635	Definitions and body measurement procedure
ISO 3636	Men's and boys' outerwear garments
ISO 3637	Women's and girls' outerwear garments
ISO 3638	Infants' garments
ISO 4415	Men's and boys' underwear, nightwear, and shirts
ISO 4416	Women's and girls' underwear, nightwear, foundation garments, and shirts

Note: ISO uses the term "outerwear" to include dresses, suits, coats, jackets, vests, skirts, shorts, trousers, sweaters, pullovers, jumpers, rompers, and swimwear.

measurement procedure for taking control measurements needed to define a specific body size. ISO defines **control measurements** as "Those body measurements, in centimeters, on which a sizing system is built, and that are used to assign an appropriately sized garment to a wearer."[24] This standard provides definitions, pictograms, and measurement procedures. **Pictograms** are illustrated body forms used to indicate the position of the body when measurements are taken. Understanding these standards and technical reports allow for more accuracy when using standards for designating size specific to garment type, gender, and age range.

ASTM International Apparel Sizing Standards

ASTM International D5219 Standard terminology relating to body dimensions for apparel sizing is available to assist in the creation or modification of garment sizing for international use in infants, men's and boys', and women's and girls' mass-produced apparel products. This standard contains specifications for taking body measurements, including both text descriptions and three-dimensional avatars to visually show where each measurement is taken on the body.[25] Body dimensions are not included in this technical report; these are found in individual ASTM International standards for size designations for clothes categorized for infants, boys, girls, juniors, misses, women's, and men's (see Table 5.3). These standards containing body measurement tables provide written procedures and three-dimensional avatars to indicate where and how body dimensions should be taken (see Figure 5.3). Measurement data is recorded in both SI units and inch-pound units. The measurement data is intended to be used with consideration for garment styling, design and functional ease, fabric type, and desired fit. According to ASTM International, it is vital for designers, product developers, and manufacturers to recognize the importance of using standardized body measurements when developing patterns and garments in an effort to be "consistent with the current anthropometric

Table 5.3 ASTM International Standards for Size Designations of Garments

Standard Number	Size Designation of Clothes
ASTM D 4910	Standard tables of body measurements for children, infant sizes—preemie to 24 months
ASTM D 5219	Standard terminology relating to body dimensions for apparel sizing
ASTM D 5585	Standard tables of body measurements for adult female misses figure type, size range 00 to 20
ASTM D 5586/D 5586M	Standard tables of body measurements for women aged 55 and older (all figure types)
ASTM D 6192	Standard tables of body measurements for girls, sizes 2 to 20 (regular and slim) and girls plus
ASTM D 6240/D 6240M	Standard tables of body measurements for mature men, ages 35 and older, sizes 34 to 52 short, regular, and tall
ASTM D 6458	Standard tables of body measurements for boys, sizes 8 to 14 slim and 8 to 20 regular
ASTM D 6829	Standard tables of body measurements for junior, sizes 0 to 19
ASTM D 6860/D 6860M	Standard tables of body measurements for boys, sizes 4H to 24H husky
ASTM D 6960	Standard tables of body measurements relating to women's plus size figure type, sizes 14W to 32W
ASTM D 7197	Standard tables of body measurements for misses maternity sizes 2 to 22
ASTM D 7878/D7878M	Standard tables of body measurements for adult female misses petite figure type size range 00P to 20P

characteristics of the population of interest . . . which should in turn reduce or minimize consumer confusion and dissatisfaction related to apparel sizing."[26]

PROTOTYPE DEVELOPMENT AND EVALUATING FIT

Trends influence the styling, fabrication, and fit of fashion products. The choices designers make when interpreting these trends for their brand ultimately affects how the garments will fit their customers. Fit is directly related to the styling, design ease, functional ease, darts, or seams used to contour curves of the body, as well as the overall aesthetic appearance and fabric grain that impacts the way the garment hangs on the body. There are different fit-types for apparel items that range from slim and form-fitting to oversized (see Table 5.4). When the garment is designed, a pattern is created and a **prototype** is constructed to evaluate the fit in addition to the overall aesthetic appearance and function of the garment. Prototypes are developed in physical form or in a virtual environment to allow for fit to be tested on a dress form, live model, or digital avatar. Proportions, drape, style, and functional ease as well as design details can be modified to improve the fit and appearance of the garment while capturing the look desired by the product developer.

Prototypes are created in **sample sizes** designated by the manufacturer for dress forms, fit models (human or digital representation of the human form), and pattern development. The sample size used is typically the one closest to the middle of the size range to achieve better proportions when the pattern pieces are graded (see Table 5.5). Although some designer and luxury brands develop and evaluate prototypes for each size in the range in an effort to increase the fit quality their customers expect, it does increase the cost. However, many customers are willing to pay more for garments that fit better. It is the brands' responsibility to figure out how much more their customers are willing to pay for a particular garment.

The initial prototype is known as the **first sample** and can be constructed of muslin or a material similar to what the finished garment will be made of. **Virtual prototypes** are digital simulations of garments developed using specialized computer software programs that convert two-dimensional pattern pieces

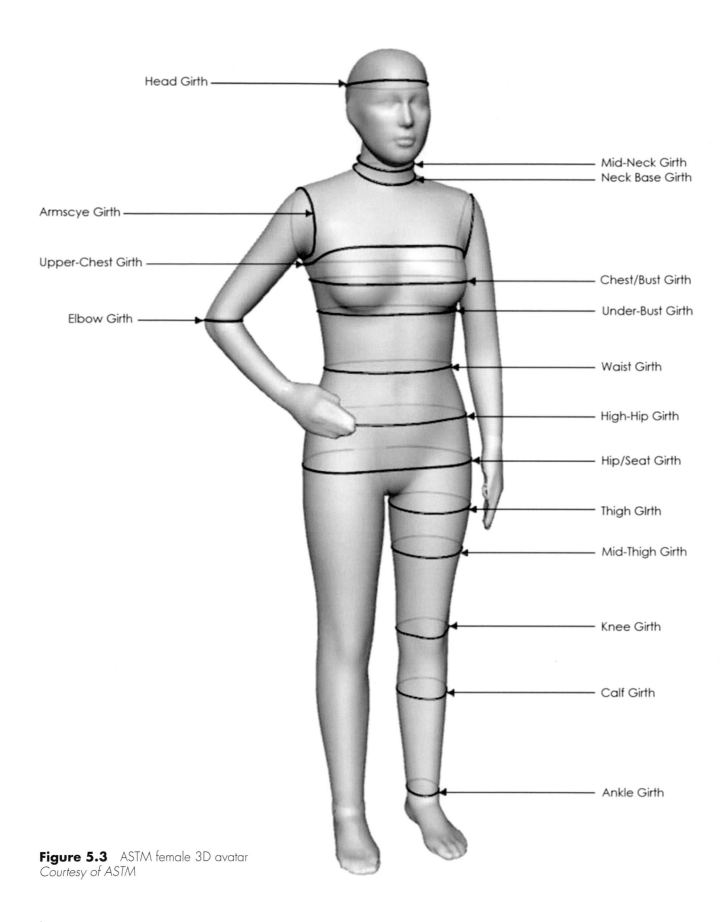

Head Girth

Mid-Neck Girth
Neck Base Girth

Armscye Girth

Upper-Chest Girth

Chest/Bust Girth

Under-Bust Girth

Elbow Girth

Waist Girth

High-Hip Girth

Hip/Seat Girth

Thigh Girth

Mid-Thigh Girth

Knee Girth

Calf Girth

Ankle Girth

Figure 5.3 ASTM female 3D avatar
Courtesy of ASTM

Table 5.4 Apparel Fit Types

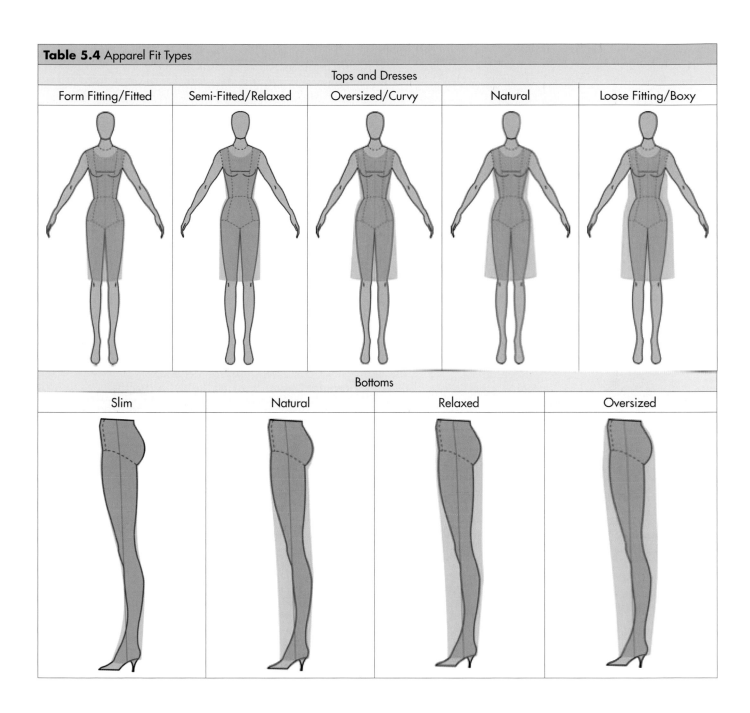

Tops and Dresses				
Form Fitting/Fitted	Semi-Fitted/Relaxed	Oversized/Curvy	Natural	Loose Fitting/Boxy

Bottoms			
Slim	Natural	Relaxed	Oversized

Table 5.5 Sample Sizes

Size Range	Sample Size	ASTM Specification
Children's		
Preemie to 24 months	3–6 months or 6 months	D4910
2–6x	5 or XS	D5826
Girl's		
2 to 20	10 or L	D6192
Junior's		
0–19	7	D6829
Boy's		
8–20 Regular	10 or L	D6458
Misses		
00–20	8, 10 or M	D5585
Women's		
14W–32W	18W or 20W	D6960
Men's		
34–52	40 jackets 34W × 32L bottoms	D6240

Sources: ASTM 2014 Online Standards.; S. Keiser and M. Garner. *Beyond Design*: The Synergy of Apparel Product Development, 3rd ed. New York: Fairchild Books, p. 351

into three-dimensional fabricated garments. Data is input or selected in the software program to simulate characteristics of the materials that will be used in the garment to accurately depict the fabric's behavior in the finished product to show how it will look in real life. The virtual prototype can then be placed onto a virtual avatar and evaluated for the same criteria as a physical sample. The advantage of using virtual prototypes is the reduction in time and resources (such as the cost savings of materials and labor because the sample is not physically being made) during the development and refinement stages of the process.

The key to proper fit is matching the garment's three-dimensional volume to the contours and volume of the body, which is easier said than done when developing apparel for mass production. Technical designers are trained to recognize fitting issues that need to be corrected when evaluating garment samples. **Drag lines** are an indication of a poor fitting garment and are identified as areas where the fabric is pulled, causing undesirable horizontal or diagonal folds in the product. These lines point to or radiate from the areas where a fitting issue must be addressed.[27] Drag lines can be seen when the contours of the body are too great for the area within the garment, requiring the addition of more fullness. They can also indicate the portions within the garment that are too tight, therefore requiring more ease. Common areas within garments where drag lines can occur are through the crotch, thigh, buttock, bustline, upper sleeve, and shoulder blades. When a garment hangs from the bust or hemline, causing **flaring** away from only one side of the body, either the front or the back, and it is not intended as part of the garment's styling, it is an indication that the horizontal balance line is not level.[28] Therefore, further adjustments are required to shape and level the garment so it will hang properly and be balanced.

In Figure 5.4, all three of the pairs of pants, sizes 8, 10, and 12, have fitting issues; however, the first (size 8) and the third (size 12) provide more challenges that need to be addressed. The first pair of pants is too small, and the virtual prototype shows there is not enough fullness to accommodate the volume of the body contours in the areas where you can see the body coming through the garment. Drag lines seen in the crotch area indicate where the pants are too tight and more ease needs to be added. The third pair of pants is too large. You can see portions of the pants standing too far away from the body at the waist and drag lines at the side seam between the waist and hip area where fullness should be removed. Drag lines in the crotch area and through the legs indicate too much fullness, and the crotch curve may need adjustment. The **break** (folds in the pant legs of trousers near the hem where it hits the instep of the foot) may need additional adjustment across the size range to ensure consistency.

The use of computer software for development of virtual prototypes allows for patterns to be quickly modified and digitally assembled and reevaluated

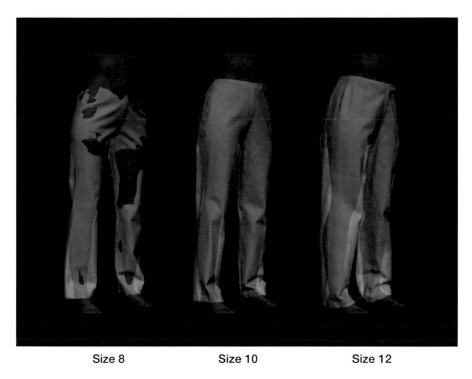

Size 8   Size 10   Size 12

Figure 5.4 Virtual prototype of pants
Cornell Body Scan Research Group, Cornell University, Ithaca, NY

until the garment pattern is corrected. **Production samples** are the final sewn garment prototypes that are tested and perfected for fit, function, and aesthetic appeal.[29] Production-ready prototypes are created based on the tech package. The prototypes are produced in the factory where the garments will be manufactured, using the same construction methods and materials used for mass production of the products; they also convey the overall quality level of the finished product.[30] When these prototypes are approved, production begins.

TECHNICAL PACKAGES AND PERFORMANCE SPECIFICATIONS

When garments are designed for mass production, they must be specified to ensure product consistency and quality. **Technical packages**, **production packages**, or

tech packs are documents prepared for a manufacturer prior to production that contain information regarding product standards and specifications for developing, assembling, and packaging the apparel item. **Product specifications** provide standards for intrinsic components of a completed product such as specifications for materials, size and fit, garment assembly, finishing, labeling, packaging, and quality standards for performance expectations, which all require approval before production begins. The complexity of the tech pack can vary from brand to brand, depending on the product and the needs of the manufacturer. Designers prepare the tech packs and discuss them with merchandisers before they are finalized and move on to the production department.[29,31]

Product Lead Sheet

A tech pack is prepared for every garment sent to production and begins with the **product lead** or

design sheet. The product lead sheet details preliminary information about the garment style in production, such as brand, company name and contact information, garment style number, season and year, color offerings, garment images, information specific to the fabric to be used, size range, stitch and seam types with locations, and delivery dates and details. Information from the product lead sheet is carried over onto all the other sheets that follow.[32]

Bill of Materials Sheets

The aesthetic and physical performance of sewn products depends on detailed specifications for materials and components used in production. The **bill of materials (BOM)** provides general information regarding all of the component parts needed to assemble a garment, such as fabric, trim, labeling, and packaging. Additional sheets are included to provide more detailed information. The **fabric sheet** is prepared for every fabric and color the garment is offered in and includes a swatch accompanied by specifications for the material used. **Fabric specifications** include fiber content, yarn composition and size, fabric density and construction, width, weight, finish, quantity in the unit of measure, color standards for manufacturing, lot number, defect tolerance, as well as performance requirements.[33]

The **component sheet** documents all of the other elements such as trim, interlining, and findings used to construct the garment. The lot or style number and the location of each component in the garment are communicated to eliminate any confusion during production. Specifications for these components are further detailed on a **trim sheet**. Depending upon the component, the following information may be included, such as fiber content or type of material (i.e., findings such a zippers, buttons, snaps, and so on), construction, size or width, quantity in the unit of measure, area and method of attachment, color standards for manufacturing and color matching, performance requirements, and any other pertinent information that needs to be communicated. For example, additional information needed for interlinings might include method and specifications for proper attachment or adhesion. Careful consideration must be taken when selecting interlining materials because they must be compatible with the garment fabric construction and weight as well as care, to avoid quality issues that can arise during use and refurbishment by consumers.

The physical performance of a sewn product also depends in large part on correct specifications for thread. Selection of sewing thread for apparel manufacturing is based on the type of garment and compatibility with the fabric (woven or knit construction and fabric weight), type of stitch, method for seam construction, and machinery used. When a garment is properly specified, the components of the seams and method of construction are planned in a manner that the thread will not break before the fabric fails or tears. Additional considerations when specifying thread type includes the garment's intended use, care, cost, desired quality level, and expected lifespan. **Thread specifications** include fiber content, yarn type and construction, thread size or ticket number, color standards for manufacturing and dye to match specifications, finish, quantity in the unit of measure, and performance requirements.[34]

Spec Sheet

Mass production of apparel products relies heavily on the accuracy of size information and dimensions communicated about a garment to ensure accuracy of design, fit, and function of the finished item. **Size specifications** designate specific dimensions and tolerances that include accurate standard dimensions of a garment that are taken at designated measurement points based on the design of the garment, desired fit, manufacturer or brand size requirements and grade rules, sizes offered in the range, and production needs. **Spec sheets** include designated **points of measurement (POM)** , garment dimensions, and tolerances pertaining to the style of the garment, grading information for all sizes in the range, and technical drawings of the front, back, and detail views including scale. **Fit history** may also be included in a tech pack to document modifications made to the garment during the sampling process as they relate to the measurements outlined in the spec sheet. Instructions for **grade rules** ensure the sizes within the range will be produced correctly. These include direction for proportionally increasing or decreasing the garment pattern pieces of the sample size, at specific locations, by designated amounts, to produce all of the sizes within the range for production.[33]

Construction, Label and Packaging Sheets

Garment assembly specifications include information pertaining to **construction details** for assembling the garment. These include stitch type, stitch width, stitches per centimeter or per inch (SPI), with +/- tolerances, top stitching details or method of application and materials used for bonding, welding, or sealing seams. Additionally, seam type and finish, hem type, instructions for matching fabrics (such as plaids, stripes, or patterns), and closure details with method of attachment are included. **Finishing specifications** provide details regarding the processes for creating the products' completed appearance, such as pressing or steaming, trimming of thread ends, and wet processing. Finishing specifications for wet processing may include color standards or abrasion tolerances, equipment settings, and compounds used to alter the garment's appearance. Details regarding placement and attachment of labels to the garment, shipping, and merchandise packaging for the products are detailed in the **label and packaging sheets**. These specifications might include the size and type of label, method of attachment and placement of labels and hangtags, instructions for blocking, folding, or hanging a garment, packaging materials and sizes, the number of garments to be packed in each shipping container, and labeling of shipping cartons or containers.[32]

Product Performance Specifications

In an effort for manufacturers to produce products that will perform at acceptable levels for customers, they should be tested and evaluated against industry standards for performance. **Performance** is defined as the ability of a product to function for its intended use. Standards and specifications for materials convey expectations for quality and performance and are indicated in industry specification documents categorized by product type and end user (i.e., women, girls, men, boys, infants). These standards provide thresholds for performance and are communicated in terms of minimum performance levels for acceptability. Table 5.6 provides possible items for inclusion in garment performance specification based on the garment type, intended use, and quality level. Standards for testing and evaluating performance of materials and finished garments using industry test methods and product specifications will be discussed in detail in Chapters 11 and 13.

Table 5.6 General Performance Specification Items for Apparel Products	
Appearance	
Abrasion	
Chemical resistance	
Acids	Laundering
Alkali	Mineral acids
Bleaching	Moisture regain
Drycleaning	Organic solvents
Insects/microorganisms	
Colorfastness	
Atmospheric contaminants	
Bleach	
Crocking	Light
Drycleaning	Perspiration
Laundering	
Dimensional stability	
Flammability	
Strength and elongation	
Thermal properties	

SUMMARY

In this chapter, the importance of body measurement data and methods used for gathering this information are discussed to further the understanding of how size standards for apparel are developed. The availability of domestic and international voluntary size standards provide retailers with sizing information that reflects the body shapes and sizes of today's consumers. Many brands have established their own sizing systems but can utilize these standards for updating their sizes. Prototype development and evaluating garment fit are important aspects in the development of apparel products that can lead to customer satisfaction or returned merchandise. As the use of 3D virtual prototyping and 3D printing technology are integrated more and more into the development and fitting process, the reduction in time and cost of sampling is significantly reduced. Technical packages and specifications for apparel products also help ensure the desired quality level and leave little for interpretation during production.

ACTIVITY

1. Select five pairs of jeans from different brands that are marked as the same size. Document the brands selected and stores where each product was found. Accurately measure and record the waist and inseam measurements for each of the brands. Compare the measurements to the appropriate ISO or ASTM standard table for size. Indicate the measurement difference for each brand, and rank them in order of closest to furthest from the labeled size.

2. Go to a retail store, select three pairs of the same jeans (brand, size, color, wash), and accurately measure and record the following critical points of measure (POM)—waist, hip, thigh, inseam, backrise, and outseam. Record each measurement for each pair of jeans in a table to compare the dimensions of each. What are the variances found for each POM that provide insight into the tolerances allowed for each measurement area?

APPAREL QUALITY LAB MANUAL

Please refer to Lab Activity 5.1 Comparison Project Garment Analysis of Size and Fit in the *Apparel Quality Lab Manual.*

ENDNOTES

1. Abram Sauer (2010). "Are Your Pants Lying to You? An Investigation." *The Esquire Style Blog,* September 7. Accessed November 17, 2012, http://www.esquire.com/blogs/mens-fashion/pants-size-chart-090710.

2. Alastair Jamieson and Tom Hadfield (2011). "Wrong Trousers on the High Street as Men Fall Victim to 'Vanity Sizing.'" *The Telegraph,* September 4. Accessed November 17, 2012. http://www.telegraph.co.uk/news/newstopics/howaboutthat/8739365/Wrong-trousers-on-the-High-Street-as-men-fall-victim-to-vanity-sizing.html.

3. Susan Reda (2011). "Manity Sizing." *NRF Stores.* Accessed November 17, 2012. http://www.stores.org/content/%E2%80%9Cmanity%E2%80%9D-sizing.

4. Stephanie Clifford (2011). "One Size Fits Nobody: Seeking a Steady 4 or a 10." *The New York Times,* April 24, p. A1.

5. Cornell University College of Human Ecology. *The 3D Body Scanner Glossary.* Accessed October 2012, www.bodtscan.human.cornell.edu/scene5b96.html.

6. National Institute of Standards and Technology (NIST). *Standardization of Women's Clothing: Short History of Ready-made Clothing.* Accessed October 2012, http://museum.nist.gov/exhibits/apparel/history.htm.

7. National Institute of Standards and Technology (NIST). *Standardization of Women's Clothing: NIST's Role.* Accessed October, 2012, http://museum.nist.gov/exhibits/apparel/role.htm.

8. Karla Peavy Simmons (2001). *Body Measurement Techniques: A Comparison of Three-Dimensional Body Scanning and Physical Anthropometric Methods.* Dissertation, NCSU, January. http://www.tx.ncsu.edu/3dbodyscan/pdf_docs/microsoft%20word%20-%20a1paper2.pdf.

9. U.S. Department of Commerce (DoC), National Institute of Standards and Technology-NIST, and the Office of Standards Services. *Body Measurements for the Sizing of Apparel.* Accessed October 2012, http://gsi.nist.gov/global/docs/stds/womens-ps42-70.pdf.

10. [TC]². *Our History.* Accessed October 2012, http://www.tc2.com/history.html.

11. Susan Ashdown, Suzanne Loker, and Margaret Rucker (2007). "Improved Apparel Sizing." National Textile Center Research Briefs. Accessed October 2012, www.human.cornell.edu/fsad/research/upload/S04-CR01-07.pdf, p. 1.

12. [TC]². *SizeUSA.* Accessed October 2012, www/tc2.com/sizeusa/html.

13. Just-style.com. *July 2010 Management Briefing: Sizing a Headache for Globalising Apparel Industry.* Accessed October 2012, http://www.just-style.com/management-briefing/sizing-a-headache-for-globalising-apparel-industry_id108359.aspx.

14. Cornell University College of Human Ecology. *The 3D Body Scanner Ready-to-Wear.* Accessed October 2012, http://www.bodyscan.human.cornel.edu/scene7354.html.

15. Christina Binkley (2013). "The Goal: A Perfect First-Time Fit." *The Wall Street Journal.* Accessed September 28, 2013, http://online.wsj.com/article/SB10001424052702304724404577293593210807790.html.

16. Barney Jopson (2012). "Clothes Shops Prepare for Body Scanning." *Financial Times.* Accessed September 29, 2013, http://www.ft.com/intl/cms/s/0/fb0ef6e2-fa0c-11e1-9f6a-00144feabdc0.html#axzz2gPC5PF5V).

17. Emma Hutchings (2011). "Full Body Scanning Kiosks Create Custom Shopping Lists." *PSFK.* Accessed September 23, 2013, http://www.psfk.com/2011/04/full-body-scan-kiosks-in-malls-tell-you-what-clothes-size-you-are.html.

18. Network World Videos (2012). "Xbox Kinect Body Scanner Helps Find the Perfect Pair of Jeans." Accessed September 29, 2013,

http://www.youtube.com/watch?v=Y1tCcWW2d2I&feature=player_embedded
http://www.bodymetrics.com/retail.php.

19. British Standards Institution (2005). *BS EN 13402-3:2004 Size Designation of Clothes—Part 3: Measurements and Intervals*, p. 5.

20. International Organization for Standardization (1991). *ISO/TR 10652 Technical Report: Standard Sizing Systems for Clothes*, p. 1.

21. International Organization for Standardization (1977). *ISO 3636 (E) Size Designation of Clothes—Men's and Boy's Outerwear Garments*, p. 3.

22. International Organization of Standardization (1977). *ISO 3637(E) Size Designation of Clothes—Women's and Girl's Outerwear Garments*, p. 3.

23. International Organization for Standardization (1989). *ISO 8599 Garment Construction and Anthropometric Surveys: Body Dimensions*, p. 1.

24. International Organization for Standardization. (1981). *ISO 3635 Size Designation of Clothes—Definitions of Body Measurement Procedure*, pp. 1–5.

25. ASTM International (2013). *5219–09 Standard Terminology Relating to Body Dimensions for Apparel Sizing*, pp. 1–13.

26. ASTM International (2013). *D5585-11e1 Standard Tables for Body Measurements Adult Female Misses Figure Type, Size Range 00–20*, pp. 1–7.

27. Sarah Veblen (2012). *The Complete Photo Guide to Perfect Fitting*. Minneapolis: Creative Publishing International, p. 21.

28. Sarah Veblen (2012). *The Complete Photo Guide to Perfect Fitting*. Minneapolis: Creative Publishing International, p. 23.

29. Apparel Design Partners. *Tech Packs*. Accessed December 1, 2012, http://www.appareldesignpartners.com/?page_id=366.

30. Apparel Design Partners. *Prototyping*. Accessed December 1, 2012, http://www.appareldesignpartners.com/?page_id=105.

31. Paula J. Myers-McDevitt (2011). *Apparel Production Management and the Technical Package*. New York: Fairchild Books, p. 73.

32. Paula J. Myers-McDevitt (2011). *Apparel Production Management and the Technical Package*. New York: Fairchild Books, pp. 97–111.

33. Janace E. Bubonia (2012). *Apparel Production Terms and Processes*. New York: Fairchild Books, pp. 94, 372–375.

34. Janace E. Bubonia (2012). *Apparel Production Terms and Processes*. New York: Fairchild Books, p. 105.

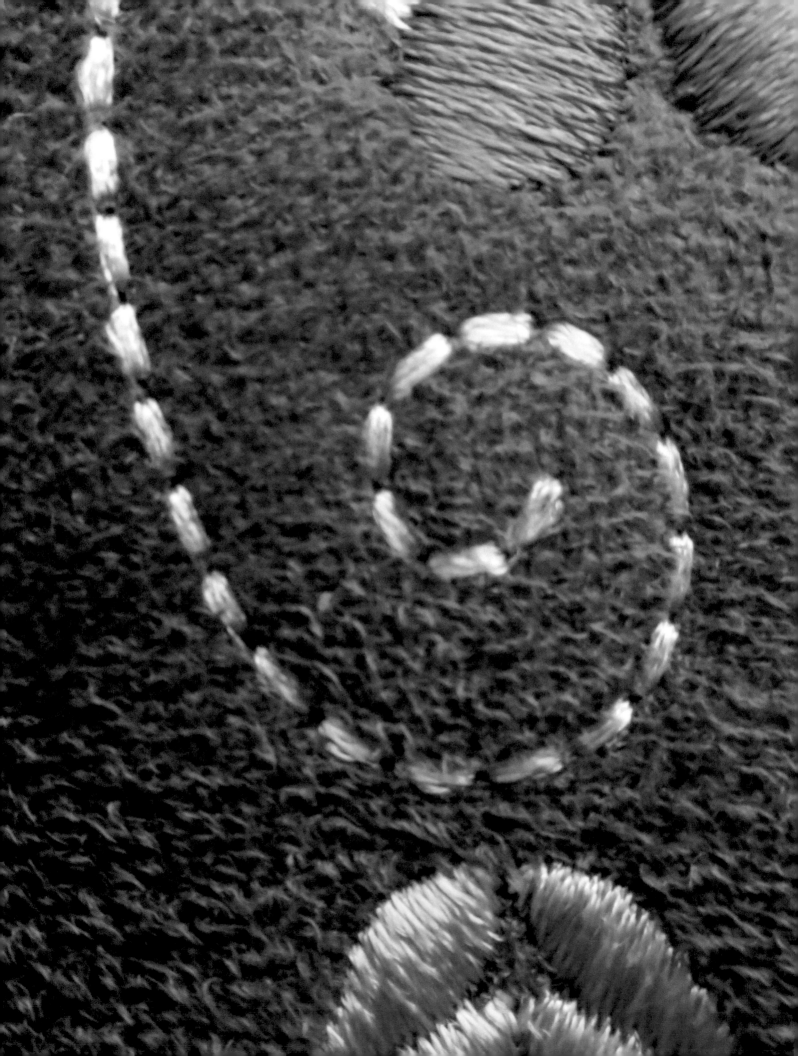

CHAPTER SIX

ASTM and ISO Stitch Classifications

Objectives:

- To review thread construction methods for creating sewing threads
- To understand thread sizing and how thread ticket numbers are determined
- To examine ASTM and ISO standards for stitch classifications and where they are used in garments
- To show the types of sewing equipment used to create the various types of stitch classes

Sewing thread is used to add decorative details to garments and assemble most apparel items in the marketplace today. The selection of sewing threads and stitch types for the assembly of apparel products is primarily driven by the fabric selected. Secondary factors include product category, styling, function, seam construction, price, and quality level. According to American & Efird, "Thread only makes up a small percent of the cost of the sewn product, but shares 50 percent of the responsibility of the seam."[1] Therefore, the type of thread, the stitch formation, and seam construction play vital roles in the quality and durability of the finished product. Standards have been developed to ensure proper communication of stitch formations required for manufacturing of apparel products to eliminate confusion between product developers and factory production personnel.

SEWING THREAD

For garments that contain stitching, thread is an essential component for garment assembly and must be properly selected. Factors that should be taken into consideration when making thread selections for garment decoration or assembly include the fiber content, construction, and weight of fabrics to be sewn; the desired seam construction and seam strength; the type of sewing equipment to be used; product end use and desired performance; and useful life of the product. These aspects can affect the garments appearance, performance, ease, and efficiency of sewing during production, and cost.

Sewing thread is a relatively strong, flexible, thin strand, or ply yarn made from staple fibers, single monofilament, multiple filaments, or cords that are bonded together.[2] Construction methods for threads used for apparel products include air entangled, core spun, monofilament, spun, and textured. **Air entangled thread** is constructed with continuous filaments that are passed through high-pressure air jets that cause them to become entwined, then twist is added. Some threads utilize a combination of staple and filament fiber types such as **core spun thread**, which is constructed with a continuous filament fiber that is wrapped with twisted spun yarn. **Monofilament thread** utilizes a process where no twist is added because the single continuous filament fiber is extruded. **Spun thread** is made from staple fibers spun into single yarns that are twisted together to create a ply. When continuous filaments are heated and texture is imparted into the fibers to provide bulk, **textured threads** are produced.[2] See Figure 6.1 for illustrations of sewing thread construction types, and see Table 6.1 for a comparison of common fiber and thread construction types, garment applications, and properties. For threads constructed using twist, there are two types of twist directions. Single-strand spun sewing threads typically possess an S-twist (right-twist) construction whereas ply yarn threads contain Z-twist (left-twist). Each of these yarns contain a specific number of turns per inch, turns per centimeter, or turns

Air entangled thread

Core spun thread

Monofilament thread

Spun thread

Textured thread

Figure 6.1 Thread construction
Courtesy of Fairchild Books

per meter to create a balanced thread; this is known as **balanced twist**. **Ply adhesion**, also known as **ply security**, is the ability of the thread to maintain its structure without unraveling during sewing. "Generally, sewing threads are made with a Z twist because most sewing machine stitch-forming devices enter the needle loop from the right-hand side, and this reduces the unplying [untwisting] of the thread during sewing."[3] Sewing

Table 6.1 Comparison of Common Fiber and Thread Construction Types, Garment Applications, and Properties

Air Entangled Thread		
Fiber Type	Use	Properties
Continuous Multifilament Polyester	Many Apparel Applications— Blouses, Dresses, Jackets, Jeans, Pants, Shirts, Shorts, Skirts	Good Abrasion Resistance Good Chemical Resistance Good Colorfastness* Excellent Seam Strength Uniform Construction
Core Spun Thread		
Staple Cotton Wrapped Around Polyester Multifilament Core	Blouses, Dresses, Jeans, Lingerie, Shirts, Overalls, Work wear	Good Abrasion Resistance Good Chemical Resistance Good Colorfastness* Excellent Seam Strength Uniform Construction Ideal for Piece Dying
Staple Polyester Wrapped Around Polyester Multifilament Core	Blouses, Dresses, Jeans, Leather Garments, Lingerie, Intimate Apparel, Shirts, Suits, Swimwear, Trousers, Uniforms, Some Embroidery	Excellent Abrasion Resistance Excellent Chemical Resistance Very Good Colorfastness* Excellent Seam Strength Strong Uniform Construction
Monofilament Thread		
Nylon Continuous Filament	Blind Hems in Garments, Leather Garments, Quilting	Excellent Abrasion Resistance Excellent Chemical Resistance Very Good Colorfastness* Excellent Seam Strength Strong Uniform Construction
Spun Thread		
Staple Cotton	Apparel to be Overdyed	Good Abrasion Resistance Good Chemical Resistance Good Colorfastness* Good Seam Strength Uniform Construction Ideal for Overdyeing
Staple Polyester	Coats, Dresses, Jeans, Lingerie, Shirts, Suits, Pants Shorts, Undergarments, Embroidery	Excellent Abrasion Resistance Good Chemical Resistance Excellent Colorfastness* Very Good Seam Strength Strong Uniform Construction
Textured Thread		
Nylon Continuous Multifilament	Blouses, Dresses, Intimate Apparel, Lingerie, Pants, Shirts, Skirts, Swimwear, Undergarments	Very Good Abrasion Resistance Excellent Chemical Resistance Good Colorfastness* Excellent Seam Strength
Polyester Continuous Multifilament	Baby Clothes, Knit Dresses, Knit Tops and Pants, Lounge Wear, Swimwear	Good Abrasion Resistance Excellent Chemical Resistance Very Good Colorfastness* Excellent Seam Strength

Note: Colorfastness to water, chlorinated water, saltwater, perspiration, drycleaning, laundering, ironing/pressing, and light.
Sources: Champion Thread Company, LLC. 2009, http://www.championthread.com/thread; American and Efird, 2009-2013, http://www.amefird.com/products-brands/industrial-sewing-thread/; Ningbo MH Yarn & Thread Factory, 1999-2013, http://www.mhthread.com/categories.html; Coats, http://www.coatsindustrial.com/en/information-hub/apparel-expertise/sewing-threads

thread must have the capability to pass through the needle(s) of industrial sewing machines at high speeds, create stitches that are consistently uniform, and be appropriate for the product's intended use.

Thread size designates the linear density or mass per unit length of the thread, also known as the thickness or diameter of the sewing thread. Thread size numbering systems are determined by a fixed weight or fixed length system. There are many sewing thread size systems, but the most common include English count (cotton count), metric count, denier, decitex, and tex. English count is commonly used to express cotton thread; metric count specifies synthetic; spun and corespun thread, and denier and decitex identify filament threads.[4] **Ticket number** is used by manufacturers to indicate thread size, and it approximates how much raw fiber is present in the unfinished sewing thread. For example, larger threads used for top stitching will have a higher ticket number than a thread used for main seaming of a garment. According to ASTM, ticket number "is based on greige thread rather than finished thread, because finishing processes such as bleaching, dyeing, stretching, mercerizing, or sewing finish application significantly change the apparent thread size so that it may become an inadequate indicator of raw fiber present. Because of the foregoing it is not practical to verify the ticket number by sizing the finished thread".[6] See Table 6.2 for conversion formulas for the various numbering systems to tex and the groups for determining the resultant ticket number. Using any of the traditional systems except for tex, along with a designated multiplier for determining thread ticket numbers, does not create an equivalency between two different types of threads. For example, a cotton 50 thread ticket is not equivalent to a core spun 50 thread ticket, which creates confusion. The tex numbering system is the new international standard for specifying thread ticket numbering for any raw fiber or thread construction of sewing thread to provide equivalencies between different types of threads. Tex, a direct yarn number system, designates the number of grams per 1,000 meters of undyed or finished thread. For example, a tex 30 yarn means there

are 30 grams of weight in 1,000 meters of thread. A higher number indicates a coarser yarn, whereas lower numbers specify finer yarns. The tex numbering system is supported by world trade institutions, the thread industry, ASTM, and ISO, because it is a metric designation and metric measurement systems are used virtually worldwide.[3,4,5] According to ASTM, "This system of sewing thread ticket numbers was developed to overcome confusion arising from the use by the thread industry of a multiple number of undefined and unrelated ticketing systems."[6] See Table 6.3 for general fabric weight designations for apparel and their corresponding thread sizes, tex yarn numbers, thread ticket numbers, and appropriate needle sizes.

Needle size for sewing thread is based on the diameter of the needle, which is measured and reported in hundredths of a millimeter. The thickness of the thread must be proportional to the size of the eye of the needle so it can pass through with the appropriate amount of tension and drag to properly form stitches. Fabric weight and type of construction as well as the type and size of thread must be carefully considered when needle size is selected.

STITCH CLASSIFICATIONS

A **stitch** is a specific repeatable loop formation of one or more sewing threads, created by machine, that intraloops, interloops, interlaces, or passes partially into or completely through one or more plies of material.[7,8] Stitches can also be formed without passing through material such as thread chains used for swing tacks (attaching free-hanging linings to shell garments), thread bars, or belt loops. In the ISO standard, three types of stitch formations are defined as intralooping, interloping, and interlacing. An **intralooping** stitch is created with one single sewing thread that forms a loop that is then looped through itself to form the stitch. A stitch formed by **interlooping** involves two or more sewing threads whereas a loop is formed by one thread that is passed through one or more loops formed by different threads. An

Table 6.2 Conversion of Numbering Systems to Tex and Groups for Determining Resultant Ticket Numbers

Conversions to Tex	
Yarn Number System	Formula to Convert to Tex
English System / Cotton Count (Ne$_c$)	$590.6 \div Ne_c$
Metric Count (N$_m$)	$591 \div N_m$
Denier (den)	$den \div 9$
Decitex (dtex)	$dtex \div 10$

Thread Ticket Number			
Resulting Tex Yarn Number After Conversion	Ticket Number	Resulting Tex Yarn Number After Conversion	Ticket Number
Up to 1.99	1	60 to 69.99	60
2 to 2.99	2	70 to 79.99	70
3 to 3.99	3	80 to 89.99	80
4 to 4.99	4	90 to 104.99	90
5 to 5.99	5	105 to 119.99	105
6 to 6.99	6	120 to 134.99	120
7 to 7.99	7	135 to 149.99	135
8 to 8.99	8	150 to 179.99	150
9 to 9.99	9	180 to 209.99	180
10 to 11.99	10	210 to 239.99	210
12 to 13.99	12	240 to 269.99	240
14 to 15.99	14	270 to 299.99	270
16 to 17.99	16	300 to 349.99	300
18 to 20.99	18	350 to 399.99	350
21 to 23.99	21	400 to 449.99	400
24 to 26.99	24	450 to 499.99	450
27 to 29.99	27	500 to 599.99	500
30 to 34.99	30	600 or greater report in steps of 100 for each 100 tex increase in resulting yarn number	
35 to 39.99	35		
40 to 44.99	40		
45 to 49.99	45		
50 to 59.99	50		

Sources: ASTM D3823-07 (2012) Standard Practice for Determining Ticket Numbers for Sewing Threads (West Conshohocken, PA); 2014, Table 1; Thread Selection Logic; American & Efird, 2014, Fabric Weight / Typical Thread Sizes / Need sizes Table, http://www.amefird.com /technical-tools/thread-education/thread-logic/; A & E Apparel Thread Size Comparison Chart; American & Efird, 2014, http://www.amefird.com/technical-tools/thread-size/apparel-chart/ Thread Numbering; Coats, http://www.coatsindustrial.com/en/apparel/expertise/thread -numbering#Communicating%20Thread%20Size%20with%20Ticket%20Numbers; "Yarn Numbering Systems Conversion Formulas for the Various Numbering systems," http://www .swicofil.com/companyinfo/manualyarnnumbering.html

Table 6.3 General Fabric Weight Designations for Apparel and Their Corresponding Thread Sizes/Tex Yarn Numbers, Thread Ticket Numbers, and Needle Sizes

Fabric Weight Range in oz/yd^2 & g/m^2	Thread Size/Tex Yarn Number	Thread Ticket Number	Metric Needle Sizes
2 to 4 oz/yd^2 68 to 136 g/m^2	Tex 16	16	60, 65
	Tex 18	18	
	Tex 21	21	
	Tex 24	24	
4 to 6 oz/yd^2 136 to 204 g/m^2	Tex 24	24	70, 75
	Tex 27	27	
	Tex 30	30	
6 to 8 oz/yd^2 204 to 272 g/m^2	Tex 30	30	80. 90, 100
	Tex 35	35	
	Tex 40	40	
8 to 10 oz/yd^2 272 to 339 g/m^2	Tex 40	40	100, 110
	Tex 45	45	
	Tex 50	50	
	Tex 60	60	
10 to 12 oz/yd^2 339 to 407 g/m^2	Tex 60	60	120, 140
	Tex 80	80	
	Tex 90	90	
	Tex 105	105	
12 to 14 oz/yd^2 407 to 475 g/m^2	Tex 105	105	140, 160
	Tex 120	120	
	Tex 135	135	
	Tex 150	150	
	Tex 180	180	180
	Tex 240	240	200
	Tex 300	300	230

Sources: ASTM D3823-07(2012) *Standard Practice for Determining Ticket Numbers for Sewing Threads* (West Conshohocken, PA); 2014, Table 1;
Thread Selection Logic; American & Efird, 2014, Fabric Weight/Typical Thread Sizes/Needle sizes Table, http://www.amefird.com/technical-tools/thread-education/thread-logic/;
A & E Apparel Thread Size Comparison Chart; American & Efird, 2014, http://www.amefird .com/technical-tools/thread-size/apparel-chart/
Thread Numbering; Coats, http://www.coatsindustrial.com/en/apparel/expertise/thread -numbering#Communicating%20Thread%20Size%20with%20Ticket%20Numbers;
Janace Bubonia. *Fashion Production Terms and Processes.* (New York: Fairchild Books, 2012)

interlacing stitch is formed by two or more sewing threads that pass through a material, forming a loop that intertwines around a different loop of thread.[8] In the ASTM standard only two stitch formations are discussed—interlooping and interlacing. ASTM uses the term *interlooping* when referring to stitch formations designated by ISO for interlacing and interlooping.

When a series of repeating stitches are formed, it is referred to as **stitching**. The length of each stitch, referred to as **stitch length**, is either measured in millimeters (mm) or designated using the number of **stitches per inch (SPI)** or **stitches per centimeter (SPC)**. See Figure 6.2 for an example of a counter used to determine the number of stitches per inch. Stitch length is adjusted depending upon the type of garment, material selected, and the seam strength required. See Table 6.4 for recommended stitches per inch typically used for a variety of woven and knitted garments. As shown in Table 6.4, there is a range of stitches per inch recommended for the

Table 6.4 Stitches Per Inch Typically Used in a Variety of Woven and Knitted Garments

Garment Type	Stitches Per Inch	Fabric Structure
Casual shirts, blouses, or tops	10–14	Woven
Children's garments	8–10	Woven
Denim jackets, jeans, or skirts	7–8	Woven
Dresses or skirts	10–12	Knit or woven
Dress shirt or blouse	14–20	Woven
Fleece garments	10–12	Knit
Infants or children's garments	10–12	Knit
Intimate apparel	12–16	Knit
Jersey T-shirts, tops, or polo shirts	10–12	Knit
Sweaters (medium to heavy)	8–10	Knit
Swimwear	12–16	Knit
Twill pants or shorts	8–10	Woven
Trousers or slacks	10–12	Woven
Underwear	12–14	Knit

Source: Amefird, "Technical Bulletin: Stitches Per Inch (SPI)—What You Should Know," February 5, 2010, accessed March 17, 2013, http://www.amefird.com/wp-content/uploads/2010/01/Selecting-the-right-SPI-2-5-10.pdf

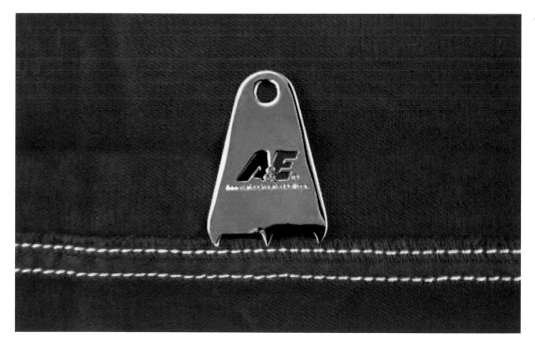

Figure 6.2 Stitch counter measuring 9 stitches per inch (SPI) *Courtesy of American & Efird LLC*

American & Efird Thread Consumption Calculator - Light Wt. Fabrics

ANECALC

Fill in the information highlighted in 'yellow'

Garment Description:

Junior's KNIT DRESS
SIZE: 10

Cost Per Garment = ___ US $

Avg. Seam Thickness: **1.2** mm

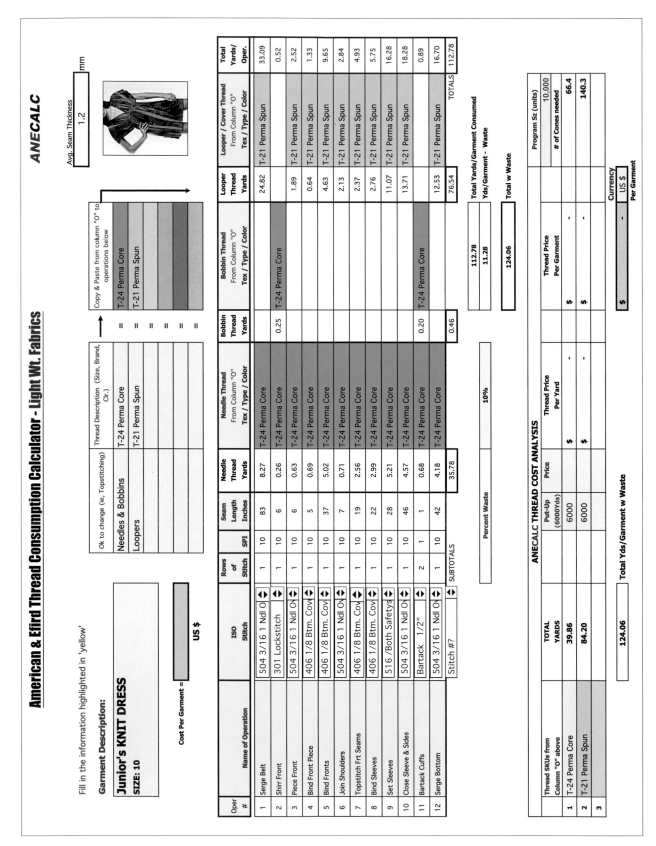

Ok to change (ie, Topstitching)	Thread Description (Size, Brand, Clr.)			
Needles & Bobbins	T-24 Perma Core	=	T-24 Perma Core	
Loopers	T-21 Perma Spun	=	T-21 Perma Spun	
		=		
		=		
		=		
		=		

Copy & Paste from column "O" to operations below

Oper #	Name of Operation	ISO Stitch	Rows of Stitch	SPI	Seam Length Inches	Needle Thread Yards	Needle Thread From Column "O" Tex / Type / Color	Bobbin Thread Yards	Bobbin Thread From Column "O" Tex / Type / Color	Looper Thread Yards	Looper / Cover Thread From Column "O" Tex / Type / Color	Total Yards/ Oper.
1	Serge Belt	504 3/16 1 Ndl O	1	10	83	8.27	T-24 Perma Core			24.82	T-21 Perma Spun	33.09
2	Shirr Front	301 Lockstitch	1	10	6	0.26	T-24 Perma Core	0.25	T-24 Perma Core			0.52
3	Piece Front	504 3/16 1 Ndl O	1	10	6	0.63	T-24 Perma Core			1.89	T-21 Perma Spun	2.52
4	Bind Front Piece	406 1/8 Btm. Cov	1	10	5	0.69	T-24 Perma Core			0.64	T-21 Perma Spun	1.33
5	Bind Fronts	406 1/8 Btm. Cov	1	10	37	5.02	T-24 Perma Core			4.63	T-21 Perma Spun	9.65
6	Join Shoulders	504 3/16 1 Ndl O	1	10	7	0.71	T-24 Perma Core			2.13	T-21 Perma Spun	2.84
7	Topstitch Frt Seams	406 1/8 Btm. Cov	1	10	19	2.56	T-24 Perma Core			2.37	T-21 Perma Spun	4.93
8	Bind Sleeves	406 1/8 Btm. Cov	1	10	22	2.99	T-24 Perma Core			2.76	T-21 Perma Spun	5.75
9	Set Sleeves	516 /Both Safetys	1	10	28	5.21	T-24 Perma Core			11.07	T-21 Perma Spun	16.28
10	Close Sleeve & Sides	504 3/16 1 Ndl O	1	10	46	4.57	T-24 Perma Core			13.71	T-21 Perma Spun	18.28
11	Bartack Cuffs	Bartack 1/2"	2	1	1	0.68	T-24 Perma Core	0.20	T-24 Perma Core			0.89
12	Serge Bottom	504 3/16 1 Ndl O	1	10	42	4.18	T-24 Perma Core			12.53	T-21 Perma Spun	16.70
	Stitch #?				SUBTOTALS	35.78		0.46		76.54		
											TOTALS	112.78

Total Yards/Garment Consumed	112.78	
Yds/Garment - Waste	11.28	
Total w Waste	124.06	

Percent Waste: **10%**

ANECALC THREAD COST ANALYSIS

	Thread SKUs from Column "O" above	TOTAL YARDS	Put-Up (6000Yds)	Price	Thread Price Per Yard		Program Sz (units)	10,000
1	T-24 Perma Core	39.86	6000	$	-		# of Cones needed	66.4
2	T-21 Perma Spun	84.20	6000	$	-			140.3
3								

			Thread Price Per Garment	
	124.06	Total Yds/Garment w Waste	$	-	Per Garment

Currency: US $

Figure 6.3 Factors that impact thread consumption and cost

different types of garments. The lowest number of SPI listed for each item represents what is found in lower price ranges such as budget and some moderate goods, whereas the highest number of SPI represents designer and some bridge-priced garments. The middle range of stitches represents garments priced at the higher end of the moderate price category, better-priced garments, and the lower end of the bridge price range. The higher the garment price, the more stitches per inch will be used for assembly. The range of SPI will also depend upon the type and weight of the fabric, the stitch construction and seam classifications selected, and the price range of the garment. For example, the number of stitches per inch used for a silk blouse in the designer price range will contain more stitches per inch than a similar style silk blouse sold in the moderate price range. This is a result of increased thread consumption, time, labor, and higher quality construction. See Figure 6.3 for the factors that impact thread consumption and thread cost for a garment. Typically the higher the stitch count, the higher the quality of the garment. The correlation among the threads that form the stitches is known as **thread tension** and can impact the appearance, durability, and quality of the stitching as well as the resulting seam construction of a garment. **Balanced thread tension** provides a smooth appearance to the stitching because the threads interlock in the middle of the fabric layers rather than at the face or on the back (see Figure 6.4). **Unbalanced thread tension** can cause a bead or loop(s) of thread between the stitches that shows in the stitch line on the face or backside. The stitches can be either too tight or too loose if tension is not properly adjusted (see Figures 6.5 and 6.6). When stitch tension is too loose seam grin occurs when tension is placed on the

seam, causing the stitches to show at the seamline. See Chapter 13 for common stitching defects found in garments. Stitches can be used for creating seams, surface decoration, or thread chains.

ASTM AND ISO STANDARDS FOR STITCHES

Standards for communicating stitch formations consistently worldwide are published by ASTM (D6193 Standard Practice for Stitches and Seams) and ISO (International Standard 4915 Textiles – Stitch Types – Classification and Terminology). These standards help designers and product developers communicate the specific numeric stitch designations for each of the areas within the garment that require stitching for assembly. All of the stitch designations require a needle carrying sewing thread to pierce or penetrate the material. As each stitch classification is discussed in this chapter, it is important to note the distinctive formation of each stitch type that is created by the mechanical actions of the specific sewing equipment required. Both ASTM and ISO standards use the same six classifications, which are referenced in terms of their configuration or overall effect. Each stitch class, 100 through 600, is identified by the first digit of a three-digit number. Individual stitches are further identified by a second and third digit designating their concatenation (series of thread configurations). ISO also accompanies each stitch class number with a name for the stitch group which includes: Class 100 chain stitches, Class 200 (originated as hand stitches), Class 300 lock stitches, Class 400 multi-thread chain stitches, Class 500 overedge chain stitches, and Class 600 covering chain stitches.

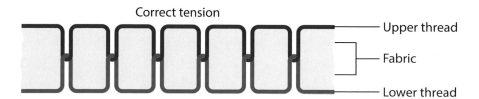

Correct tension

— Upper thread

— Fabric

— Lower thread

Figure 6.4 Balanced thread tension
Illustration by Q2A Media Services Private Limited

Unbalanced thread tension in apparel items

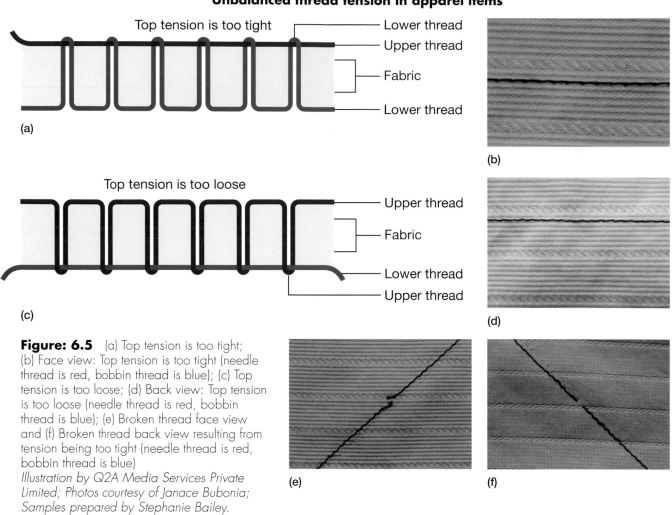

Top tension is too tight
— Lower thread
— Upper thread
— Fabric
— Lower thread

(a)

(b)

Top tension is too loose
— Upper thread
— Fabric
— Lower thread
— Upper thread

(c)

(d)

(e)

(f)

Figure: 6.5 (a) Top tension is too tight; (b) Face view: Top tension is too tight (needle thread is red, bobbin thread is blue); (c) Top tension is too loose; (d) Back view: Top tension is too loose (needle thread is red, bobbin thread is blue); (e) Broken thread face view and (f) Broken thread back view resulting from tension being too tight (needle thread is red, bobbin thread is blue)
Illustration by Q2A Media Services Private Limited; Photos courtesy of Janace Bubonia; Samples prepared by Stephanie Bailey.

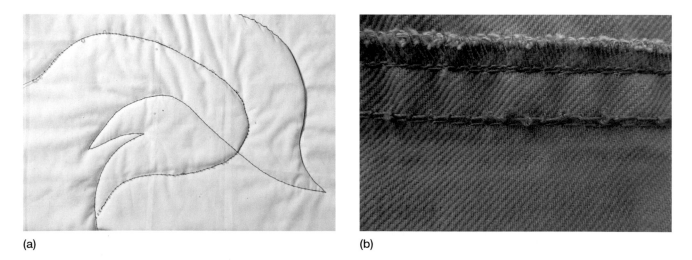

(a)

(b)

Figure 6.6 Unbalanced thread tension in apparel Items
(a) © Ken Cavanagh Photo courtesy of KenCavanagh.com; (b) Photo courtesy of Janace Bubonia

100 Class Chain Stitches

For apparel production, the **100 chain stitches** classification is used primarily for attaching buttons, creating blind hems, and for basting tailored apparel. Although this stitch class is very economical, its use is limited in apparel because it can easily unravel when broken or cut and can be removed by pulling on an unlocked thread end. This stitch class does not provide strength and security; therefore, its use is limited. The 100 Class of chain stitches are formed by the intralooping (ISO term) or interlooping (ASTM term) of one needle threads that passes through the fabric and is held in place by the subsequent loop(s).[7,8] There is one exception to this in the ISO standard, which is stitch 102. The 102 stitch is formed with two needle threads that form loops that are passed through the fabric, and the threads intraloop on the other side. See Figure 6.7 for the most commonly used ASTM and ISO 100 Class

Most commonly used ASTM & ISO 100 Class chain stitches for apparel

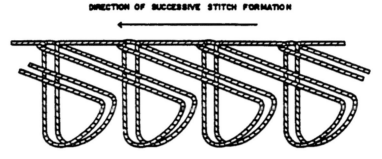

NOTE 1—This type of stitch shall be formed with one needle thread, which shall interloop with itself on the top surface of the material. The thread shall be passed through the top ply and horizontally through portions of the bottom ply without penetrating it the full depth.

(a)

Stitch Type 103

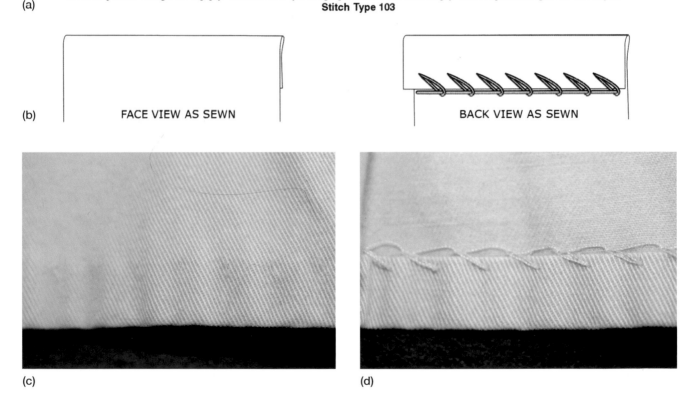

(b) FACE VIEW AS SEWN   BACK VIEW AS SEWN

(c)   (d)

Figure 6.7 a–d (a) ASTM 103 Blindstitch; (b) ASTM 103, ISO 103 Blindstitches; (c) ASTM 103, ISO 103 Blindstitches face view; (d) ASTM 103, ISO 103 Blindstitches back view
Illustrations of stitch formations from ASTM D 6193. Illustrations of stitches showing face and back views courtesy of Fairchild Publications. Photos courtesy of Janace Bubonia.

continued

Most commonly used ASTM & ISO 100 Class chain stitches for apparel

DIRECTION OF SUCCESSIVE STITCH FORMATION

NOTE 1—This type of stitch shall be formed with one needle thread which shall interloop with itself on the undersurface of the material.

(e)   **Stitch Type 104**

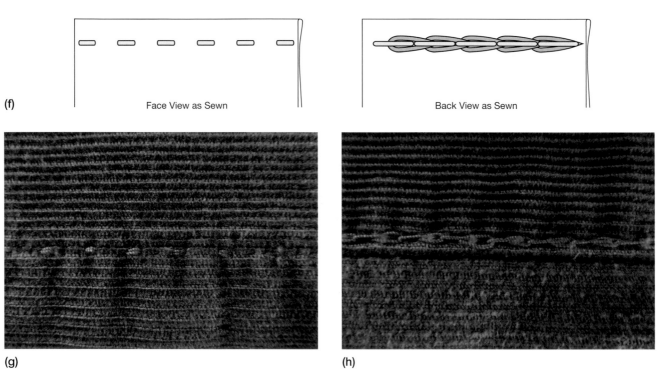

Face View as Sewn	Back View as Sewn

(f)

(g)   (h)

Figure 6.7 e–h (e) ASTM 104 Blindstitch; (f) ASTM 104, ISO 104 Blindstitches; (g) ASTM & ISO 104 Blindstitches face view; (h) ASTM & ISO 104 Blindstitches back view
Illustrations of stitch formations from ASTM D 6193. Illustrations of stitches showing face and back views courtesy of Fairchild Publications. Photos courtesy of Janace Bubonia.

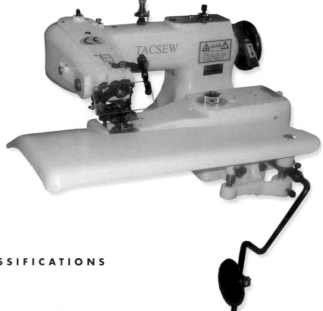

Figure 6.8 Chain stitch machine
Courtesy of www.sewinggold.com

chain stitches for apparel. This stitch classification utilizes chain stitch machines (see Figure 6.8).

200 Class (Originated as Hand Stitches)

The **200 stitch class** is limited in its use for mass production due to the high labor cost of forming stitches by hand or increased expense of specialized sewing equipment and training required when hand stitches are simulated by machine. These stitches, while limited in practice, are used primarily for decorative purposes. The 200 Class of stitches are made by one or more needle threads that pass through the fabric in a single line thread formation that is held in place by the single line of thread weaving or interlooping in and out of the fabric, or by the threads interlooping with themselves. It is important to note that when two or more threads are used to form a stitch, all of the threads traverse the same needle punctures through the fabric.[7,8] See Figure 6.9 for the most

Most commonly used ASTM & ISO 200 Class stitches for apparel

DIRECTION OF SUCCESSIVE STITCH FORMATION

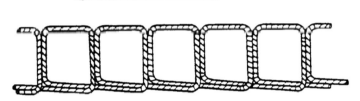

NOTE 1—This type of stitch shall be formed with one needle thread, which shall be passed through the material brought forward two stitch lengths, passed back through the material and brought back one stitch length before being passed through the material a third time.

(a)   **Stitch Type 202**

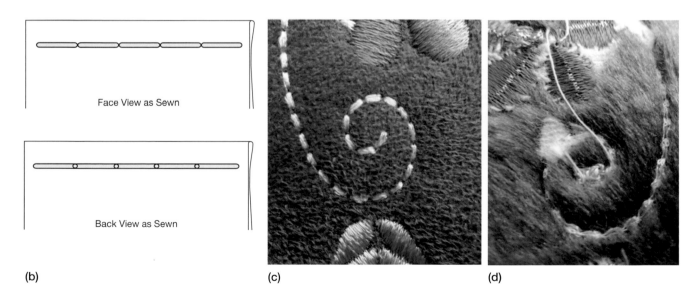

Face View as Sewn

Back View as Sewn

(b)   (c)   (d)

Figure 6.9 a–d (a) ASTM 202 Hand stitch; (b) ASTM 202, ISO 202 Hand stitches; (c) ASTM 202, ISO 202 Hand stitches face view; (d) ASTM 202, ISO 202 Hand stitches back view
Illustrations of stitch formations from ASTM D 6193. Illustrations of stitches showing face and back views courtesy of Fairchild Books. Photos courtesy of Janace Bubonia.

continued

Most commonly used ASTM & ISO 200 Class stitches for apparel

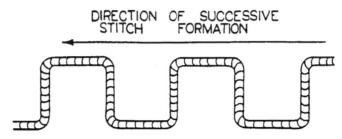

NOTE 1—This type of stitch shall be formed with one or more needle threads and has for a general characteristic that the thread does not interloop with itself or any other thread or threads. The thread is passed completely through the material by means of a double pointed center eye needle and returned by another path. This class of stitch simulates hand stitching.

Stitch Type 205

(e)

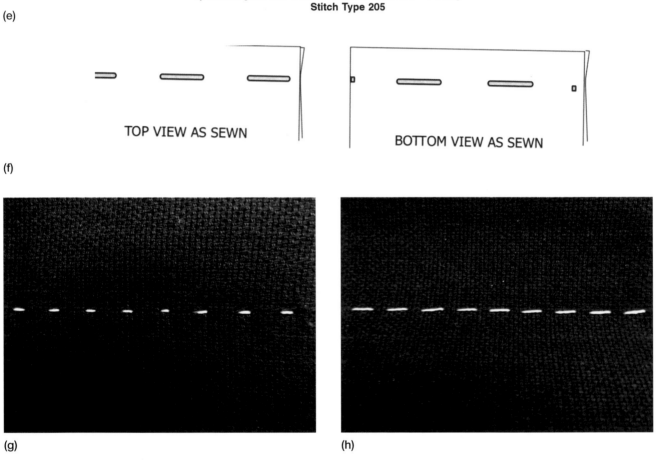

(f)

(g)   (h)

Figure 6.9 e–h   (e) ASTM 205 Hand stitch; (f) ASTM 205, ISO 205 Hand stitches; (g) ASTM 205, ISO 205 Hand stitches face view; (h) ASTM 205, ISO 205 Hand stitches back view
Illustrations of stitch formations from ASTM D 6193. Illustrations of stitches showing face and back views courtesy of Fairchild Books. Photos courtesy of Janace Bubonia.

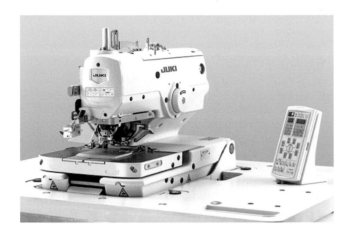

Figure 6.10 Hand stitch machine
© Juki juki.com

300 Class Lockstitches

The **300 lockstitches** classification is the most widely used for assembly of apparel products. Lockstitches are selected for securing buttons, forming buttonholes and bar tacks, main seaming and hemming of garments, attaching elastic and trims, embroidery, and top stitching. It is important to note that this stitch class, while strong and secure, does not offer stretch or extendibility. The 300 Class of lockstitches are formed with a bobbin thread and one or more needle threads that pass through the fabric and interlace together to secure each stitch. This stitch class offers straight stitching and zigzag patterns, as well as blind hem stitch formations that offer greater security than 100 Class stitches.[7,8] See Figure 6.11 for the most commonly used ASTM and ISO 300 Class lock stitches in apparel. This stitch classification utilizes lockstitch machines (see Figure 6.12)

commonly used ASTM and ISO 200 Class stitches in apparel. This stitch classification utilizes hand-stitch machines (see Figure 6.10).

Most commonly used ASTM & ISO 300 Class lock stitches for apparel

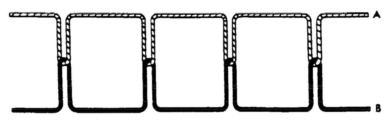

NOTE 1—This type of stitch shall be formed with two threads: one needle thread, A, and one bobbin thread, B. A loop of thread A shall be passed through the material and interlaced with thread B. Thread A shall be pulled back so that the interlacing shall be midway between surfaces of the material or materials being sewn.

(a)
Stitch Type 301

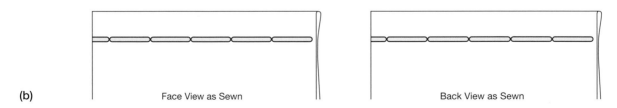

(b) Face View as Sewn   Back View as Sewn

Figure 6.11 a–b (a) ASTM 301 Lock stitch; (b) ASTM 301, ISO 301 Lock stitches
Illustrations of stitch formations from ASTM D 6193. Illustrations of stitches showing face and back views courtesy of Fairchild Books. Photos courtesy of Janace Bubonia.

continued

Most commonly used ASTM & ISO 300 Class lock stitches for apparel

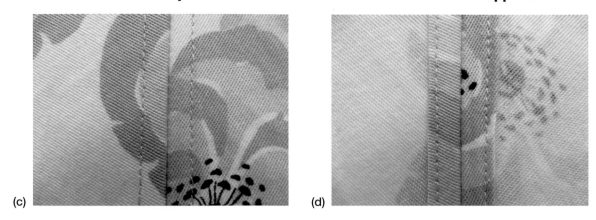

(c)　　　　　　　　　　　　　　(d)

DIRECTION OF SUCCESSIVE STITCH FORMATION

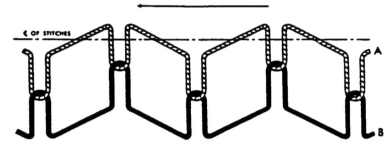

NOTE 1—This type of stitch shall be formed with two threads: one needle thread, A, and one bobbin thread, B. This stitch type is exactly the same as stitch type 301 except that successive single stitches form a symmetrical zigzag pattern.

(e)　　　　　　　　　　**Stitch Type 304**

Face View as Sewn　　　　　　　　Back View as Sewn

(f)

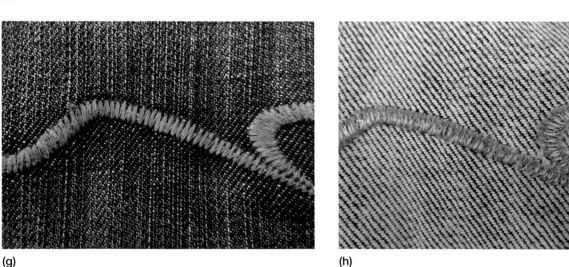

(g)　　　　　　　　　　　　　　(h)

Figure 6.11 c–h　(c) ASTM 301, ISO 301 Lock stitches face view; (d) ASTM 301, ISO 301 Lock stitches back view; (e) ASTM 304 Zigzag lock stitch; (f) ASTM 304, ISO 304 Zigzag lock stitches; (g) ASTM 304, ISO 304 Zigzag lock stitches face view; (h) ASTM 304, ISO 304 Zigzag lock stitches back view
Illustrations of stitch formations from ASTM D 6193. Illustrations of stitches showing face and back views courtesy of Fairchild Books. Photos courtesy of Janace Bubonia.

Figure 6.12 Lock stitch machine
© Juki juki.com

400 Class Multi-thread Chain Stitches

The **400 multi-thread chain stitches** classification is a close competitor to the 300 Class of stitches in its use in apparel production; however, it is stronger and offers flexibility that lock stitches do not provide. This group of stitches is used for main seams in woven garments, felling, button loop construction, top stitching, hems of knitted garments, attaching bindings, elastic, and trims. The 400 Class of stitches are made with a looper thread and one or more needle threads that pass through the fabric and interlace with loops that interloop on the underside of the material. This stitch class offers straight stitching and zigzag patterns that provide greater security than 300 Class stitches.[7,8] See Figure 6.13 for the most commonly used ASTM and ISO 400 Class multi-thread chain stitches in apparel. Lock stitch machines are utilized for sewing both 300 Class lock stitches and 400 multi-thread chain stitches (see Figure 6.12).

500 Class Overedge Chain Stitches

The **500 overedge chain stitches** classification is used for main seaming, finishing raw edges, decorative hem edges, and attaching elastic and trims. The 500 Class of stitches is formed with one or more thread groups. One group of threads pierces through the fabric and are held in place by intralooping (ISO term) or interlooping (ASTM term) with itself to cover the edge of the material, whereas subsequent loops pass through the fabric to form the stitch. The threads can also be secured by one group of threads interlooping with loops formed by one or more interlooped groups before subsequent loops from the first group are passed back through the fabric to cover the edge and form the stitch.[7,8] ASTM designates safety stitches as part of this classification, which are formed by the simultaneous sewing of two parallel independent rows of stitches. One row of lock stitches or multi-thread chain stitches is positioned at a specified distance from the overedge chain stitch. This combination of stitches provides strength, durability, and elasticity.[7,8] See Figure 6.14 for the most commonly used ASTM and ISO 500 Class overedge chain stitches in apparel. Overedge chain stitches are created with overlock machines (see Figure 6.15).

600 Class Covering Chain Stitches

The **600 Class covering chain stitches** classification is primarily used for main seaming in knitted garments because they are strong and provide flexibility and extendibility. This particular group of stitches is used in seams of tight-fitting garments such as swimwear, shapewear, athletic apparel, and thermal underwear. This class of stitches is made using two or more groups of threads that enclose the raw edges of both surfaces of the fabric plies by covering them. The threads are cast on the surface of the fabric and then interlooped with loops of thread formed on the underside of the fabric.[7,8] See Figure 6.16 for the most commonly used ASTM and ISO 600 Class covering chain stitches in apparel. Stitches within this classification are formed using cover stitch machines (see Figure 6.17). It is important to note that this stitch class uses the most thread of all of the classifications, which increases the cost of the garment.

Most commonly used ASTM & ISO 400 Class multi-thread chain stitches in apparel

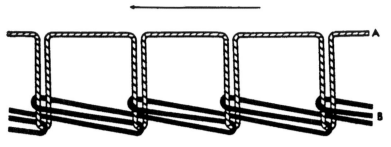

DIRECTION OF SUCCESSIVE STITCH FORMATION

NOTE 1—This type of stitch shall be formed with two threads: one needle thread, A, and one looper thread, B. Loops of thread A shall be passed through the material and interlaced and interlooped with loops of thread B. The interloopings shall be drawn against the underside of the bottom ply of material.

(a)

Stitch Type 401

(b)

Face View as Sewn

Back View as Sewn

(c)

(d)

Figure 6.13 a–d (a) ASTM 401 Multi-thread chain stitch; (b) ASTM 401, ISO 401 Multi-thread chain stitches; (c) ASTM 401, ISO 401 Single needle multi-thread chain stitches face view; (d) ASTM 401, ISO 401 Single needle multi-thread chain stitches back view
Illustrations of stitch formations from ASTM D 6193. Illustrations of stitches showing face and back views courtesy of Fairchild Books. Photos courtesy of Janace Bubonia.

Note 1—This type of stitch shall be formed with three threads: two needle threads A and A′ and one looper thread, B. Loops of threads A and A′ shall be passed through the material and interlaced and interlooped with loops of thread B. The interloopings shall be drawn against the underside of the material.

(e)

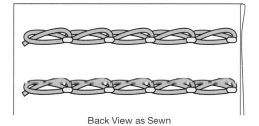

(f)   Face View as Sewn   Back View as Sewn

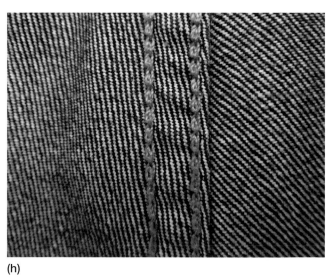

(g)   (h)

Figure 6.13 e–h   (e) ASTM 402 Double/twin needle multi-thread chain stitch; (f) ASTM 402, ISO 402 Double/twin needle multi-thread chain stitches; (g) ASTM 402, ISO 402 Double/twin needle multi-thread chain stitches face view; (h) ASTM 402, ISO 402 Double/twin needle multi-thread chain stitches back view
Illustrations of stitch formations from ASTM D 6193. Illustrations of stitches showing face and back views courtesy of Fairchild Books. Photos courtesy of Janace Bubonia.

continued

Most commonly used ASTM & ISO 400 Class multi-thread chain stitches in apparel

DIRECTION OF SUCCESSIVE STITCH FORMATION

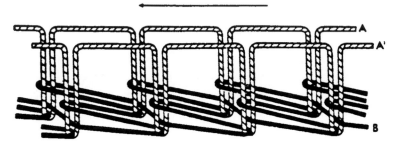

NOTE 1—This type of stitch shall be formed with three threads: two needle threads, A and A′ and one looper thread, B. Loops of threads A and A′ shall be passed through the material and interlaced and interlooped with loops of thread B. The interloopings shall be drawn against the underside of the material.

(i)

Stitch Type 406

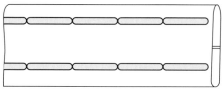

(j)   Face view as shown

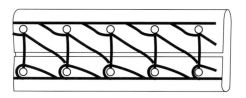

Back view as shown

(k)

(l)

Figure 6.13 i–l (i) ASTM 406 Double/twin needle bottom cover stitch; (j) ASTM 406, ISO 406 Double/twin needle bottom cover stitch; (k) ASTM 406, ISO 406 Double/twin needle bottom cover stitches face view; (l) ASTM 406, ISO 406 Double/twin needle bottom cover stitches back view
Illustrations of stitch formations from ASTM D 6193. Illustrations of stitches showing face and back views courtesy of Fairchild Books. Photos courtesy of Janace Bubonia.

Most Commonly used ASTM & ISO 500 Class overedge chain stitches in apparel

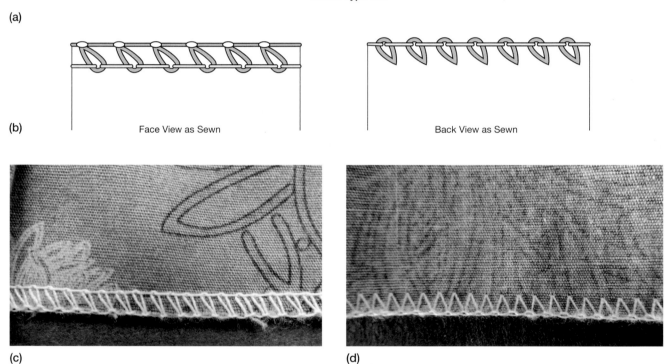

DIRECTION OF SUCCESSIVE STITCH FORMATION

NOTE 1—This type of stitch shall be formed with two threads: one needle thread, A, and one looper thread, B. Loops of thread A shall be passed through the material and brought to the edge where they shall be interlooped with thread B. The loops of thread B shall be extended from this interlooping to the point of needle penetration of the next stitch and there interlooped with thread A.

Stitch Type 503

(a)

(b)

Face View as Sewn | Back View as Sewn

(c)   (d)

Figure 6.14 a–d   (a) ASTM 503 Two-thread overedge chain stitch with single purl on edge; (b) ASTM 503, ISO Two-thread overedge chain stitches with single purl on edge; (c) ASTM 503, ISO Two-thread overedge chain stitches with single purl on edge face view; (d) ASTM 503, ISO Two-thread overedge chain stitches with single purl on edge back view
Illustrations of stitch formations from ASTM D 6193. Illustrations of stitches showing face and back views courtesy of Fairchild Books. Photos courtesy of Janace Bubonia.

continued

Most Commonly used ASTM & ISO 500 Class overedge chain stitches in apparel

DIRECTION OF SUCCESSIVE STITCH FORMATION

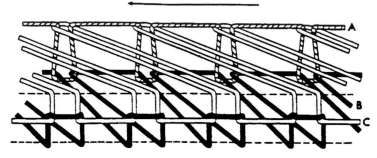

NOTE 1—This type of stitch shall be formed with three threads: one needle thread, A; one looper thread, B; and one cover thread, C. Loops of thread A shall be passed through the material and interlooped with loops of thread B at the point of penetration on the underside of the material. The loops of thread B shall be extended to the edge of the material and there interlooped with loops of thread C. Loops of thread C shall be extended from this interlooping to the point of needle penetration of the next stitch and there interlooped with thread A.

(e)   **Stitch Type 504**

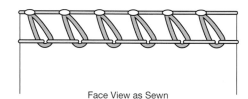

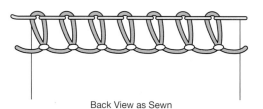

(f)   Face View as Sewn   Back View as Sewn

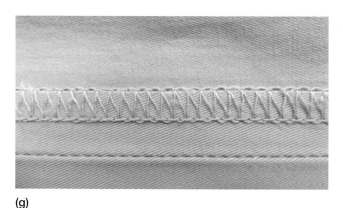

(g)   (h)

Figure 6.14 e–h   (e) ASTM 504 Three-thread overedge chain stitch; (f) ASTM 504, ISO 504 Three-thread overedge chain stitches; (g) ASTM 504, ISO 504 Three-thread overedge chain stitches face view; (h) ASTM 504, ISO 504 Three-thread overedge chain stitches back view
Illustrations of stitch formations from ASTM D 6193. Illustrations of stitches showing face and back views courtesy of Fairchild Books. Photos courtesy of Janace Bubonia.

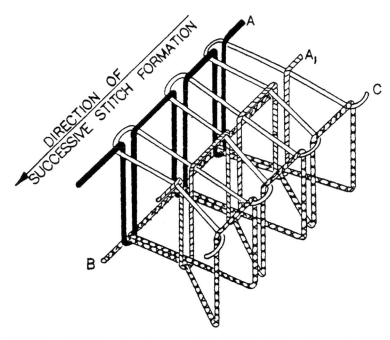

NOTE 1—This type of stitch shall be formed with four threads: two needle threads, A and A′; one looper thread, B; and one cover thread, C. Loops of threads A and A′ shall be passed through the material where they shall be interlooped at the lower point of penetration with lops of thread B. The loops of thread B shall be brought around the edge of the material and interlooped with loops of thread C. The loops of thread C shall be extended to the point of needle penetration of threads A and A′ at the next stitch where they shall be entered by loops of these threads.

(i)

Stitch Type 514

(j)

Face View as Sewn

Back View as Sewn

(k)

(l)

Figure 6.14 i–l (i) ASTM 514 Four-thread overedge chain stitch; (j) ASTM 514, ISO 514 Four-thread overedge chain stitches; (k) ASTM 514, ISO 514 Four-thread overedge chain stitches face view; (l) ASTM 514, ISO 514 Four-thread overedge chain stitches back view

Illustrations of stitch formations from ASTM D 6193. Illustrations of stitches showing face and back views courtesy of Fairchild Books. Photos courtesy of Janace Bubonia.

continued

Most Commonly used ASTM & ISO 500 Class overedge chain stitches in apparel

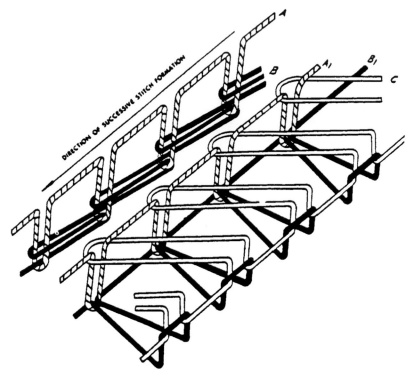

NOTE 1—This type of stitch shall be formed by simultaneously sewing one row of stitch type 401 a specified distance from the edge of the material, and one row of stitch type 504 on the edge of the material.

(m)

Stitch Type 516

(n)

Face View as Sewn

Back View as Sewn

(o)

(p)

Figure 6.14 m–p (m) ASTM 516 Five-thread overedge safety stitch; (n) ASTM 516 Five-thread overedge safety stitch; (o) ASTM 516 Five-thread overedge safety stitches face view; (p) ASTM 516 Five-thread overedge safety stitches back view *Illustrations of stitch formations from ASTM D 6193. Illustrations of stitches showing face and back views courtesy of Fairchild Books. Photos courtesy of Janace Bubonia.*

Figure 6.15 Overlock machine
© *Juki juki.com*

Most commonly used ASTM & ISO 600 Class covering chain stitches in apparel

DIRECTION OF SUCCESSIVE STITCH FORMATION

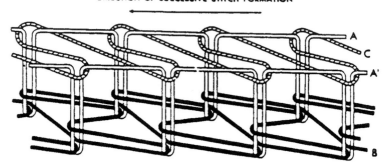

Note 1—This type of stitch shall be formed with four threads: two needle threads, A and A'; one looper thread, B; and one cover thread, C. Loops of threads A and A' shall be passed through loops of thread C already cast across the top surface of the material, and then through the material where they shall be interlooped with loops of thread B on the underside.

(a)   **Stitch Type 602**

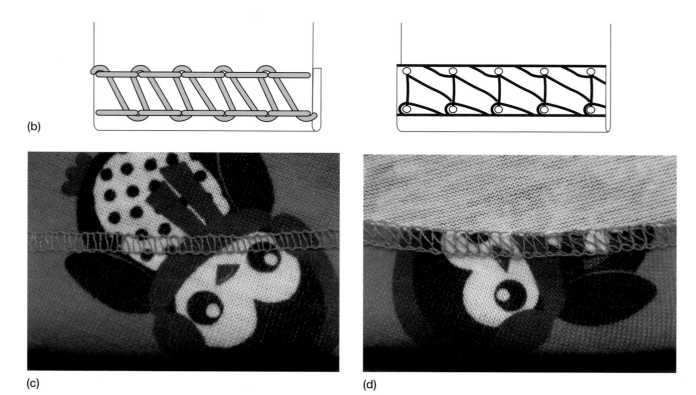

(b)

(c)   (d)

Figure 6.16 a–d (a) ASTM 602 Two-needle four-three coverstitch; (b) ASTM 602, ISO 602 Two-needle four-three coverstitch; (c) ASTM 602, ISO 602 Two-needle four-three coverstitch face view; (d) ASTM 602, ISO 602 Two-needle four-three coverstitch back view

Illustrations of stitch formations from ASTM D 6193. Illustrations of stitches showing face and back views courtesy of Fairchild Books. Photos courtesy of Janace Bubonia

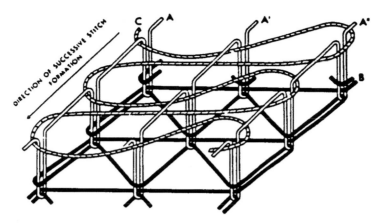

NOTE 1—This type of stitch shall be formed with five threads: three needle threads, A, A', and A''; one looper thread, B; and one cover thread, C. Loops of threads A, A', and A'' shall be passed through loops of thread C already cast on the top surface of the material and then through the material where they shall be interlooped with loops of thread B on the underside.

(e)

Stitch Type 605

(f)

Face view as shown

Back view as shown

(g)

(h)

Figure 6.16 e–h (e) ASTM 605 Three-needle five-thread coverstitch; (f) ASTM 605, ISO 605 Three-needle five-thread coverstitches; (g) ASTM 605, ISO 605 Three-needle five-thread coverstitches face view; (h) ASTM 605, ISO 605 Three-needle five-thread cover stitches back view
Illustrations of stitch formations from ASTM D 6193. Illustrations of stitches showing face and back views courtesy of Fairchild Books. Photos courtesy of Janace Bubonia

continued

Most commonly used ASTM & ISO 600 Class covering chain stitches in apparel

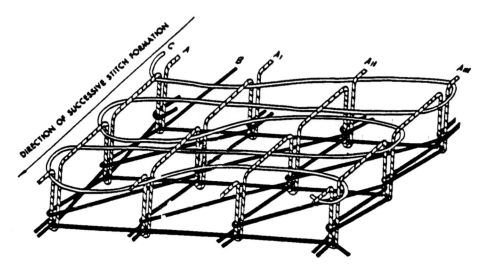

NOTE 1—This type of stitch shall be formed with six threads: four needle threads, A, A', A'', and A'''; one looper thread, B; and one cover thread, C. Loops of threads A, A', A'', and A''' shall be passed through loops of thread C already cast on the surface of the material, and then through the material where they shall be interlooped with loops of thread B on the underside.

(i)

Stitch Type 607

(j)

Face view as shown

Back view as shown

(k)

(l)

Figure 6.16 i–l (i) ASTM 607 Four-needle five thread cover stitch; (j) ASTM 607, ISO 607 Four-needle five thread cover stitches; (k) ASTM 607, ISO 607 Four-needle five thread cover stitches face view; (l) ASTM 607, ISO 607 Four-needle five thread cover stitches back view
Illustrations of stitch formations from ASTM D 6193. Illustrations of stitches showing face and back views courtesy of Fairchild Books. Photos courtesy of Janace Bubonia

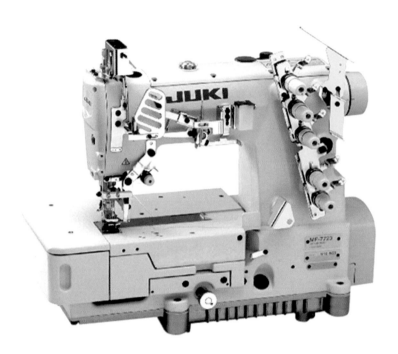

Figure 6.17 Coverstitch machine
© Juki juki.com

SUMMARY

This chapter focused on methods for thread construction and standards used in the fashion industry for designating stiches for garment specifications. Knowledge of thread construction, fiber types, and desirable properties aid designers and product developers in making choices appropriate for the assembly of apparel items. Thread ticket numbers and thread sizes were discussed to provide a foundation as to how thread is designated for ordering. Both ISO and ASTM standards for classifying stitches were discussed, and examples were provided to help visualize the stitches as they appear in real life. See Table 6.5 for a comparison summary of ISO and ASTM stitches. The industry machines used to create these stitches were also featured. Ability to communicate using standards for stitch designation and knowing typical applications within garments is important for designers. There is a wide assortment of stitches within each classification that range in complexity and thread consumption to provide options for every price category of merchandise. There are no classifications that are strictly reserved for designer or budget price classifications. Stiches from each major classification can be found in all price ranges. The more complex the stitch formation, and the more thread used, the more the cost of the garment will increase.

Table 6.5 Comparison Summary of Commonly Used ASTM and ISO Stitch Designations

Stitch Class	ASTM Stitch Designation	ISO Stitch Designation
100	103	103
	104	104
200	202	202
	205	205
300	301	301
	304	304
400	401	401
	402	402
	406	406
500	503	503
	504	504
	514	514
	516	516
600	602	602
	605	605
	607	607

Sources: ISO. *International Standard 4915:1991, Textiles—Stitch Types—Classification and Terminology*, printed in Switzerland; ASTM International *Online Standards 2014:D6193-11 Standard Practice for Stitches and Seams*

ACTIVITIES

1. Convert the following to tex, and indicate the resultant ticket number using Table 5.1. Example: 20 Ne$_c$ to tex = 29.5 tex. Resultant thread ticket number is 27.

   - 30 Ne$_c$ to tex
   - 693 den to tex
   - 34 N$_m$ to tex
   - 270 dtex to tex

2. Select and compare two items from your wardrobe (one made of woven fabric and one made of knitted fabric). Identify the main stitch classes (100–600) within each garment. Specify the location for each. Count the number of stitches per inch or stitches per centimeter for each garment. Discuss the differences in stitches within each class and the number of SPI (SPC) based on price point of the garments selected. Which stitches require more thread? Which stitches take longer to construct? How does this impact the cost of the garment?

3. Compare two similar garments (both woven or both knitted) from different price categories, and identify the stitch classifications and locations for each garment. Discuss the similarities and differences of the stitch class selections based on fabrication, style, and performance for the intended use of the product.

4. Open the ANE CALC Apparel Guidelines, American & Efird Thread Consumption Calculator for the Missy's Knit Dress. Using Table 6.6, find the price for 6,000 yards /5,000 meters for each of the thread types used in this garment and enter the pricing next to the respective thread type at the bottom, middle of the page. The following information will be provided:

   - Thread price per yard
   - Thread price per garment
   - Number of cones of thread needed for each thread type

- Needle thread yards, bobbin thread yards, looper thread yards, and total yards per operation
- Total yards per garment consumed, yards per garment of waste, and total yards per garment including waste
- Cost per garment

Print a copy of the thread calculation. Now change the ISO stitches in the drop down menu to see how the thread consumption and thread cost per garment has changed. Change all 504 3/16 Ndl Overedge stitch to 602 3/16 2 Ndl Coverstitch. Change the 301 Lock stitch to a 401 Chainstitch. Change all 406 1/8 Btm Cover stitch to 503 1/8 2Thd Serge stitch. Print a copy of the revised thread calculation. Compare the two thread calculations. Are there differences in the cost of thread per garment, thread price per yard, thread price per garment, and the number of cones needed? Is the cost difference significant?

Table 6.6 Thread Pricing for American and Efird Thread Consumption Calculator

Thread Type	Yards per Cone	Putup Price per Cone—White thread	Putup Price Per Cone—Colored Thread
T-18 Perma core	6000 yards	$4.88	$5.93
T-21 Perma spun	6000 yards	$3.37	$3.74
T-24 Perma core	6000 yards	$5.57	$6.08
T-27 Perma spun	6000 yards	$3.42	$3.94
T-40 Perma Core	6000 yards	$7.06	$7.79
T-18 Wildcat Plus	26800 yard in white	$6.64	
25,423 yard in colors			$12.69
T-24 Wildcat Plus	20247 yards in white	$6.64	
18355 yards in colors			$12.69

Sources: American & Efird, 2014

APPAREL QUALITY LAB MANUAL

Please refer to Lab Activity 6.1 Comparison Project Garment Identification of Stitches and Seams; and Lab Activity 6.2 Comparison Project Garment Thread Consumption Calculations in the *Apparel Quality Lab Manual*. These activities will correspond to both Chapters 6 and 7 of this book.

ENDNOTES

1. American & Efird, Inc. *Thread Science—Choosing the Right Thread from Fiber to Finishing*. Accessed July 31, 2012, http://www.amefird.com/technical -tools/thread-education/thread-science/.

2. American & Efird, Inc. *Thread Science—Thread Construction*. Accessed July 31, 2012, http://www .amefird.com/technical-tools/thread-education /thread-science/.

3. American & Efird, Inc. *General Thread Terms Glossary*. Accessed July 31, 2012, http://www .amefird.com/technical-tools/thread-education /general-textile-terms-glossary/.

4. Coats Industrial. *Thread Numbering: Bulletin 5*. Accessed August 2, 2012, http://www.coats industrial.com/en/apparel/expertise/thread -numbering#Communicating%20Thread%20 Size%20with%20Ticket%20Numbers.

5. Coats India. *International Tex Numbering System: Bulletin 24*. Accessed August 2, 2012, http://www .coatschina.com/Ticket_number_BP_24.pdf.

6. ASTM International. *Online Standards 2013:D3823-07 (2012) Standard Practice for Determining Ticket Numbers for Sewing Threads*. Accessed October 20, 2013, http://myastm1 .astm.org/DOWNLOAD/D3823.1593794-1.pdf.

7. International Organization for Standardization. *International Standard 4915:1991, Textiles – Stitch Types – Classification and Terminology*. Printed in Switzerland, pp. 1–48.

8. ASTM International. *Online Standards 2013:D6193-13 Standard Practice for Stitches and Seams*. Accessed October 20, 2013, http://myastm1.astm.org/DOWNLOAD /D6193.1593794-1.pdf.

ASTM and ISO Seam Classifications

CHAPTER SEVEN

Objectives:

- To define the role of seams within a garment
- To examine ASTM and ISO standards for seam classifications and where they are used in garments
- To identify the stitches used to create seam constructions within each classification
- To introduce alternative stitchless seam constructions and seamless garments

Garment construction requires some method of securing one or more plies of fabric together. The most common method used in the apparel industry today to secure seams is with stitches. The quality of seam construction in this case is shared by the thread and stitch configurations selected. There are also evolving technologies for forming seams that do not contain stitches. Application of these alternative technologies has been limited to use in performance-based athletic and outdoor apparel as well as undergarments. There are also existing technologies for producing seamless garments. This chapter will cover both existing and evolving technologies for seam construction and use.

SEAM OVERVIEW

A **seam** is formed by joining together two or more layers of fabric by stitching, sealing, welding, or thermal bonding. The primary function of a seam is to secure garment panels and components together, and provide the appropriate amount of strength, durability, and extendibility for the apparel item without causing failure of the fabric or seam when pressure or force is applied. The effectiveness of a seam relies upon the balance between the construction and strength of the seam which must be able to endure the stress and pressure applied during intended wear and refurbishment. If the construction of the seams used in a garment restricts body movement or presses uncomfortably into the skin during wear, the user will not want to continue to wear the garment. The seam construction must provide the appropriate level of extendibility for the material in order to provide a little more elasticity in the seam than what is present in the fabric to which it is joined.[1] If this balance is not achieved, the stitching can break when the fabric is stretched, or the garment area may be so restricted that it cannot be worn. For example, a children's jersey knit turtleneck has a small ruffle that has been stitched onto the top edge of the turtleneck portion that folds down. The combination of the thread, stitch, and seam construction in this area do not offer any level of extendibility; therefore, the turtleneck cannot be worn because the neck opening will not allow the head to pass through. **Seam efficiency**, as defined by ASTM International, is "the ratio of seam strength to fabric strength."[2] Seams also provide a means for shaping and fitting the garment to body contours and by offering design features or decorative details.

Garments engineered with seams require seam allowances. The planned measured distance between the stitchline of the seam to the fabric's raw edge of the garment panels is referred to as **seam allowance** (see Figure 7.1). The width of the seam allowance depends upon the type of seam and seam finish

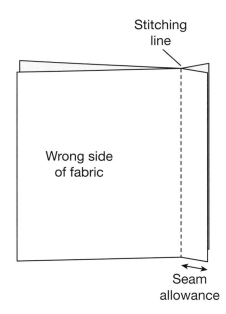

Figure 7.1 Seam allowance
Illustration by Q2A Media Services Private Limited

desired for the design of the garment. The type of seam, stitch configuration, thread type and construction, thread tension, number of stitches per inch, and the construction and strength of the selected materials all play important roles in the strength and functionality of the garment and must carefully be selected to maintain product quality and avoid problems with seam failure, seam slippage, or fabric failure. **Seam failure** can happen in high stress areas of a garment when the thread and seam construction are not appropriately matched with the fit of the garment, fabric type, and construction. Seam failure can also occur due to abrasion. **Seam slippage** can appear at high stress areas of a garment where the warp yarns within the material become displaced, causing them to slide away from the seam, exposing the filling yarns, and therefore weakening the fabric and compromising the appearance (see Figure 7.2). Over time, the warp yarns will completely pull out of the seam and cause a hole. When the yarns of the material become ruptured it is referred to as **fabric failure** (see Figure 7.3). This can be caused when the construction of a seam is disproportionately stronger

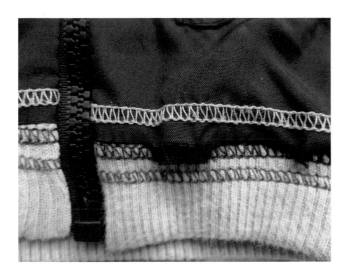

Figure 7.2 Seam slippage
Photo courtesy of Janace Bubonia

Figure 7.3 Fabric failure
Photo courtesy of Janace Bubonia

or less elastic than the apparel items selected material. Failure of the fabric can also be attributed to lack of functional ease at a critical stress point in a garment, or if the stitches per inch are too dense, causing the needle penetrations to damage the material. See Chapter 13 for common garment defects related to stitching and seaming. Typical stress areas within apparel items include seams at the crotch/seat area, armholes, closures such as zippers and button plackets, pockets, collars, seam end points, and areas that utilize bartacks for additional support and added

strength. Thread failure can also occur, impacting the durability and strength of the seam. Careful pairing of the fiber content, construction, finish, and size of the thread in relation to the type of fabric, weight, construction, durability, and strength, as well as the stitch and seam configurations desired for the garment can avoid problems with thread, seam, or fabric failure. Failure of any aspect of a garment's seam construction will deem the item unacceptable, therefore causing consumer dissatisfaction with product quality. It is important for designers and product developers to consider all of these aspects when selecting seams for different portions of the garment to ensure the appropriate seam efficiency and ease are achieved for the fabric selected. Additionally, it is important to consider the type of seam construction in relation to its position within the garment and ease of movement.

SEAM CLASSIFICATIONS

Industry standards are used to communicate specific seam configurations for use in production assembly operations. Unlike the stitch classification standards established by ASTM and ISO, the seam standards are categorized differently. ASTM designates six classes of seams, whereas ISO delineates eight classes. Appropriate seam selection is reliant upon the fabric, intended use of the garment, position and placement of the seam within the apparel item, method of care, and retail price. These standards help designers and product developers communicate using the specific number-letter designations for each of the areas within the garment that require seams for assembly.

ASTM Seam Classifications

ASTM International's designation D6193, Standard Practice for Stitches and Seams, provides standardized seam constructions for use in the apparel industry with focus on stitched seam assemblies. In this standard, each seam class is identified by two or more uppercase letters that classify the seam, followed by one or two lowercase letters identifying the type of seam within the class, and one or more numbers indicating the number of rows of stitching within the seam.[3]

SS Superimposed Seam Class

Superimposed-class seams are designated with the uppercase letters SS. This seam classification contains 55 different seam configurations and is the most commonly used in the construction of apparel products. Two or more plies of fabric are overlaid, one on top of another with their raw edges aligned and stitched together at a specified distance from the raw edge, with one or more rows of stitching. Single- or two-step operations can be used to produce superimposed seams. When the seam is assembled in a single action, the plies of the material are overlaid one on top of another with their raw edges aligned, and they are joined with stitching on the designed seam line. The seam allowance of a superimposed seam can be pressed open. For two-step seam assemblies, the raw edges are folded and concealed or hidden within the layers of material that compose the seam. These are known as enclosed seams. For example, the simplest superimposed seam having only two or more plies of fabric joined together at the seam line with one row of stitching is indicated as SSa-1 (see Figure 7.4). If the same seam had two rows of stitching, it would be identified as SSa-2 (see Figure 7.5).[3] Superimposed seams are used for assembling main seams in woven garments and cut-and-sew knits, linings, attaching interlinings, piping, seaming outer edges of necklines,

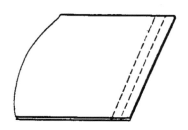

Figure 7.5 ASTM SSa-2 Seam with two rows of stitching
Courtesy of ASTM D 6193 Standard Practice for Stitches and Seams

collars, cuffs, waistlines, and waistbands, and setting the fly on pants. The standardized ASTM and ISO stitch classifications that can be selected for assembly of superimposed seams include 100 Chain stitches, 300 Lock stitches, 400 Multi-thread chain stitches, and 500 Overedge chain stitches. The most frequently used superimposed seam types include SSa, SSh, SSk, SSab, SSae, SSag, and SSaw (see Figure 7.6).

LS Lapped Seam Class

Lapped-class seams are designated with the uppercase letters LS. This seam class offers 101 variations. Lapped seams are constructed with two or more plies of material that are overlapped with the raw edges exposed or the seam allowance is folded under and joined with one or more rows of stitching. For example, the simplest lapped seam having two or more plies of fabric joined together at the seam line with one row of stitching is specified as LSa-1. If the same seam had two rows of stitching, it would be identified as LSa-2.[3] Lapped seams are used for assembling main seams in unlined garments such as jeans, denim jackets, side seams of some dress shirts, casual pants, and casual skirts constructed of sturdy woven fabrics such as denim and chino, as well as materials that will not unravel such as leather and suede. Lapped seams are also used for crotch seams on jeans and chinos, setting sleeve seams, attaching elastic, setting patch pockets or pocket flaps, side seams in dress

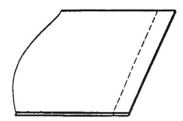

Figure 7.4 ASTM SSa-1 Seam with one row of stitching
Courtesy of ASTM D 6193 Standard Practice for Stitches and Seams

Most frequently used ASTM superimposed seam types

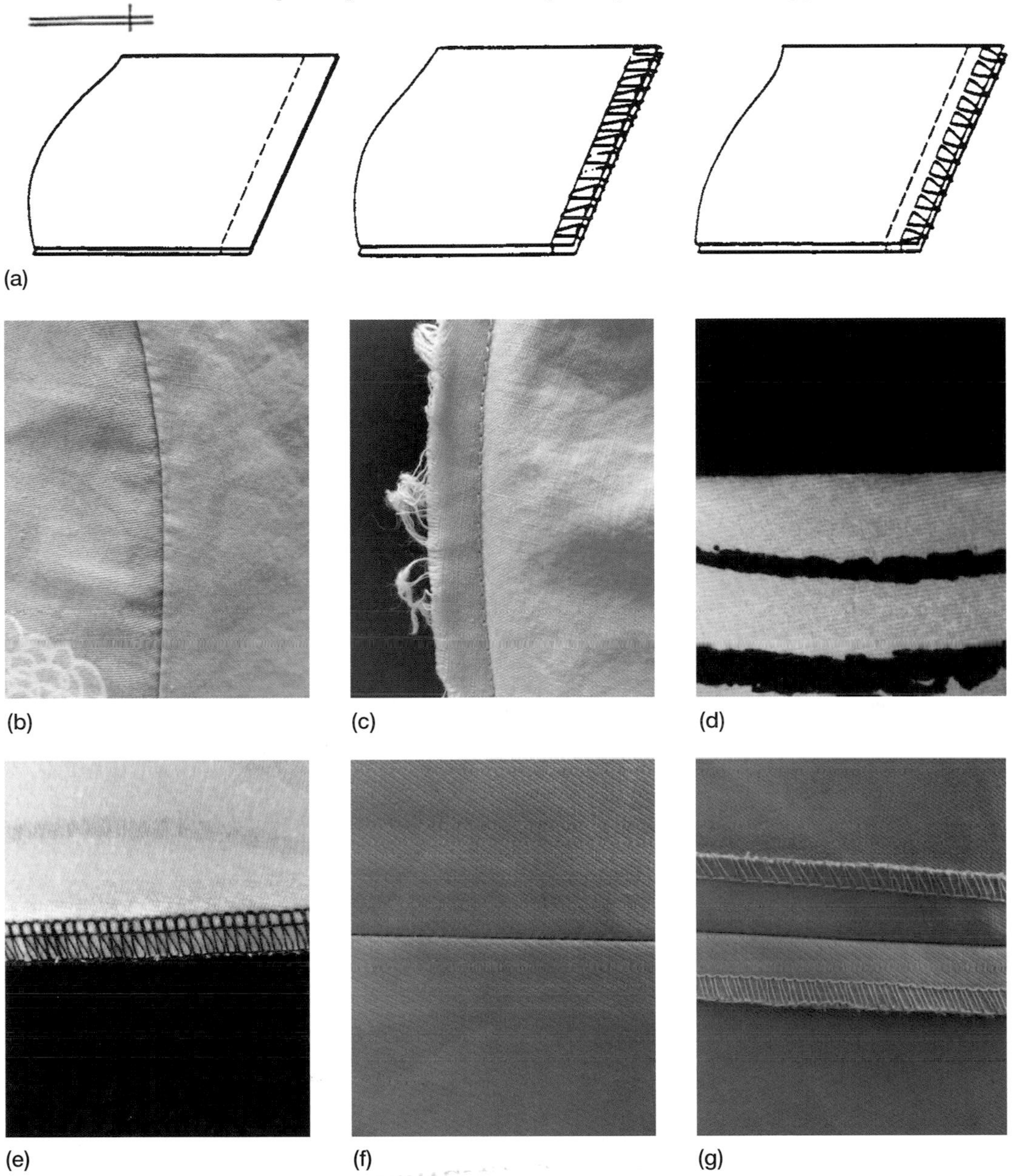

(a)

(b)

(c)

(d)

(e)

(f)

(g)

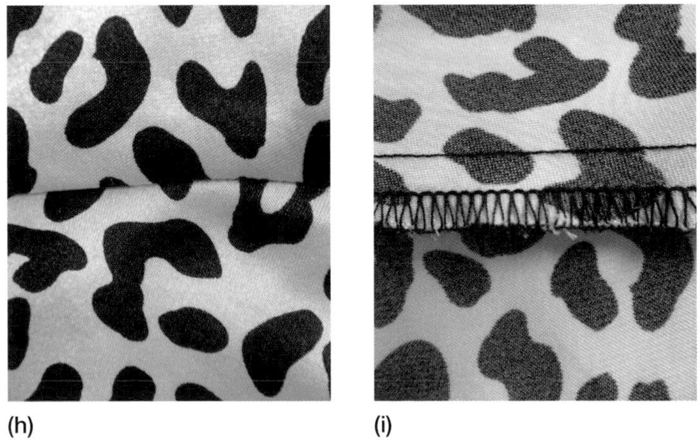

(h)

(i)

Figure 7.6 a–i (a) ASTM SSa Seams; (b) ASTM SSa Single row stitching with raw edge face view; (c) ASTM SSa Single row stitching with raw edge back view; (d) ASTM SSa Overedge face view; (e) ASTM SSa Over edge back view; (f)ASTM SSa Over edge with seam pressed open face view; (g) ASTM SSa Over edge with seam pressed open back view; (h) ASTM SSa Safety stitch face view *Courtesy of ASTM D 6193 Standard Practice for Stitches and Seams. Photos courtesy of Janace Bubonia.*

Most frequently used ASTM superimposed seam types

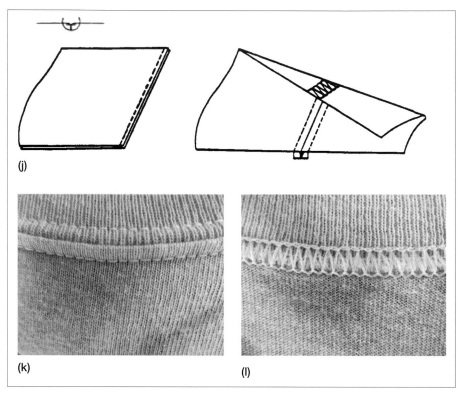

(j)

(k)

(l)

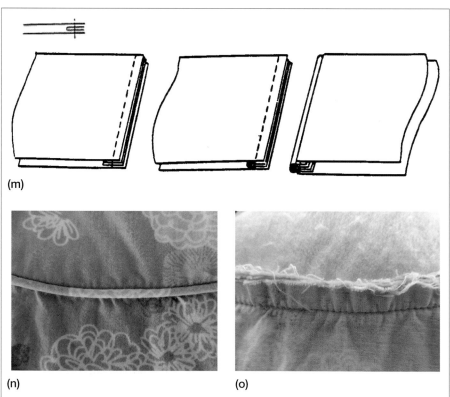

(m)

(n)

(o)

Figure 7.6 j–o (j) ASTM SSh; (k) ASTM SSh Face view; (l) ASTM SSh Back view; (m) ASTM SSk; (n) ASTM SSk Face view; (o) ASTM SSk Back view.
Courtesy of ASTM D 6193 Standard Practice for Stitches and Seams. Photos courtesy of Janace Bubonia.

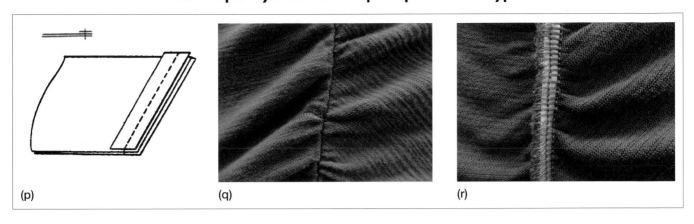

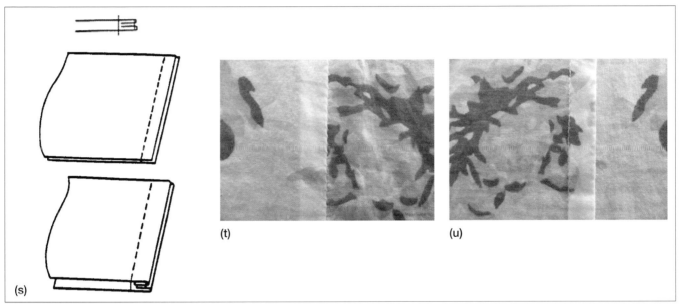

Figure 7.6 p–x (p) ASTM SSab; (q) ASTM SSab Face view; (r) ASTM SSab Back view; (s) ASTM SSae; (t) ASTM SSae Face view; (u) ASTM SSae Back view; (v) ASTM SSag; (w) ASTM SSag Face view; (x) ASTM SSag Back view
Courtesy of ASTM D 6193 Standard Practice for Stitches and Seams. Photos courtesy of Janace Bubonia.

Most frequently used ASTM superimposed seam types

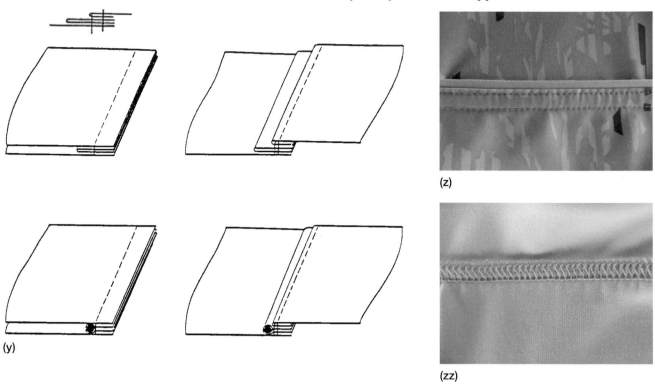

(z)

(y)

(zz)

Figure 7.6 y–zz (y) ASTM SSaw; (z) ASTM SSaw Double needle face view; (zz) ASTM SSaw Double needle back view *Courtesy of ASTM D 6193 Standard Practice for Stitches and Seams. Photos courtesy of Janace Bubonia.*

shirts, attaching yokes, and where stitching is desired as a decorative finish to the garment. The standardized ASTM and ISO stitch classifications that can be selected for assembly of lapped seams include 300 Lockstitches, 400 Multi-thread chain stitches, and 500 Overedge chain stitches. The most frequently used lapped seam types for apparel include LSc, LSd, and LSbm (see Figure 7.7).

BS Bound Seam Class

Bound-class seams are designated with the uppercase letters BS. This seam class offers 18 variations. Bound seams are constructed with the raw edges of the seam allowance of one or more plies of fabric covered with a binding and stitched with one or more rows of

stitches. For example, the simplest bound seam having two or more plies of fabric covered with a binding that is joined together at the seam line with one row of stitching is indicated by BSa-1. If the same seam had two rows of stitching it would be indicated as BSa-2.[3] Bound seams are used for finishing necklines, sleeve openings, hems, the inside of waistbands in trousers and pants, and seams of unlined jackets and coats. This seam class is selected when finishing raw edges. The standardized ASTM and ISO stitch classifications that can be selected for assembly of bound seams include 300 Lockstitches, 400 Multi-thread chain stitches, and 600 Covering chain stitches. The most frequently used bound seam types for apparel include BSa, BSb, BSc, and BSm (see Figure 7.8).

Most frequently used ASTM lapped seam types

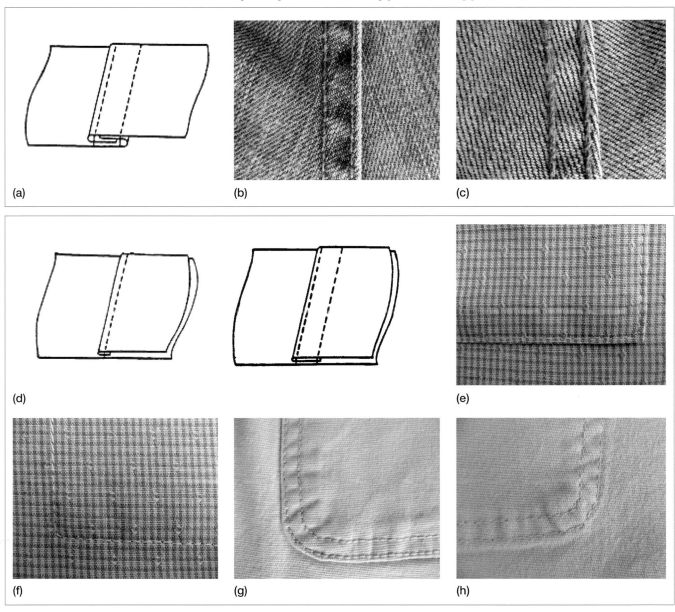

Figure 7.7 a–h   (a) ASTM LSc; (b) ASTM LSc Two rows of stitching face view; (c) ASTM LSc Two rows of stitching back view; (d) ASTM LSd; (e) ASTM LSd One row of stitching face view; (f) ASTM LSd One row of stitching back view; (g) ASTM LSd Two rows of stitching face view; (h) ASTM LSd Two rows of stitching back view.
Courtesy of ASTM D 6193 Standard Practice for Stitches and Seams. Photos courtesy of Janace Bubonia.

Most frequently used ASTM lapped seam types

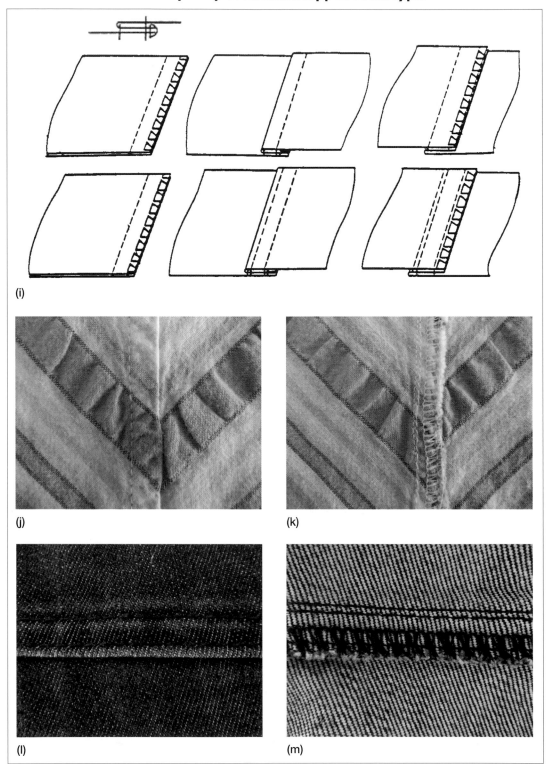

Figure 7.7 i–m (i) ASTM LSbm; (j) ASMT LSbm One row of stitching face view; (k) ASTM LSbm One row of stitching back view; (l) ASTM LSbm Two rows of stitching face view; (m) ASTM LSbm Two rows of stitching back view. *Courtesy of ASTM D 6193 Standard Practice for Stitches and Seams. Photos courtesy of Janace Bubonia.*

Most frequently used ASTM bound seam types

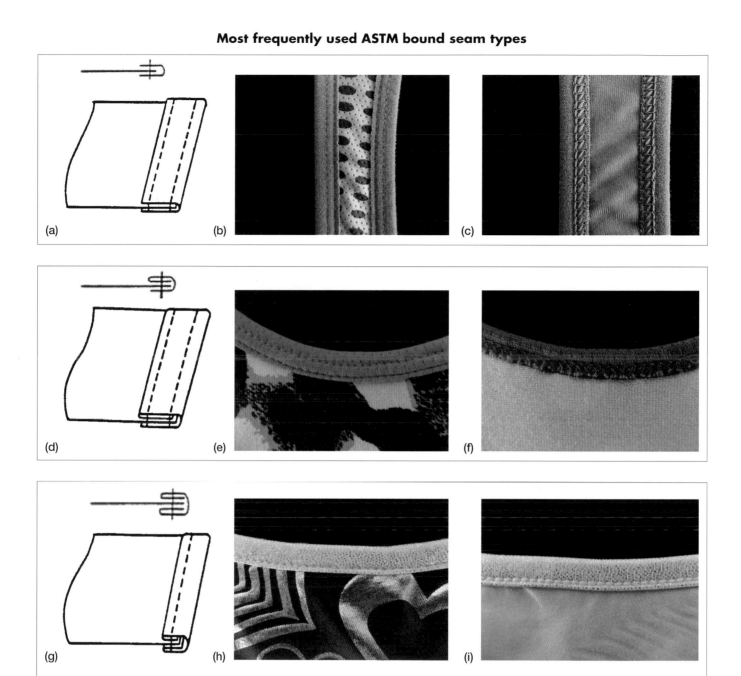

Figure 7.8 a–i   (a) ASTM BSa; (b) ASTM BSa Face view; (c) ASTM BSa Back view; (d) ASTM BSb; (e) ASTM BSb Face view; (f) ASTM BSb Back view; (g) ASTM BSc; (h) ASTM BSc Face view; (i) ASTM BSc Back view. *Courtesy of ASTM D 6193 Standard Practice for Stitches and Seams. Photos courtesy of Janace Bubonia.*

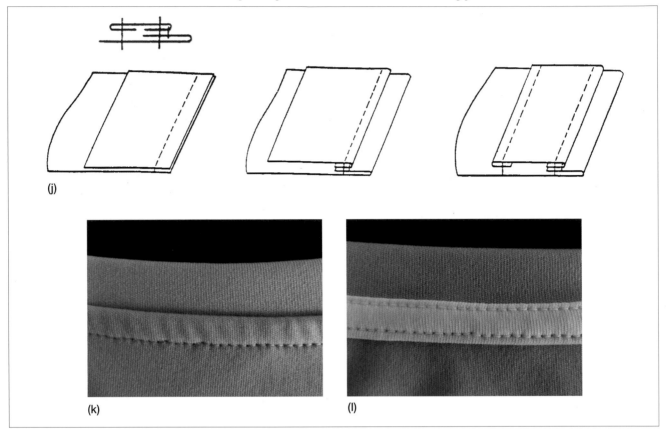

Figure 7.8 j–l (j) ASTM BSm; (k) ASTM BSm Face view; (l) ASTM BSm Back view
Courtesy of ASTM D 6193 Standard Practice for Stitches and Seams. Photos courtesy of Janace Bubonia.

FS Flat Seam Class

Flat-class seams are designated with the uppercase letters FS. This seam class offers six variations. Flat seams are constructed with the raw edges of the material plies abutted or slightly overlapped and joined together with stitching that covers the joint.[3] These seams do not contain seam allowances, so they produce a low profile seam and thus minimal bulk. This seam class is selected for close-fitting garments where the seam allowance may put pressure on the body and when the bulkiness of a seam needs to be minimized such as in athletic apparel, shapewear, undergarments, lingerie, swimwear, and for seaming pelts of fur. The standardized ASTM and ISO stitch classifications that can be selected for assembly of

flat seams include 300 Lockstitches, 400 Multi-thread chain stitches, and 600 Covering chain stitches. The most frequently used flat seam type for apparel is FSa (see Figure 7.9).

OS Ornamental Seam Class

Ornamental-class seams are designated with the uppercase letters OS. This seam class offers eight variations and adds ornamentation to one or more plies of material by means of a series of stitches expressed in a straight, curved, or designated design for the purpose of adding decoration to a garment.[3] Examples of these seams include tucking, pleating, piping, and decorative stitching details. The standardized ASTM and ISO stitch classifications that can be

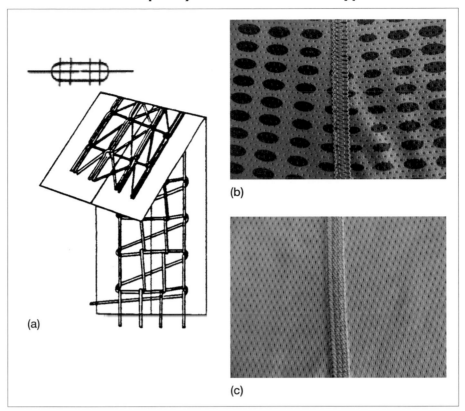

Figure 7.9 a–c (a) ASTM FSa; (b) ASTM FSa Face view; (c) ASTM FSa Back view *Courtesy of ASTM D 6193 Standard Practice for Stitches and Seams. Photos courtesy of Janace Bubonia.*

selected for assembly of ornamental seams include 100 Chain stitches, 200 class (originated as hand stitches), 300 Lock stitches, and 400 Multi-thread chain stitches. The most frequently used ornamental seams include OSa, OSe, and OSf (see Figure 7.10).

EF Edge Finish Seam Class

Edge-finish-class seams are designated with the uppercase letters EF. This seam class offers 32 variations. Edge finish seams are constructed with one or two plies of fabric that are used to finish the edge of a garment. Within this classification there are three types of assembly that can be used. The first method of assembly joins a folded edge to the shell fabric by stitching it onto the face or back. The second assembly type employs stitching to be used at the garment's

edge or to cover the raw edges of the fabric, and may or may not have a folded construction. For the third assembly type, a narrow strip of single or double ply of fabric is folded and stitched to form a tube or flat strap where the raw edges are concealed inside or visible on the back side. Edge-finish seams are used for hems, facings, seaming shoulder straps, seaming belt loops, and drawstrings.[3] This seam class is selected when finishing garment edges. The standardized ASTM and ISO stitch classifications that can be selected for assembly of edge finish seams include 100 Chain stitches, 200 class (originated as hand stitches), 300 Lock stitches, 400 Multi-thread chain stitches, and 500 Overedge chain stitches. The most frequently used edge finish seam types for apparel include EFa, EFb, EFc, EFd, EFh, and EFu (see Figure 7.11).

Most frequently used ASTM ornamental seam types

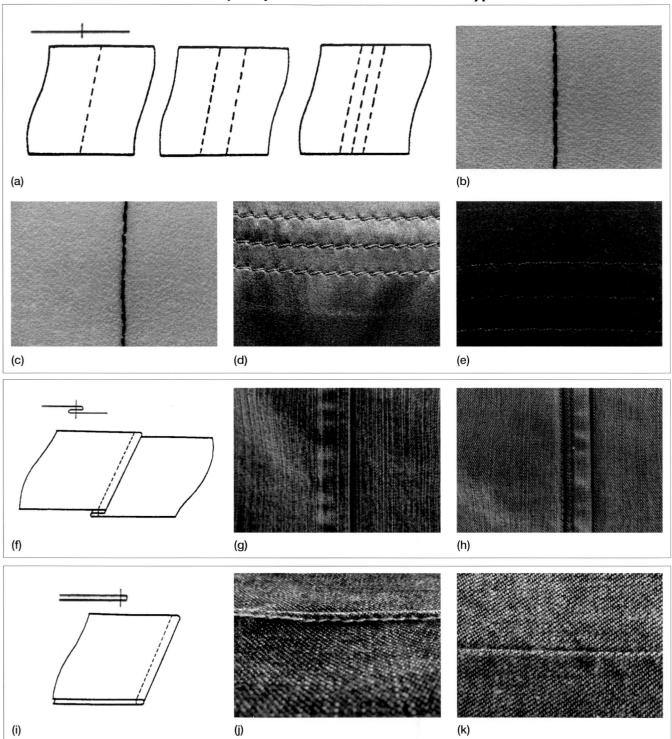

Figure 7.10 a–k (a) ASTM OSa; (b) ASTM OSa One row of stitching face view; (c) ASTM OSa One row of stitching back view; (d) ASTM OSa Three rows of stitching face view; (e) ASTM OSa Three rows of stitching back view; (f) ASTM OSe; (g) ASTM OSe Face view; (h) ASTM OSe Back view; (i) ASTM OSf; (j) ASTM OSf Face view; (k) ASTM OSf Back view. *Courtesy of ASTM D 6193 Standard Practice for Stitches and Seams. Photos courtesy of Janace Bubonia.*

Most frequently used ASTM edge finish seam types

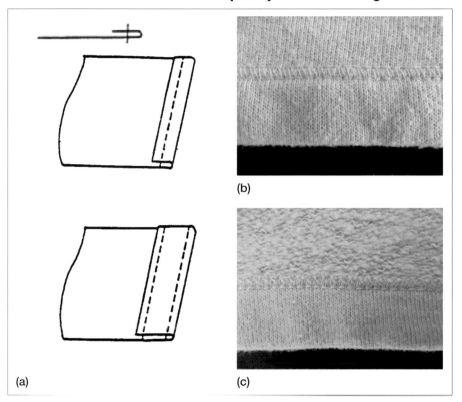

(a)

(b)

(c)

Figure 7.11 a–h (a) ASTM EFa;
(b) ASTM EFa Face view; (c) ASTM
EFa Back view; (d) ASTM EFb;
(e) ASTM EFb One row of stitching
face view; (f) ASTM EFb One row
of stitching back view; (g) ASTM
EFb Two rows of stitching face view;
(h) ASTM EFb Two rows of stitching
back view
*Courtesy of ASTM D 6193
Standard Practice for Stitches and
Seams. Photos courtesy of Janace
Bubonia.*

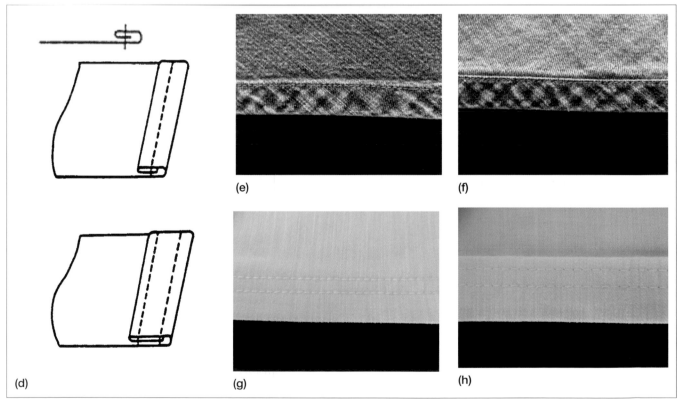

(d)

(e)

(f)

(g)

(h)

Most frequently used ASTM edge finish seam types

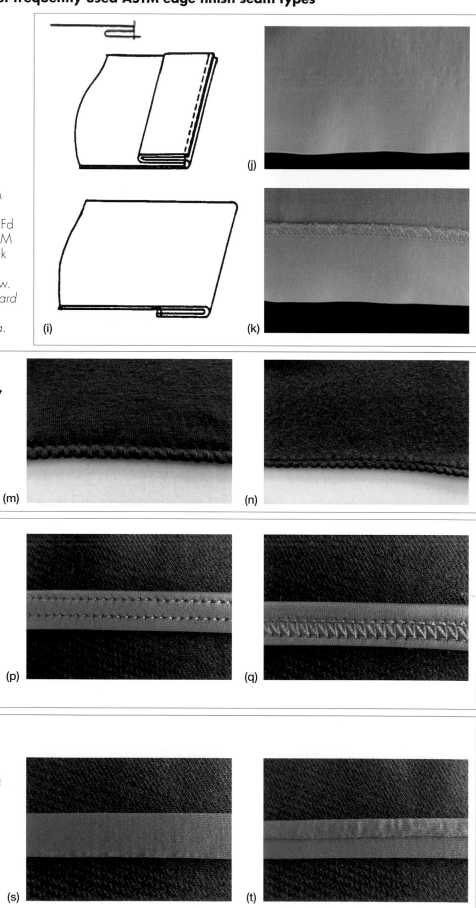

Figure 7.11 i–t (i) ASTM EFc; (j) ASTM EFc Face view; (k) ASTM EFc Back view; (l) ASTM EFd; (m) ASTM EFd Face view; (n) ASTM EFd Back view; (o) ASTM EFh; (p) ASTM EFh Face view; (q) ASTM EFh Back view; (r) ASTM EFu; (s) ASTM EFu Face view; (t) ASTM EFu Back view. *Courtesy of ASTM D 6193 Standard Practice for Stitches and Seams. Photos courtesy of Janace Bubonia.*

ISO Seam Classifications

ISO 4916 International Standard for Textiles—Seam types—Classification and terminology provides standardized seam constructions for use in the apparel industry for stitched seam assemblies. In this standard, each seam class is identified by a numeric sequence composed of five digits. The first numeral, a single digit, designates the seam class (1 to 8) and is followed by a period. The second and third double digit numbers (01 to 82) are used to indicate differences in fabric configurations/arrangements relating to the number of components within the seam. The fourth and fifth double digit numbers (01 to 12) are separated from the previous digits by a period and specify the variations in the positioning of needle penetrations or passages through the fabric to create the seam. It may also indicate if the seam contains a mirror image of the arrangement of the fabric which is specified by the second and third numbers of the classification type. Within each seam classification, ISO may use the terms limited or unlimited, which refer to the width of the pieces of fabric composing the seam. Limited means the component fabric is a specified width within the seam construction. Unlimited means the component fabric extends beyond the specified seam area.[4]

Seam Class 1

Class 1 seams are designated with 1.01 to 26.01 (seam class. fabric configuration and number of components within the seam) followed by .01 to .05 (specifies the specific needle position[s] and penetrations to create the seam) and includes 26 variations. These seams are constructed with two or more plies of fabric of which two are limited in width on the side where the seam is constructed. Any additional plies may be limited in the same manner as the first two, or they can be restricted in width on two sides, in the case of piping, cording, or seam taping.[5] This class contains seam constructions ASTM identifies primarily as superimposed, although there are some lapped seams included here as well. Applications of Class 1 seams include main seaming in woven garments and cut-and-sew knits, attaching collars, cuffs, yokes, piping, setting the fly on pants, waistlines, and waistbands. The standardized ASTM and ISO stitch classifications that can be selected for assembly of Class 1 seams include 100 Chain stitches, 300 Lock stitches, 400 Multi-thread chain stitches, and 500 Overedge chain stitches. The most frequently used Class 1 seam types include 1.01.01, 1.01.02, 1.01.04, 1.01.05, 1.06.03, 1.12.01, and 1.23.01.

Seam Class 2

Class 2 seams are designated with 1.01 to 46.01 (seam class. fabric configuration and number of components within the seam) followed by .01 to .09 (specifies the specific needle position[s] and penetrations to create the seam) and include 46 variations. These seams are constructed with two or more plies of material that are limited in the width on opposite sides from each other where they join into the seam. One of the plies of fabric is positioned below the other and then they are overlapped. If an additional ply is required for the seam construction, it will mirror one of the previous plies discussed or will be limited in the width on both sides.[5] This class contains the seam construction ASTM identifies as lapped seams. Applications of Class 2 seams include main seams in unlined garments constructed of sturdy woven fabrics, such as denim and chino, as well as materials that will not unravel, such as leather and suede. Class 2 seams are also used for crotch seams on jeans and chinos, setting sleeve seams, attaching elastic, sewing side seams of dress shirts, setting patch pockets or pocket flaps, and attaching yokes. The standardized ASTM and ISO stitch classifications that can be selected for assembly of Class 2 seams include 300 Lock stitches and 400 Multi-thread chain stitches. The most frequently used Class 2 seam types include 2.02.03, 2.02.05, 2.04.01, and 2.19.02.

Seam Class 3

Class 3 seams are designated with 1.01 to 32.01 (seam class fabric configuration, and number of components within the seam) followed by .01 to .12 (specifies the specific needle position[s] and penetrations to create the seam), and include 32 variations. These seams are constructed with a minimum of one ply of fabric that is limited in width on one side and a binding that is limited in width on two sides that wraps over the raw edge of the other ply of material to finish the edge. Any additional components included in the seam will be in the form of the fabric ply or the binding.[5] This class contains the seam construction ASTM identifies as bound seams. Applications of Class 3 seams include finishing necklines, sleeve openings, hems, the inside of waistbands in trousers and pants, and seams of unlined jackets and coats. This seam class is selected when finishing raw edges. The standardized ASTM and ISO stitch classifications that can be selected for assembly of Class 3 seams include 300 Lockstitches, 400 Multi-thread chain stitches, and 600 Covering chain stitches. The most frequently used Class 3 seam types for apparel include 3.01.01, 3.03.01, and 3.05.01.

Seam Class 4

Class 4 seams are designated with 1.01 to 14.01 (seam class, fabric configuration, and number of components within the seam) followed by .01 to .04 (specifies the specific needle position[s] and penetrations to create the seam), and include 14 variations. These seams are constructed with a minimum of two pieces of material that are limited in width having the raw edges abutted and stitched to cover over the joint.[5] Class 4 seams are low profile, having very little bulk because they do not contain seam allowances. This seam class is selected for close-fitting garments where the seam allowance may put pressure on the body and when the bulkiness of a seam needs to be minimized, such as in athletic apparel, shapewear, undergarments, lingerie, swimwear, and for seaming pelts of fur. This class contains the seam construction ASTM identified as flat seams. The standardized ASTM and ISO stitch classifications that can be selected for assembly of Class 4 seams include 300 Lock stitches and 400 Multi-thread chain stitches, although 600 Covering chain stitches is the most popular. The Class 4 seam types most frequently

used for apparel are 4.01.02, 4.01.02, 4.03.03, and 4.10.01.

Seam Class 5

Class 5 seams are designated with 1.01 to 45.01 (seam class, fabric configuration, and number of components within the seam) followed by .01 to .10 (specifies the specific needle position[s] and penetrations to create the seam), and include 45 variations. These seams are constructed with a minimum of one ply of fabric that is unlimited on two sides, and any other fabric integrated into the seam can be limited on one or two sides.[5] This class contains seam constructions ASTM identifies as ornamental seams but also contains some lapped and superimposed seam types. Applications of Class 5 seams include tucking, pleating, piping details, decorative stitching details, setting patch pockets, flaps, and facings. The standardized ASTM and ISO stitch classifications that can be selected for assembly of Class 5 seams include 100 Chain stitches, 200 class (originated as hand stitches), 300 Lock stitches, and 400 Multi-thread chain stitches. The Class 5 seam types most frequently used for apparel include 5.01.01, 5.02.01, 5.31.01, 5.31.05, and 5.45.01.

Seam Class 6

Class 6 seams are designated with 1.01 to 08.01 (seam class, fabric configuration, and number of components within the seam) followed by .01 to .08 (specifies the specific needle position[s] and penetrations to create the seam) and include eight variations. These seams are constructed with one ply of fabric that is limited in width on either the right or left side.[5] This class contains seam constructions ASTM identifies as edge finish seams but includes some ornamental seams. The edge finishing seams in this classification are assembled by either joining a folded edge to the shell fabric by stitching on either the face or back or by covering the raw edges of the fabric, which may then be folded or remain flat. The standardized ASTM and ISO stitch classifications that can be selected for assembly of Class 6 seams include 100 Chain stitches, 200 class (originated as hand stitches), 300 Lock stitches, 400 Multi-thread chain stitches, and 500 Overedge chain stitches. Applications of Class 6 seams include seaming of garment panel edges, dart panels, and hems. The Class 6 seams types most frequently for apparel include 6.01.01, 6.02.01, 6.03.01, 6.03.08, and 6.06.02.

Seam Class 7

Class 7 seams are designated with 1.01 to 26.01 (seam class, fabric configuration, and number of components within the seam) followed by .01 to 09 (specifies the specific needle position[s] and penetrations to create the seam) and include 82 variations. These seams are constructed with at least two pieces of material where one is limited in width on one side (on the right or the left side) and the other pieces being limited on two of the sides.[5] This class contains seam constructions ASTM identifies as edge finish seams but includes some bound, lapped, and superimposed. The edge finishing seams in this classification are assembled by applying a binding to a single ply of a seam allowance to finish the raw edges. The standardized ASTM and ISO stitch classifications that can be selected for assembly of Class 7 seams include 300 Lock stitches, 400 Multi-thread chain stitches, and 500 Overedge chain stitches. Applications of Class 7 seams include hems where elastic is inserted, attaching zipper tape, and attaching waistbands. The Class 7 seams type most frequently for apparel is 7.40.01.

Seam Class 8

Class 8 seams are designated with 1.01 to 26.01 (seam class, fabric configuration, and number of components within the seam) followed by .01 to .08 (specifies the specific needle position[s] and penetrations to create the seam), and include 32 variations. These seams are constructed with a minimum of one ply of fabric that is limited in width on two sides and any additional components are equally limited in width on two sides.[5] This class contains primarily seam constructions ASTM identifies as edge finish seams. The

standardized ASTM and ISO stitch classifications that can be selected for assembly of Class 8 seams include 100 Chain stitches, 200 class (originated as hand stitches), 300 Lock stitches, 400 Multi-thread chain stitches, and 500 Overedge chain stitches. Applications of Class 8 seams include seaming shoulder straps, belts, and drawstrings. The Class 8 seams types most frequently for apparel include 8.02.01, 8.03.03, and 8.06.01 (see Figure 7.12).

Most frequently used ISO seam 8 types

(a)

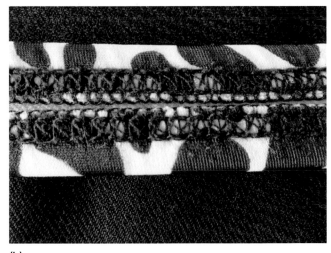

(b)

Figure 7.12 (a) ISO 8.02.01 Face view; (b) ISO 8.02.01 Back view
Photos courtesy of Janace Bubonia

ALTERNATIVES TO STITCHED SEAMS

Since the 19th century, technology has existed for producing circular knits, which were initially used for creating hosiery and socks, has led to the production of **seamless garments** today. Seamless knitting machines have made knit-and-wear garments possible. As discussed in Chapter 2, knit-and-wear garments are of the highest quality and can be expensive to produce, depending upon the product. Although this technology is currently limited in its use to undergarments, shapewear, performance, and athletic apparel, it is moving in the direction for use in producing general wearing apparel.[6] The cost is a major factor. For the majority of apparel manufacturers today, producing a cut-and-sew garment or full-fashioned knitted garment is less expensive, provides faster throughput volume, and can be produced with existing equipment employees are already trained to use. The benefits of seamless garments include a smooth appearance and increased comfort, because there are no seams to put pressure on the body, and bulkiness of seam allowances and seams are eliminated. This technology also greatly reduces fabric waste. The finished product is aesthetically appealing. See Figure 7.13 for an example of seamless garment technology.

Although seamless technologies provide increased comfort and wearability, so do stitchless options. When seams are required but sewn stitches are not desirable, alternative **stitchless** technologies that can be used for apparel production include thermal bonding, laser welding, and ultrasonic sealing. **Thermal bonded seams** utilize thermoplastic film adhesives made from polyvinylchloride (PVC), polyurethane (PU), polyethylene fabric (PE), or polypropylene (PP) to glue seam components together.[7] It is important for the garment materials and the adhesives to be compatible so the bond is strong enough to last for the useful life of the product. Thermal bonded seams

Figure 7.13 Seamless garment
Cesare Citterio/cifra-spa.net

can be used in outerwear to keep the body dry but are no longer limited to this application. Some companies are using bonded seams in conjunction with traditionally stitched seams to reduce the cost of the finished garment.[8] When thermal bonded seams were first introduced, they were used for garments made from synthetic materials; however, there are now many different adhesive formulations that have been developed for different types of fibers including cellulose and protein based textiles.[9] When seams are formed with bonding technology rather than stitches, the seam strength is evaluated for adhesion level, which is composed of a chemical bond or a mechanical bond.

Chemical bonding relates to the level of compatibility of the garment fabric with the formulation of the adhesive compound to create a covalent bond. A **covalent bond** is formed when a chemical reaction occurs and pairs of electrons are shared between atoms. Adhesion problems related to chemical bonding can occur when the formulation of the adhesive is not properly matched to the fiber content selected for the garment's materials. Also, the application of fiber lubricants and fabric finishes used to provide performance benefits can also inhibit adhesion.[10] The ability of the adhesive to permeate the fabric and establish a strong bond is referred to as a **mechanical bond**. Proper mechanical adhesion is reliant upon the conditions used for bonding (specified time, temperature, and level of pressure applied), the viscosity of the thermoplastic film adhesive, and the construction of the garment fabric. For performance outerwear, water repellant finishes can pose challenges for thermal bonded seams in regard to both chemical and mechanical adhesion properties. For mechanical bonding the adhesive must be able to penetrate the material to produce a good quality lasting seam. The chemical bond must be appropriately matched so the adhesive used will adhere properly to fabrics having silicone finishes.[10] Bemis Associates Inc., a global manufacturer of specialty films and seam tape, has found that replacing stitched seams with thermal bonded seams has reduced the weight of some garments by up to 15%.[11] Thermal bonded seams are a popular choice for performance athletic wear and outerwear because when engineered properly, the seams produced can provide greater stretch and recovery, reduced garment weight, enhanced appearance and shaping of the product, and increased comfort due to their flat construction. In addition, labor costs are often reduced because thermal bonded seams allow for several garment components to be adhered together in one step, which reduces the production period and provides faster throughput time.

Laser welding offers another method for creating seams without using stitches. This seam formation method is utilized on materials made from thermoplastic fibers and does not require the use of additional films or adhesives. **Laser welding** seals the seam through the use of infrared laser technology and a laser-absorbing fluid. A specially formulated fluid is applied to the contact area(s) of the fabric where the seam will be formed. The infrared laser is then transmitted through the material to heat fibers only where the laser-absorbing fluid has been applied, thereby melting a portion of the fabrics surface where it will be joined together.[12] This sophisticated technology is controlled to avoid distortion or changes in appearance on the surface of the garment. Although this technology is limited in its use, laser welding produces clean finished, strong sealed flat seams that can accommodate curves better than thermal bonding. Laser-welded seams also offer flexibility and cannot be penetrated by liquids or gasses, so they are desirable in waterproof performance outerwear garments.[12,13] According to the Hohenstein Textile Testing Institute (2011), "only a few textiles, made of thermoplastic fibers, absorb laser radiation in the near-infrared range. This means that, with many textiles, absorbers have to be used which are specifically designed to absorb the infrared light. However, these substances can cause discoloration or colour changes round the seams"[13] Laser-welded seams produce a high-quality seam when produced under the correct specified conditions. See Figure 7.14 for laser-welding equipment and Figure 7.15 for examples of laser-welded seam technology.

The remaining stitchless seam method uses ultrasonic sealing, which requires materials to be constructed with thermoplastic fibers. This technology is different than the others in that it does not require any additional adhesives or agents to create the seam. **Ultrasonic sealing** bonds thermoplastic materials together by means of pressure and high-frequency sound waves deployed at frequencies above 20,000 Hz. These focused vibrations cause friction between the fibers of the fabric, generating heat to melt the material just enough to fuse it together within seconds.[14,15] Ultrasonic seaming produces a fast, clean finish to a garment. These seams cannot be penetrated by liquids, which makes them useful for waterproof performance outerwear garments. **Ultrasonic slitting** can be used simultaneously with ultrasonic seaming or on a single layer of fabric to seal the edge.[16] For this process the ultrasonic sound wave is used to cut the fabric and seal the edge in one step to avoid raveling and does not produce a hard bead

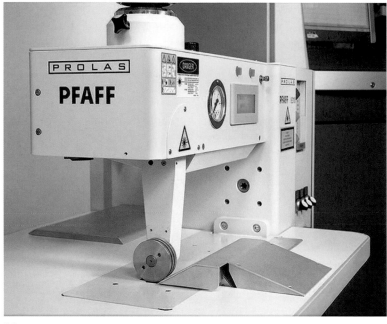

(a)

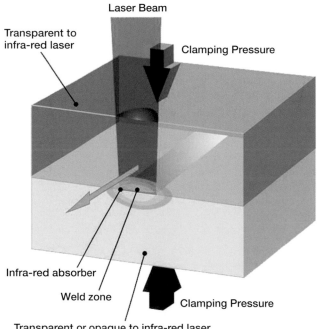

Laser Beam

Transparent to
infra-red laser

Clamping Pressure

Infra-red absorber

Weld zone

Transparent or opaque to infra-red laser

Clamping Pressure

(b)

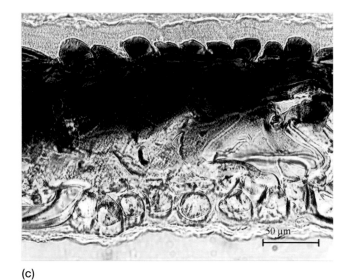

50 μm

(c)

Figure 7.14 a–c
Laser welding equipment
Images courtesy Coleg Sir Gar/twi.co.uk

(a)

(b)

Figure 7.15 a and b Laser-welded seams
(a) © Patagonia; (b) Image courtesy of NASA

(see Figure 7.18). Ultrasonic technology is the most environmentally friendly method because it is the easiest to recycle; it does not contain multiple components made from other materials. See Figure 7.16 for ultrasonic sealing equipment and Figure 7.17 for an example of ultrasonic sealed seam technology.

Research and development of stitchless technologies used for apparel continues to be refined. Currently, the majority of this technology is compatible only with fabrics containing thermoplastic fibers, and use is limited to the assembly of undergarments and performance-based athletic apparel and outerwear. These technologies have the potential to become more

economical, produce less waste, and make lighter-weight garments than traditional sewing methods using stitches. Although these new technologies provide many benefits to the aesthetic and functional performance of products, they require new equipment, training of employees, and time to perfect the methods required to produce high-quality bonds, welds, and seals. The apparel industry's primary method for garment assembly for general wearing apparel remains with traditional methods of stitches and seams, as supported by ISO and ASTM stitch and seam construction classifications.

(a)

(b)

(c)

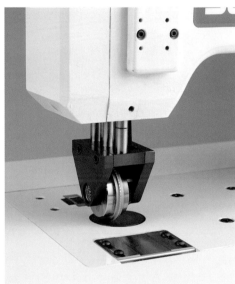

(d)

Figure 7.16 a–d Ultrasonic welding/sealing equipment
Courtesy of Sonobond Ultrasonics

(a)

(b)

Figure 7.17 a and b   Ultrasonic welded/sealed seams and fabrics
Courtesy of Sonobond Ultrasonics

Figure 7.18   Ultrasonic slitting
Courtesy of Sonobond Ultrasonics

SUMMARY

This chapter focused on methods for seam construction and standards used in the fashion industry for designating seams for garment specifications. Knowledge of thread and fabric construction, stitch classifications, and seam efficiency in relation to the garment's end use help designers and product developers make choices appropriate for the assembly of apparel items. Stitchless seam constructions were introduced along with seamless garments. Both ASTM and ISO standards for classifying seams were discussed, and examples were provided to help visualize the seam configurations as they appear in real life. See Table 7.1 for a comparison summary of ISO and ASTM seams. The classifications of stitches that can be used to assemble the various seam configurations were identified along with garment applications. The ability to communicate using standards for seam designations and knowing typical applications within garments is important for designers when preparing specifications for production. There is a wide assortment of seams within each classification that range in complexity and thread consumption to provide options for every price category of merchandise. There are no classifications that are strictly reserved for designer or budget price classifications. Seams from each major classification are found in all price ranges. The more complex the seam formation and the more thread used will increase the cost of the garment.

Table 7.1 Comparison Summary of Commonly Used ASTM and ISO Seam Classifications

ASTM Seam Classification	ISO Seam Classification
SSa	1.01
SSh	4.03
SSk	1.12
SSab	1.23
SSae	1.06
SSag	4.10
SSaw	2.19
LSc	2.04
LSd	5.31
LSbm	2.02
BSa	3.01
BSb	3.03
BSc	3.05
BSm	7.40
FSa	4.01
OSa	5.01
OSa	5.02
OSf	5.45
EFa	6.02
EFb	6.03
EFc	6.06
EFd	6.01
EFh	8.03
EFu	8.06

Sources: ISO. *International Standard 4916:1991, Textiles—Seam Types—Classification and Terminology,* printed in Switzerland; ASTM International. *Online Standards 2014:D6193-11 Standard Practice for Stiches and Seams.*

ACTIVITIES

1. Select a garment from your wardrobe that has a minimum of two types of stitch classes and a minimum of two types of seam classifications designated by ISO or ASTM. Take photographs of the entire garment (front and back). Then visually inspect the product to determine each stitch and seam used in the garment, and document through a photo as well as written description the location of each.

2. Complete this activity by once again using two similar garments for two different price categories (budget, moderate, better, bridge, or designer). Compare and contrast the seam construction methods and SPI/SPC (if stitches are used) in relation to your perception of quality.

3. Evaluate the garments in your wardrobe to see if you own any garments possessing stitchless technologies. If you do not have any, visit a store that sells high-performance athletic or outerwear garments. Look at the construction of the garment, and determine which stitchless method was used for assembly of the garment. Try the garment on. Compare this garment to one that is assembled using traditional stitch and seam construction. Can you tell a difference in the weight of the garment? Is there a difference in comfort level of the garment? What is the difference in price? What performance properties does the stitchless product promote?

APPAREL QUALITY LAB MANUAL

Please refer to Lab Activity 6.1 Comparison Project Garment Identification of Stitches and Seams; and Lab Activity 6.2 Comparison Project Garment Thread Consumption Calculations in the *Apparel Quality Lab Manual*. These activities will correspond to both Chapters 6 and 7 of this book.

ENDNOTES

1. ASTM International. *Online Standards 2013:D6193-11 Standard Practice for Stitches and Seams.* Accessed October 27, 2013, http://myastm1.astm.org/DOWNLOAD /D6193.1593794-1.pdf, p. 4.

2. ASTM International. *Online Standards 2013:D6193-11 Standard Practice for Stitches and Seams.* Accessed October 20, 2013, http://myastm1.astm.org/DOWNLOAD /D6193.1593794-1.pdf, p. 1.

3. ASTM International. *Online Standards 2013:D6193-11 Standard Practice for Stitches and Seams.* Accessed October 20, 2013, http://myastm1.astm.org/DOWNLOAD /D6193.1593794-1.pdf, pp. 1–143.

4. International Organization for Standardization. *International Standard 4916:1991, Textiles – Seam types – Classification and Terminology.* Printed in Switzerland, pp. 1–64.

5. International Organization for Standardization. *International Standard 4916:1991, Textiles – Seam Types – Classification and Terminology.* Printed in Switzerland, p. 2.

6. Michael Quante (2010). "Garment Seams: Stitched, Stitchless, or Seamless?" *AATCC* (August 3). Accessed July 28, 2010, http://aatcc .informz.net/admin31/content/template.asp?sid =10180&ptid=99&brandid=4199&uid=1004906 425&mi=938683.

7. Textile Exchange (2012). *Fabric Welding.* Accessed October 12, 2012, http://www.teonline .com/knowledge-centre/fabric-welding.html.

8. Bemis Associates Inc. (2007). *Sew Free Bonded Apparel Construction.* Accessed July 28, 2012, http://www.bemisworldwide.com/applications /apparel/apparel1.html.

9. Emily Walzer (2011). "The Glue Guys: Bemis Takes Bonded Tech to the Limit." *Textile Insight* (May/June): 18–19. Accessed 2012, http://digital .turn-page.com/issue/31744.

10. Luca Mosso and Amir Nankali (2011). "Ask the Expert: Bonding Technology in Apparel." *WSA: The International Magazine for Performance and Sports Materials,* 17, no. 2 (March/April): 24–28.

11. Bemis Associates Inc. (2007). *Sew Free Bonded Apparel Construction.* Accessed July 28, 2012, http://www.bemisworldwide.com/applications /apparel/apparel1.html.

12. Ian Jones (2007). *EC Contract Coop-CT-2005-017614 ALTEX: Automated Laser Welding for Textiles.* Cambridge, UK: TWI Ltd. Accessed October 12, 2012, http://cordis.europa.eu /documents/documentlibrary/121406901EN6.pdf.

13. Hohenstein Textile Testing Institute. *Mechanically and Visual Perfect Seams: New Absorber Systems to Improve the Quality of Laser Welded Seams on Technical Textiles.* Accessed October 12, 2012, http://www.hohenstein.de/en/inline/pressrelease _8464.xhtml.

14. Sonobond Ultrasonics Inc. (2012). *Ultrasonic Technology.* Accessed October 12, 2012, http:// www.sonobondultrasonic.com/ultra_tech.asp.

15. Renuk Kadoro Reddy (2007). "Ultrasonic Seaming of PET, PET/Cotton Blend, and Spectra Fabrics." *Masters Theses and Doctoral Dissertations.* Paper 177, http://commons.emich .edu/theses/177.

16. Emerson Industrial Automation (2012). *Textiles and Film Processing.* Accessed July 28, 2012, http://www.emersonindustrial.com/en-US /branson/Products/plastic-joining/ultrasonic -plastic-welders/textile-and-film-processing /Pages/default.aspx.

CHAPTER EIGHT

Sourcing, Assembly, and Mass Production of Sewn Products

Objectives:

- To provide an overview of the organizational structure of the global apparel industry
- To gain awareness of infrastructures and their impact

on sourcing factory locations for apparel production
- To understand the organization of factory layouts and production processes used in apparel manufacturing

Mass-produced apparel items are sourced and manufactured around the globe. **Sourcing** is the process of investigating, assessing, and procuring resources to acquire materials or apparel products manufactured by domestic or offshore factories that can provide raw materials or produce finished sewn products at the negotiated price, volume, and quality level within the designated delivery time frame. The quality produced by a factory relies upon the level of technology, skills of the operators, types of equipment, plant capacity, and time to market. Cost of

materials and labor are the two most expensive components in apparel production; therefore, sourcing managers are continuously seeking places to manufacture products in countries with low total costs that can produce apparel products at the desired quality level consumers expect from the brands they shop while maintaining profitability. A **sourcing agent** acts as an integral liaison between the manufacturer, factory, and retailer to oversee production and monitor quality according to product specifications for sewn products produced around the globe.

OVERVIEW OF THE ORGANIZATIONAL STRUCTURE OF THE GLOBAL APPAREL INDUSTRY

The structure of the global apparel industry is composed of four levels:

- Manufacturers of raw materials
- Apparel manufacturers and retail product developers
- Retail
- End consumers

Raw materials manufacturers produce fabrics, findings, and trimmings for use in sewn products. Apparel manufacturers and retail product developers are involved in varying degrees with the design, development, production, merchandising, and marketing processes of apparel products. Traditional manufacturers own factories that produce the sewn product lines they design, develop, merchandise, and market to consumers. Retail product developers and some manufacturers use contractors to complete all or part of the design, development, and manufacturing aspects to produce a product or apparel line. The retail level then provides sales channels for distribution of products to consumers whether through websites, mobile and social channels, brick-and-mortar stores, catalogues, or shopping networks. The end consumer is the last level but is at the core of the entire organizational structure of the apparel industry. It is the customer who drives the success or failure of products in the marketplace.

Apparel manufacturing poses many challenges due to the wide variety of raw materials used, expanse of product offerings and sizes, varying manufacturing technologies and production volumes, time to market, and range in quality expectations across price classifications. Fashion trends and increasing consumer demand for constant flow of new products into the marketplace are driving manufacturers to produce products faster, speeding up time-to-market

by reducing supply chain inefficiencies from the initial concept to the end consumer. A **supply chain** is the network of suppliers, manufacturers, and retailers responsible for one or more aspects of producing (production of raw materials, garment assembly and finishing), handling, and distributing a particular product to the end consumer. The term *supply chain* is sometimes confused with the word **logistics**, which focuses solely on the distribution and warehousing processes for a product.

Managing the supply chain requires careful analysis with increased demand for integration of technology. Optimization of the supply chain can be achieved through the use of advances in information technology such as PLM- (product lifecycle management) and PDM- (product data management) integrated technology systems. PLM and PDM are used to significantly reduce communication time across the global supply chain by making information immediately available via an internet interface. **Product lifecycle management (PLM)** is a software system that allows for real-time interaction and collaboration for managing and communicating information about a digital representation of a product, with respect to product data management and supply chain processes throughout the product's lifecycle. PLM allows digital files to be accessed and shared among individuals or teams around the globe who are responsible for each of the various phases of the development, manufacturing, and distribution processes, starting from the initial concept and ending with the consumer.[1,2,3] A key benefit of PLM is the creation of one source for product information. All parties involved with the development or production processes use PLM as their primary information resource. A key objective of PLM is to minimize the amount of time in the development and production processes while also minimizing mistakes from occurring. An important component of PLM is **product data management (PDM)**, which utilizes software that can be integrated with the PLM system to monitor and track information regarding product documents such as specifications for raw materials, design development, and line planning, as well as process-related files for manufacturing and sourcing.[3,4,5,6] As changes are made, the records are updated to provide efficient flow of information and reduce time to market. This technology provides an efficient platform for companies to track costs associated with producing a product. These advances in communication have allowed companies to reduce the time-to-market cycle by up to 50% and streamline the supply chain for greater efficiency, thereby bringing goods to the consumer faster.[7] Fast-fashion and speed-to-market programs have become increasingly important as companies seek ways to meet consumer demand and reduce the product development cycle; therefore, responsive suppliers that provide agility are critical. A challenge that companies often face with fast-fashion is compromised quality. Kathleen Mitford, vice president of product and market strategy at PTC (PLM software vendor), explained, "Everyone can see the latest version of a product, know when it's been modified, or if it's been dropped from the line, avoiding manufacturing errors and improving product quality."[8] PLM can also streamline sourcing. According to just-style.com, a leader in online resources for the apparel and textiles industries and major publisher of market research indicated, "A manufacturer can quickly and easily see a product's spec to draft with a cost estimate and send a product sample to the retailer. The retailer can then review the sample and enter any modifications into the PLM system for the manufacturer to sew a final sample."[6]

MANUFACTURERS AND FACTORIES

The global supply chain for apparel products is primarily driven by low-cost wages in developing countries. **Offshore** production refers to apparel products manufactured in a different country than they will be consumed. If the manufacturing country is located in close geographic proximity to the country the goods will be distributed and sold, the term **nearshore** can

be used. Offshore production of apparel products has increased significantly over the last 20 years due to de-regulation of international trade of goods; the elimination of quotas, which created a more competitive global marketplace; technological advances in communication as companies utilize PLM and PDM systems; and increased developments in transportation of goods.[9,10] **Domestic sourcing** of apparel products in the United States and the EU has decreased significantly over the years, but recently there are movements to bring manufacturing back to these areas due to consumer demand. There are few companies producing garments **onshore**, meaning manufactured domestically.

Location and Infrastructure

According to Plunkette Research, Ltd., "China's textile and clothing exports soared from $16.89 billion in 1990 to $206.74 billion in 2010…and $253.2 billion in 2011."[11] When looking specifically at garments and removing textiles from this equation, China's apparel exports to the world have grown from $113.02 billion in 2008 to $148.30 billion in 2012, a growth rate of 31.21%.[12] As the cost of manufacturing along the coastline in China increases, manufacturing is moving further inland to towns and villages. Ease of transportation from the factory to the final destination is critical when sourcing production around the globe because any delay in getting goods to market can impact a brand's profitability. Adequate infrastructures must be in place to make factories in low-wage countries desirable. Some infrastructure factors that must be considered include the distance from the factory to the port, the quality and capacity of the roads goods will be transported on, and accessibility and reliability of utilities such as electricity, telecommunication networks, and water. These factors can impact time and time is of the essence when producing fashion driven apparel products. For example, while India has a large pool of skilled workers and low cost labor, the country's infrastructure needs improvement to provide the same level of sourcing completion as

China.[13] Bureaucracy, instability, and corruption can also be barriers and lead to delays in shipment of goods when sourcing products internationally. See Table 8.1 for examples of estimated port to port shipping times from China to the United States, Europe, Australia, and Canada.

As costs increase in China, companies are seeking alternative places to source goods at lower costs such as Pakistan, India, Bangladesh, Sri Lanka, Indonesia, and Africa.[14,15] In 2011, Ethiopia was close to tripling its apparel and textile exports and will see continued growth over the next five years as more clothing and textile companies invest in Ethiopia.[16] Ninety-four percent of Ethiopia's exports in this sector are shipped to "Turkey, Germany, Italy, the United Arab Emirates, United States, United Kingdom, Netherlands, China, Australia, Belgium, and Sudan".[17] Considerations for sourcing decisions should include careful evaluation of supply chain, product costs, and profits in relation to labor rates, productivity, quality-level capability, plant capacity and minimum requirements, production time and delivery, transportation, tariffs, trade regulations and incentives, exchange rates, and economic and political stability.[15,18]

Sourcing apparel production in developing countries can be challenging when communicating quality needs. Perceptions of quality can be quite different in developing countries versus those that are developed. There are parts of the world that are known for specializing in certain products, such as sweaters from Peru, and sourcing in these areas can help ensure quality standards will be met. Communication between the designer or product developer and the factory is critical. Product specifications should be clearly documented in technical packages that accompany accurate garment prototypes so that garment details or quality standards are not left to interpretation. The skill of the workforce and their ability to work with a variety of materials across product categories are important factors to consider in addition to the type of equipment and training employees receive. Production capacity should not be overlooked in this quality equation. A factory's **demonstrated capacity** is measured by the total quantity of component parts or finished products it is able to produce at a particular quality level, within a specific time period. If a factory cannot accommodate the needed volume of garments, they may subcontract the work to another vendor, which may or may not maintain the same level of quality expected.

Time-Based Manufacturing Strategies

The evolution of mass production and time-based approaches to manufacturing have allowed for the acceleration of apparel supply chain management today. Manufacturers need to be able to quickly

Table 8.1 Estimated Port-to-Port Shipping Times from Shanghai and Hong Kong to Various Destinations

United States Port Designations		
Starting Port	Destination Port	Number of Days
Hong Kong	Los Angeles	12
Shanghai	Los Angeles	14
Hong Kong	Chicago	20
Hong Kong	New York	26
Shanghai	New York	28
Hong Kong	Miami	28
Shanghai	Miami	30
Canadian Port Destinations		
Hong Kong	Vancouver	19
Hong Kong	Toronto	26
European Port Destinations		
Hong Kong	Barcelona	21
Hong Kong	Antwerp	23
Australian Port Destinations		
Hong Kong	Sydney	11
Hong Kong	Brisbane	18

NOTE: Estimated shipping days do not include the following which can take an additional 3–4 days: loading and unloading shipping containers, clearance of shipment through customs, or transfer of shipment to warehouses. Additional time is also required if the shipping vessel stops at another port prior to the final destination.
Source: *Shipping Times*; Manufacturing Sourcing from China and Asia, accessed December 14, 2012, http://manufacturingsourcing.com /shipping/

respond to customer needs and fluctuations in the marketplace. The concept of **lean manufacturing** has evolved from just-in-time (JIT) and focuses on reducing product waste, from raw materials through delivery of the finished product, by producing the smallest quantities of product closest to the time needed, in an effort to reduce in-process inventory and carrying costs without compromising quality. Core apparel products also known as *basics* are well suited for lean manufacturing because there is less demand for styling changes and the selling period is considerably longer than fashion or trend-right products. Agile manufacturing has evolved from quick response (QR) and focuses on speed and flexibility to deliver the product to the consumer faster through the use of technology systems. This streamlines processes and eliminates unnecessary steps that do not add value, in an effort to decrease lead times and provide greater flexibility when there is demand for style changes. Fashion or trend-right apparel products are well suited for agile manufacturing due to high demand for style changes and the rapid selling periods.[19] Both lean and agile manufacturing strategies handle production needs based on actual orders placed and not projections, which can lead to markdowns and loss of profits.

Factory Direct Sourcing

Sourcing products can range from contracting simple assembly of garments or component parts to comprehensive design and production of apparel items. The three factory-direct sourcing options include CMT, OEM, and ODM. The simplest form is **cut-make-trim (CMT)** sourcing, which utilizes vendors who are contracted to spread and cut fabric and then assemble the component parts into garments according to specifications provided by the contracting firm. CMT contractors charge a fee for constructing the garments and are not responsible for designing the garment or providing the materials needed to assemble the product. These contractors provide skill, labor, and equipment used for assembling products. The contracting firm is responsible for designing the garments, providing technical packages containing specifications, sourcing and purchasing the materials, and delivering them to the factory where the garments will be cut and assembled. Cut-make-trim contractors are typically found in less-developed locations such as Cambodia and Vietnam because little capital investment is required.[20,21,22]

As investments are made in developing countries, opportunities for upgrading value are made possible. The middle tier in the factory-direct sourcing chain is **original equipment manufacturing (OEM)**, also known as a **package contractor**. In this business model, the contracting firm designs the garments and provides technical packages containing specifications for materials. The OEM contractor is then responsible for financing and sourcing fabrics and component parts needed for garment assembly based on contracted specifications. In addition to obtaining materials and assembling the products, they also finish and package garments for delivery to the retail destination. Increased technology for coordination, logistics, and machinery as well as a higher level of production expertise are expected from this type of contractor. Examples of OEM sourcing locations include Bangladesh, Sri Lanka, Indonesia, and Mexico.[20,21,22]

Original design manufacturing (ODM), also referred to as **full package**, is the third tier of the factory-direct sourcing, which offers a comprehensive range from product design through distribution. In this business model, ODM contractors are responsible for designing the product, developing and approving the patterns and prototypes, grading, marker making, cutting, assembling, finishing, packaging, and distributing the product. They are also responsible for financing and sourcing fabrics and component parts needed for garment assembly, packaging, and distribution of the finished product. Among the factory-direct sourcing options, ODM contractors have the most responsibility in the design and manufacturing of apparel products and carry the largest financial burden. Examples of ODM sourcing locations include China, Turkey, and India.[20,21, 22]

When the product is made offshore, this supplier would be considered a **landed duty paid (LDP)** supplier. LDP suppliers are responsible for the landed value of a product plus any import duties, such as shipping, duty, delivery, insurance, and customs clearance costs.

Factory Layouts

The manner in which the physical space within a manufacturing plant is allocated and arranged dictates the **factory layout** and its level of efficiency. This layout accommodates areas for administrative offices, production, utilities, storage, raw materials, inspection, quality control, finishing, packaging, transportation, and employee services (i.e., restrooms, break room, and so on). The layout of equipment within a factory will impact how garments flow through the production process and at what speed. The objective of an efficient factory is to produce a garment in the shortest time frame with a minimum cost per unit. The productivity and profitability of a factory is based on the efficient movement of materials and assembly processes. Within manufacturing plants there are two types of production layouts—**product layout (line layout)** and **process layout (skill center)**. Although many factories rely on one type of layout for production, some possess both product and process arrangements. In a product layout, also known as an *assembly line*, the manufacturing equipment is arranged according to the sequential order of garment assembly, not a specific garment style. Product layouts are particularly efficient for manufacturing large volumes of identical garments. A process layout utilizes a spatial arrangement of manufacturing equipment that is grouped and placed into work areas according to the operations needed to produce a specific garment style. Garment component parts are grouped by assembly operation, and the production equipment is arranged by each of the procedures to be completed. Process layouts offer greater flexibility for fast fashion brands because of their efficiency in manufacturing a variety of garment styles in small volumes.

GARMENT PRODUCTION PROCESSES

Apparel production can be divided into three segments—pre-assembly, assembly, and finishing operations. Pre-assembly processes are completed in preparation for garment construction. The pre-assembly and production operations require the greatest investment in materials, labor, and equipment. The selection of materials, skill of the labor, and types of equipment ultimately impact the overall quality level of the finished product. Finishing operations allow for garments to be prepared for shipment and distribution. Quality perception can also be compromised if finishing steps are not properly conducted.

Pre-Assembly Operations

In order for production to begin there are a few processes that must be completed prior to garment assembly. Garments are designed, and the finalized sized production patterns are arranged into a marker to prepare for cutting. A **marker** is a planned layout of pattern pieces used for cutting the fabric for prototypes and for mass production. Most markers today are digitally prepared, although some manually drawn markers do exist, mainly for use in cutting prototypes (see Figure 8.1). All of the garment pattern pieces in all sizes in the range are strategically arranged with regard to the materials structure, design, and width to maximize fabric utilization and minimize **fabric fallout** or waste that remains on the cutting table after garment pieces are removed. Markers allow for fabric yardage to be more accurately estimated when ordering for production. The manner in which the fabric will be spread on the cutting table must be taken into consideration when a marker is planned. Directional or one-way fabrics such as one-way print designs, knits, brushed, pile, looped and satin materials need special consideration when planning a marker because if the garment pieces are cut in different directions the color or surface texture

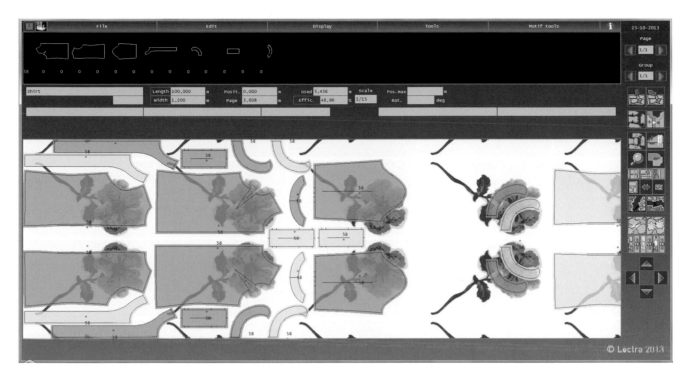

Figure 8.1 Lectra's Diamino software for marker making
© LECTRA

can appear different, thereby compromising the aesthetic quality of the garment. Grainline must also be carefully aligned on the marker to avoid skewing of the fabric in the finished garment. When stripes and plaid fabrics are used, the final garment appearance can be greatly impacted and influence a customer's perception of quality when the pattern does not match at the seams and closures. In an effort to reduce mismatched stripes or plaids, portions of the garment such as plackets, yokes, cuffs, and pockets can be planned to be cut on the bias.

Fabric spreading is the next step to begin the production process. Before fabric is spread, the material is inspected. This inspection takes place when the materials are received. They are evaluated for flaws and compliance with negotiated specifications. Chapter 13 will discuss in more detail the various levels and types of inspection that occur throughout the development and manufacturing processes. Material is laid

using a manual or automated spreader. It is important for fabric to be spread without tension, with each layer aligned at the selvedge. If the fabric is stretched during spreading, it will be too tight; likewise, if the spread has too much slack, ripples will be visible that cause fabric folds. Both of these spreading issues will negatively impact the quality of the garment pieces when cut. The layup (total number of plies to be cut) should be free of defects and on-grain (see Figure 8.2). Any of these problems can compromise the quality of the garment and may render it unsalable. After the material is spread and allowed to relax (if applicable), a paper marker is placed on the layup and cut manually with a knife blade or cutting machine, or the digital marker is sent to a computerized automated cutting machine and the garment pieces are cut. Cutting must be accurate because it can impact the assembly of garment pieces and how they line up when stitched. Notching and drill holes must be properly marked

Figure 8.2 Fabric spreading
© RIA Novosti/TopFoto/The Image Works

and cut to assist workers with the assembly of apparel products. If a drill hole or notch is cut in the wrong place, the garment pieces will not align properly when assembled. If the notch is cut too deep, it will not be contained within the seam allowance and the cut hole will show on the face of the garment. These are indications of poor quality that can be avoided. After the cutting process has concluded, the garment pieces are offloaded, counted, marked, and bundled or grouped according to the production process that will be used. See Figure 8.3 for offloading and Figure 8.4 for shade marking. Fusing garment parts such as interlining is typically completed in the cutting room, or the pieces can either be sent out for fusing or the fabric yardage can be block- or roll-to-roll fused prior to cutting.

Assembly Production Systems

A **production system** is defined as the combination of allocated resources and sequencing of work flow needed for manufacturing a finished salable apparel item. From beginning to end, **work flow** is the planned sequence for the specific movement of garment component pieces and materials through the production process. No matter which type of process a factory uses, all production systems employ individuals responsible for managing the handling of materials, findings, and component parts, workforce, equipment for production, assembly, finishing, and packaging, and planning the efficient sequence for the movement of materials and garment parts during

Figure 8.3 Offloading
Photo by Jeff Giberstein, courtesy of Exacta

Figure 8.4
Shade marking
Mouse in the House/Alamy

manufacturing. See Table 8.2 for garment and construction assembly operations for men's, women's, and children's garments. Throughout the course of assembly there can be varying degrees of **work in progress** or **work in process**, which is the quantity of incomplete products during manufacturing that can vary depending upon the production process selected and the volume of garments in production.

Production systems for assembly of apparel products include make-through/whole garment production, modular production, and assembly-line systems such as progressive bundle and unit production. See

Table 8.2 Garment Construction and Assembly Operation Sequences

Construction Sequence for Men's Short Sleeve T-shirt

Operation Description	Stitch Type	Seam Type	Estimated Units Per Hour	Garment Illustration
1. Blind hem sleeves	503	EFc-1	480	
2. Close sleeves	504	SSa-1	144	
3. Blind hem bottom	503	EFc-1	300	
4. Join right shoulder	504	SSa-1	360	
5. Attach neckband inserting label	504	SSa-1	288	
6. Close left shoulder	504	SSa-1	336	
7. Tape neck and shoulder seams	401	SSag-2 (inv)	144	
8. Set sleeves	504	SSa-1	72	
9. Trim and inspect				

Construction Sequence for Women's Full Fashioned Cardigan Sweater

Assembly Operations				
1. Close right shoulder	504	SSa-1	84	
2. Attach collarette	504	SSa-1	84	
3. Close left shoulder	504	SSa-1	84	
4. Set top of sleeve	504	SSa-1	84	
5. Set under arm portion of sleeves	504	SSa-1	84	
6. Close sleeves and sides	504	SSa-1	60	
7. Close collarette	504	SSa-1	48	
8. Attach button and buttonhole Facings	401	SSa-1	36	
9. Attach label	101		180	
10. Front buttonholes			60	
11. Sew front buttons	101		60	

Construction Sequence for Women's Knit Dress

Assembly Operations				
1. Close sleeves	504	SSa-1	204	
2. Finish bottom of collar	301	SSa-1	240	
3. Join shoulder	504	SSa-1	216	
4. Attach collar to neck opening	504	SSa-1	72	
5. Stich neck seam	406	SSh-2	216	
6. Finish ends of collar	301	SSa-1	96	
7. Sew front dart	301	SSa-1	120	
8. Close sides	504	SSa-1	60	
9. Set sleeves	504	SSa-1	72	
10. Tack label to neck opening	101		300	
11. Sew buttons to collar	101		300	
12. Tack collar	101		300	
13. Hem bottom	101	EFl-1	60	
14. Trim and inspect				

Construction Sequence for Men's Casual Work Shirt

Collar Operations			
1. Runstitch collar	301	SSa-1	192
2. Trim collar points	540		
3. Trim and press collar	240		
4. Topstitch collar	301	SSe-2(b)	192
5. Hem collar band	301	EFa-1	420
6. Attach collar band to collar	301	SSa-1	192
7. Topstitch collar band to collar	301	SSq-2(b)	240
8. Buttonhole collar band	900		
9. Button sew collar band	101	900	
Cuffs Operations			
10. Runstitch	301	SSa-1	216
11. Topstitch cuffs	301	SSe-1(b)	180
12. Buttonhole cuffs	360		
13. Button sew cuffs	101	360	
Pockets and Flaps Operations			
14. Precrease flaps		192	
15. Make pocket flaps	301	SSc-2	90
16. Buttonhole flaps	360		
17. Hem pocket top	301	EFa-1	180
18. Precrease pocket	300		
19. Button sew pocket		101	360
Fronts, Backs, and Sleeves Operations			
20. Hem button stay or fuse	401	EFb-1 (inv)	360
21. Attach center plait	401	LSa-2	300

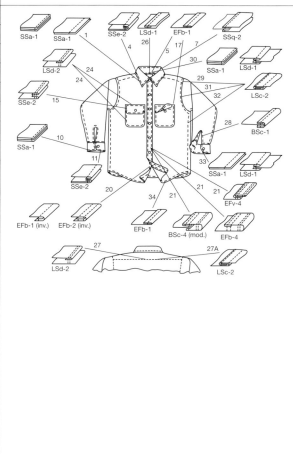

Construction Sequence for Men's Jeans

Preliminary Operations			
1. Make belt loops	406	EFh-1	420
2. Hem top of hip pocket	401	EFb-2 (inv)	216
3. Decorative stitch hip pockets	401	OSa-2	216
4. Hem ruler, watch and right front pocket facing	401	EFa-2 (inv)	216
5. Sew facings to front pockets	301	LSd-1	144
6. Bag front pockets	515	SSa-2	216
Fronts and Backs Operations			
7. Set front swing pocket	301	SSl-2	96
8. Attach and stitch down right fly facing	301	EFb-1 (mod)	96
9. Attach zipper to right fly and finish crotch	301	SSa-1	120
10. Attach left zipper, hem left fly and finish crotch	301	EFb-1 (mod)	120
11. Fell risers to backs	401	LSc-3	180
12. Set ruler pocket	301	LSd-2	120
13. Set hip pockets	301	LS-2	60
14. Seat seam	401	LSc-3	156
Assembly Operations			
15. Side seam	401	LSc-3	84

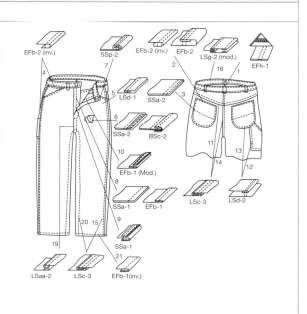

Table 8.2 (continued)

			Construction Sequence for Children's Unlined Jacket	
Operation Description	Stitch Type	Seam Type	Estimated Units Per Hour	Garment Illustration
Preliminary Operations				
1. Fuse collar and cuffs				
2. Runstitch collar	301	SSa11	180	
3. Trim and turn collar				
4. Runstitch cuffs	301	SSa-1	144	
5. Turn cuffs				
6. Hem left and right front facings	301	EFb-1	96	
Assembly Operations				
7. Bind pocket opening	301	BSc-10	120	
8. Attach zipper and facing to left front	301	SSj-1	60	
9. Attach zipper and facing to right front	301	SSj-1	60	
10. Tack down top of right and left front facings and edgestitch	301	SSq-2(b)	36	
11. Cord pocket openings and close side pockets	301	LSd/SSa-1	60	
12. Join shoulders	401	LSc-2	180	
13. Set sleeves	401	LSc-2	72	
14. Close sleeves and sides	401	LSc-2	108	
15. Sew collar on and down inserting Label and topstitching	301	SSe-2(b)	60	
16. Attach cuffs	301	LSq-3(b)		
17. Sew cuffs down	301	SSa-1	108	
18. Attach elastic to waist	301	SSa-1	108	
19. Hem bottom	301	EFb-1		
20. Bartacks				
21. Cuffs buttonholes				
22. Sew button on cuffs	101		180	
23. Trim and inspect				

Source: Union Special

Table 8.3 for a comparison of production processes. The quality level produced will depend on the expertise of the factory, skill level of the workers, and the equipment used.

The method that requires the highest level of skill and produces the smallest volume is the **make-through** or **whole garment production system**, which has severe production limitations and is used in making the highest-priced, highest-quality apparel. Entire garments are assembled by individuals—one person sews the garment from start to finish. An individual is given a bundle of garment components to construct the garment based on their logical progression of assembly. Although this system offers great flexibility

Table 8.3 Comparison of Production Processes across Decision Considerations

Make-Through Production System				
Response Time	Flexibility	Labor Cost	Labor Skill Level	Plant Equipment Investment and Management Cost
Quick	High	High	High	Low
Modular Production System				
Quick	High	Moderate	Moderate to Low	High
Progressive Bundle System				
Slow	Low	Low	Low	High
Unit Production System				
Slow	Low	Low	Low	High

Source: Just-style.com, *Production Management Goes Back to the Future,* March 19, 2004, accessed December 22, 2012, http://www.just-style.com /analysis/production-management-goes-back-to-the-future_id93130.aspx; V. Ramesh Babu, "Garment Production Systems," *The Indian Textile Journal,* October 2006. Accessed December 22, 2012, http://www.indiantextile journal.com/articles/FAdetails.asp?id=28

for very small exclusive production runs, it has the highest labor cost and requires the utmost skilled workers who possess great versatility. [23,24] Workers are compensated by the number of finished garments produced.

Modular production involves teams of individuals working together to assemble a garment. Members of the team are cross trained to complete different continuous operations or sometimes all operations within the unit. The modular system provides the most flexibility and is well suited for small volume production runs of a wide variety of garment styles. The equipment is arranged in a U-shaped layout based on the needs of the style, and workers typically stand to complete operations. This production method is well suited for better-, bridge-, and designer-priced merchandise where a small quantity of garments requires speed to market. The modular production system is the best option for meeting market needs for frequent style changes requiring proportionately smaller production runs. This system provides the ability to efficiently change over to new styles in a minimal amount of time. Workers have the ability to identify and correct quality problems as they occur, thereby significantly reducing the amount of second quality garments produced. Compensation is based on the completed garments produced by the team. This method requires the collaborative effort of all team members to maintain a consistent work flow and output of finished garments. [23,24,25,26] See Figure 8.5 for modular production layouts.

(a)

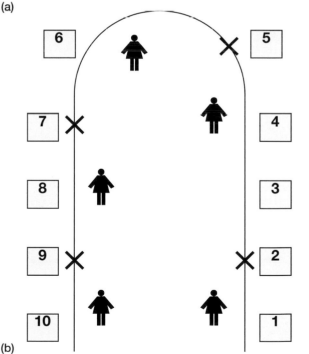

(b)

Figure 8.5 Modular production system
(a) Courtesy of Sandra Keiser; (b) Courtesy of Fairchild Books

The **progressive bundle system** utilizes assembly line production methods. Components of garments are bundled and manually moved according to the sequential order of machines and operations for assembly. Cut component parts for garments are matched and bundled in the cutting room to include pieces for completing a particular operation or consecutive assembly operations for portions of a garment and include bundle tickets. A **bundle ticket** is a master list of operations for the bundle that includes coupons or smart cards that correspond to each assembly operation, routing information, piece rate, and identification information regarding the style number, size, and shade number. **Bundle coupons** are retained by each worker to turn in at the end of their shift, and their pay is calculated based on the pieces completed. **Smart cards** or **electronic bundle tickets** are used by some manufacturers. The electronic bundle ticket is swiped through a card reader and work completed by a sewing operator is electronically monitored. When used, these electronic cards are paired with identification cards containing information provided in the bundle ticket. In this system, sewing operators complete the same operation day after day and become highly efficient. Bundles are manually moved from one operation to the next so the apparel item is progressively constructed as it moves through sequential sub-assembly and main assembly operations. The progressive bundle system is well suited for high volume orders of identical garments and does not offer the level of flexibility for frequent style changes like the previous methods discussed. This system also produces a high level of work in progress due to the volume of garments in production at any given time. Factory workers are compensated based on how many pieces they complete within a particular shift, which is known as **piece rate**. The progressive bundle system is the most widely utilized production method around the globe for producing apparel products.[23,25,26] See Figure 8.6 for progressive bundle system layouts.

The other production system that utilizes assembly line methods is the **unit production system**. This production method utilizes a single garment as the "unit of production" unlike the progressive bundle system that uses bundles of cut components for many garments. The component parts for a single garment are loaded into a carrier and moved from one work station to the next by means of transporters or conveyers that are connected to overhead power rail systems. These electric-powered tracks are laid out to provide the mechanical movement of component pieces of a garment in an effort to eliminate the need for manual movement of goods thereby providing greater efficiency for flow of goods through the plant. In this system, sewing operators complete the same operation day after day and become highly efficient. A computer system is used to control the routing and flow of garments to each workstation and records productivity of the sewing operator as garments are moved from one operation to the next along the production floor. This computerized system is used to track workers' compensation as they are also paid piece rate. The unit production system is well suited for high volume orders of similar garments and does not offer the flexibility for frequent style changes like modular production. This system also produces a high level of work in progress due to the volume of garments in production at any given time.[23,25,26] See Figure 8.7 for unit production system layouts.

Finishing Processes

When garments are assembled they may be sent for wet processing (i.e., garment dyeing, washing, application of finishes) to enhance the aesthetic or functional performance of the apparel item. In some cases findings may be damaged during processing, therefore requiring them to be attached after wet processing. During the finishing process loose threads are trimmed, garments are inspected for defects, and repairs are made if possible. Inspection will be discussed in more detail in Chapter 13. Garments are then pressed, tags are attached, and items are folded or hung and packaged for shipment according to

(a)

(b)

Two examples of progressive bundle plant layouts

Figure 8.6 Progressive bundle production system
(a) AFP/Getty Images; (b) Courtesy of Fairchild Books

specifications outlined in the technical package. Details as simple as loose threads on a garment or improper pressing can convey poor quality to a consumer and may impact whether they purchase the product or not; therefore, attention to every detail is important when producing quality apparel. Some flaws may be overlooked by the customer if the garment is inexpensive and quality expectations are low.

(a)

(b)   Two examples of unit production systems

Figure 8.7   Unit production system
(a) Courtesy of WWD; (b) Courtesy of Fairchild Books

INDUSTRY SCENARIO 8.1 Sustainability and Environmental Impact of Manufacturing Apparel

Sustainability is an important topic in the apparel industry and will be for years to come. Stephen Jesseph, president and CEO of Worldwide Responsible Accredited Production (WRAP), stated, "By the year 2050, we will have almost 10 *billion* people competing for limited clean water, nonrenewable *and* renewable resources, land to grow food, and energy to sustain their businesses, families, and lifestyles."[27] According to Cotton Incorporated, "Every stage of a textile product's life cycle has environmental impacts—from fiber production through manufacturing and retailing to laundering and disposal by consumers. Of particular concern is the use of water, energy, and chemicals (WEC) in textile processing—an area where technological advances offer significant savings in resources and environmental benefits."[28] Fashion brands and their supply chain must evaluate ways to minimize their environmental impact on the planet and the human race. Fashion companies are seeking new or alternative technologies to replace processes that deplete natural resources, pollute water systems, the air, and the ground as well as cause harm to workers handling the materials during processing. Many well-known brands are making conscious efforts to reduce the consumption of natural resources and eliminate toxic chemicals used to produce their products in an effort to protect the environment and workers. Limiting the use of natural resources, careful materials selection and utilization of dyeing processes that use CO_2 rather than water are ways Nike is creating an ecofriendly product. "Nike is differentiating itself from its competitors using the power of sustainability strategies. It is emerging as one of the strongest global sustainable brands."[29]

- What are some other brands that are focusing their efforts on the environment and sustainable practices?
- What are some ways that fashion brands can produce more sustainable products?
- How can fashion brands reduce consumption of natural resources along the supply chain?
- What are governments around the world doing to help protect the environment that impact textile and apparel production?

SUMMARY

In this chapter the organizational structure of the apparel industry, sourcing, and production of apparel products were discussed in relation to the factors that impact quality. Optimization of the supply chain through use of technology systems is changing the way product information is communicated and exchanged throughout the development and production processes. This up-to-the-minute information exchange is helping to minimize errors and streamline communication. Manufacturing strategies and sourcing play critical roles in securing the appropriate resources for producing apparel products at the targeted price, in the quantities and quality levels desired, all while meeting critical timing deadlines. Additionally, the impact infrastructure has on selection of factory locations is an important consideration when sourcing goods. Factory layouts and production processes used for manufacturing apparel products provide a basis for understanding the flow of raw materials to the finished end product. Maintaining and monitoring quality throughout the production phase allows for factories to minimize product flaws from reaching the consumer.

ACTIVITIES

1. Identify two major manufacturing trends, and explain how these are impacting apparel production.

2. Research factors that impact the sourcing of apparel goods. Sources to get started include *WWD*, *the Sourcing Journal* online, and *Just-style.com*.

3. Research a company that is focused on sustainable practices. Write a brief summary, and list the ways they are reducing their impact on the environment and workers.

4. Randomly select 15 garments from your wardrobe. Create a list of the items and include the country of origin for each. How many countries have the apparel products been sourced from?

ENDNOTES

1. Ruth E. Glock and Grace I. Kunz (2005). *Apparel Manufacturing: Sewn Product Analysis*, 4th ed. Upper Saddle River, NY: Pearson/Prentice Hall, pp. 7–11.
2. Paula J. Myers-McDevitt (2011). *Apparel Production Management and the Technical Package*. New York: Fairchild Books, p. 40.
3. Visionet Systems, Inc. *Collaborative PLM Capability*. Accessed December 8, 2012, http://www.vsiapparel.com/product_lifecycle _management.htm.
4. Siemens. *Product Data Management*. Accessed December 8, 2012, http://www.plm.automation .siemens.com/en_us/plm/pdm.shtml.
5. Jim McKinney (2012). "PDM & PLM: What's the Difference?" *PLM on My Brain,* March 5. Accessed December 8, 2012, http://plmjim .blogspot.com/2012/03/pdm-plm-whats -difference.html.
6. Paula J. Myers-McDevitt (2011). *Apparel Production Management and the Technical Package*. New York: Fairchild Books, p. 81.
7. just-style.com. *About PLM*. Accessed December 8, 2012, http://just-style.com/plm/introduction -to-PLM.aspx.
8. just-style.com. *About PLM: How Does PLM Work?* Accessed December 8, 2012, http://just -style.com/plm/how-does-PLM-work.aspx.
9. European Foundation for the Improvement of Living and Working Conditions. *EU Textiles and Clothing Sector: Location Decisions*. Accessed December 8, 2012, http://www.eurofound .europa.eu/pubdocs/2008/48/en/1/ef0848en.pdf.
10. U.S. Department of Commerce Office of Textiles and Apparel. *Going Global: Export Guide for Textile and Apparel*. Accessed November 30, 2012, http://otexa.ita.doc.gov/pdfs/goingglobal .pdf .
11. Plunkett Research, Ltd. (2013). *Introduction to the Apparel and Textile Industry*. Accessed October 20, 2013, http://www.plunkettresearch .com/apparel-textiles-clothing-market-research /industry-and-business-data.
12. Fibre2fashion (2013). "China outshines India in apparel export growth," March 22. Accessed October 20, 2013, http://www.fibre2fashion .com/news/apparel-news/newsdetails.aspx? news_id=122603.
13. Manufacturingsourcing.com. *Promises and Perils of Sourcing from India*. Accessed December 14, 2012, http://manufacturingsourcing.com /sourcing-from-india/.
14. Ben Hanson (2012). *Freak'n Fashionomics: The New Economics of Fashion,* November 7. Accessed October 20, 2013, http://www.infor .com/content/whitepapers/freak-n-fashionomics .pdf/?view=Standard&ok=yes.
15. Richard Woodard (2012). "Emerging Asian Countries Hold Apparel Sourcing Key." *just.style.com*, June 26. Accessed December 2, 2012, http://www.just-style.com/comment /emerging-asian-countries-hold-apparel -sourcing-key_id114691.aspx.
16. Johnathan Dyson (2012). "Ethiopia Pushes on with Textile and Clothing Expansion Plan." *just.style.com,* December 11. Accessed December 17, 2012, http://www.just-style.com/analysis /ethiopia-pushes-on-with-textile-and-clothing -expansion-plan_id116368.aspx.
17. Barrie Leonie (2011). "ETHIOPIA: Textile and Clothing Exports Reach $62.2m." *just.style.com*, August 17. Accessed December 17, 2012, http://www.just-style.com/news/textile-and -clothing-exports-reach-622m_id111909.aspx.
18. Stig Yding Sørensen (2008). *EU Textiles and Clothing Sector: Location Decisions*. European Foundation for the Improvement of Living and Working Conditions. Accessed December 14, 2012, http://www.eurofound.europa.eu/pubdocs /2008/48/en/1/ef0848en.pdf , p. 2.
19. Grace Kunz and Myrna Garner (2011). *Going Global: The Textile and Apparel Industry*, 2nd ed. New York: Fairchild Books, p. 145–146.

20. Gary Gereffi and Stacey Frederick (2010). "The Global Apparel Value Chain, Trade, and the Crisis: Challenges and Opportunities for Developing Countries." In *Global Value Chains in a Postcrisis World: A Development Perspective*, edited by Olivier Cattaneo, Gary Gereffi, and Cornelia Staritz. Washington DC: The International Bank for Reconstruction and Development/The World Bank, pp. 157–208.

21. Grace Kunz and Myrna Garner (2011). *Going Global: The Textile and Apparel* Industry, 2nd ed. New York: Fairchild Books, pp. 136–137.

22. Sandra Keiser and Myrna Garner (2012). *Beyond Design: The Synergy of Apparel Product Development*, 3rd ed. New York: Fairchild Books, pp. 472–471.

23. V Ramesh Babu (2006). "Garment Production Systems." *The Indian Textile Journal.* October. Accessed December 22, 2012, http://www .indiantextilejournal.com/articles/FAdetails .asp?id=28.

24. Just-style.com (2004). "Production Management Goes Back to the Future," *Just-style.com,* March 19. Accessed December 22, 2012, http://www.just -style.com/analysis/production-management -goes-back-to-the-future_id93130.aspx.

25. Janace Bubonia (2012). *Apparel Production Terms and Processes*. New York: Fairchild Books, pp. 277–279.

26. Sandra Keiser and Myrna Garner (2012). *Beyond Design: The Synergy of Apparel Product Development*, 3rd ed. New York: Fairchild Books, pp. 441–442.

27. Maria C. Thiry (2011). "Staying Alive: Making Textiles Sustainable." *AATCC Review,* (November/ December). Accessed October 21, 2013, http:// www.aatcc.org/media/read/documents/sustain 1111.pdf.

28. Cotton Incorporated (2010). "Sustainable Dyeing Solutions." *Supply Chain Insights.* Accessed October 21, 2013, http://www.cottoninc.com /corporate/Market-Data/SupplyChainInsights /sustainable-dyeing-solutions/Sustainable-Dyeing -Solutions-02-10.pdf.

29. Aarti Sharma (2013). "Swoosh and Sustainability: Nike's Emerging as a Global Sustainable Brand." *Sustainable Brands,* May 17. Accessed October 21, 2013, http://www.sustainablebrands.com /news_and_views/supply_chain/swoosh-and -sustainability-nikes-emergence-global -sustainable-brand.

Labeling Regulations and Guidelines for Manufactured Apparel

CHAPTER NINE

Objectives:

- To examine garment labeling regulations for key major consumer markets around the globe

- To gain awareness of regulatory bodies overseeing and enforcing labeling regulations for apparel items

Textile and garment labeling is regulated by governments in an effort to protect consumers and provide them with information about apparel products. By doing so, consumers can make informed purchase decisions and properly maintain the garments. The variance in textile labeling regulations has become a challenge for apparel brands exporting merchandise to different countries around the globe. When apparel items are imported or manufactured within a country and then sold to a consumer, there are specific labeling regulations for that country that must be met before goods can be sold. Currently, there is

no international standard for labeling that is accepted worldwide, so firms must carefully navigate through the variance of regulatory complexity. Each country or area around the globe has standards and regulations with which they must comply in order to ship goods into that country or region and sell them. Some countries do not require labeling to be affixed to garments at the point of entry when they are cleared through customs. In these instances, the goods must either be accompanied by documentation providing the necessary information or provided with the contact information for the labeler. Inspections are required to be completed after labeling has been affixed and approved prior to the sale of any products. Mandatory labeling regulations for textile and apparel products require compliance and are enforced by government. These regulations must be taken very seriously to avoid fines and delays in shipment and delivery of goods to their retail destinations or to the final consumer. If mandatory regulations are not met within a specified amount of time, the goods can be confiscated.

Although some countries may not require disclosure of care labeling for garments to legally enter into commerce, it is important for product developers to consider their prominence in relation to quality and customer satisfaction. During the product development process, designers select materials for use in finished garments. The fiber content and care of all of the garment components must carefully be considered to avoid compatibility problems with the finished products that compromise quality. Fiber content and care methods for garment parts can be tested to ensure compatibility. When fiber content and proper-care labeling instruction is determined during the design process, this information can be conveyed to the merchandising and quality assurance departments, as well as importers, wholesalers, and retailers who should consider the quality in serviceability and provide this information to consumers.

OVERVIEW OF LABELING ACTS AND REGULATIONS

Garment labeling regulations for the United States, Canada, the European Union, and Japan will be summarized in this chapter. For a comprehensive chart and links to labeling requirements for a variety of other countries, visit the International Trade Associations Office of Textiles and Apparel (OTEXA) website and select labeling requirements (http://otexa.ita.doc .gov/). Mandatory labeling content can vary depending upon the country, but at minimum includes disclosure of fiber content. Content that is not enforceable by law but can be included to assist the customer when making purchases and maintaining

the product is known as voluntary or non-required content. Information disclosed on garment labels can influence a buyer's or customer's decision of whether to purchase a product and also provide cues that will impact their perception of quality. If any information on a garment label is misrepresented or misleading, it is punishable by law.

United States Garment Labeling Regulations

In the United States, the Federal Trade Commission (FTC) oversees the Textile Fiber Products Identification Act, the Wool Products Labeling Act, Fur Products Labeling Act, and the Rule on Care Labeling of Textile Wearing Apparel and Certain Piece Goods. Labeling content required under these Acts (excluding the Care Labeling Rule) includes accurate disclosure of fiber content, country of origin, and identification of the manufacturer, importer, or distributer. Guidelines for refurbishment are inclusive of the Care Labeling Rule. Enforcement of these regulations is shared by the FTC as well as the U.S. Customs and Border Protection Agency (CBP).[1]

Textile Fiber Products Identification Act

In section 16 of the Code of Federal Regulations (CFR), part 303, the rules under the **Textile Fiber Products Identification Act (TFPIA)** are defined for labeling garments and advertising textile products.[2] English terms must be used for disclosure of all required content but can be accompanied by other languages. Labeling requirements do not apply until a product is finished and ready to be sold. If components or garments are shipped at an intermediate stage of production and, therefore, are not yet labeled with the required information, the shipment must be accompanied by an invoice that discloses the following information: fiber content, country of origin, name and address of the company issuing the invoice, and the manufacturer or dealer's identity. Garment labels must be permanently affixed for the useful life of the product and located in a conspicuous area on the inside or outside of the product. If the garment has a neckline, the label must be attached to the center of the neck on the inside of the item. Information required by law for inclusion under this act should be disclosed in the following order: fiber content, registered identification number or identity of manufacturer, or importer, distributor or retailer, and country of origin. All required information must appear in the same lettering style and be of equal size without using abbreviations.[2,3] There is one exception to this rule: Abbreviations are accepted for use for specific country names when designating country of origin (such as USA, and GT. Britain).[3] The abbreviation of the name should clearly indicate the country without causing any confusion as to the origin of the product.

Rules for listing fiber content are very specific. Fiber content can be listed on the front or back side of the label as long as it is easily visible to the consumer. Generic fiber names are required to be used for identification on fiber content labels but can be accompanied by the respective trademarked fiber name—brand names of fibers cannot be used alone. For example, a fiber content label can state 90% Cotton, 10% Spandex, or 90% Cotton, 10% Lycra® Spandex. The percentage of each fiber must be listed in order of predominance by weight, starting with the highest percentage and progressing to the lowest. If a garment contains 5 percent or more of a hair or fur fiber (skin removed) derived from an animal "other than the sheep, lamb, Angora goat, Cashmere goat, camel, alpaca, llama, or vicuna," the name of the animal can be stated but is not required.[2,3] Examples of acceptable disclosures include 80% Rabbit hair, 20% Acrylic; 80% Wool, 20% Mink fiber; or 60% Nylon, 40% Fur fiber." For disclosure requirements for listing fiber content of wool or fur (skin attached) from animals, see the following sections summarizing the Wool Products Labeling Act or the Fur Products Labeling Act. Any fiber(s) less than 5 percent should be designated as Other fiber or combined and listed as Other fibers. According to the Bureau of Consumer Protection Business Center, a division of the FTC, "If there are multiple, non-functionally significant fibers present in amounts of less than 5 percent each, they should be designated with their aggregate

percentage, even if it is greater than 5 percent".[3] For example, a garment can be labeled as 70% Cotton, 20% Polyester, 10% Other fibers. If a fiber is less than 5 percent of the weight of the product but serves a significant function such as adding stretch, durability, or warmth to a garment, the fiber can be listed as a percentage less than 5 percent, but must adequately serve the function in the quantities contained within the product. However, the function does not have to be disclosed on the label. For example, a pair of leggings may be labeled as 97% Cotton, 3% Spandex. The function of the spandex fiber is to assist with stretch and recovery of the fabric so the garment will move with the wearer and maintain its shape better than a pair of leggings containing 100 percent cotton. The term *percent*, *per centum*, or the percent symbol (%) must follow the fiber name on the label except if the product is composed of only one fiber, in which case it can be listed as "All" followed by the fiber name. For example, a t-shirt composed solely of cotton fiber can be listed on the fiber content label as All Cotton or 100% Cotton. In the case where a garment contains different fiber compositions for different parts of the garment, the fiber content should be disclosed in distinct sections, such as Body 100% Cotton, Sleeves 80% Cotton, 20% Polyester. A 3 percent tolerance is allowed for fiber content percentages when more than one fiber is listed on a garment label. However, if any fiber percentage contains a variance greater than 3 percent of the fiber's total weight that is listed on the label it is deemed as non-compliant because the fiber content is misrepresented.[2,3]

There are components of garments that are excluded from fiber content disclosure rules if they meet specific parameters. Items for exclusion include structural components, trimmings, non-fibrous materials, and minimal quantities of ornamentation. Thread, elastic materials, linings, interlinings, filling, and padding materials do not have to be disclosed if they only serve a structural function. However, if the lining, interlining, filling, or padding is used to add warmth to the garment, the fiber content must be disclosed. For example, the filling adds warmth to a ski jacket; therefore, it must be disclosed on the label as

Shell 100% Nylon, Filling 100% Polyester. Garment trimmings such as collars, cuffs, waistbands, wristbands, leg bands, gussets, gores, welts, braiding, rick-rack, binding, tape, belting, labels, and elastic materials that add structural support, reinforcement, or a means for holding a garment or section in place are also exempt from this regulation. Garment components composed of non-fibrous materials such as buttons, zippers, beads, sequins, leather patches, and painted designs do not have to be disclosed. Decoration on an apparel item includes trim, embroidery, appliques, or overlays. The words *Exclusive of Decoration* should be listed on a fiber content label when trim is composed of a different fiber than the shell fabric and accounts for less than 15 percent of the products surface area. Ornamentation is defined by the FTC as "any fibers or yarns imparting a visibly discernable pattern or design to a yarn or a fabric."[2] The words *Exclusive of Ornamentation* should be stated when the fiber ornamentation does not exceed 5 percent of the product's fiber weight. Furthermore, if the decorative trim or ornamentation or decorative pattern or design exceeds 15 percent of the surface area of the product and 5 percent of the fiber weight, the fiber content must be disclosed. The words *Exclusive of Elastic* should be used when the elastic material is an integral part of the shell fabric of the product and does not exceed 20 percent of the surface area. If the elastic exceeds 20 percent of the surface area, the fiber must be disclosed.[2,3]

The second requirement for disclosure of information on a garment label is the name of the company or **registration number (RN)** issued and registered by the FTC for the purpose of identifying the manufacturer, importer, or distributor of apparel products. Registered identification numbers are only issued to U.S. businesses that handle textile, wool, or fur products by means of manufacturing, importing, marketing, distributing, or selling textile, wool or fur products. This identification number can be used only by the company it is issued to; therefore, the number is not transferable. If a business taking part in one of the previously listed functions does not possess an

RN, they can still operate using the full name of the company. When the name of the company is used in lieu of an RN, all business documents must use this same name. There are several options for disclosing this information on the labels of imported garments, which include the name of the foreign manufacturer or the RN or the name of the importer, wholesaler, or retailer.[2,3] If the retailer's RN is used there must be consent to avoid misrepresentation. According to the Bureau of Consumer Protect, a division of the FTC, a business cannot use "a trademark, trade name, brand, label, or designer name—unless that name is also the name under which the company is doing business."[3] The FTC has the right to terminate the use of an RN number if a business has violated regulations for use or if they see it is in the best interest of protecting the consumer.[2,3] At one time the FTC issued **wool products labeling (WPL) numbers** for businesses manufacturing, importing, or distributing wool products. Although WPL numbers are no longer issued, businesses can still use their assigned number because only one RN or WPL number can be issued to a company. The FTC provides an online directory for RN and WPL numbers, so anyone can look up a U.S. business manufacturing, importing, distributing, or selling textile, wool, or fur apparel products.[2,3,4] This database can be found at http://business.ftc.gov /content/registered-identification-number-database. Under the regulations set forth in the Textile Fiber Products Identification Act, RN, WPL number, or business name can be located on the front or back of the label as long as it is in a conspicuous location that is easily accessible to the consumer.

The last required item for disclosure on a garment label is country of origin, which must be located on the front of the label. Country of origin must state where the textile fiber, fabric, and product were processed or manufactured. When a product is manufactured in a different country than the fabric or the yarn, in case of knits, the label should state the origin of the yarn or fabric and the country where the garment was produced. For example, a sweater made in the United States from yarn imported from Italy would be listed as Made in USA of Imported Yarn, or Knitted in USA of Imported Yarn. Another example would be a pair of trousers manufactured in China from fabric made in Italy. The label could state Made in China, Fabric Made in Italy. All countries must be listed using the designated English name with exception of variant spellings such as Brasil (Brazil) or Italie (Italy), which are accepted.[2,3]

Wool Products Labeling Act of 1939

In Section 16 of the Code of Federal Regulations (CFR) part 300, the rules under the **Wool Products Labeling Act of 1939** govern the accurate disclosure of information on labels affixed to garments containing any amount of wool fiber.[3] The basic rules of the Textile Fiber Products Identification Act for listing RN, WPL number, company name, country of origin, and most fiber content disclosure requirements remain consistent; however, there are differences for listing fiber content specifically related to disclosure of wool fibers outlined under the Wool Products Labeling Act. This section will focus on the distinct differences for wool products labeling.

According to the FTC, "the term *wool* may be used for fiber made from the fleece of the sheep or lamb, and the hair of the Angora goat [listed as mohair], Cashmere goat [listed as cashmere], camel, alpaca, llama, or vicuna."[3] However, when the fur or hair is attached to the skin of the animal, it is governed under the Fur Products Labeling Act. Specialty fiber names can be listed in lieu of the generic term wool. If a manufacturer chooses to specify the specialty fibers contained in a garment, they must be designated by specific percentages by weight. For example, a sweater can be labeled All Wool, 100% Wool, or when specialty fibers are designated by percentage, 86% Wool, 14% Cashmere can be used. If any wool fiber is reprocessed the term *recycled* must accompany the fiber name and percentage on the garment label, such as 100% Recycled Wool. The terms *virgin* or *new* can be used only on a wool garment label when all of the fiber is derived from virgin or new fiber. For products containing wool fiber, the Wool Products Labeling Act requires any amount of wool, including weights less than 5 percent, to be disclosed by name; "Other fiber" cannot be used. For example, a sweater containing a blend of fibers should be listed as 67% Wool, 30% Nylon, 3% Cashmere. Additionally, wool products containing linings, interlinings, paddings, stiffening, and trim must be separately disclosed on the label.[2,3]

Fur Products Labeling Act

In section 16 of the Code of Federal Regulations (CFR) part 301, the rules under the **Fur Products Labeling Act (FPLA)** govern the accurate disclosure of information on labels affixed to garments containing any amount of fur fiber.[6] As with the Wool Products Labeling Act, the basic disclosure rules of the Textile Fiber Products Identification Act for listing fiber content, RN, WPL number, or company name, and country of origin remain consistent with some differences specifically related to disclosing fur fibers and country of origin outlined under the Fur Products Labeling Act. This section will focus on the distinct differences for fur products labeling.

The size and contents of the actual label for use in products containing fur are very specific. The smallest allowed size for a fur product label is 13/4 inches by 23/4 inches, or 4.5 cm by 7 cm, and must be easily visible and securely attached to the product until it is purchased by the customer. The typeface used on the label must be a minimum font size of 12 point and use a consistent size lettering and style for all information disclosed.[6,7] Labeling content required for fur products must all be located on one side of the label. The style number or lot and the garment size are the only additional contents that can be stated on the label side containing the required information. All other content must be located on a different side. The label must state the following information in this exact order. The term *natural* should appear on the label if the color of the fur has not been altered. Otherwise, one of the following terms should be used to designate the color treatment of the fur such as *pointed, bleached, tip-dyed*, or *dyed*. If the fur has been altered through sheering, plucking, or letting-out, this can be indicated on the label; however, it is not required. The name of the fur-bearing animal must be disclosed using the appropriate name designated by the Fur Products Name Guide. The animal's originating country, stated in adjective form, can be listed preceding the animal name but is not required. For example, mink fur from Russia can be listed as Russian Mink. When the product consists of pieces of fur exceeding 10 percent of the garment's surface area being comprised "in whole of backs or in whole or in substantial part of paws, tails, bellies, sides, flanks, gills, ears, throats, heads, scrap pieces, or waste fur," this information can be voluntarily listed following the name of the animal.[6,7] The fur fiber content descriptions and origin are followed by country of origin. When the originating country is listed as part of the animal's origin it cannot be used in place of separately listing country of origin of the fur on the garment label. For example, the country of origin for mink fur from Russia should be listed as Fur Origin: Russia. The RN or company name can be listed before the fiber content information on the garment label or listed following country of origin.[6,7] If a garment is composed of other fibers in addition to fur they will be listed in accordance with the Textile Products Fiber Identification Act or the Wool Products Labeling Act.

The sale of garments made with fur from endangered species or from dogs or cats is prohibited in the United States. In 2000, the Dog and Cat Protection Act was put in place to forbid the import, export, distribution, or sale of any product made with fiber derived from domestic cat (genus-species felis catus) or dog (genus-species canis familiaris) fur.[6,7] The U.S. Congress also passed the Truth in Fur Labeling Act in December of 2010. Prior to this legislation, any fur product having a component value of less than $150 or was sold at a retail cost of $150 or less was exempt from the requirements of disclosure under the Fur Products Labeling Act. Any products sold after March 2012 containing any amount of fur must be disclosed on the label and be in full compliance with the Fur Products Labeling Act.

Care Labeling of Textile Wearing Apparel and Certain Piece Goods

In section 16 of the Code of Federal Regulations (CFR) part 423 **Care Labeling of Textile Wearing Apparel and Certain Piece Goods** outlines required content and order of placement for non-harmful routine refurbishment methods for disclosure on labels. Care labels provide instructions for cleaning that will not cause damage to the item and must be permanently affixed and legible for the useful life of the product. Symbols may be used on garment labels and can be accompanied by terms to provide clarification for consumers. *ASTM D5489 Standard Guide for Care Symbols for Care Instructions on Textile Products* is approved for use in the United States. and is also used by other NAFTA countries (Canada and Mexico).[8,9,10,11] See Figure 9.1 for the ASTM Guide to Care Symbols. Applicable care label content should be listed in the following order: wash, bleach, dry, iron, dryclean. Washing instructions or drycleaning should be designated on the label. In the case where a garment cannot be safely drycleaned or washed without causing harm to it, the label must state Do Not Dryclean, Do Not Wash. Warnings must be stated on the care label to caution consumers if there is a procedure they might use during refurbishment that will cause damage to the product. Warnings can include do not wash, do not bleach, do not machine dry, do not dryclean, do not wring, do not steam, do not iron decoration, wash before wearing, wash separately, wash with like colors, wash inside out, do not spin, do not wring, and so on.[8,10]

When washing is appropriate for the routine care of a garment, washing, bleaching, drying, ironing, and warning instructions must be disclosed on the care label as applicable. The washing method—machine wash or hand wash—and water temperature—cold, warm, or hot—must be included unless the hottest water can be routinely used without harming the apparel item. In this case the temperature of the wash bath does not have to be listed. Wash modifiers can also be used such as delicate/gentle or permanent press cycles. Bleach instructions are not required if all types of consumer bleach, chlorine or oxidizing both,

Valued Quality. Delivered.

American Care Labeling

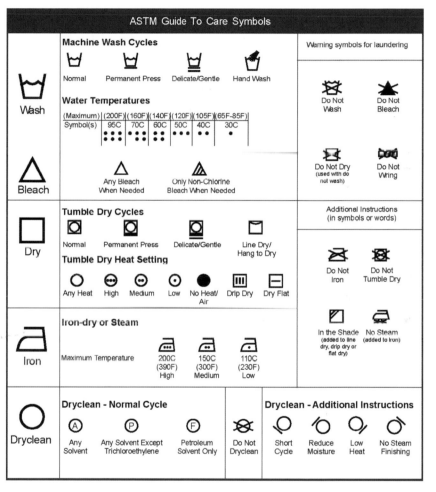

Note: This figure illustrates the symbols to use for laundering and drycleaning instructions. As a minimum, laundering instructions should include, in order, four symbols: washing, bleaching, drying and ironing; drycleaning instructions shall include one symbol. Additional words may be used to clarify the instructions.

Figure 9.1 ASTM guide to care symbols
Courtesy of Intertek

can safely be used on a routine basis without harming the product. When bleach will damage the product the label should state Nonchlorine Bleach Only or Do Not Bleach. The method for drying—machine, line/hang to dry, or dry flat—must be designated. If machine dry is designated it must state Tumble Dry and be accompanied by temperature, air/no heat, low, permanent/durable press, or medium, unless the hottest temperature can be used on a routine basis without damaging the product. Drying modifier can also be used such as remove promptly, drip dry, line dry in shade, line dry away from heat, block or reshape to dry, or smooth by hand. If the apparel item requires routine ironing to maintain the appearance, the term *iron accompanied by temperature, cool/lowest setting, or warm* must be disclosed unless the hottest iron will not harm the garment. Ironing modifiers can be listed, such as iron inside out/wrong side, dry iron, steam press/iron, or steam only.[8,10] When the term *dryclean* is used on a care label, it must be accompanied by the type of solvent, perchlorethylene, petroleum, or fluorocarbon, unless any solvent can safely be used. The phrase *dryclean only* cannot be used on a garment label if the item can be safely washed.[8,10] The words *leather clean* should be used for leather and suede products requiring special care methods for these types of animal derived materials.[12]

Canadian Garment Labeling Regulations

In Canada, the Competition Bureau (Bureau de la Concurrence Canada) oversees the Textile Labelling Act R.S.C., 1985, c.T-10 and Textile Labelling and Advertising Regulations (TLAR) C.R.C., c.1551, which are enforced by the Minister of Justice.[13,14,15] In the Legislation Revision and Consolidation Act, subsections 31(1) and (3), the rules under the Textile Labelling Act are explained for labeling garments and textile products.[13] Guidelines for adhering to this act are found in the **Textile Labelling and Advertising Regulations**. Label content must be stated in a bilingual manner using both English and French terms.

Words should be legible and stated using the same lettering style and size and all required information must be located on one side of the label. Garment labels must be permanently affixed to the apparel item in a conspicuous area at the time of sale and must remain legible for a minimum of ten cleanings.[14,15] A manufacturer, processes, or finisher of apparel can import textile products into Canada that are not yet labeled with the required disclosures if information regarding the following is provided prior to or at the time of entry: a statement of intention to import of goods that provides the date and location if importation; the quantity and type of product; and the physical address where the products will be labeled for compliance with the Textile Labeling Act and Regulations for Labelling and Advertising Regulations. When the goods are properly labeled they must be inspected to confirm compliance prior to sale.[14,15]

Labeling content required under the Textile Labelling and Advertising Regulations includes accurate disclosure of fiber content and identification of the manufacturer, importer, or distributor. Information that is not mandatory for inclusion on a garment label in Canada includes trademark names, size, and care.[15] Although these items are not required, they can be voluntarily disclosed to assist the customer in making purchasing decisions or maintaining a garment after purchase. Any voluntary item disclosure on a label must be accurate.[14,15] When care instructions are provided they should comply with the National Standard of Canada—Care Labelling of Textiles (CAN/CGSB-86 1-2003) for disclosure of washing, bleaching, drying, ironing, and drycleaning instructions and warnings. Country of origin does not have to be disclosed for any products made and sold in Canada; however, any apparel product imported and sold in Canada must state the country in which it was manufactured with the words *Made in* followed by the country name. The Canadian Border Service Agency is responsible for monitoring country of origin compliance for imported goods.[16]

Rules for listing fiber content are closely paralleled with those outlined in the U.S. Textile Fiber

Products Identification Act. Generic fiber names are required for the identification of fibers represented in the amount of 5 percent or more. Each fiber must be listed by its percentage in order of predominance by weight, beginning with the highest percentage by weight to the lowest. If a garment contains hair or fur fiber derived from an animal "other than that of a sheep, lamb, angora or Kashmir goat, alpaca, vicuna, camel or llama," it must be disclosed on the label with the name of the animal accompanied by one of these terms as appropriate: *hair, fibre,* or *fur fibre.*[15] The following examples show how hair or fur fiber can be listed on a care label: wool fiber blended with mink fur fiber can be listed as 80% Wool/Laine, 20% Mink fur fibre/Vison fur fibre; or a wool garment blended with angora rabbit hair can be listed as 80% Wool/Laine, 20% Angora rabbit hair/Poil de lapin angora. If recycled fibers are used in a garment the fiber must appear on the label along with one of the following terms: *reclaimed, reprocessed,* or *reused.* Use whichever term best represents how the fibers were produced, such as 100% Reclaimed Wool/ Laine Récuperée.[15] If a garment contains only one fiber it can be listed using the word *All* or *Pure* in lieu of 100 percent and must be followed by the generic fiber name. Any fiber(s) less than 5 percent should be designated by Other fibre/Autre fibre or listed as Other fibres/Autre fibres. For example, if a garment is composed of cotton, metallic, and spandex fibers, those less than 5 percent can be reported in the aggregate such as 92% Cotton/Coton 8% Other fibers/Autres fibres.[15] If an elastic fiber is less than 5 percent of the weight of the product, it can be listed as a percentage less than 5 percent (for example, 98% Cotton/ Coton 2% Spandex or 98% Cotton/Coton 2% Other fibre/Autre fibre).[9,10] According to the Competition Bureau, "an elastic yarn present in an amount of less than 5 percent may be disclosed as 'Exclusive of Elastic,' provided that the total of the other fiber(s) disclosed equals 100%."[14,15]

Structural components such as interlinings, linings, fillings, or paddings do not require disclosure of fiber content unless they are added to the garment for warmth. When added for warmth they must be disclosed separately from the shell garment fabric, such as Outer shell/Extérieur: 100% Cotton/Coton, Filling/Remplissage: 100% Polyester.[15] Reinforcement yarns can be disclosed using the term *Exclusive of Reinforcement* when the yarn is less than 5 percent of the weight of the product. When the reinforcement yarn is present in quantities greater than percent, the generic fiber name and percentage must be listed. Ornamentation is defined by the Competition Bureau as "textile fibre product that is present as an integral part of the article for a decorative purpose, that imparts a visibly discernable overall pattern or design, and that differs in fiber content from the remainder of the article."[15] The words *Exclusive of Ornamentation* should be stated when the fiber ornamentation does not exceed 5 percent of the product's fiber weight, as long as the total fiber weight of the product equals 100 percent. The words *Exclusive of Trimming* should be listed on a fiber content label when the trim added for decorative purposes is composed of a different fiber than the shell fabric and accounts for less than 15 percent of the product's surface area. Trim includes "embroidery, applique, braid, lace, ribbon, smocking threads, patch pockets, ruffles, piping, belts, rick rack, collars, and cuffs."[15] Findings are excluded and do not require disclosure on a garment label. A 5 percent tolerance is allowed for fiber content percentages when more than one fiber is listed on a garment label (excluding down and feather). If any fiber percentage contains a variance greater than 5 percent of the fiber's total weight listed on the label, it is deemed as non-compliant because the fiber content is misrepresented.[14,15]

The other mandatory requirement for disclosure on a garment label is the name of the company or identification number known as the **CA number** issued by the Competition Bureau for the purpose of identifying the manufacturer, importer, or distributor of apparel products. CA numbers are issued only to Canadian businesses that handle textile products by means of manufacturing, importing, marketing, distributing, and selling. This identification number can be used only by the business it is issued to but can be transferable if the Competition Bureau is notified in writing. If a business does not have a CA number it can still operate using the full name and postal address as the dealer's identity. When this information is used, the address provided on the product label must comply with Canadian post guidelines.[14,15] CA numbers can be accessed through an online directory so anyone can look up a Canadian business manufacturing, importing, or distributing apparel products. This database can be found on the Competition Bureau's website www.competitionbureau.gc.ca.

European Union Garment Labeling Regulations

On October 18, 2011, a new regulation for the labeling of textile products was enacted for the United Kingdom (UK) and all member states as well as the European Union (EU), repealing all other previous EU and UK regulations for labeling textile products. Enforcement of the **Textile Products (Labelling and Fibre Composition) Regulations** began May 18, 2012; however, any product on the market labeled in compliance with previous regulations can be sold until November 9, 2014, at which time the product would need to be relabeled to meet the new regulation prior to sale.[17,18] The European Commission oversees this regulation that is monitored and enforced by the Secretariat-General, the Local Weights and Measure authorities of Great Britain, and the Department of Enterprise and Trade and Investment in Northern Ireland.[17,19]

Labeling content required under the Textile Products (Labelling and Fibre Composition) Regulations 2012 includes accurate disclosure of fiber content only. The following items slated for future consideration of the European Parliament and the Council for unified (union-wide) regulatory compliance for all members in the union include standards for origin labeling designating country of origin and traceability of textile products (i.e., manufacturer, importer, or distributor), a system for uniform size labeling, coordinated care labeling system, disclosure of allergenic substances, and electronic labeling.[18] Currently each member country of the EU must comply with the fiber content labeling requirements under the new Textile Products Regulations; all other labeling content varies by country as to additional mandatory and voluntary content for garment labels. Any voluntarily disclosed item on a label must be accurate.[19,20] See Table 9.1 for a summary of mandatory and voluntary garment labeling content requirements for each EU member country and the language required. When care labeling is required the ISO standard 3758 recommends the use of the GINETEX care system. GINETEX is the International Organization for Textile Care Labeling. The GINETEX care system is composed of care symbols that are registered as international trademarks; therefore, a contract specifying the license agreement is required for use. The GINETEX care symbols are accepted by most European and Asian countries (see Figure 9.2) for disclosure of washing, bleaching, drying, ironing, and drycleaning instructions and warnings.[11,21] All required information should be disclosed in the same lettering style and size without using any abbreviations. Labels must be durable and attached to the garment in an area readily visible to the consumer. This regulation does not require labels to be permanently affixed to the garment by means of stitching or directly printing onto the garment. Gummed labels, swing tickets, or printed packaging are acceptable methods for conveying this information.[17]

Generic fiber names are required for disclosure on content labels using the English language and cannot be abbreviated. The percentage of each fiber must be listed in order of predominance by weight, starting with the highest percentage and progressing to the lowest. If a garment contains only one fiber it can be listed using the word *All* or *Pure* in lieu of 100 percent and followed by the generic fiber name. For example, it can be listed as 100% Cotton, All Cotton, or Pure Cotton. Any fiber present in an amount less than 5 percent should be designated by Other fiber. Furthermore, if these individual fibers (less than 5 percent of the weight of the garment) collectively represent no more than 15 percent, they can

Table 9.1 Summary of Garment Labeling Content Requirements for EU Members

Country	Language	Origin (Country, Manufacturer Importer, Trader, Retailer Identification)	Care	Size
Austria	German	Voluntary	Mandatory	Voluntary
Belgium	Official Language of Region*	Voluntary	Voluntary	Voluntary
Bulgaria	Bulgarian**	Voluntary	Voluntary	Voluntary
Cyprus	Greek	Voluntary	Mandatory	Voluntary
Czech Republic	Czech	Mandatory (Country)	Mandatory	Mandatory
Denmark	Danish	Voluntary	Voluntary	Voluntary
Estonia	Estonian	Mandatory (Country and Manufacturer)	Mandatory	Mandatory
Finland	Finnish or Swedish	Mandatory (Country, Manufacturer, and Importer)	Voluntary	Voluntary
France	French	Voluntary	Voluntary	Voluntary
Germany	German	Voluntary	Voluntary	Voluntary
Greece	Greek	Mandatory Manufacturer and Trademark Country for Wool Yarns only	Voluntary	Voluntary
Hungary	Hungarian	Mandatory Country	Mandatory	Mandatory
Ireland	Irish or English	Voluntary	Voluntary	Voluntary
Italy	Italian	Mandatory Manufacturer, Importer, or Retailer	Voluntary	Voluntary
Latvia	Latvian	Voluntary	Voluntary	Voluntary
Lithuania	Lithuanian	Mandatory Country	Mandatory	Mandatory
Luxembourg	French or German	Voluntary	Voluntary	Voluntary
Malta	English or Maltese	Voluntary	Voluntary	Voluntary
Netherlands	Dutch	Voluntary	Voluntary	Voluntary
Poland	Polish	Mandatory Country, Manufacturer	Mandatory	Mandatory
Portugal	Portuguese	Mandatory Country	Voluntary	Voluntary
Romania	English or Romanian	Mandatory Country	Mandatory	Voluntary
Slovak Republic	Slovak	Voluntary	Voluntary	Voluntary
Slovenia	Slovenia	Mandatory Country	Mandatory	Mandatory
Spain	Spanish	Mandatory Manufacturer, Importer, or Trader	Voluntary	Voluntary
Sweden	Swedish	Voluntary	Voluntary	Voluntary
United Kingdom	English	Voluntary	Voluntary	Voluntary

Note: Language specifies the language(s) required or acceptable for use on garment labels.

*Belgium requires labeling to be disclosed in the official language of the region where the product is sold (i.e., French, Dutch, German).

**English, German, and French languages are also accepted.

Sources: http://web.ita.doc.gov/tacgi/overseasnew.nsf/d1c13cd06af5e3a9852576b20052d5d5/fad8900a6a29da2b8525789d0049ea04?OpenDocument; http://web.ita.doc.gov/tacgi/overseasnew.nsf/annexview/EU+Member+Labeling+Requirements

Valued Quality. Delivered.

European Care Labeling

The ISO care labeling standard ISO 3758 was prepared by Technical Committee ISO/TC 38, Textiles, Subcommittee SC2, Cleansing, finishing, and water resistance tests. The care symbols used in this standard was established based on the GINETEX care labeling system, the symbols are registered as international trademarks. GINETEX has 18 member countries, the national committees are given a mandate to represent GINETEX to insure the correct use of the care symbols in their national territory. For details, please visit http://ginetex.info/ginetex/.

The first and second editions ISO 3758 were published in 1991 and 2005. The third edition ISO 3758:2012 has been published and replaces the previous version of the standard (ISO 3758:2005). Key changes are the addition of symbols for natural drying processes and the change of 'Do not bleach' symbol. The previous version used a blackened triangle; in the 2012 version this has now reverted back to a lined version. The care symbols used in ISO 3758: 2012 consist of 5 main treatments and shall appear in the order washing, bleaching, drying, ironing and professional textile care.

Symbol	Washing Process
95	- maximum washing temperature 95°C normal process
70	- maximum washing temperature 70°C normal process
60	- maximum washing temperature 60°C normal process
60	- maximum washing temperature 60°C mild process
50	- maximum washing temperature 50°C normal process
50	- maximum washing temperature 50°C mild process
40	- maximum washing temperature 40°C normal process
40	- maximum washing temperature 40°C mild process
40	- maximum washing temperature 40°C very mild process
30	- maximum washing temperature 30°C normal process
30	- maximum washing temperature 30°C mild process
30	- maximum washing temperature 30°C very mild process
(hand)	- wash by hand maximum temperature 40°C
⊠	- do not wash

Symbol	Bleaching Process
△	- any bleaching agent allowed
⚠	- only oxygen / non-chlorine bleach allowed
⊠	- do not bleach

Symbol	Tumble Drying Process
⊙ (two dots)	- tumble drying possible - normal temperature - maximum exhaust temperate 80°C
⊙ (one dot)	- tumble drying possible - drying at lower temperature - maximum exhaust temperature 60°C
⊠	- do not tumble dry

Symbol	Natural Drying Process
▯	- line drying
▯▯	- drip line drying
—	- flat drying
＝	- drip flat drying
◩	- line drying in the shade
◩	- drip line drying in the shade
◲	- flat drying in the shade
◲	- drip flat drying in the shade

Symbol	Ironing Process
⊿ (···)	- iron at a maximum sole-plate temperature of 200°C
⊿ (··)	- iron at a maximum sole-plate temperature of 150°C
⊿ (·)	- iron at a maximum sole-plate temperature of 110°C without steam steam ironing may cause irreversible damage
⊠	- do not iron

Symbol	Professional Textile Care Process
Ⓟ	- professional dry cleaning in tetrachloroethene and all solvents listed for the symbol F normal process
Ⓟ	- professional dry cleaning in tetrachloroethene and all solvents listed for the symbol F mild process
Ⓕ	- professional dry cleaning in hydrocarbons (distillation temperature between 150°C and 210°C, flash point between 38°C and 70°C) normal process
Ⓕ	- professional dry cleaning in hydrocarbons (distillation temperature between 150°C and 210°C, flash point between 38°C and 70°C) mild process
⊠	- do not dry clean
Ⓦ	- professional wet cleaning normal process
Ⓦ	- professional wet cleaning mild process
Ⓦ	- professional wet cleaning very mild process
⊠	- do not professional wet clean

Figure 9.2 ISO/GINETEX care symbols
Courtesy of Intertek

be listed in the aggregate as Other fibers. Fiber from the fleece of sheep or lamb, as well as hair fibers from alpaca, llama, camel, Cashmere goat, Angora goat, Angora rabbit, vicuna, yak, guanaco, Cashgora goat, beaver, and otter[18] can be labeled as wool. For example, a garment containing a mixture of fibers from a sheep fleece and fibers from an angora goat can be listed in one of two ways: 100% Wool, or can express the mohair content separately as in 60% Mohair 40% Wool. If the terms *Fleece Wool* or *Virgin Wool* are used on a label, the fiber comprising the garment must be 100 percent wool fiber and cannot have been recycled or reclaimed from another finished garment. The phrase *Contains non-textile parts of animal origin* must be used on a garment label when the product contains any portion of an animal such as horn, bone, fur (skin attached), or leather.[17] In the case where a garment contains different fiber compositions for different parts of the garment, the fiber content should be disclosed in distinct sections such as Body 100% Cotton, Sleeves 80% Cotton 20% Polyester. A 2 percent tolerance is allowed for fiber content percentages listed on a garment label unless they have been through a carding process prior to spinning, in which case a 5 percent tolerance is allowed. However, if any fiber percentage contains a variance greater than the allowed percent of the fiber's total weight that is listed on the label, it is deemed as non-compliant because the fiber content is misrepresented.[17]

Garment components that are excluded from fiber content disclosure labels include fiber decoration and certain parts of garments. Fibers used in a garment to create a specific visible decorative effect in amounts less than 7 percent of the weight of the product do not have to be disclosed. Apparel products that have fibers added in amounts less than 2 percent for the specific function of static prevention do not have to be listed. Additionally, product parts that are not an integral part of the product can be excluded from fiber content labels. Product parts that do not have to be disclosed include labels, trim, findings, elastic, decoration, thread, interlinings, and reinforcements.[17]

Japanese Garment Labeling Regulations

In Japan, The Minister of Economy oversees and enforces the **Textile Goods Quality Labeling Regulations** for apparel products that are published in the *Household Goods Quality Labeling Law Handbook*. When on-site inspections are required they are conducted by the Bureau of Economy, Trade and Industry.[22,23] Labeling content required for inclusion under this regulation includes accurate disclosure of fiber content, country of origin, water repellency, manufacturer identification information, and care. All required information should be disclosed on the sewn-in label using the Japanese language, but country of origin disclosure can be made in English. Generic fiber names are required for disclosure of fiber composition on labels and can be accompanied by the brand name stated in parentheses. "For items using fillings [jackets, overcoats, topcoats, raincoats, and other coats], the cover fabric, lining fabric and filling materials (with exception of auxiliary materials used in pockets, elbows, collars etc. to partially adjust the shape) shall be indicated."[22] The percentage of each fiber must be listed in order of predominance by weight starting with the highest percentage and progressing to the lowest. Fibers such as sheep wool, Angora rabbit hair, Cashmere, mohair, camel, and alpaca can be listed as wool on a garment label.[22] All coats are required to be labeled if they are water repellant and only those labeled as such can be designated as raincoats. Country of origin must also be disclosed on apparel product labels. The manufacturer or labeler name and address or phone number must be listed prominently on the label where it is easily visible to the customer.[22,23]

Appropriate instructions for refurbishment are required to be disclosed on garment labels and must comply with the *Japanese Industrial Standard JIS L 0217-1995 Care Labelling of Textile Goods*. Under this regulation JIS care symbols (see Figure 9.3) are mandated for communicating instructions, which must be listed in the following order from left to right:

Valued Quality. Delivered.

Japanese Care Labeling

Japanese care instructions, like other care label systems, must be in a specified order. This order is washing, bleaching, ironing, dry-cleaning, wringing, and drying.

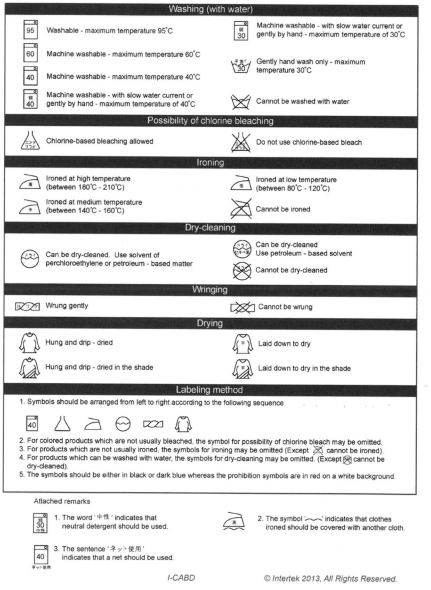

Washing (with water)		
95 — Washable - maximum temperature 95°C	弱 30 — Machine washable - with slow water current or gently by hand - maximum temperature of 30°C	
60 — Machine washable - maximum temperature 60°C	手洗 30 — Gently hand wash only - maximum temperature 30°C	
40 — Machine washable - maximum temperature 40°C		
弱 40 — Machine washable - with slow water current or gently by hand - maximum temperature of 40°C	Cannot be washed with water	

Possibility of chlorine bleaching	
エンソ サラシ — Chlorine-based bleaching allowed	Do not use chlorine-based bleach

Ironing	
高 — Ironed at high temperature (between 180°C - 210°C)	低 — Ironed at low temperature (between 80°C - 120°C)
中 — Ironed at medium temperature (between 140°C - 160°C)	Cannot be ironed

Dry-cleaning	
セキユ系 — Can be dry-cleaned. Use solvent of perchloroethylene or petroleum - based matter	セキユ系 — Can be dry-cleaned Use petroleum - based solvent
	Cannot be dry-cleaned

Wringing	
Wrung gently	Cannot be wrung

Drying	
Hung and drip - dried	平 — Laid down to dry
Hung and drip - dried in the shade	平 — Laid down to dry in the shade

Labeling method

1. Symbols should be arranged from left to right according to the following sequence

40 △ ⌐ ◡ ⋈ 👕

2. For colored products which are not usually bleached, the symbol for possibility of chlorine bleach may be omitted.
3. For products which are not usually ironed, the symbols for ironing may be omitted (Except ⊠ cannot be ironed).
4. For products which can be washed with water, the symbols for dry-cleaning may be omitted. (Except ⊗ cannot be dry-cleaned).
5. The symbols should be either in black or dark blue whereas the prohibition symbols are in red on a white background.

Attached remarks

弱 30 中性 — 1. The word ' 中性 ' indicates that neutral detergent should be used.

高 — 2. The symbol '〰' indicates that clothes ironed should be covered with another cloth.

40 ネット使用 — 3. The sentence ' ネット使用 ' indicates that a net should be used.

I-CABD

Figure 9.3 JIS care symbols
Courtesy of Intertek

washing, bleaching, ironing, drycleaning, wringing, and drying. Symbols must be communicated in blue or black with the exception of warnings, which must be listed in red. It is mandatory that warnings be stated on the care label to caution consumers if there is a procedure they might use during refurbishment that will cause damage to the product. Warnings can include the following: cannot be washed with water, do not use chlorine bleach, cannot be ironed, cannot be drycleaned, and cannot be wrung.[11,24]

When routine garment care is washing with water, the method, machine or hand wash, accompanied by the maximum water temperature, reported in Celsius, is included, followed by a symbol communicating whether chlorine bleach can safely be used. Ironing temperatures accompanied by ranges stated in Celsius should be disclosed unless ironing will damage the item and in such cases the statement "cannot be ironed" is used. Drycleaning instructions and solvent type, perchloroethylene, or petroleum, are included if the item can be safely cleaned using this method. Instructions for whether the item can be wrung are provided, followed by drying methods that include hang/drip dry, line dry, or dry flat in shade.[24]

Regardless of the country, all mandatory and voluntary labeling content must be accurately disclosed to provide consumers with information to make informed decisions regarding purchasing and care of apparel products. Manufacturers, importers, distributors, or labelers are responsible for providing documentation/proof that the method instructed on the care label will not damage the product. The proof must be gathered by means of testing the product to ensure the garment or component parts will not be adversely affected.

INDUSTRY SCENARIO 9.1 Disclosure of Country of Origin on Luxury Coats

A product developer for a prominent Italian luxury brand is designing misses' coats. The coats are made of 100 percent Cashmere with a 100 percent silk lining. The coats are manufactured in Italy and China. The garments manufactured in China are not labeled with country of origin and are only shipped to countries that do not require disclosure of country of origin on the garment label. The garments manufactured in Italy are labeled with Italy as the manufacturing country and shipped to locations that require country of origin disclosure. The quality of the finished products is comparable.

- Why would a brand manufacture the same products in China and Italy?
- Why would a brand sell only the merchandise manufactured in China to countries that do not require disclosure of country of origin on a garment label?
- Where does the brand want the customer to assume the products are made when the origin is not stated?
- Although there is nothing illegal about what this brand is doing, how does this make you feel about brands that use this type of practice?

INDUSTRY SCENARIO 9.2 Fiber Content Labeling for Fur Trimmed Parkas

A moderate wholesale brand is selling parkas for girls and boys to retailers in the United States. The parka's fiber content reads as follows Shell: 100% Nylon, Fiber Fill: 100% Polyester, Lining: 100% Polyester, Hood Trim: Natural Raccoon Fur. After several customers have questioned the fur trim, the retailer sent the parkas to a lab for testing. It is discovered that the fur on the hood is actually raccoon dog, a member of the Canidae family (dog—genus-species Canis familiaris), which is illegal to sell in the U.S. market.

- What action should the retailer take?
- What if the hood trim was, in fact, natural raccoon fur but was labeled as faux fur? What action would need to be taken for the garments to comply with fiber content labeling regulations so the parkas could be sold in the United States?

SUMMARY

In this chapter, garment labeling regulations for the major consumer markets were presented to provide a means of comparison between each country's mandatory and voluntary regulations. Manufacturers that sell apparel to different countries around the world are choosing to integrate the highest regulatory standards into their products to ensure individual mandatory regulations for labeling are being met. The regulatory bodies that oversee and enforce labeling regulations for apparel products were also introduced to increase understanding of who monitors the goods that enter into commerce.

ACTIVITIES

1. Select 15 items from your wardrobe, and read the labeling content. Does each label comply with the appropriate government standards mandated for content on garment labels? Record the labels that are not in compliance and rewrite them so they meet the standards.

2. Using the garments from activity number 1, look up the RN for each product using the FTC's RN database (http://business.ftc.gov/content/registered-identification-number-database) and record the company's name, the product line (if stated), and business type.

3. Write a care label using symbols for a garment that you own that does not provide symbols on the label.

APPAREL QUALITY LAB MANUAL

Please refer to Lab Activity 7.1 Comparison Project Garment Label Compliance; and Lab Activity 7.2 Garment Care in the *Apparel Quality Lab Manual*.

ENDNOTES

1. Keith Nuthall (2012). "just-style Management Briefing: Global Labeling Legislation a Challenge," *just-style.com*, September 3. Accessed December 24, 2012, http://www.just-style .com/management-briefing/global-labelling -legislation-a-challenge_id115444.aspx.

2. Federal Trade Commission. *Rules and Regulations Under the Textile Fiber Products Identification Act: 16 CFR Part 303*. Accessed November 14, 2012, http://www.ftc.gov/os /statutes/textile/rr-textl.shtm.

3. Bureau of Consumer Protection Business Center. *Threading Your Way Through the Labeling Requirements Under the Textile and Wool Acts*. Accessed November 14, 2012, http://business .ftc.gov/documents/bus21-threading-your-way -through-labeling-requirements-under-textile -and-wool-acts.

4. Federal Trade Commission. *Registered Identification Database*. Accessed December 24, 2012, http://www.ftc.gov/bcp/rn/index.shtml.

5. Federal Trade Commission. *Rules and Regulations Under the Wool Products Labeling Act: 16 CFR Part 300*. Accessed November 14, 2012, http://www.ftc.gov/os/statutes/textile/ woolact.htm.

6. Federal Trade Commission. *Rules and Regulations Under the Fur Products Labeling Act: 16 CFR Part 301*. Accessed November 14, 2012, http://www.ftc.gov/os/statutes/textile/furact.htm.

7. Bureau of Consumer Protection Business Center. *In-FUR-mation Alert: How to Comply with the Fur Products Labeling Act*. Accessed November 14, 2012, http://business.ftc.gov/documents /alt006-fur-mation-alert-how-comply-fur -products-labeling-act.

8. Federal Trade Commission. *Care Labeling of Textile Wearing Apparel and Certain Piece Goods, As Amended Effective September 1, 2000*. Accessed December 30, 2012, http://www.ftc .gov/os/statutes/textile/carelbl.shtm.

9. Federal Trade Commission. *16 CFR 423 Trade Regulation Rule on Care Labeling of Textile Wearing Apparel and Certain Piece Goods*. Accessed December 30, 2012, http://www.ftc .gov/os/2000/07/carelabelingrule.htm.

10. Bureau of Consumer Protection Business Center. *Clothes Captioning: Complying with the Care Labeling Rule*. Accessed December 30, 2012, http://business.ftc.gov/documents/bus50-clothes -captioning-complying-care-labeling-rule.

11. Intertek (2012). *Care Labeling: Caring About the Consumers Beyond the Label*. Accessed November 14, 2012, http://www.intertek.com /uploadedFiles/Intertek/Divisions/Consumer _Goods/Media/PDFs/Services/Low%20Res%20 CompleteCareLabelling.pdf.

12. Federal Trade Commission. *Care Labeling of Textile Wearing Apparel and Certain Piece Goods, as Amended Effective September 1, 2000: 19 CFR 423*, last modified June 24, 2011. Accessed December 30, 2012, http://www.ftc.gov/os /statutes/textile/carelbl.shtm.

13. Minister of Justice of the Canadian Government. *Textile Labelling Act.* Accessed December 27, 2012, http://www.laws.justice.gc.ca/eng/acts /T-10/FullText.html.

14. Minister of Justice of the Canadian Government. *Textile Labelling and Advertising Regulations.* Accessed December 27, 2012, http://www.laws .justice.gc.ca/eng/regulations/C.R.C.,_c._1551 /FullText.html.

15. Competition Bureau Office of Industry Canada. *Guide to the Textile Labelling and Advertising Regulations.* Accessed December 27, 2012, http://www.competitionbureau.gc.ca/eic/site /cb-bc.nsf/eng/01666.html#Bilingual.

16. International Trade Administration, Office of Textiles and Apparel (OTEXA). *Market Reports/ Tariffs: Textiles, Apparel, Footwear and Travel Goods Canada.* Accessed December 28, 2012, http://web.ita.doc.gov/tacgi/overseasnew.nsf /alldata/Canada#Labeling.

17. Department for Business Innovation & Skills (BIS) (July 2012). *Textile Labeling Regulations: Guidance on the Textile Products (Labeling and Fibre Composition) Regulations 2012.* Accessed November 14, 2012, http://webarchive .nationalarchives.gov.uk/+/http://www.bis.gov .uk/assets/biscore/consumer-issues/docs/t/12 -791-textile-labelling-regulations-guidance.pdf, pp. 1–17.

18. European Parliament and the Council. "Regulation (EU) No 1007/2011 of the European Parliament and of the Council of the 27 September 2011 on Textile Fibers and Related Labelling and Marking of the Fiber Composition of Textile Products." *Official Journal of the European Union.* Accessed December 29, 2012, http://eur-lex.europa.eu/LexUriServ/LexUriServ .do?uri=OJ:L:2011:272:0001:0064:en:pdf, pp. 1–64.

19. European Commission. *Application of EU Law.* Accessed December 29, 2012, http://ec.europa /eu/eu_law/index_en.htm.

20. International Trade Administration, Office of Textiles and Apparel (OTEXA). *EU Member Labeling Requirements.* Accessed December 29, 2012, http://web.ita.doc.gov/tacgi/overseas new.nsf/annexview/EU+Member+Labeling +Requirements.

21. GINETEX. Care Symbols. Accessed October 20, 2013, http://www.ginetex.net/labelling/care -labelling/care-symbols/.

22. Ministry of Economy, Trade, and Industry (METI) (October 2010). *Household Goods Quality Labeling Law Handbook.* Accessed December 29, 2012, http://ec.europa.eu/enterprise/tbt/tbt_repository /JPN303_EN_1_1.pdf.

23. International Trade Administration, Office of Textiles and Apparel (OTEXA). *Market Reports /Tariffs: Textiles, Apparel, Footwear and Travel Goods Japan.* Accessed December 29, 2012, http://web.ita.doc.gov/tacgi/overseasnew.nsf /alldata/Japan#Labeling.

24. Japanese Standards Association. "Japanese Industrial Standard: Care Labeling of Textile Goods, JIS L 0217-1995, 3rd ed." *Standardization Journal,* Tokyo, pp. 1–13.

Safety Regulations and Guidelines for Wearing Apparel

CHAPTER TEN

Objectives:

- To examine safety regulations for key major consumer markets around the globe
- To gain awareness of regulatory bodies overseeing and enforcing

safety regulations for apparel items
- To understand the importance of consumer safety regulations in relation to apparel products and the harm they may cause

When consumers purchase apparel products, they don't always think about the hazards involved with wearing garments such as toxicity, flammability, and strangulation. A product can be assembled from the highest-quality materials using the best construction techniques, but if it is not safe it is perceived by the consumer as poor quality, which can ultimately impact the reputation of the brand. The best way to prevent unsafe products from entering the marketplace is through educating and informing designers, product developers, buyers, and

manufacturers about testing products to ensure they are safe and will not cause harm to the consumer.

Consumer safety is a top priority for governments of major consumer markets in numerous countries. Manufacturers are not only responsible for producing apparel products according to designers' specifications and desired quality levels, but they must also meet the mandatory standards for safety. Factories in emerging markets are aware they need to meet safety standards in the countries in which the products will be sold. Governmental regulations have been established in an effort to provide consumers with products that are safe. Some regulations are mandatory, whereas others are voluntary. Many apparel producers choose to meet voluntary guidelines for product safety to reduce liability and provide consumers with products that will not cause them harm. Enforcement of these regulations is critical to prevent products from entering the marketplace that can injure consumers.

The responsibility of consumer safety is shared across the supply chain. Governments develop and enforce mandatory regulations or provide voluntary guidelines to help the industry provide products that are safe for sale and use by consumers. Mills, converters, finishers, and importers of materials must ensure their goods meet all applicable requirements for flammability and toxicity for the country, state, or area in which they will be sold. Designers, product developers, and manufacturers are responsible for creating products that are safe for consumer use through the design, selection, and purchase of materials, as well as providing assembly and finishing processes that comply with mandatory regulations. Garment designs should not pose strangulation or choking hazards to consumers, nor should they include materials possessing toxicity or flammability hazards. Buyers and retailers are responsible for knowing the legal requirements for goods to be sold in the locations in which their products will be sold. Lastly, it is the consumer's responsibility to read all labels and hangtags related to safety so they can be informed when making purchases. Consumers should also be knowledgeable as to how to use and care for the product to avoid causing injury to themselves or harm to others.

Safety regulations can vary greatly from country to country, and those that are mandatory in one may be voluntary in another. Although safety issues surrounding wearing apparel remain the same around the globe as well as the liability of the maker for injury to a consumer, it is surprising that all known safety hazards are not governed under compulsory regulations. The mandatory safety regulations and voluntary guidelines for garments sold in the United States, Canada, the European Union, and Japan will be discussed in this chapter.

TOXICITY REGULATIONS FOR WEARING APPAREL

Toxicity is a safety hazard resulting from wearing some apparel products. Materials containing certain types of dyes, finishes, containments, or metals that come in contact with the wearer's skin can cause mild to severe allergic reactions or dermatitis for those individuals with skin sensitivity and worse some substances have been found to be carcinogenic. Chemical substances are identified by CAS (Chemical Abstract Service) numbers, which are registration designations assigned to individual chemical substances located in the CAS database to provide information specific to a wide range of substances. CAS numbers are assigned by the American Chemical Society. The chemical substances of particular concern by one or more countries include nickel, lead, certain azo dyes, formaldehyde, fluorinated organic compounds, and certain flame retardants used in wearing apparel.

Nickel

According to the Health Protection Agency of the UK, **nickel** (CAS # 7440-02-0) is a naturally occurring chemical element found in the crust of the earth; therefore, it is detected in the air, soil, water, and atmosphere.[1,2] Consumers may also come in contact with nickel through wearing apparel containing findings made of this metal. Extended skin contact with nickel can cause excessive itching and irritation known as contact dermatitis or nickel dermatitis.[1] Nickel compounds are known to be "potent skin sensitizers," and the International Agency for the Research on Cancer (IARC) has found it to cause cancer in humans.[2]

In 2000, the UK implemented the Nickel Directive, which regulated the release of nickel from consumer products containing this metal that would have direct and prolonged exposure with the skin. In 2004, this became the EU Nickel Directive, which restricts the use of nickel in consumer products sold in the European Union. The European Commission oversees this regulation that requires compliance in all

European Union (EU) member locations in which goods will be sold.[3,4] Entry 27 Nickel Annex XVII CAS No 7440-02-0 EC No 231-111-4 states that nickel and its compounds "shall not be used: . . . (b) in products intended to come into direct and prolonged contact with the skin such as:— rivet buttons, tighteners, rivets, zippers, and metal marks, when these are used in garments, if the rate of nickel release from the parts of these articles coming into direct and prolonged contact with the skin is greater than $0.5\mu g/cm^2/week$ (0.5 microgram per square centimeter per week)."[5] Although nickel allergies and nickel dermatitis have not been totally eliminated, this directive has been credited with significantly reducing consumer medical issues throughout Europe and the UK resulting from prolonged exposure to consumer products containing nickel.[2,6]

Compliance with this regulation requires testing using the European Union harmonized standard EN 1811:2011 and EN 16128:2011, ANNEX XVII of REACH. These new standards have replaced EN 1811:1998 + A1:2008.[7] **REACH** is the European Community Regulation that stands for Registration, Evaluation, Authorization, and restriction of CHemical substances. It regulates the safe use of chemicals and publishes a directive for restricted substances found in EC 1907/2006 Annex XVII Restrictions on the Manufacture, Placing on the Market and Use of Certain Dangerous Substances, Mixtures and Articles. The REACH regulation requires manufacturers and importers to enter information into a centralized database overseen by the European Chemicals Agency (ECHA) in an effort to provide consumers and industry professions with information on managing hazardous substances.[8] At the time of publication, the United States, Canada, and Japan do not have regulations on the use of garment findings containing nickel.

Lead

Lead (CAS # 7439-92-1) is a naturally occurring chemical element found in the crust of the earth.[9] It is highly toxic, and according to the National Toxi-

cology Program in the Department of Health and Human Sciences, "lead and lead compounds are reasonably anticipated to be human carcinogens based on limited evidence from studies in humans and sufficient evidence of carcinogenicity from studies in experimental animals."[10] Exposure to lead in wearing apparel when present is through dermal contact and can be found in findings made from metal or plastic, or in textiles treated with surface coatings or printing.

Lead content in children's products for ages 12 and under is regulated and enforced by the U.S. Consumer Products Safety Commission (CPSC) under the Consumer Product Safety Improvement Act (CPSIA) and title 16 of the Code of Federal Regulations section 1303 Ban of Lead-Containing Paint and Certain Consumer Products Bearing Lead-Containing Paint.[11,12] After August 14, 2011, the total lead content for all children's wearing apparel (intended for children ages 12 and under) became restricted to a maximum of 100 ppm (parts per million).[12,13,14] The Consumer Product Safety Improvement Act stipulates that apparel made from textiles containing natural and manufactured fibers do not exceed the regulated limit for lead content if they have not been treated with screen prints, transfers, or other types of prints.[14] See Table 10.1 for a list of untreated materials that do not exceed the lead content limits. When additional treatments are used on the product that can introduce or increase the lead content, it must be tested for compliance to ensure the required lead limit is not exceeded.[15]

This regulation requires testing and certification of compliance with lead content levels of component parts (must be the same as what will be used in the finished garment) and finished products that must be completed by a third-party testing laboratory accredited by the CPSC or an approved accreditation body. Compulsory children's product certificates, as well as general conformity certificates required for other regulations, must be prepared in English but can be accompanied by another language, to identify the "manufacturer or private labeler of the product, the testing laboratory, and the date and place of manufacturing and testing the product."[16] Under this

Table 10.1 Untreated Textile Materials that Do Not Exceed Lead Content Limits*

Natural Fibers Dyed or Undyed	Manufactured Fibers Dyed or Undyed	Other Plant or Animal Materials
Cotton	Rayon	Nut shells (beads & buttons)
Kapok	Azlon	Bone (buttons, toggles)
Flax/Linen	Lyocell	Feathers
Jute	Acetate	Leather
Ramie	Triacetate	Fur
Hemp	Rubber	
Kenaf	Polyester	
Bamboo	Olefin	
Coir	Nylon	
Sisal	Acrylic	
Wool from sheep	Modacrylic	
Alpaca	Aramid	
Llama	Spandex	
Mohair		
Cashmere		
Angora rabbit hair		
Camel		
Horse		
Yak		
Vicuna		
Qiviut		
Guanaco		

Note:*Textile materials or finished garments that have not been altered/ treated by means of screen printing, transfers, or other means that could introduce lead in excess of the allowed limit.
Source: U.S. Government Printing Office (GPO), "Title 16: Commercial Practices Part 1500—Hazardous Substances and Articles; Administration and Enforcement Regulations," *Electronic Code of Federal Regulations*, January 10, 2013, http://www.ecfr.gov/cgi-bin/text-idx?c=ecfr&rgn=div8 &view=text&node=16:2.0.1.3.73.0.1.38&idno=16

regulation, any children's apparel product exceeding the allowed lead limit cannot be sold in the United States. Additionally, "the certificate must accompany the product or product shipment and must be available to CPSC and Customs and Border Protection upon request. Failure to furnish the certificate or furnishing

a false certificate can subject the manufacturer or private labeler to civil and criminal penalties."[16] At the time of publication, Canada, the EU, and Japan do not have regulations limiting the lead content in children's wearing apparel. According to the Office of Textile and Apparel (OTEXA), "Lead in buttons—Although Japanese law does not currently prohibit lead, there is a movement to ban lead in accessories."[17]

Certain Azo Dyes

According to the Chemical Inspection and Regulation Service (CIRS) of Europe, "**Azo dyes** are the name of the group of synthetic dyestuffs based on nitrogen that are often used in the textile industry. Some Azo dyestuffs may separate under certain conditions to produce carcinogenic and allergenic aromatic amines."[18] This separation is known as reductive cleavage and occurs when the azo dye is cleaved or broken down into amines. Azo dyes are used significantly for textile and leather products, accounting for 60 to 80 percent of all organic colorants, so it is important to note that only those colorants that contain aromatic amines are prohibited and account for less than 4 percent of azo dye structures.[19]

In 2002 the European Parliament and the European Union agreed to harmonize regulations for azo dyes, which became effective in September 2003. The EU AZO Colourants Directive 2002/61/EC was replaced by REACH (EC 1907/2006) under Annex XVII Restrictions on the Manufacture, Placing on the Market and Use of Certain Dangerous Substances, Mixtures and Articles, in an effort to harmonize regulatory legislation of chemicals to protect consumers. This regulation prohibits the use of certain Azo dyes "which by reductive cleavage of one or more azo groups, may release one or more of the aromatic amines (see Table 10.2) in detectable concentrations above 30 ppm in finished articles or in the dyed parts thereof, according to the test methods listed . . . shall not be used in textile and leather articles which may come into direct and prolonged contact with the human skin."[20]

Table 10.2 Azo Colorants Aromatic Amines on the REACH Restriction List

No.	Substances	CAS Number
1	biphenyl-4-ylamine-aminobiphenyl xenylamine	92-67-14
2	benzadine	92-87-5
3	4-chloro-o-toluidine	95-69-2
4	2-naphthylamine	91-59-8
5	o-aminoazotoluene 4-amino-2', 3-dimethylazobenzene 4-o-tolylazo-o-toluidine	97-56-3
6	nitro-o-toluidine	99-55-8
7	4-chloroaniline	106-47-8
8	4-methoxy-m-phenylenediamine	615-05-04
9	4,4'-methylenedianiline 4,4'-diaminodiphenylmethane	101-77-9
10	3,3'-dichlorobenzidine 3,3'-dichlororbiphenyl-4,4'-ylenediamine	91-94-1
11	3,3'-dimethoxybenzidine o-dianisidine	119-90-4
12	3,3'-dimethylbenzidine 4,4'-bi-o-toluidine	119-93-7
13	4,4'methylenedi-otoluidine	838-88-0
14	6-methylenedi-o-toluidine	120-71-8
15	4,4'-methylene-bis-(2-chloro-aniline) 2,2'-dichloro-4,4'-methylene-dianiline	101-14-4
16	4,4'-oxydianiline	101-80-4
17	4,4'-thiodianiline	139-65-1
18	o-toluidine 2-aminotoluene	95-53-4
19	4-methyl-m-phenylenediamine	95-80-7
20	2,4,5-trimethylaniline	137-17-7
21	o-ansidine 2-methozyaniline	90-04-0
22	4-amino azobenzene	60-09-3

Note: CAS (Chemical Abstract Service) number is a registration designation assigned to individual chemical substances located in the CAS database to provide information specific to a wide range of substances. CAS numbers are assigned by the American Chemical Society
Source: American Chemical Society, *CAS Registry and CAS Registry Number FAQs,* accessed January 15, 2013, http://www.cas.org/content/chemical-substances/faqs;
The European Parliament and the Council, *Regulation (EC) No 1907/2006 of the European Parliament and of the Council,* January 6, 2012, 2006R 1907 — 01.06.2012 — 012.001, accessed January 5, 2013, http://eur-lex.europa.eu/LexUriServ/LexUriServ.do?uri=CONSLEG:2006R1907:2012060 1:EN:PDF, p.512

As with nickel, the REACH regulation requires manufacturers and importers of garments containing certain azo dyes to comply by entering information into a centralized database that is overseen by the European Chemicals Agency (ECHA), in an effort to provide consumers and industry professions with information on managing hazardous substances.[8] At this time, the United States, Canada, and Japan do not have mandatory regulations restricting the use of any azo dyes used in wearing apparel; however, in 2010, the Japan Textile Federation published voluntary standards for use of azo dyes in the Voluntary Standards on Nonuse of Harmful Substances for Textiles and Clothing. This voluntary standard states that apparel products cannot contain levels of the specific aromatic amines (see Table 10.2) in amounts greater than 30 mg/kg.[21] An important aspect to note here is that voluntary standards are not enforceable.

Formaldehyde

The chemical known as **formaldehyde** (CAS # 50-00-0) is composed of hydrogen, oxygen, and carbon. According to the American Chemical Council, "All organic life forms—bacteria, plants, fish, animals and humans—make formaldehyde at various levels. Formaldehyde does not accumulate in the environment or within plants, animals or people, as metabolic processes quickly break it down in the body and the atmosphere."[22] Formaldehyde can be used as a binder for dyes and pigments when combined with other compounds or applied as a finish for some wrinkle free apparel items because it "acts as a cross-linking agent to make an easy-care finish, intended to prevent shrinkage, and gives the product crease resistant and smooth-dry properties."[23] When formaldehyde is released into the air, it can cause health related problems due to "irritation of mucous membranes and the respiratory tract."[23]

In Japan, use of a detectable level of formaldehyde or formalin, meaning 20 mg/kg or 20 ppm (.002 percent), is banned in infant clothing for ages 0–24 months under the Law for Control of Household Products

Containing Harmful Substances. Additionally, any textile product containing levels of formalin exceeding 75 ppm (.0075 percent) cannot be sold in Japan.[17] Compliance with this regulation requires testing using Japanese Law 112 or JIS L1041. Mandatory standards in Japan must be met and certified for compliance prior to sale. Japan's restricted limits for formaldehyde are much more stringent than other countries.

According to the August 2010 report, *Formaldehyde in Textiles,* published by the United States Government Accountability Office (GOA), "Formaldehyde levels in clothing and other textiles that come into contact with the skin are not regulated."[24] That said, the document goes on to state, "Formaldehyde is one of five substances [the] CPSC has identified as a strong sensitizer—a substance that can cause hypersensitivity through reoccurring contact—under the Federal Hazardous Substances Act. Therefore, formaldehyde and any products containing 1 percent of formaldehyde or more (10,000 parts per million) are required to bear a warning label . . . this reporting level for formaldehyde far exceeds amounts likely to be found in clothing."[24] The American Apparel and Footwear Association publishes a *Restricted Substance List* that states the only countries other than Japan that regulate formaldehyde in apparel products include "Poland, China, Russia, Finland, Norway, France, Netherlands, Austria, Lithuania, Germany, New Zealand, South Korea, Vietnam, [and] Taiwan."[25] For these countries, the regulated level of formaldehyde allowed in children's apparel for ages 0–36 months old is 75 ppm (0.0075 percent) which is tested for compliance using ISO 17226 or JIS L1041 test method.[25] To date, there is no harmonized EU regulation for the restricted use of formaldehyde in wearing apparel for children or adults. Canada does not regulate the use of this substance in apparel either.

Fluorinated Organic Compounds

The chemical substances known as perfluorooctane sulfonates (PFOS) (CAS # 45298-90-6) and perfluorooctanic acids (PFOA) (CAS # 335-67-1) are **fluorinated organic compounds** that do not occur naturally in the environment and are man-made.

The U.S. Environmental Protection Agency (EPA) reported in 2012 that these compounds do not break down under environmental conditions; therefore, they are invasive and exist for exceedingly long periods of time in the environment and have been found to reside in the human body for approximately four years.[26] Furthermore, these substances are shown to be "readily absorbed after oral exposure and accumulate primarily in the serum, kidney, and liver. Toxicology studies on animals indicate potential developmental, reproductive, and systematic effects."[26] These particular fluorinated organic compounds are used in apparel products to provide water, oil, or grease resistance.

Canada passed legislation that became effective June 1, 2009 to ban PFOS under the Perfluorooctane Sulfinate Virtual Elimination Act S.C. 2008, c. 13.[27] Currently there are no restrictions for the use of perfluorooctanic acids in Canada. Perfluorooctane sulfinate is also banned in the EU. This substance was originally banned under the 2006/122/EC Marketing and Use Directive that became effective in June 2008. This directive was harmonized under the Annex XVII of the REACH regulation in June 2009.[28] In January 2010, the European Commission reported that the use of PFOA in consumer products do not pose risks to the health of humans.[29,30] The U.S. "EPA intends to propose actions in 2012 under the Toxic Substances Control Act (TSCA) Section 6 to address the potential risks from long-chain PFCs such as PFOS and PFOA. TSCA Section 6 provides authority for the EPA to ban or restrict the manufacture (including import), processing and use of these chemicals."[26] Whereas the industry is in a period of voluntary phase-out of the use of PFOA, the EPA is predicted to ban the use of this chemical by 2015.[30, 31] Japan does not currently have any restrictions on the use of PFOS and PFOA substances in wearing apparel.

Certain Flame Retardants

Flame retardant is a chemical finish that is applied to provide textiles with flame resistance so that when the material comes in contact with a flame it should prevent the spread of fire. There are a number of flame retardant chemical compounds that are banned for use in products designated as undergarments or sleepwear and an increasing number of formulations are currently being evaluated to determine if they are safe for use. Flame retardants are primarily used in children's sleepwear in an effort to meet strict mandatory flammability standards. According to Intertek, "commonly used flame retardants are TRIS, TEPA, Bis (2,3-dibiomopropyl) phosphate, and Polybrominated Diphenylether (PBDE). Prolonged contact to high doses of flame retardants can cause impairment of the immune system, hypothyroidism, memory loss and joint stiffness.[23] Prolonged contact with the skin allows for these chemicals to be absorbed into the body. The toxicity of these substances are very dangerous to the health of humans.

The EU and Japan both prohibit the use of TRIS –Tris (2,3 dibromopropyl) phosphate (CAS number 126-72-7), TEPA –Tris (aziridinyl) phosphineoxide (CAS number 545-55-1), and PBB – Polybromobiphenyles, Polybrominatedbiphenyls 48 (CAS number 59536-65-1) in textile products that come in direct contact with the skin. These substances are banned in accordance with Japanese Law 112 for the control of household products containing harmful substances and regulated in the EU under the Annex XVII of the REACH regulation.[17,28] Mandatory standards in the EU and Japan must be met and certified for compliance prior to sale. Additionally, the use of PentaBDE (PBDE) is restricted in the EU for use as a flame retardant, but is occasionally used for textile products.[28,32] Canada only prohibits the use of TRIS –Tris (2,3 dibromopropyl) phosphate and is regulated for compliance under the Canada Consumer Product Safety Act under Schedule 2.[34]

In 1977, polychlorinated biphenyls (PCBs) (CAS # 1336-36-3) were found to be toxic, causing thyroid problems, cancer, and damage to organs. As a result of these findings, PCBs were banned in the United States. In this same year, chlorinated Tris (tris(1,3-dichloro-2-propyl) phosphate or TDCPP (CAS # 13674-87-8) was voluntarily removed from use in children's sleepwear because it was suspected to be carcinogenic. Polybrominated diphenyl ether

(PBDEs) (CAS # 32534-81-9) flame retardants came into use as PentaBDE, OctaBDE, or DecaBDE, which are banned in the EU and Japan. The use of PDBE flame retardants will be phased out and no longer acceptable for use in the US by the end of 2013. In Canada, PBDEs are strictly controlled and future actions for restricting the use of certain PBDEs are planned.[33] Additionally, bis(2-ethylhexyl)phthalate, or DEHP, (CAS # 117-81-7) has been banned for use in children's products in the United States due to its toxic effects on human development and its classification as a cancer causing agent.[35]

FLAMMABILITY REGULATIONS FOR WEARING APPAREL

A material's ability to ignite and burn is known as **flammability**. With very few exceptions, fabrics used for general wearing apparel and sleepwear will ignite when introduced to a flame. There are several factors that can affect the flammability of textile products such as fiber content, construction, density, finish, surface prints, trim, and fit. Some fabrics will burn quickly when a flame is introduced whereas others will melt as they slowly burn and some even recede from the flame as they melt. Additionally, there are fabrics that will self-extinguish when removed from the flame. When trims, surface embellishments, prints, or finishes are applied to materials they can change the burning characteristics of a garment. The density of the fabric as well as the fit of the garment can impact the ignition and burn time. For example, open weave or knitted fabrics allow more airflow as do loose-fitting garments, which can increase the ignition and flame spread time because there is more oxygen present to sustain the flame. On the other hand, the risk of ignition of a tight fitting garment is greatly reduced because the airflow is limited to what is trapped between the wearer's body and the garment. Tight-fitting garments are also less likely to come in contact with an ignition source.

Flammability of wearing apparel is a very serious matter. The age groups possessing the highest risk for burn related injuries or deaths include infants and children ages four and under and adults ages 65 and older.[36] According to the Centers for Disease Control, in the United States, "Every day, over 300 children ages 0 to 19 are treated in emergency rooms for burn-related injuries and two children die as a result of being burned."[37] Flammability standards for general wearing apparel are regulated by the United States and Canada but not the EU or Japanese governments. However, flammability standards for children's sleepwear and nightwear are strictly regulated by the United States, Canada, and the EU governments. Products not meeting the designated flammability standards cannot be sold within the respective country. Surprisingly, Japan does not have any compulsory regulations for flammability levels of wearing apparel for adults or children.[38]

Textile Flammability for General Wearing Apparel

In the United States, the Consumer Product Safety Commission (CPSC) oversees the flammability regulations and compliance for wearing apparel. In title 16 of the Code of Federal Regulations (CFR), volume 2, part 1610 disclose flammability requirements for general wearing apparel sold in the United States.[39,40,41] The purpose for these mandatory regulations "is to reduce danger of injury and loss of life by providing, on a national basis, standard methods of testing and rating the flammability of textiles and textile products for clothing use, thereby prohibiting the use of any dangerously flammable clothing textiles."[39]

Textile flammability standards for general wearing apparel, regulated by the CPSC under 16 CFR 1610 Standard for the Flammability of Clothing Textiles, requires testing and certification of compliance in order for goods to be sold or imported for sale in the United States. Three classifications have been established for documenting the level of flammability of textiles used for wearing apparel. Before the flammability classifications can be discussed, one must first understand how fabrics and terms are defined within this standard. **Plain surface materials** are defined by the CPSC as "any textile fabric which does not have an intentionally raised fiber or yarn surface such as a pile or nap, or tuft, but shall include those fabrics that have fancy woven, knitted, or flock-printed surfaces."[39] Furthermore, **raised fiber surface materials** are described as "any textile fabric with an intentionally raised fiber or yarn surface, such as pile, including flocked pile, nap, or tufting."[39] A **base burn** or **base fabric ignition** refers to "the point at which the flame burns the ground (base) fabric of a raised surface textile fabric and provides a self-sustaining flame."[39] A **surface flash** is described as "rapid burning of pile fibers and yarns on a raised fiber surface textile that may or may not result in base burning."[39] Lastly, **burn time** or **flame spread time** specifies "the time elapsed from ignition until the stop thread is severed as measured by the timing mechanism of the test apparatus."[39]

Class 1, Normal Flammability, is used to designate acceptability of textiles for wearing apparel. Plain surface fabrics must possess a minimum burn time of 3.5 seconds to be considered Class 1. Raised fiber surface fabrics designated as Class 1 can either possess a minimum burn time of 7 seconds or a maximum surface flash burn time of 7 seconds without a resulting base burn. **Class 2, Intermediate Flammability**, is not applicable to plain surface fabrics and is used to designate acceptable burn times of raised surface fabrics for apparel products. Raised surface fabrics are designated as Class 2 when they possess a burn time between 4 to 7 seconds and result in a base burn. Textiles designated as either Class 1 or Class 2 flammability meet the mandatory regulations for compliance for use in wearing apparel. **Class 3, Rapid and Intense Burning**, is used to designate highly flammable fabrics that have been deemed dangerous because they possess a burn time of less than 4 seconds and result in a base burn. Textiles designated with Class 3 flammability cannot be used in wearing apparel that is sold in the United States due to their hazardous flammable nature.[39]

Textile Flammability Regulations SOR/2011-22 is published by the Minister of Justice and Health Canada is the governmental oversight for compliance for wearing apparel sold in Canada under the Consumer

Product Safety Act and the Hazardous Products Act. Schedule 1, part 1, item 4 of the Hazardous Products Act (HPA), requires textiles to be tested for compliance with this regulation to determine if the materials used for apparel are safe for import and sale.[42,43] Canadian regulations do not categorize flammable materials into classes like the United States but rather focus on material burn times and material types. For plain weave fabrics to comply with mandatory flammability regulations they must have a flame spread time greater than 3.5 seconds, and for raised fabric surfaces the flame spread time must exceed 4 seconds and not exhibit a base burn in order to be deemed acceptable.[43] Any general wearing apparel item that does not meet these compulsory standards is prohibited for sale in Canada.

Children's Sleepwear and Nightwear Flammability Regulations

According to the U.S. Fire Administration, "clothing fires are a significant cause of fire injuries to children."[44] In title 16 of the Code of Federal Regulations (CFR), volume 2, parts 1615 Standard for the flammability of children's sleepwear: Sizes 0 through 6X and 1616 Standard for the flammability of children's sleepwear: Sizes 7 through 14 disclose flammability requirements for compliance of children's sleepwear sold in the United States.[45,46] Under these compulsory regulations, children's sleepwear is defined as "any product of wearing apparel up to size 14, such as nightgowns, pajamas, or similar related items such as robes, intended to be worn primarily for sleeping or activities related to sleeping except: (1) diapers and underwear, (2) 'infant garments,' [and] (3) tight-fitting garments."[45,46] Infant garments are exempt from meeting these regulations if they are labeled as a size expressed as 9 months or less, such as 0 to 3 months, 3 to 6 months, or 6 to 9 months. Additionally, the length of one-piece garments cannot be longer than 25.75 inches (64.8 cm) and for two-piece styles no garment can be longer than 15.75 inches (40 cm) to be exempt as an infant garment. Tight-fitting garments are also exempt if they comply with

the maximum specified garment dimensions for the chest, upper arm, wrist, waist, seat, thigh, and ankle according to the designated garment sizes as outlined in these regulations (see Figure 10.1 and Table 10.3).

For children's sleepwear, compliance with the regulations requires testing to determine char length. The CFR defines **char length** as "the distance from the original lower edge of the specimen exposed to the flame in accordance with the procedure in §1615.5 [or §1616.4] *Test procedure* to the end of the

Figure 10.1   Children's tight-fitting sleepwear
© Wee Woollies Children's Apparel

Table 10.3 Maximum Dimensions Required for Children's Tight-Fitting Sleepwear Exemption Under 16 CFR 1615 and 1616 Standards for Flammability

Maximum Dimensions for Garment Areas by Size						
Size	Chest	Upper Arm	Wrist	Waist	Seat	Thigh	Ankle
9–12 Months	19 inches (48.3 cm)	5⅝ inches (14.3 cm)	4⅛ inches (10.5 cm)	19 inches (48.3 cm)	19 inches (48.3 cm)	10½ inches (26.7 cm)	5⅛ inches (13 cm)
12–18 Months	19½ inches (49.5 cm)	5⅞ inches (14.9 cm)	4⅛ inches (10.5 cm)	19½ inches (49.5 cm)	20 inches (50.8 cm)	11⅛ inches (28.3 cm)	5⅛ inches (13.1 cm)
18–24 Months	20½ inches (52.1 cm)	6⅛ inches (15.6 cm)	4¼ inches (11 cm)	20 inches (50.8 cm)	21 inches (53.3 cm)	11⅝ inches (29.5 cm)	5⅜ inches (13.6 cm)
2	20½ inches (52.1 cm)	6⅛ inches (15.6 cm)	4½ inches (11.4 cm)	20 inches (50.8 cm)	21 inches (53.3 cm)	11¾ inches (29.8 cm)	5½ inches (14 cm)
3	21 inches (53.3 cm)	6⅜ inches (16.2 cm)	4⅝ inches (11.7 cm)	20½ inches (52.1 cm)	22 inches (56 cm)	12⅜ inches (31.4 cm)	5⅞ inches (14.9 cm)
4	22 inches (56 cm)	6⅝ inches (16.8 cm)	4¾ inches (12.1 cm)	21 inches (53.3 cm)	23 inches (58.4 cm)	13 inches (33 cm)	6¼ inches (15.9 cm)
5	23 inches (58.4 cm)	6⅞ inches (17.5 cm)	4⅞ inches (12.4 cm)	21½ inches (54.6 cm)	24 inches (61 cm)	13⅝ inches (34.6 cm)	6⅝ inches (16.8 cm)
6	24 inches (61 cm)	7⅛ inches (18.1 cm)	5 inches (12.7 cm)	22 inches (56 cm)	25 inches (63.5 cm)	14¼ inches (36.2 cm)	7 inches (17.8 cm)
6X	24¾ inches (62.9 cm)	7⅜ inches (18.7 cm)	5⅛ inches (13 cm)	22½ inches (57.2 cm)	25¾ inches (65.4 cm)	14⅞ inches (37.8 cm)	7⅜ inches (18.7 cm)

Maximum Dimensions for Garment Areas by Gender Size						
Gender Size	Chest	Upper Arm	Wrist	Waist	Seat	Thigh	Ankle
Boys 7	25 inches (63.5 cm)	7⅜ inches (18.7 cm)	5⅛ inches (13 cm)	23 inches (58.4 cm)	26 inches (66 cm)	14⅝ inches (37.2 cm)	7⅜ inches (18.7)
Girls 7	25 inches (63.5 cm)	7⅜ inches (18.7 cm)	5⅛ inches (13 cm)	23 inches (58.4 cm)	26½ inches (67.3 cm)	15¼ inches (38.7 cm)	7⅜ inches (18.7)
Boys 8	26 inches (66 cm)	7⅝ inches (19.4 cm)	5¼ inches (13.3 cm)	23½ inches (59.7 cm)	26½ inches (67.3 cm)	15⅛ inches (38.4 cm)	7½ inches (19.1 cm)
Girls 8	26 inches (66 cm)	7⅝ inches (19.4 cm)	5¼ inches (13.3 cm)	23½ inches (59.7 cm)	28 inches (71.1 cm)	16¼ inches (41.3 cm)	7½ inches (19.1 cm)
Boys 9	27 inches (68.6 cm)	7⅞ inches (20 cm)	5⅜ inches (13.7 cm)	24 inches (61 cm)	27¼ inches (69.2 cm)	15⅝ inches (39.7 cm)	7⅝ inches (19.4 cm)
Girls 9	27 inches (68.6 cm)	7⅞ inches (20 cm)	5⅜ inches (13.7 cm)	24 inches (61 cm)	29 inches (73.7 cm)	16¾ inches (42.6 cm)	7⅝ inches (19.4 cm)
Boys 10	28 inches (71.1 cm)	8⅛ inches (20.6 cm)	5½ inches (14 cm)	24½ inches (62.2 cm)	28 inches (71.1 cm)	16⅛ inches (41 cm)	7¾ inches (19.7 cm)
Girls 10	28 inches (71.1 cm)	8⅛ inches (20.6 cm)	5½ inches (14 cm)	24½ inches (62.2 cm)	30 inches (76.2 cm)	17¼ inches (43.8 cm)	7¾ inches (19.7 cm)
Boys 11	39 inches (73.7 cm)	8¼ inches (21 cm)	5⅝ inches (14.3 cm)	25 inches (63.5 cm)	29 inches (73.7 cm)	16⅝ inches (42.2 cm)	7⅞ inches (20 cm)
Girls 11	39 inches (73.7 cm)	8¼ inches 21 cm)	5⅝ inches (14.3 cm)	25 inches (63.5 cm)	31 inches (78.7 cm)	17¾ inches (45.1 cm)	7⅞ inches (20 cm)
Boys 12	30 inches (76.2 cm)	8½ inches (21.6 cm)	5¾ inches (14.6 cm)	25½ inches (64.8 cm)	30 inches (76.2 cm)	17⅛ inches (43.5 cm)	8 inches (20.3 cm)
Girls 12	30 inches (76.2 cm)	8½ inches (21.6 cm)	5¾ inches (14.6 cm)	25½ inches (64.8 cm)	32 inches (81.3 cm)	18½ inches (46.7 cm)	8 inches (20.3 cm)

Maximum Dimensions for Garment Areas by Size							
Size	Chest	Upper Arm	Wrist	Waist	Seat	Thigh	Ankle
Boys 13	31 inches (78.7 cm)	8¾ inches (22.2 cm)	5⅞ inches (14.9 cm)	26 inches (66 cm)	31 inches (78.7 cm)	17⅝ inches (44.8)	8⅛ inches (20.6 cm)
Girls 13	31 inches (78.7 cm)	8¾ inches (22.2 cm)	5⅞ inches (14.9 cm)	26 inches (66 cm)	33 inches (83.8 cm)	18¾ inches (47.6 cm)	8⅛ inches (20.6 cm)
Boys 14	32 inches (81.3 cm)	9 inches (22.9 cm)	6 inches (15.2 cm)	26½ inches (67.3 cm)	32 inches (81.3 cm)	18⅛ inches (46 cm)	8¼ inches (21 cm)
Girls 14	32 inches (81.3 cm)	9 inches (22.9 cm)	6 inches (15.2 cm)	26½ inches (67.3 cm)	34 inches (86.4 cm)	19½ inches (49.5 cm)	8¼ inches (21 cm)

Note: Garments sizes 7 to 14, not specifically designated as girls, must not exceed the maximum measurement designations for boys garments outlined in this table.

Sources: U.S. Government Printing Office (GPO), *Code of Federal Regulations Annual Edition 2012: 16 CFR 1615-Standard for the Flammability of Children's Sleepwear: Sizes 0 through 6X (FF 3-71)*, accessed January 7, 2013, http://www.gpo.gov/fdsys/pkg/CFR-2012-title16-vol2/pdf/CFR-2012-title16-vol2-part 1615.pdf, p. 712

U.S. Government Printing Office (GPO), *Code of Federal Regulations Annual Edition 2012: 16 CFR 1616-Standard for the Flammability of Children's Sleepwear: Sizes 7 through 14 (FF 5-74)*, accessed January 7, 2013, http://www.gpo.gov/fdsys/pkg/CFR-2012-title16-vol2/pdf/CFR-2012-title16-vol2 -part1616.pdf, p. 743–744

tear or void in the charred, burned, or damaged area, the tear being made in accordance with the procedure specified."[45,46] The average char length of five specimens cannot be greater than 7 inches (17.8 cm) and no one specimen can have a char length of 10 inches (25.4 cm), which is the length of the full specimen.[45,46]

The United States also requires conspicuously displayed hangtags affixed to the garments regarding flammability for all sleepwear garments covered under these regulations (see Figure 10.2). These hangtags must comply with the following specifications:

1. Hangtag dimensions must be 1½ inches by 6¼ inches (3.81 by 15.88 cm).

2. The standard safety yellow color designated by ANSI Z535.1-1998 (Hue 5.OY; Value/Chroma 8.0/12) must be used for the background of the hangtag.

3. Text must be printed in black using Arial or Helvetica in an 18 point font and contained within a rectangular outline/box having dimensions of 1 inch by 5¾ inches (2.54 cm by 14.61 cm).

4. Text for the hangtag must state "For child's safety, garment is not flame resistant. Loose-fitting garment is more likely to catch fire."[45,46]

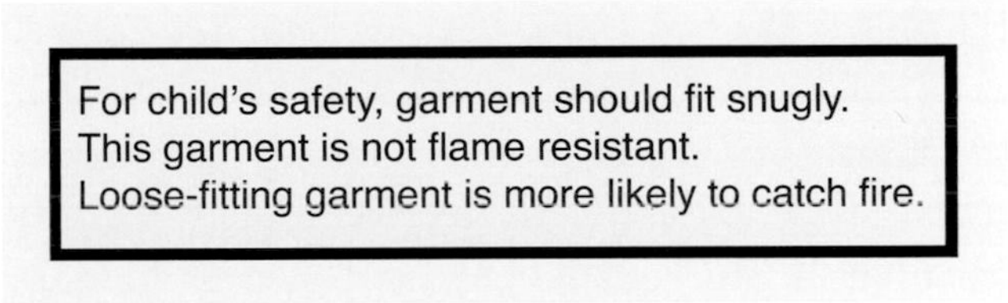

> For child's safety, garment should fit snugly.
> This garment is not flame resistant.
> Loose-fitting garment is more likely to catch fire.

Figure 10.2 Required hangtags for children's sleepwear sold in the United States
Illustration by Q2A Media Services Private Limited

Only these warning statements can appear on one side of the hangtag. It is allowable to print sizing information on the reverse side of this flammability safety hangtag, but any other information is prohibited. The placement of the hole in the hangtag used for attaching it to the garment must also not interfere or obstruct the text. In addition, for snug fitting sleepwear, the following information must be printed on the garment label located at the center back and listed directly below the size (see Figure 10.3).

1. The text color should contrast the background of the label and be no smaller than a 5-point sans serif font using all capital letters to make it easily distinguishable from the rest of the label content.

2. The text on the garment label must state "Wear Snug-fitting. Not Flame Resistant."[45,46]

Figure 10.3 Labeling required for tight-fitting children's sleepwear
Illustration by Q2A Media Services Private Limited

Figure 10.4 Children's loose-fitting sleepwear
Absodels/Getty Images

The U.S. government requires general certificates of conformity for clothing and textiles products to provide verification that garments sold within the country are in compliance with compulsory regulations for flammability.

Children's Sleepwear Regulations SOR/2011-15 is published by the Minister of Justice, and Health Canada is the governmental oversight for compliance under the Consumer Product Safety Act and the Hazardous Products Act regarding flammability requirements for children's sleepwear sold in Canada. Schedule 1, part 1, item 5, and part 2, item 40 of the Hazardous Products Act (HPA), and Section 37 of the Canadian Consumer Product Safety Act requires garments to be tested for compliance with this regulation to determine if they are safe for import and sale.[43,47]

In Canada, both tight- and loose-fitting sleepwear are defined in the regulation. **Tight-fitting sleepwear** is categorized in Canada as "any children's sleepwear in sizes up to and including 14X other than loose-fitting sleepwear. It includes (a) sleepwear designed for infants weighing up to 7 kg; (b) sleepwear designed for use in a hospital; (c) polo pyjamas; and (d) sleepers."[47] Compliance requires testing and certification documenting the tested specimens had a flame spread greater than 7 seconds. **Loose-fitting sleepwear** refers to "children's nightgowns, night shirts, dressing gowns, bathrobes, housecoats, robes, pyjamas and baby-doll pyjamas in sizes up to and including 14X, other than sleepwear designed for infants weighing up to 7 kg [15.43 pounds], sleepwear designed for use in a hospital or polo pyjamas."[47] See Figure 10.4 for an example of loose-fitting children's sleepwear. **Char length** is defined by Canadian standards as the "maximum extent of the damaged length of a material that has been subjected to the test conditions set out in these Regulations [Children's Sleepwear Regulations SRO/2011-15]."[47] Compliance of loose-fitting sleepwear requires a char length average for five specimens that does not exceed 178 mm (7 inches) and no one specimen can have a char length the length of the full specimen. If loose-fitting sleepwear is treated with a flame retardant finish, it must comply further with the following requirements to be in compliance. When a flame retardant is applied to children's loose-fitting sleepwear, it cannot be the cause any of the following negative health effects:

a) acute lethality as a result of oral exposure to a dose of 500 mg/kg body weight or less when tested for acute oral toxicity or acute dermal toxicity in accordance with section 1 or 2, respectively of Schedule 2;

b) an effect graded at a mean greater than 1 for erythema formation or for edema formation measured at any specified time when tested for dermal irritation in accordance with section 3 of Schedule 2;

c) When tested for dermal sensation in accordance with section 4 of Schedule 2, a response in greater than 15 percent of the test animals when using the Draize Test or the Buehler Test or in greater than 30 percent of the test animals when using one of the five other tests, in which an adjuvant is incorporated, that are specified in the OECD [Organization for Economic Development] Test Guideline No. 406 that is referred to in that section;

d) Gene mutation or chromosomal aberration when tested for mutagenicity in accordance with section 5 of Schedule 2; or

e) Tumors when tested for tumorigenicity in accordance with section 6 of Schedule 2.[47]

Canada requires children's sleepwear to bear a permanently affixed label if it has been treated with a flame retardant. The information on the label must be presented in both English and French languages and state "flame retardant" and "ignifugeant" accompanied by care instructions to prevent a consumer from using any care methods that would break down or negate the flame resistant finish on the garment.[47]

The European Committee for Standardization (CEN) approved and published a harmonized flammability standard EN 14878:2007 Textiles – Burning Behavior of Children's Nightwear – Specification to provide mandatory guidelines for compliance of children's sleepwear products imported and sold within the EU. The EU General Product Safety Directive utilizes this standard to determine compliance with regulations and to evaluate the level of risk of injury to consumers.[48,49] The EU specification defines **nightwear** as "garments that are either sold as nightwear or intended to be worn as nightwear, e.g., bathrobes, dressing gowns, night shirts, nightdresses and pyjamas."[49] **Pyjamas** are described as "either two or several piece nightwear garment[s] comprising trouser, shorts or briefs and top. It may also comprise one-piece pyjama type[s] with [the] top integral to [the] trouser. The trouser may be with or without feet."[49]

The EU flammability specification classifies nightwear garments by age group and garment type and minimum flammability requirements are designated for each. **Class A** designates children's nightwear other than pyjamas made for children over 6 months old up to 14 years of age, having a height of 68 cm (26.77 inches) up to 176 cm (69.29 inches) for girls and up to 182 cm (71.65 inches) for boys. Nightwear, not pyjamas, designated as Class A exhibit a flame spread of less than 15 seconds, having a char length less than 520 mm (20.47 inches) and not breaking the third marker thread when tested. This class cannot exhibit **surface flash**, which occurs when a flame quickly spreads across the surface of the fabric but ignition of the base materials does not occur. **Class B** designates children's pyjamas for this same age group and height range. Pyjamas designated as Class B exhibit a flame spread of less than 10 seconds having a char length less than 520 mm (20.47 inches), not breaking the third marker thread when tested. Additionally, both Class A and B garments cannot exhibit a surface flash when tested. **Class C** indicates babies' nightwear produced for infants up to 6 months old and up to 68 cm (26.77 inches) in height. Class C products do not require testing; therefore, there are no minimum requirements in this classification.[49]

Design specifications regarding critical measurement areas of pajama tops, jackets, and trousers are outlined in this regulation. The lower hem of pajama tops and jackets must not exceed a length of 10 cm (3.94 inches) below the crotch and the hem circumference must not be greater than 20 percent of the hip measurement for the designated size. If sleeves extend below the elbow, no part of the sleeve circumference shall exceed 50 cm (19.67 inches); and if cuffs are part of the sleeve design, the cuff hem circumference shall not exceed 40 cm (15.74 inches). The lower leg portion of pajama trouser legs must not exceed the width measurement at the knee. When the previously described design specifications are not met for children's pyjamas, they must meet the requirements for Class A products. When a flame retardant finish is applied to improve flame resistance of a garment in order to conform to the regulation, it must resist degradation throughout the useful life of the garment. Any flame retardant used for children's apparel must also comply with toxicity regulations. At this time, labeling is not mandatory as part of this regulation, but if a voluntary label is used it must state the following words in red, "WARNING – keep away from fire," followed by the fabric Class A, B, or C and EN 14878.[49]

Annex C, A-deviations, of this flammability specification allow for national departures from this standard for CEN/CENELEC countries (i.e., United Kingdom) when stricter provisions are required and shall remain active until they have been removed. Under this deviation, the United Kingdom children's sleepwear must also meet strict regulations under UK legislation for The Nightwear (Safety) Regulations 1985. Children's sleepwear sold in the UK is bound to comply with BS EN 14878:2007 regulations. British Standard 5722:1991 Specification for Flammability Performance of Fabrics and Fabric Combinations Used in Nightwear Garments is utilized to assess performance and determine compliance. The minimum performance criteria for acceptability under EN 14878:2007 are less stringent than BS 5722:1991; therefore, the later prevails. This UK standard requires flammability testing in accordance with EN 1103 Textiles – Fabrics for Apparel – Detailed Procedure to Determine the Burning Behaviour and EN ISO 6941:2003 Textile Fabrics – Burning Behaviour

– Measurement of Flame Spread Properties of Vertically Oriented Specimens (British Standard).

Babies' garments are defined in the UK standard as nightwear possessing a "chest measurement not exceeding 53 centimeters [20.87 inches] and which would normally be worn only by a child under the age of 3 months" rather than 6 months of age and a height of 68 cm, as defined by EN 14878.[49,50] The following flammability performance requirements designated in BS 5722 supersede EN 14878. Children's nightwear is described under The Nightwear (Safety) Regulation as garments intended for sleepwear by boys and girls under the age of 13. Schedule 1 of this regulation specifies maximum dimensions for design requirements of specific nightwear garments that cannot be exceeded. The maximum chest measurement for night dresses is 91 cm [35.83 inches] and the length cannot exceed 122 cm [48.03 inches]. The maximum chest measurement for dressing gowns, bathrobes and other comparable garments is 97 cm [38.19 inches] and the sleeve length cannot exceed 69 cm [27.17 inches].[50]

Performance standards for acceptability and compliance in the UK require night dresses, dressing gowns, and robes (not constructed of cotton terry toweling), for children 6 months to 13 years of age, to demonstrate minimum flammability performance levels in one of the following ways. When tested, the garment exhibits a flame spread of less than 10 seconds that does not exceed 520 mm (20.47 inches) and break the trip thread. Additionally, the garment dimensions must not exceed the maximum measurements for design specification requirements. The other option for compliance is for the garment to exhibit a flame spread of less than 15 seconds that does not exceed 520 mm (20.47 inches) and break the trip thread.[49]

Although EN 14878 does not require warning labels, there are very strict requirements for labeling both children's and adult nightwear under UK legislation for The Nightwear (Safety) Regulations 1985. According to these regulations "pyjamas, babies' garments, terry toweling, bath robes, and adult's nightwear are required to be labeled to show whether or not the fabric from which they are made is capable of complying with those flammability performance requirements (Regulation 7 and Schedule 3)."[50] Labels must comply with the following requirements:

1. Pyjamas, babies' garments, and cotton terry toweling bath robes (being children's nightwear) and adults' nightwear which are not made of fabric of a kind which after having been washed in accordance with Regulation 11 is capable of complying with the flammability performance requirements shall bear a label on which the following wording shall appear in red letters: KEEP AWAY FROM FIRE.

2. Pyjamas, babies, garments, and cotton terry toweling bathrobes (being children's nightwear) and adults' nightwear other than that described in paragraph 1 [listed above] shall bear a label on which shall appear

   a. in black letters, 'LOW FLAMMABILITY TO BS 5722'; or
   b. the wording prescribed by paragraph 1; or
   c. the wording prescribed by both paragraph 1 and sub-paragraph (a).

3. All wording required by this Schedule [2] shall appear on—

   a. a label securely attached to the inside of the neck of the garment; or
   b. a label securely attached to the garment immediately adjacent to any other label attached to the garment and giving details of the size of the garment; or
   c. any label securely attached to the garment and giving details of the size of the garment, in which case the wording required by this Schedule [2] shall appear immediately under the details of the size of the garment.

4. All wording required by this Schedule [2] shall be in the medium letters of 10 point in uppercase and shall be set out in legible and durable form on a background of a sufficiently different colour to enable the letters readily to be seen. Any label on which such wording appears shall itself be durable.[50]

For nightwear garments that have been treated with flame retardant chemicals they must possess a label using black text in 6-point font, using capital letters stating DO NOT WASH AT MORE THAN 50°C. CHECK SUITABILITY OF WASHING AGENT. The label must also comply with the same standards as listed above in numbers 3a, b, and c, and 4.[50]

GUIDELINES FOR DRAWSTRINGS ON CHILDREN'S GARMENTS

According to RAPEX Weekly Notifications, (the EU's rapid alert system for consumer product safety), during the first 32 weeks of 2010 there were 196 strangulation deaths of children due to drawstrings in garments.[51] Children's garments containing drawstrings or cords are a significant hazard because they can get caught in playground equipment, moving bicycle parts, doors of vehicles, ski lifts, escalators, elevators, and automatic doors that can lead to injury and in some cases death.[52] Drawstring compliance is a serious safety issue that clothing manufacturers face when producing product to be sold in different parts of the world. The United States, Canada, and the EU have adopted standards or guidelines in an effort to reduce the risk of accidental injury or strangulation due to clothing items containing drawstrings or cords. At the time of publication, Japan does not have any regulations or guidelines regarding the use of drawstrings in children's apparel.

In the United States, the CPSC has determined that the use of drawstrings or cords in children's garments poses a serious safety hazard; therefore, a voluntary standard has been imposed. Under ASTM F1816-97 (reapproved 2009), this voluntary standard prohibits drawstrings to be used in the neck or hood areas of children's outerwear garments size 2T (age 18 months) up to size 12 (age 10) that cover the upper portion of the body. Upper outerwear is defined by ASTM F1816-97 as "clothing such as jackets and sweatshirts, generally intended to be worn on the exterior of other garments."[53] The length of any drawstrings used in the waist or bottom of children's upper outerwear garments sizes 2T (age 18 months) up to size 16 (age 14) cannot extend beyond 3 inches (75 mm) outside of the drawstring casing when the garment is fully extended. In situations where one continuous string is used, it must be securely stitched through the garment at the midpoint by means of a bar tack to prevent it from being pulled through the casing. Additionally, use of any attachment at the ends of the drawstrings or cords such as knots or toggles is prohibited.[53,54] Manufacturers are encouraged to use alternative closures at the head and neck area of upper outwear garments (i.e., Velcro, snaps, buttons, or elastic) to provide safer options to consumers.[54] See Figure 10.5 for alternative hood/neck closures recommended by the CPSC.

In Canada, similar voluntary standards for consumer product safety are recommended for all children's upper outerwear garments.[55] The length of any drawstrings used in the waist or bottom of children's garments should not extend beyond 8 cm (3.14 inches) outside of the drawstring casing when the garment is fully extended, and if it consists of one continuous string it must be securely stitched through the garment to prevent it from being pulled through the casing. Additionally, use of any attachment at the ends of the drawstrings or cords such as knots or toggles is not advised. Drawstrings should not be used in the hood or neck area of children's garments and manufacturers are encouraged to use closures such

as Velcro, snaps, buttons, or elastic to provide safer alternatives to consumers.[55]

In the EU the harmonized standard EN 14682 Safety of Children's Clothing: Cords and Drawstrings on Children's Clothing Specifications has been adopted for children's clothing containing drawstrings and cords in an effort to ensure product safety for girls and boys up to the age of 14. Compliance requirements are divided by age group. Apparel intended for children up to 7 years of age and no taller than 134 cm [52.76 inches] should not contain drawstrings or cords in the neck or hood, and alternative closures such as Velcro, buttons, or snaps should be used. For children ages 7 to 14 that are taller than 134 cm [52.76 inches] having a height up to 176 cm [69.29 inches] for girls and up to 182 cm for boys, all cords or drawstrings contained within the neck or hood of a garment cannot exceed 75 mm [2.95 inches] in length. Elastic draw cords are prohibited for use in the neck and hood of garments (excluding halter and shoulder straps) for children ages 7 to 14 due to eye injuries caused by these types of cords.[56] This standard also restricts the length of ties, belts, or sashes placed in the front portion of children's apparel to 360 mm [14.17 inches] or less to avoid entanglement. Furthermore, strings and draw cords positioned on the backside of garments also pose a hazard of entanglement and should not hang below the sleeve or bottom hem of the garment. If a drawstring or cord is placed at the hem of trousers, it must be contained or restricted to the inside of

Figure 10.5 CPSC recommended alternative hood and neck closures for upper outerwear children's garments *Illustration by Q2A Media Services Private Limited*

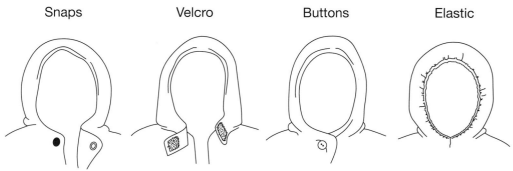

Snaps　　Velcro　　Buttons　　Elastic

the garment to avoid entanglement. Children's garments that are not in compliance with this standard are banned for sale in EU countries under the General Product Safety Directive (Directive 2001/95) that requires all products sold in the marketplace be safe for consumer use.[56]

OEKO-TEX ASSOCIATION

It is very important to prevent garments containing harmful substances from reaching the marketplace. The OEKO-TEX Association is composed of 15 textile research and testing institutes in Europe and Japan with offices in 60 countries around the world.[57] This organization developed and maintains the OEKO-TEX Standard 100, which "is an independent test and certification system for textile raw, intermediate and end products at all stages of processing."[58] For apparel products to be certified under this standard all garment components must be tested for harmful substances and are categorized into one of three product classes:

- Product class I: Textile items for babies and toddlers up to 3 years
- Product class II: Textiles used close to the skin
- Product class III: Textiles used away from the skin[58]
- For the latest information and list of harmful substances included in testing, visit www.oeko-tex.com.

INDUSTRY SCENARIO 10.1 Flammability Recall of Children's Sleepwear

Over the past few years there have been several recalls regarding children's sleepwear that do not meet flammability regulations and pose a burn risk. According to the U.S. Consumer Product Safety Commission, on September 17, 2013, the United States and Canada jointly recalled 41,280 footed pajamas (38,000 in the United States and 3,280 in Canada) that were produced in three styles that did not meet flammability standards for tight-fitting pajamas. The recalled pajamas were offered in different sizes, depending upon the style, ranging from 9–12 months up to 3T. No injuries were reported.[59]

- Could this recall have been prevented?
- In what stages of development and manufacturing could this have been detected?
- What measures could have been taken to correct this problem?

SUMMARY

The goal of brands around the globe is to design, manufacture, distribute, and sell products that are compliant with relevant governmental regulations for apparel products that will not cause intentional harm to consumers. The mandatory safety regulations and voluntary guidelines for apparel sold in the United States, Canada, the European Union, and Japan were discussed in this chapter as well as the regulatory bodies overseeing and enforcing safety regulations

Table 10.4 provides a summary of the safety regulations by country. Education of industry professionals is vital to ensuring products are developed and tested to certify they are safe for the useful life of the product. Additionally, consumers need to be educated as well so they can make informed decisions when purchasing apparel products as well as use and maintenance of garments that may pose risk to one's safety.

Table 10.4 Summary of Safety Regulations by Country

Regulation	Country			
	U.S.	Canada	Harmonized EU	Japan
Nickel	N	N	R	N
Lead	R	N	N	N
Certain Azo Dyes	N	N	R	N
Formaldehyde	R	N	N	R
Fluorinated Organic Compounds	V	R	R	N
Certain Flame Retardants	R	R	R	R
Flammability				
General Wearing Apparel	R	R	N	N
Children's Sleepwear	R	R	R	N
Drawstrings in Children's Apparel	V	V	R	N

Note:
R = Required Regulation
V = Voluntary Regulation
N = No Regulation to Date

ACTIVITIES

1. Visit three retail stores that sell children's outerwear garments. Carefully evaluate the outerwear products for compliance with drawstring regulations. If you find a product(s) that is not compliant, list the violation(s). For those that are compliant, record the alternative neck/hood closures used.

2. Visit a retail store that sells children's sleepwear. Locate a pair of pajamas that are made of 100 percent cotton that meet the tight-fitting garment requirement for flammability. Read the garment labels and hangtags that are required by law to be displayed on these garments. Now find a pair of loose-fitting pajamas that have a flame retardant finish. Read the garment labels and hangtags that are required by law to be displayed on these garments. Compare both the tight- and loose-fitting pajamas in the same size, and document the differences in the overall appearance, fit, construction, and design of the garments. Take photos of the garments side by side for visual documentation.

3. Select a country not covered in this chapter, and research the safety regulations for one of the topics discussed to determine if there are requirements for compliance in order for certain products to be sold within the selected country.

APPAREL QUALITY LAB MANUAL

Please refer to Lab Activity 8.1 Garment Safety Regulations and Compliance in the *Apparel Quality Lab Manual.*

ENDNOTES

1. EPA. *Nickel Compounds: Hazard Summary -Created in April 1992; Revised in January 2000.* Accessed January 10, 2013, http://www.epa.gov /ttnatw01/hlthef/nickel.html.

2. K. Foxall (2009). *Health Protection Agency Nickel Toxicology Overview.* Accessed January 10, 2013, http://www.hpa.org.uk/webc/HPAwebFile/HPA web_C/1236757324101.

3. The Commission of the European Communities. "Commission Directive 2001/96/EC of 27 September 2004." *Official Journal of the European Union,* 28.9.2004, L301/51-52. Accessed January 4, 2013, http://eur-lex.europa.eu/LexUriServ/LexUri Serv.do?uri=OJ:L:2004:301:0051:0052:EN:PDF.

4. The European Parliament and the Council of the European Union. "European Parliament and Council Directive 94/27/EC of 30 June, 1994." *Official Journal of the European Communities,* 28.9.2004, L301/51-52. Accessed January 4, 2013, http://eur-lex.europa.eu/LexUriServ/LexUriServ .do?uri=OJ:L:1994:188:0001:0002:EN:PDF.

5. Milieu Ltd. (March 7, 2012). *Implementation and Enforcement of Restrictions Under Title VIII and Annex VXII to REACH in the Member States.* Accessed January 10, 2013, http://ec.europa.eu/ enterprise/sectors/chemicals/files/reach/review 2012/final-report-restrictions_en.pdf, pp. 130–137.

6. Jacob P. Thyssen, Wolfgang Uter, John McFadden, Torkil Menné, Radoslav Spiewak, Martine Vigan, Ana Gimenez-Arnau, and Carla Lindén (2001). "The EU Nickel Directive Revisited—Future Steps Toward Better Protection Against Nickel Allergy." New York: John Wiley & Sons A/S. *Contact Dermatitis,* 64: 121–125. Accessed January 8, 2013, http://www .radoslawspiewak.net/2011-3.pdf.

7. Intertek. *EU Nickel Release—New Official Test Methods.* Accessed January 10, 2013, http://www .intertek.com/uploadedFiles/Intertek/Divisions /Consumer_Goods/Media/PDFs/Sparkles/2012 /sparkle623.pdf.

8. European Commission. *REACH.* Accessed January 10, 2013, http://ec.europa.eu/environment /chemicals/reach/reach_intro.htm.

9. The National Institute of Environmental Health Sciences (NIEHS). *Lead.* Accessed January 12, 2013, http://www.niehs.nih.gov/health/topics /agents/lead/.

10. National Toxicology Program, Department of Health and Human Services. "Lead and Lead Compound CAS No. 7439-92-1 (Lead)." *Report on Carcinogens,* 12th ed. Accessed January 12, 2013, http://ntp.niehs.nih.gov/ntp/roc/twelfth /profiles/Lead.pdf, p. 251.

11. Mary F. Toro. *U.S. Consumer Product Safety Commission Requirements: An In Depth Review.* Accessed January 12, 2013, http://www.cpsc.gov/ businfo/intl/textilepp.pdf.

12. American Apparel & Footwear Association (AAFA) (2012). *Restricted Substances List,* 11th ed. https://www.wewear.org/assets/1/7/RSLRelease 11.pdf.

13. U.S. Consumer Product Safety Commission. *Total Lead Content.* Accessed January 12, 2013, http://www.cpsc.gov/info/toysafety/lead.html.

14. US Government Printing Office (GPO). "Title 16: Commercial Practices Part 1500—Hazardous Substances and Articles; Administration and

Enforcement Regulations." *Electronic Code of Federal Regulations*. Accessed January 10, 2013, http://www.ecfr.gov/cgi-bin/text-idx?c=ecfr&rgn=div8&view=text&node=16:2.0.1.3.73.0.1.38&idno=16.

15. U.S. Government Printing Office (GPO) (November 8, 2011). "Title 16: Commercial Practices [16 CFR] Part 1109—Conditions and Requirements for Relying on Component Part Testing or Certification, or Another Party's Finished Product Testing, or Certification, to Meet Testing and Certification Requirements." Accessed February 2, 2013, http://www.ecfr.gov/cgi-bin/text-idx?c=ecfr&SID=db72b2a853d671ea0265fa340efc7e3a&rgn=div5&view=text&node=16:2.0.1.2.29&idno=16.

16. U.S. Consumer Product Safety Commission (September 28, 2008). *Section 102. Mandatory Third Party Testing for Certain Children's Products*. Accessed February 2, 2013, http://www.cpsc.gov/en/Regulations-Laws—Standards/CPSIA/CPSIA-Topics/Section-102-Mandatory-Third-Party-Testing-for-Certain-Childrens-Products/.

17. Office of Textiles and Apparel (OTEXA). *Market Reports/Tariffs: Textiles, Apparel, Footwear and Travel Goods Japan*. Accessed January 27, 2013, http://web.ita.doc.gov/tacgi/overseasnew.nsf/alldata/Japan.

18. Chemical Inspection and Regulation Service (CIRS Europe). *Azo Dye Testing: Textile Testing*. Accessed January 10, 2013, http://cirs-reach.com/Testing/AZO_Dyes.html.

19. A. Püntener and C. Page (January 5, 2004). *European Ban on Certain Azo Dyes*. Accessed January 11, 2013, http://www.tfl.com/web/files/eubanazodyes.pdf.

20. Official Journal of the European Union (May 29, 2007). *Annex XVII*. Accessed January 14, 2013, http://www.reach-compliance.eu/english/REACH-ME/engine/sources/reach-annexes/launch-annex17.html.

21. Intertek (2010). *Japan—Voluntary Requirements on Harmful Substances for Textiles and Clothing*.

Accessed February 3, 2013, http://www.intertek.com.cn/resource/newsparkle-en.aspx?kc=454.

22. American Chemical Council. *Formaldehyde, The Simple Molecule*. Accessed January 27, 2013, http://www.formaldehydefacts.org/.

23. Intertek. (2012). *Eco-Textile Services: For Brands that Care from Make to Wear*. Accessed January 4, 2013, http://www.intertek.com/uploadedFiles/Intertek/Divisions/Consumer_Goods/Media/PDFs/Services/Eco-Textiles.pdf.

24. U.S. Government Accountability Office (GOA). *Formaldehyde in Textiles: While Levels in Clothing Generally Appear to be Low, Allergic Contact Dermatitis is a Health Issue for Some People, GOA-10=875, August 2010*. Accessed February 2, 2013, http://www.gao.gov/assets/310/308673.pdf.

25. American Apparel & Footwear Association (AAFA) (October 2012). *Restricted Substances List*, 11th ed. Accessed January 9, 2013, https://www.wewear.org/assets/1/7/RSLRelease11.pdf.

26. U.S. EPA (May 2012). *Emerging Contaminants—Perfluorooctane Sulfante (PFOS) and Perfluorooctanoic Acid (PFOA)*. EPA 505-F-11-002. Accessed February 16, 2013, http://www.epa.gov/fedfac/pdf/emerging_contaminants_pfos_pfoa.pdf.

27. Minister of Justice (2008). *Perfluorooctane Sulfonate Virtual Elimination Act*. S.C. c. 13. Accessed February 3, 2013, http://laws-lois.justice.gc.ca/PDF/P-8.3.pdf.

28. The European Parliament and the Council of the European Union. *Regulation (EC) No 1907/2006 of the European Parliament and of the Council of 18 December 2006 Concerning the Registration, Evaluation, Authorisation and Restriction of Chemicals (REACH), Establishing a European Chemicals Agency, Amending Directive 1999/45/EC and Repealing Council Regulation (EEC) No 793/93 and Commission Regulation (EC) No 1488/94 as Well as Council Directive 76/769/EEC and Commission Directives 91/155/EEC, 93/67/EEC, 93/105/EC and 2000/21 EC, 3006R1907 – EN – 01.06.2012 – 012.001*. Accessed January 1, 2013,

http://eur-lex.europa.eu/LexUriServ/LexUriServ.do?uri=OJ:L:2006:396:0001:0849:EN:PDF.

29. RPS Advies B.V. "Analysis of the Risks Arising from the Industrial Use of Perfluorooctanic Acid (PFOA) and Ammonium Perfluorooctanoate (APFO) and From Their Use in Consumer Articles. Evaluation of the Risk Reduction Measures for Potential Restrictions on the Manufacture, Placing on the Market, Placing on the Market and Use of PFOA and APFO," January 14, 2010, Final Report (20.12.2008-20.10.2009). Accessed February 16, 2013, http://ec.europa.eu/enterprise/sectors/chemicals/files/docs_studies/final_report_pfoa_pfos_en.pdf.

30. Revati (January 28, 2010). *European Commission Publishes PFOA and PFOS Risk Assessment.* Accessed February 16, 2013, http://reach-rohs-blog.tantraconsulting.org/2010/01/european-commission-publishes-pfoa-and.html.

31. Patagonia. "PFOS, PFOA, and Other Fluorochemicals." *The Foot Print Chronicles.* Accessed February 16, 2013, http://www.patagonia.com/pdf/en_US/pfoa_and_flourochemicals.pdf.

32. CBI Market Information Database (2012). *EU Legislation: Flame Retardants in Textiles.* Accessed February 3, 2012, http://www.miepo.md/public/files/cbi/eulegislation.nonfood/2012_EU_legislation_Flame_retardants_in_textiles.pdf.

33. Health Canada (August 2009). *PBDE Flame Retardants and Human Health.* Accessed February 4, 2013, http://www.hc-sc.gc.ca/hl-vs/alt_formats/pdf/iyh-vsv/environ/pbde-eng.pdf.

34. Minister of Justice (June 20, 2011). *Canada Consumer Product Safety Act*, S.C. 2010, c 21. Accessed 1/3/2013, http://laws-lois.justice.gc.ca/pdf/c-1.68.pdf.

35. M. Hawthorne, K. Nieland, and D. Eads (May 10, 2012). "Flame Retardants and Their Risks." *Chicago Tribune.* Accessed February 3, 2013, http://media.apps.chicagotribune.com/flames/chemical-similarities-and-history-of-flame-retardants.html.

36. Centers for Disease Control and Prevention (October 11, 2011). "Fired Deaths and Injuries: Fact Sheet." Accessed January 7, 2013, http://www.cdc.gov/homeandrecreationalsafety/fire-prevention/fires-factsheet.html.

37. Centers for Disease Control and Prevention (April 12, 2012). "Burns Safety: The Reality." Accessed February 17, 2013, http://www.cdc.gov/safechild/Burns/index.html.

38. Just-style.com (September 27, 2010). *September Management Briefing: Part I – Protecting Clothing and Textile Consumers from Harm.* Accessed January 4, 2013, http://www.just-style.com/management-briefing/part-i-protecting-clothing-and-textile-consumers-from-harm_id109039.aspx.

39. U.S. Government Printing Office (GPO). *Code of Federal Regulations Annual Edition 2012: 16 CFR 1610-Standard for the Flammability of Clothing Textiles.* Accessed January 7, 2013, http://www.gpo.gov/fdsys/pkg/CFR-2012-title16-vol2/pdf/CFR-2012-title16-vol2-part1610.pdf, p. 670–699.

40. U.S. Consumer Product Safety Commission. CFR 1610. Accessed January 6, 2013, http://www.cpsc.gov/businfo/frnotices/fr07/clothingflammstd.pdf.

41. U.S. Consumer Product Safety Commission Office of Compliance. Requirements for Clothing Textiles, 16 C.F.R. Part 1610. Accessed January 6, 2013, http://www.cpsc.gov/businfo/regsumwearapp.pdf

42. Minister of Justice (December 31, 2012). *Textile Flammability Regulations, SOR/2011-22.* Accessed January 8, 2013, http://laws-lois.justice.gc.ca/pdf/SOR-2011-22.pdf.

43. Health Canada. *Flammability of Textile Products in Canada 2009.* Accessed January 8, 2013, http://www.hc-sc.gc.ca/cps-spc/alt_formats/hecs-sesc/pdf/pubs/indust/flammability-inflammabilite/flammability-inflammabilite-eng.pdf.

44. U.S. Fire Administration. "Children and Fire." Accessed January 7, 2013, http://www.usfa.fema.gov/downloads/pyfff/children.html.

45. U.S. Government Printing Office (GPO). *Code of Federal Regulations Annual Edition 2012: 16 CFR*

1615-Standard for the Flammability of Children's Sleepwear: Sizes 0 through 6X (FF 3-71). Accessed January 7, 2013, http://www.gpo.gov/fdsys/pkg /CFR-2012-title16-vol2/pdf/CFR-2012-title16 -vol2-part1615.pdf, p. 710–741.

46. U.S. Government Printing Office (GPO). *Code of Federal Regulations Annual Edition 2012: 16 CFR 1616-Standard for the Flammability of Children's Sleepwear: Sizes 7 through 14 (FF 5-74.* Accessed January 7, 2013, http://www.gpo.gov/fdsys/pkg /CFR-2012-title16-vol2/pdf/CFR-2012-title16 -vol2-part1616.pdf, p. 741–775.

47. Minister of Justice (December 31, 2012). *Children's Sleepwear Regulations, SOR/2011-15.* Accessed January 8, 2013, http://laws-lois.justice .gc.ca/pdf/SOR-2011-15.pdf.

48. Intertek. "New European Flammability Standard, EN 14878-2007 'Textiles — Burning Behavior[1] of Children's Nightwear — Specification.'" Accessed March 3, 2013, *SPARKLE, Vol. 287, July 2007,* http://www.intertek.com/uploaded Files/Intertek/Divisions/Consumer_Goods /Media/PDFs/Sparkles/2007/sparkle287.pdf.

49. BSI. *Textiles — burning behavior of children's nightwear — Specification BS EN 14878:2007, Incorporating Corrigendum January 2009.* ISBN 978 0 580 63991 3[2].

50. Crown (December 20, 1985). *1985 No. 2043 Consumer Protection: The Nightwear (Safety) Regulations 1985.* Accessed January 7, 2013, http://www.legislation.gov.uk/uksi/1985/2043 /contents/made.

51. Just-style.com (September 30, 2010). "September management briefing: Part IV — Clothing safety data." Accessed January 4, 2013, http://www .just-style.com/management-briefing/part-iv -clothing-safety-data_id109059.aspx.

52. Just-style.com (September 27, 2010). September management briefing: Part 1 - Protecting clothing and textile customers from harm. Accessed January 4, 2013, http://www.just-style

.com/management-briefing/part-i-protecting -clothing-and-textile-consumers-from-harm _id109039.aspx.

53. ASTM International (December 15, 2009). *ASTM F1816-97(Reapproved 2009) Standard Safety Specification for Drawstrings on Children's Upper Outerwear.* DOI: 10.1520/F1816-97R09.

54. U.S. Consumer Product Safety Commission (June 2012). "Drawstrings in Children's Upper Outerwear: Frequently Asked Questions." Accessed January 4, 2013, http://www.cpsc .gov/en/Business—Manufacturing/Business -Education/Business-Guidance/Drawstrings-in -Childrens-Upper-Outerwear/Frequently-Asked -Questions-FAQs/.

55. Health Canada. "Potential Strangulation from Drawstring's on Children's Outerwear." Accessed March 11, 2013, http://schools.hwdsb.on.ca /dundana/files/2011/12/Playground-Strangulation -Alert.pdf.

56. Europa (March 23, 2010). *Questions and Answers on Cords and Drawstrings.* Accessed January 4, 2013, http://europa.eu/rapid/press-release_MEMO -10-98_en.htm.

57. OEKO-TEX Association. "OEKO-TEX Association." Accessed November 2, 2013, https://www.oeko-tex.com/en/manufacturers /philosophy/oeko_tex_association/oeko_tex _association.xhtml.

58. OEKO-TEX Association. "OEKO-TEX Standard 100." Accessed November 2, 2013, https://www .oeko-tex.com/en/manufacturers/concept/oeko _tex_standard_100/oeko_tex_standard_100 .xhtml.

59. U.S. Consumer Product Safety Commission (September 17, 2013). "The Children's Place Recalls Footed Pajamas Due to Violation of Federal Flammability Standard." Accessed November 3, 2013, http://www.cpsc.gov/en /Recalls/2013/The-Childrens-Place-Recalls -Footed-Pajamas/.

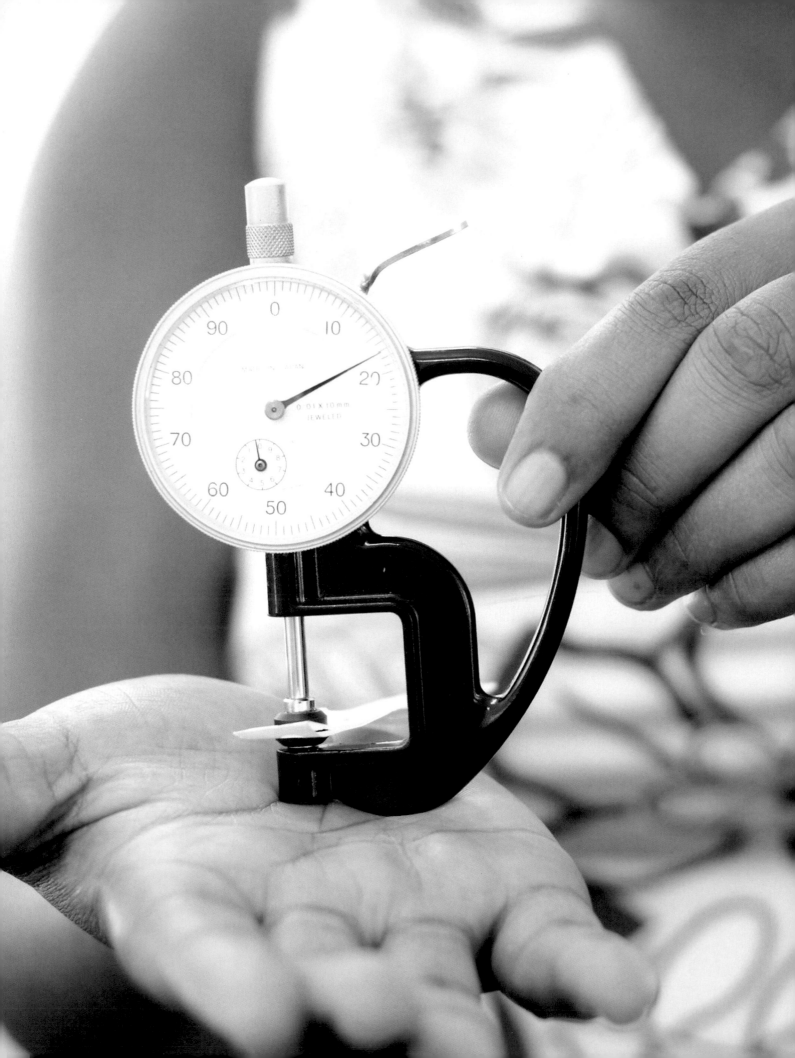

CHAPTER ELEVEN

Measuring Product Quality Through Testing

Objectives:

- To discuss ways to obtain reliable and reproducible test results
- To provide an overview of the contents of a test method
- To describe sample selection and specimen preparation for testing
- To identify commonly used tests for determining fiber or fabric properties

Consumer perception plays an important role in determining whether a product is of desirable quality for them to purchase at the given price. As you have learned so far, quality must be considered when designing and developing products, selecting materials and component parts, and determining methods for construction and finishing. Quality is measured through testing and evaluation during the development and manufacturing phases to ensure specifications and standards are being met, as well as complying with mandatory or voluntary regulations. Understanding the importance of testing and how samples are selected, specimens prepared, tested, and evaluated allows for individuals to make informed

decisions when purchasing garment materials and components. Taking the extra time and investing in standardized testing to evaluate and verify these materials ultimately leads to better quality products in the marketplace and customer satisfaction.

This chapter and the next are a little more technical, given the scientific nature of textile testing. That said, after working through Chapters 11 and 12, you will have a better understanding of the importance of standardized testing, how it is conducted, what is measured, and how the information is used to improve the quality of materials and products. The data collected provides insight into problems that should be remedied during development to avoid unexpected product failures and customer dissatisfaction. You will also gain a better understanding of the problems encountered with your own clothes that could have been avoided if testing had been conducted.

OVERVIEW OF STANDARDS FOR TESTING AND SAMPLING SEWN PRODUCTS

Testing provides useful information and can be a predictor of whether a garment or material is going to have safety, appearance, or performance problems that will ultimately lead to customer dissatisfaction if not corrected. Some tests can be equated to real-life conditions and time frames whereas others do not provide a direct correlation between hours tested and when failure will occur. But for the tests that do not provide direct correlations between time tested and time in use, they do effectively predict if product performance or appearance will be a significant concern that needs to be addressed prior to the manufacturing or sale of the garment. Testing requires an investment of both time and money from textile and apparel companies, and without it there would be no way of predicting or evaluating how a product would perform as it was intended prior to consumer purchase and use.

Routine testing is an integral part of fiber, yarn, fabric, and finished garment production, which allows companies to produce consistent products at expected quality levels. **Testing** refers to the procedures for evaluating materials, component parts, and completed garments. This process encompasses sample preparation, experimentation, evaluation, and analysis of data to determine if the materials or products meet appearance, performance, safety, and quality expectations for their intended use.

Reliability and Reproducibility

It is of the utmost importance to use standardized test methods when evaluating product performance and assessing quality. **Standardized test methods** are detailed procedures for conducting experiments, examining, and evaluating textile materials and apparel products. Standards are developed and maintained by international, national, and federal organizations and agencies (see Chapter 1) to ensure consistent quality and compliance with compulsory and safety regulations. Use of standards provides **reliability**, which offers consistent, dependable, and reproducible test method procedures and results obtained during testing. When a standard test method is repeatedly performed on the same material or garment, anywhere in the world, the data collected should be consistent and therefore **reproducible**.

Utilizing a standard test method alone will not totally ensure that the results obtained will be reliable. Testing equipment must be properly calibrated, maintained, and verified to ensure it is working properly. ASTM defines **calibration** as the process used to "determine and record the relationship between a set of standard units of measure and the output of an instrument or test procedure."[1] Standard calibration fabrics are used to verify if the data obtained from testing equipment is reliable. These fabrics provide a means for technicians to verify that a piece of equipment is functioning properly and the data obtained from tested specimens is reliable and consistent. If equipment is not maintained, the test results obtained may not be accurate, and it could be only a matter of time before the machine or apparatus stops working or fails to operate properly. In the meantime, the data provided could result in rejection of materials or products based on incorrect data—or worse—products that should have been flagged as failing could be approved and sold to consumers, resulting in dissatisfaction or product recalls when safety is an issue.

Another factor when ensuring reliability and reproducibility is the textile testing technician. People must be properly trained to perform test methods according to standards and must know how to utilize the testing apparatus or equipment to obtain accurate results. Test methods can be difficult to understand and most require additional training to conduct the test procedure properly with accuracy and reliability. When the same test is conducted by different people on the same fabric the resulting data should be comparable or relatively precise. **Precision** is the "degree of agreement within a set of observations or test results, obtained as directed in a test method."[2]

Although many types of testing equipment are now available with digital readouts or computer generated data, there is equipment still in existence that utilizes a dial and pointer. **Technician error** or **observer error** can also occur if the technician misreads the digital output display or when the pointer on a dial is read from a slight angle rather than directly in front. The latter is known as **parallax error**. Figure 11.1 shows an example of the occurrence of parallax error when the dial is read from the side rather than directly in front, at eye level.

Error can also occur if the technician miscalculates or rounds up the data to a whole number that may no longer accurately represent the results when multiple decimal places are required for analysis. When testing multiple specimens an average of the results is typically calculated to obtain the **mean (x-bar or $\bar{x}$)**. The formula used for calculating mean is $\left[\bar{x} = \dfrac{\sum x_i}{n} \right]$. The Σ symbol represents the sum. The number of individual observations is represented in the equation as (x_i) and n symbolizes the overall number of observations. The number of **significant figures** (the number of known reliable figures) providing a degree of accuracy and certainty that should be reported is typically outlined in the calculation section of the test method. For example, if the result is 9.3 it has two significant figures, 9.25 has three significant figures, and 19.65 has four significant figures.

The remaining factor that can impact reliability is the environmental conditions where the test is conducted. Standard atmospheric conditions for testing will be discussed in this chapter following the section on sampling.

Components of a Standard Test Method

The contents of test methods follow similar formats regardless of the developing source (i.e., ISO, ASTM, AATCC, EN, BS, JIS, and so on), although the heading for each topic covered within a test method may vary slightly. Depending upon the specific test method selected, there may be additional contents or some portions may be excluded. The basic framework of a test method will be discussed to provide an understanding of the contents included.

Each standard will indicate the developing source and be designated by a test method name and number. The **test method name** distinguishes the type of test covered within the standard. **Test method number** is used to identify an individual standard, and the numeric configuration will vary by the developing organization.

Scope is the first section of a test method, and it summarizes the purpose of the test and the materials covered by the standard. **Referenced documents**, also known as **normative references**, follow and present additional standards that are related to the selected test method. Important terms used within the test standard are defined in the **terminology** section. The **summary of test method, summary of practice,** or **principle** follows next to provide a concise

Figure 11.1 Parallax error shown on this dial reading that has been viewed from the side rather than straight on
Getty Images

explanation of the procedure to be performed. Not all test methods will contain a section on **significance and use**, but for those that do, information regarding acceptance testing procedures and how the data gathered should be used is explained. **Acceptance testing** is conducted to determine if a material or product meets the specified criteria for approval.

Apparatus describes the type of machine or equipment used for conducting the test. If the equipment requires preparation or calibration prior to testing, additional guidelines will be outlined. Reagents and materials required to perform the test may also be discussed with the apparatus or in their own respective section. A **reagent** is a substance or compound used for testing in order to produce a chemical reaction. Some test methods will contain **safety precautions** or **hazards** detailing precautions that should be taken to ensure the lab technician's safety when conducting the procedure.

The **sampling** or **test specimens** section contains detailed procedures for taking and preparing specimens such as dimensions, the number required, and the methods for preparing them prior to testing. **Conditioning** is another component that is included in many test methods and involves exposing specimens and materials to standard atmospheric conditions to prepare them for testing.

The **procedure** section includes specific instructions for how to perform the test. After the data is collected, the **calculation** portion provides clear instructions and formulas when applicable for computing test results. Test methods may include an **evaluation** category rather than calculation when ratings using photographic standards, visual standards, or gray scales are required. The **report** section typically follows and offers direction for documenting the procedures used for testing and calculation of data or standards used for rating, accompanied by a statement of results. Some standards contain information regarding **precision and bias**. If contained in the method, it provides statistical data for determining if a significant difference exists and if there are factors that may influence

test results. **Key words** may also be listed for important terms used within the testing standard.

Sampling

Testing and evaluation allows for conclusions to be drawn regarding appearance, performance, and safety from small portions of a lot sample to represent the larger population of materials or garments. When materials or garments are tested, **samples** must be acquired for observation and evaluation in order to provide a means for drawing conclusions about the population from which textile fibers, yarns, yardage, apparel components, or finished products are drawn.[3] **Lot samples** are randomly selected garments or materials taken from one or more main stock or production lot shipments to be utilized for conducting acceptance testing. **Lab samples** are then obtained from the lot sample to supply specimens for testing.[4] See Figure 11.2 for an example of how samples are selected from a production lot to obtain lab samples and specimens. Some test methods require a **control**, which can be a fabric sample or a garment that is used as a standard for drawing comparisons. The individual portion of a lab sample used for conducting a test is known as a **specimen**. Specimens can be fibers, yarns, sewing thread, material, garment sections, or component parts.

The strategic arrangement and procedure for obtaining test specimens from the sample is known as a **sample plan** (see Figure 11.3). When creating a sample plan it is important to read all of the standards that will be required for testing. This determines how many specimens are needed for each test, dimensions of the specimens, and the direction of grain required on each, as well as additional preparation requirements to get the specimens ready for testing. Knowing this information allows the sample preparer to create a physical or conceptual plan for accurately taking specimens from the lab sample to avoid making errors and to provide the best utilization of the material or garment sample. When a physical sample plan is desired, it can be created on graph paper to maintain accurate dimensions for

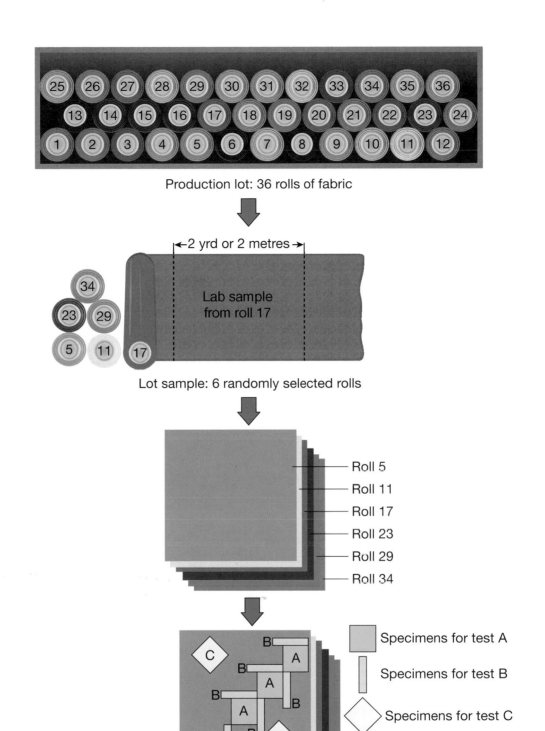

Figure 11.2 Example showing how samples are selected from a production lot to obtain lab samples and specimens
Illustration by Q2A Media Services Private Limited

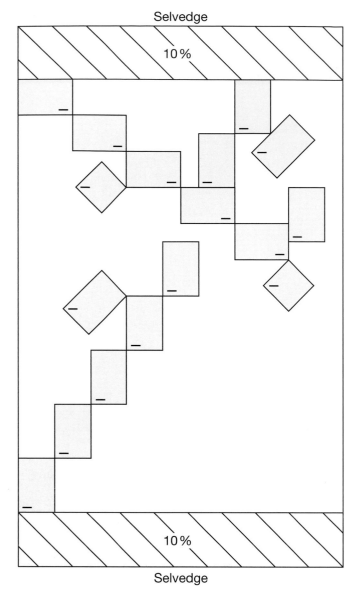

Figure 11.3 Example of a sample plan
Illustration by Q2A Media Services Private Limited

the sample and each of the specimens integrated into the plan.

There are specific rules to abide by when creating a sample plan and obtaining specimens from a sample. These rules are as follows:

1. Take specimens no closer to the selvedge than 10 percent of the fabric width. For example, if the fabric width is 60 inches wide (152.4 cm), specimens should not be taken closer to the fabric edge than 6 inches (15.24 cm). For fabric having a width of 45 inches (114.3 cm) specimens should not be cut closer to the selvedge than 4.5 inches (11.43 cm). The fabric selvedge is constructed differently and is typically denser and can be slightly thicker or thinner than the rest of the material. The selvages of woven materials and warp knitted fabrics are not commonly used in manufactured apparel and are part of the fabric fallout after cutting is completed. Therefore, it is important that test specimens not be taken from these areas because they are not representative of the variations that can be found within the area of the fabric that is used in garments.

2. Take all of the specimens for one test from different parts of the sample in order to capture a variety of areas within the material and to represent an assortment of warp or machine direction yarns and filling or cross direction yarns in fabrics. Specimens for one test should be diagonally staggered to achieve results that are representative of the sample. This is important because lot samples are randomly selected in an effort to provide representative lab samples that reflect the entire production run of goods. This goal should be maintained when specimens are taken.

3. Cut the number of specimens according to the testing standard. Some test methods will require more filling specimens than warp. For example, ASTM D5034 Standard Test Method for Breaking Strength and Elongation of Textile Fabrics (Grab Test) requires five specimens are tested in the warp/machine direction and eight specimens are tested in the filling/cross direction.[5] This particular test has been proven to provide greater variation in the filling or cross direction of the sample; therefore, more specimens are evaluated. Testing more specimens in the filling/cross direction provides

for greater accuracy when calculating the mean and analyzing results.

4. Cut the specimens on the designated grain according to the testing standard. If test specimens are cut off-grain, the results obtained may not be accurate. Additionally, if specimens need to be cut on the bias and they are prepared on straight grain, the data collected from testing may not accurately reflect the performance of the fabric.

5. Use an indelible ink pen to make all identifying marks on the specimens unless otherwise stated in the testing standard. Some methods require samples or specimens to be tested in solutions that can cause markings to dissolve or disappear, making it difficult to finish the evaluation if the testing area measurement points have been removed.

6. Mark the grain in the warp direction on each specimen with a small line or arrow (approximately $1/2$ inch or 1.27 cm in length). Keep all markings out of critical test areas of the specimens. Marking a specimen in a critical test area can deem it unusable before testing ever begins, because the results will be compromised.

7. Mark all specimens before removing them from the sample to avoid confusion as to which specimens were taken from the warp and filling directions or those cut on the bias.

8. Avoid taking specimens containing seams, buttons, buttonholes, or attached decorative elements unless the specific element is being tested (i.e., button impact, seam strength, seam slippage, and so on).

9. Avoid taking specimens from wrinkled, creased, or folded areas of the material or garment sample because they may impact testing and evaluation.

10. Cut accurately. If the specimen template is traced off precisely but careless cutting changes the dimensions of the specimen, it can make it unusable for testing.

Failure to follow any of these guidelines can result in compromised test results, which increase the cost of testing because new samples may need to be obtained, new specimens prepared, tested and evaluated, and valuable time is lost.

Conditioning

Conditioning plays an important role when it is required for testing because it controls the atmospheric conditions in the testing laboratory in order to provide reproducible, more reliable results. The **standard atmospheric conditions** for testing are 70° Fahrenheit, plus or minus (±) 2 degrees (21° Celsius ± 1 degree) and 65 percent relative humidity ± 2 percent. The allowance of ± 1 or 2 degrees (20°–22° Celsius or 68°–72° Fahrenheit) and the ± 2 percent **relative humidity** (63%–67% RH) provides for a small amount of fluctuation to occur within the testing environment.[6,7] Relative humidity (RH) of air is defined by ASTM International as "the ratio of the pressure of water vapor present to the pressure of saturated water vapor at the same temperature."[6] In other words, RH is the quantity of water vapor present in the air that is represented as a percentage of the maximum volume that the air can support at any specified temperature. See Table 11.1 for formulas for converting Fahrenheit to Celsius and the inverse.

There are some fibers that absorb moisture and in turn lose strength, whereas others may become stronger. Some fibers may not be affected at all by the humidity in the air; therefore, physical properties such as strength, elongation, and abrasion can be impacted as well as aesthetic properties such as color. The amount of time required for test specimens in standard atmospheric conditions to reach **moisture equilibrium** depends upon the fiber content. Moisture

Table 11.1 Conversion Formulas for Temperatures	
Temperature to Convert	Conversion Formula
Celsius to Fahrenheit	$1.8 \times °C + 32 = °F$
Fahrenheit to Celsius	$°F - 32 \div 1.8 = °C$

equilibrium is achieved when the material can no longer absorb moisture from the atmosphere or in the converse, lose moisture to the atmosphere.[6] See Table 11.2 for standard conditioning times for textiles used in apparel products.

Some samples or specimens may require pre-conditioning to reduce the amount of moisture content prior to conditioning. The **standard atmosphere for pre-conditioning textiles** is 122°F ± 2 degrees (50°C ± 1 degree) with relative humidity between 5 and 25 percent having a tolerance of ± 2 percent. The specific relative humidity used should be selected based on the amount of drying required prior to conditioning.[6]

A **conditioning room**, **chamber**, or **cabinet** is required to bring samples or specimens up to the designated standard atmospheric conditions for testing. Racks are used to expose all of the surfaces of each sample or specimen to the conditioned environment for the designated period of time, as stated in Table 11.2. The device used for measuring the temperature and relative humidity of the air is a **psychrometer**. This type of **hygrometer** possesses a wet-bulb thermometer that is kept moist through ventilation by aspiration and a dry-bulb thermometer. The dry-bulb measures the air temperature. The moisture content of the air is indicated by the difference between the two thermometer readings. Handheld sling psychrometers can also be used to measure the air temperature and relative humidity. The wet-bulb in this device is wetted and the device is then swung in the air to obtain the measurements. See Figure 11.4 for examples of psychrometers.

The other major component that comprises the standard atmospheric conditions required for testing many apparel products is **air temperature**. The temperature of air is defined by the *Dictionary of Scientific and Technology Terms* as "the temperature of the atmosphere which represents the average kinetic energy of the molecular motion in a small region and is defined in terms of a standard or calibrated thermometer in thermal equilibrium with the air."[8] **Molecules** are made up of bonded atoms. An **atom** is the smallest unit of an **element**, which is the simplest chemical substance that is the basis for building molecular structures and cannot be further broken down using chemical means. See Figure 11.6 for a periodic table of elements. Chemical compounds are composed of a minimum of two elements.

Textile fibers contain molecules. When the air temperature rises it causes their atoms to move at a more rapid pace; conversely, when the temperature is lowered, their movement slows. The molecular structures that comprise textile fibers are long and thin, which allows them to be more densely packed together. Intermolecular bonds are what hold the fiber molecules together. Fibers contain both crystalline and amorphous regions. The **crystalline regions** are the sections of molecules that are aligned and parallel to each other, having consistent strong intermolecular bonds of the same length. When the air temperature is increased the rapid movement of the atoms within these crystalline regions is not significantly impacted due to the strength of the intermolecular bonds. However, **the amorphous regions** of the fiber structure are not as clearly defined. There are fewer intermolecular bonds found within the amorphous regions, and they

Table 11.2 Standard Conditioning Times for Testing Textiles for Apparel

Fiber Content	Minimum Conditioning Time Required (in hours)
Animal and Protein Fibers	8
Cellulose Fibers	6
Viscose	8
Acetate	4
Manufactured Fibers	2
Blended Fibers	The fiber component within the blend that requires the longest conditioning period shall be used when determining the minimum conditioning time required.

Sources: ASTM International, 2014, "ASTM D1776-08e1 Standard Practice for Conditioning and Testing Textiles," *2014 Online Standards*; British Standards Institute, BS EN ISO 139: 2005 + A1: 2011, *Textiles Standard Atmosphere for Conditioning and Testing*

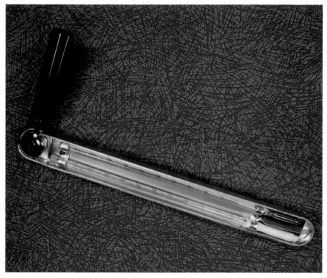

(b)

Figure 11.4 a and b Stationary and sling psychrometers; (a) Stationary psychrometer; (b) Sling psychrometer
(a) Stretch/Shutterstock; (b) RUNK/SCHOENBERGER/ Grant Heilman Photography

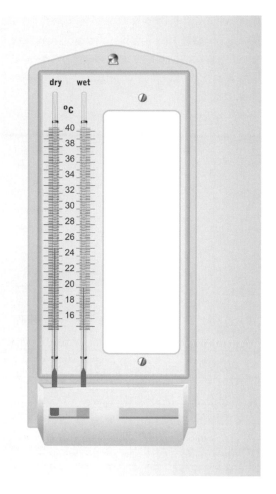

(a)

vary in length, causing them to be weaker and less stable than in the crystalline regions. See Figure 11.5 for an example of a fiber structure showing both crystalline and amorphous regions. When the air temperature is raised the rapid movement of the atoms within the amorphous regions can cause the weaker intermolecular bonds to break. Changes in temperature can affect the color, drape, flexibility, strength, elongation, and abrasion properties of textile products. Chemical changes may also occur due to reactions resulting from the deviations in atmospheric conditions. Utilizing a controlled environment during laboratory testing ensures the data collected will provide more reproducible, reliable results.

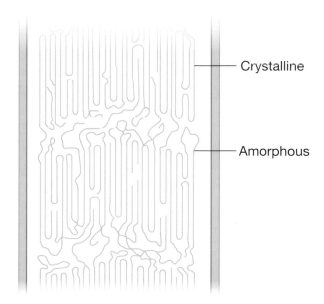

Crystalline

Amorphous

Textile fiber

Figure 11.5 Crystalline and amorphous regions within a fiber
Illustration by Q2A Media Services Private Limited

RAW MATERIALS AND SEWN PRODUCTS TESTING

Test methods can be categorized into two groups—nondestructive and destructive. When measurements can be taken directly on the lab sample without causing aesthetic or physical damage, it is classified as a **nondestructive test**. On the other hand, **destructive tests** require testing directly on the sample or specimens to be cut in order for testing and evaluation to occur. During this type of test, the sample or specimen is destroyed, and the method cannot be repeated without a new sample or preparation of new specimens.

Testing most often occurs within a laboratory setting on individual component materials as well as garments to assist in appropriate selection during the development process. Materials testing allows for individual fabrics and components to be tested

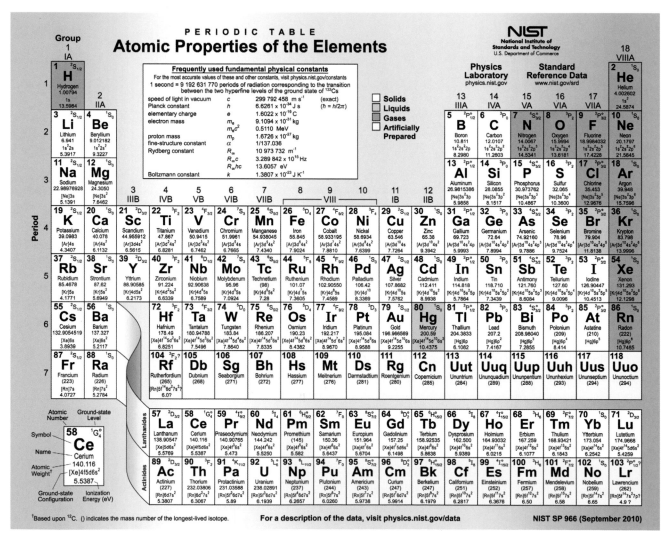

Figure 11.6 Periodic table of elements
Courtesy of NIST, nist.gov

independent of each other to determine physical, appearance, and performance characteristics. Testing of materials prior to incorporation into garments allows designers and product developers to make informed selection decisions based on established quality standards for the brand, product category, use, care, and performance expectations of their customers. Test data offered by mills or fabric suppliers allows for designers and product developers to make more informed purchase decisions. Aesthetic and performance requirements can be analyzed and comparisons made to determine compatibility of components and quality level prior to integrating them into a garment.

Laboratory testing is also completed on finished products after production to ensure the goods being shipped meet established quality and performance standards, as well as safety regulations. Product testing is important to determine the compatibility of component materials when actually assembled into a garment. This allows for testing and evaluation of fit, performance, construction, and care to determine if the interaction between component parts is acceptable.

Laboratory testing does not always equate to real-life use and time-in-use; however, it can be utilized as a predictor of customer dissatisfaction due to poor performance, adverse aesthetic appearance, or compromised fit due to wear and care. Laboratory testing provides a foundation for determining defects and problematic performance issues that need to be addressed prior to committing to production yardage/meters. Poor performing materials and products may be replaced by those that meet specifications or designers can work with mills, converters, or manufacturers to make improvements to increase the quality and performance to the desired levels.

In addition to laboratory testing, garments can also be worn to evaluate the expected performance of a product in the environment in which the consumer will use it. This is known as **wear testing** or **wear-service conditions**. Standards are still used when garments are evaluated through wear testing.

For example, ASTM International provides specific guidelines for this type of testing under D3181 Standard Guide for Conducting Wear Tests on Textiles.[9] Wear testing requires people who have agreed to don the garment to test the fit, aesthetic appearance, function, and performance for its intended use for a specified period of time, as well as refurbish the item as part of the testing. This type of testing typically requires more garments but provides actual results of garment behavior in normal use conditions that laboratory testing cannot fully simulate.

Characterization Testing

There are standard tests performed to determine the properties of the components utilized for sewn products. It is important for manufacturers to verify that the fibers, yarns, or fabrics they are purchasing meet designated specifications. The tests most commonly used to characterize materials include fiber identification, yarn construction, fabric count, weight, and thickness.

Fiber Identification

Verification of fiber content is a critical part of quality testing. Accurate disclosure of fiber content on apparel labels is a compulsory regulation around the globe for products to legally enter into commerce. Burning behavior can help classify fibers into broader categories of cellulose and protein while more specific information can be gathered for synthetic fibers. Factors to consider as part of the evaluation include the reaction of the fiber or yarn when introduced to a flame and when it is removed, the odor, and the characteristics of the ash or char that remains can all provide clues to fiber identification (see Chapter 3, Table 3.3). However, burning behavior cannot provide evidence regarding the specific species of natural fibers present with any level of certainty or provide specific information regarding fiber percentages when different fibers are blended together. For example, if the burning behavior is representative of a protein-based fiber, one cannot distinguish through this means if the fiber is wool, cashmere, mohair, llama, or a blend of two or more of these fibers. When fiber blends are present, each fiber needs to be separated and tested to determine its percentage in weight within the fabric's overall composition. Common standard methods used in testing labs to identify the fibers present in textile products include microscopic observation and chemical analysis. Natural fibers are typically identified by their physical shape, whereas manufactured fibers are best distinguished by their chemical structure.

Observation using a microscope allows for longitudinal or cross-sectional views to determine the specific type of cellulose or protein fiber based on length, diameter, and shape. Fiber specimens can be mounted in air, mineral oil, or other mounting liquid to prepare for observation. **Microscopic observation** provides the highest level of accuracy when identifying cellulose and protein-based fibers. This method requires a compound microscope with the ability to magnify 100 to 500 times, having eye pieces matched to the objectives, and equipped with a polarizer and analyzer (see Figure 11.7).[10,11] **Microscope objectives** are the primary means for forming the image and determining the level of image quality that can be produced by the equipment.[12] The **polarizer** and **analyzer** (an additional polarizer) allow for the maximum amount of light to be transmitted so the lab technician can observe the fiber or yarn specimens.[13] See Figure 11.8 for photomicrograph of cellulose fiber cross-section and longitudinal views.

The compound microscope with polarizer can also provide additional observations when specimens are prepared by immersing them in a drop of liquid possessing a reflective index of 1.55 (i.e., mixture of chloronaphthalene and centane or equivalent) and positioning the longest dimension of the fiber to align with 12 and 6 o'clock.[10] The polarized light beams are reflected in two opposing directions (one positioned at 12 o'clock and the other positioned at 6 o'clock), causing the rays to align. The observation of the refractive indices and birefringence can be used to help distinguish the subtle differences in fibers that can otherwise be more difficult to discern

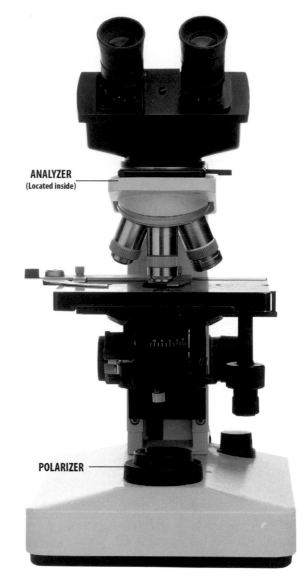

ANALYZER (Located inside)

POLARIZER

Figure 11.7 Microscope with polarizer
Stockbyte/Getty Images

using other tests. A fiber's **refractive index** is measured by the speed in which the polarized light wave of the microscope travels through the mounted fiber specimen when compared to the speed of light in a vacuum. The reflective index of a fiber's optical property is dependent upon the direction and transmittance of polarized light, which is known as **birefringence** or **double refraction**. During testing, the lab technician observes the silhouette or outline

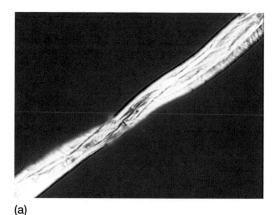

(a)

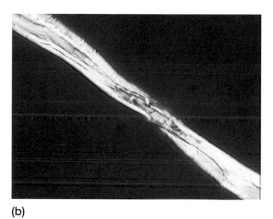

(b)

Figure 11.8 Photomicrographs of cotton
Courtesy of AATCC

of the fiber structure and adjusts the focus to determine the manner in which the light is reflected through the specimen.

Manufactured fibers are best identified through means of determining the chemical nature through solubility, infrared spectroscopy, and density tests. Solubility tests are useful for determining the fiber content of manufactured fibers because they can be dissolved in reagent solutions. The process of dissolving fibers in chemical substances or reagents is known as **solubility**, which is particularly reliable for accuracy in identifying the specific manufactured fiber(s) present within a material. Small specimens of fiber are weighed and then submerged in a chemical solvent. The testing vessel is shaken vigorously and left to stand

for a designated period of time and is then repeated at specified intervals. When this phase of testing has concluded the solution containing the fiber specimens is filtered. The remaining fiber or residue is dried and re-weighed to determine its solubility with the particular reagent tested. This process is completed with the different reagents until the fiber content is identified. It is critical for each solution to be fresh to avoid any residual from another fiber to interfere with the test results. The results from testing a variety of reagents are compared to generic classes of fibers in which the solubility to various chemical solutions is known. This comparison of data provides a means for identifying the specific fiber being tested. See Table 11.3 for common reagents used for solubility testing.

Infrared spectroscopy (IR spectroscopy) is another method for chemically analyzing fiber specimens through measurement of "infrared absorption spectra associated with rotational and vibrational energy levels of molecules."[14] The infrared radiation is revealed/displayed through wavelengths within the

Table 11.3 Commonly Used Reagents for Solubility Testing

Reagent	Chemical Formulation
Acetic Acid	(CH_3COOH)
Acetone	(CH_3COCH_3)
Ammonium Thiocyanate Solution	$(NH4SCN)$ (70%)
Chloroform	$(CHCI^3)$
m-Cresol	$(CH_3C_6H_4OH)$
Cyclohexane	(C_6H_{12})
nn'-Dimethylformamide	$(HCON(CH_3)_2)$ (DMF)
Formic Acid	$(HCOOH)$ (98%)
Hydrochloric Acid	$(HCL)^*$
Lead Acetate Solution	$(Pb(CH_3COO)_2)$ (2.0%)
Methylene Chloride	(CH_2CI_2)
Sodium Hydroxide Solution	$(NaOH)$ (5.0%)
Sulfuric Acid Solution	(H_2SO_4) (75%)
Trichloroethylene	$(CHCI:CCI_2)$

Note: *Mix with distilled water at a ratio 1 + 1
Source: ASTM International, 2014, "ASTM D276-12 Standard Test Methods for Identification of Fibers in Textiles," *2014 Online Standards*

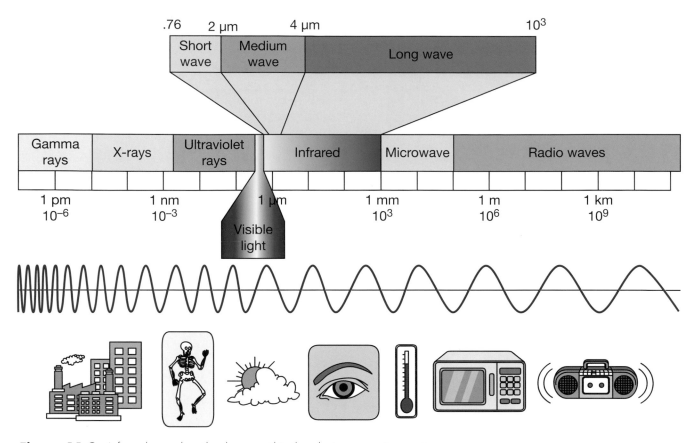

Figure 11.9 Infrared wavelengths shown within the electromagnetic spectrum
Illustration by Q2A Media Services Private Limited

infrared spectrum (see Figure 11.9). This wavelength of concentrated radiation is absorbed by the specimen and dispersed into the spectrum and the interaction is documented on a graph for comparative analysis, evaluation, and identification. The infrared absorption spectrum graphs are then compared to standards to determine which manufactured fiber is represented in the specimen. The apparatus used for measuring the electromagnetic radiation to determine the presence and strength of chemical compounds comprising the specimen is a FTIR or double-beam **infrared spectrophotometer** (see Figure 11.10). This apparatus is calibrated to scan a range of 2.5 to 15 μm (micrometers) to detect and quantify electromagnetic radiation.[10,11]

Fiber identification can be verified by evaluating density and melting point. **Fiber density** is described as the mass per unit volume which can be measured

Figure 11.10 FTIR infrared spectrophotometer
© Charles Anderson/AndersonMaterials.com

by first weighing a specimen in the air and then again after immersion in a lower density liquid than the fiber itself. This allows for thorough wetting of the fiber specimen so conclusions can be drawn regarding its density.[10,11] The force applied from beneath the submerged fiber specimen by the lower density liquid is known as **buoyant force**. "Its magnitude is equal to the weight of the fluid displaced" by the fiber specimen which allows for fiber density to be determined.[15]

Manufactured fibers can also be tested for melting point to help verify the type of fiber. **Melting point** is the "temperature at which the material [fiber specimen] begins to lose its shape or form and becomes molten or liquefies."[16] Heat is applied to a fiber specimen; it is then monitored for changes, and any temperature variation is documented. The melting point is then compared to those outlined in the standard to identify the fiber specimen. See Table 11.4 for the melting points of fibers used in apparel items.

Yarn Construction

Yarn number, the method for measuring a yarn's fineness, is an important aspect of evaluating yarns and fabrics. The two types of yarn number systems used in apparel are direct and indirect. The **direct yarn number system** is used for measuring filament yarns made of manufactured fiber or silk. This system measures the mass/weight per unit length of filament yarn. The larger the yarn the higher the yarn number will be. Furthermore, a finer yarn is designated by a low yarn number. There are more specific designations within the direct yarn number system, depending upon the content and construction of the yarn, such as denier, tex, decitex, and kilotex. The **indirect yarn number system** is used for measuring the length per unit of mass/weight of spun yarn made from staple fibers. The finer the yarn, the higher the yarn number will be, and a thicker yarn is designated by a lower yarn number. There are several designations within the indirect yarn number system, including cotton count, linen lea, metric count, woolen run, and worsted count. See Table 11.5 for the yarn number systems and the units of measurement for expressing linear density in relation to mass/weight.

Table 11.4 Melting Points of Fibers Commonly Used in Apparel

Fiber	Melting Point °F	°C
Acetate	500	260
Acrylic	DNM	DNM
Cotton	DNM	DNM
Flax	DNM	DNM
Modacrylic	DNM	DNM
Nylon 6	426	219
Nylon 6,6	489	254
Olefin-Polyethelene	275 or 338	135 or 170
Polyester		
2 GT (Ethylene glycol)	493	256
4 GT (1,4-butanediol)	441	227
CHDM-T (1,4-cyclohexandimethanol)	437	225
Rayon	DNM	DNM
Silk	DNM	DNM
Spandex	446	230
Triacetate	550	288
Wool	DNM	DNM

Note: DNM = Does Not Melt
Source: ASTM International, 2014, "ASTM D276-12Standard Test Methods for Identification of Fibers in Textiles," *2014 Online Standards*

Yarn construction refers to the structure of the yarn. Yarn construction for single spun yarns is reported in the following order: (1) yarn number and name of system, (2) twist direction, and (3) number of turns per inch, per centimeter, or per meter. If known, additional information can be included in parentheses such as fiber length, average linear density of fibers, and percentage of fibers for yarns comprised of a blend of different fibers. For example, a cotton-spun single yarn having a yarn number of 24, reported using cotton count (indirect yarn number system), with Z-twist and 15 turns per inch is reported as 24 Ne_c Z 15 tpi. Yarn construction for single filament yarns is reported in the following order: (1) yarn number and name of system, (2) number of filaments in the yarn, (3) twist direction, and (4) number of turns per inch, per centimeter, or per meter. For example, a polyester-filament single yarn

Table 11.5 Yarn Number Systems

Direct Yarn Number Systems		
System	Mass Per Unit Length	Fiber Type
Denier (den)	grams/9,000 meters	Filament yarns from silk or manufactured fiber
Tex (tex)	grams/1,000 meters	Spun yarns from silk or manufactured fiber
Kilotex (ktex)	kilograms/1,000 meters	Thick spun yarns from silk or manufactured fiber
Decitex (dtex)	grams/10,000 meters	Fine filament yarns from silk or manufactured fiber
Indirect Yarn Number Systems		
System	Linear Density in Length	Fiber Type Per Unit Mass
Cotton Count (cc or Ne_c)	840 yd lengths/lb	Cotton and cotton blend yarns
Linen Lea (lea)	300 yd lengths/lb	Linen and linen-like yarns
Metric Count (mc or Nm)	1,000 meters/gram	All spun yarns
Woolen Run (wr or Nw_e)	1,600 yd lengths/lb	Coarse woolen and woolen blend yarns
Worsted Count (wc or Nw_w)	560 yd lengths/lb	Fine worsted wool, worsted wool blends, and acrylic yarns

Sources. ASTM International, 2014. *Online Standards 2014: D1244-98 (2011) Standard Practice for Designation of Yarn Construction;* ASTM International, 2014. *Online Standards 2014: D2260-03 (2013) Standard Tables of Conversion Factors and Equivalent Yarn Numbers Measured in Various Numbering Systems;* ISO, 1973. *ISO Standard 2947 Textiles-Integrated Conversion Table for Replacing Traditional Yarn Numbers by Rounded Numbers in the Tex System.* ISO, 1–13; http://www.nexisfibers.com/spip.php?rubrique76

having a yarn number of 100, reported using denier count (direct yarn number system), composed of 34 filaments, with S-twist and 2.5 turns per inch is reported as 100 den f34 S 2.5 tpi. The same filament yarn having zero twist is reported as 100 den f34 t0. For designating plied yarns, a single-to-ply notation is used. When the plied yarns have identical components, the first group of data is reported as stated in the previous examples followed by the multiplication sign (×) when reporting using the direct yarn number system, or a backslash symbol or solidus (/) for reporting using the indirect yarn number system. The second group of data reports the information regarding the ply which includes: (1) number of single yarns comprising the plied yarn, (2) ply twist direction, and (3) number of turns per inch, per centimeter, or per meter of plied yarn. For example, a cotton-spun two-ply yarn reported in single-to-ply notation, having a yarn number of 24, reported using cotton count (indirect yarn number system), with Z-twist and 15 turns per inch, and the ply contains two identical single yarns having S-twist and twisted with 9 turns per inch is stated as 24 Ne_c Z 15 tpi/2 S 9 tpi. When the plied yarns do not have identical components, the first group of data are reported as stated in the above examples followed by the sequence of single yarns

separated by plus signs (+) rather than the multiplication or backslash symbol. This portion of the yarn construction is enclosed in braces ({}) followed by the overall twist and turns per inch for the yarn. This designation of yarn construction is reported as {24 Ne_c Z 15 tpi (cotton) + 10 c.c. Z 23 tpi (cotton)} S 8 tpi.[17]

Fabric Count

Fabric count is determined by counting the number of threads per 1 inch or per 25 mm in both the warp and fill directions or the number of wale loops and course loops per inch or per 2.5 cm. When reporting fabric count, the average number of warp yarns or wale loops is listed first followed by the × (times) symbol or word "by" and then the average number of filling yarns or course loops is stated. For example, a woven fabric having 58 warp yarns per inch (25 mm) and 42 filling yarns per inch (25 mm) would be expressed as 58 × 42 or 58 by 42. For a knitted fabric having 34 wale loops per inch or 2.5 cm and 24 course loops per inch or 2.5 cm, it is expressed as 34 × 24 or 34 by 24.[18,19,20] Sometimes fabric count is reported as the combined totals of yarns or loops in both directions (warp and filling or wales and courses) that appear within a 1 inch or 2.5 cm area. For example, fabric count can be expressed as 420 thread count, meaning there could be 300 warp yarns and 120 filling yarns within a one inch or 25 mm square area (300w + 120f = 420 fabric count). The problem with reporting data this way is that the numbers of yarns occurring in either direction are not independently disclosed. A fabric pick counter (digital or manual), linen tester/ pick glass, or ruler and pointer can be used to count the number of yarns or loops in five representative areas staggered along the length of the fabric to capture different shuttle changes (see Figure 11.11). It is important not to take a count closer to the selvedge than 10 percent of the fabric width because the yarns are typically denser near the selvedge. Fabric count can also be determined through destructive testing. Destructive testing is when a sample is unraveled and each yarn within the area of fabric is removed and counted. Fabric count provides information regarding a material's density by indicating the compactness of the yarns. The openness or compactness of yarns in a fabric provides cues to cost and quality. The more yarns per inch or per 2.5 cm typically indicates higher quality and cost because more fiber is required than a similar fabric having fewer yarns. Higher-density fabrics are typically more durable due to their finer yarns and compact structure that does not allow for yarns to slide or easily ravel.

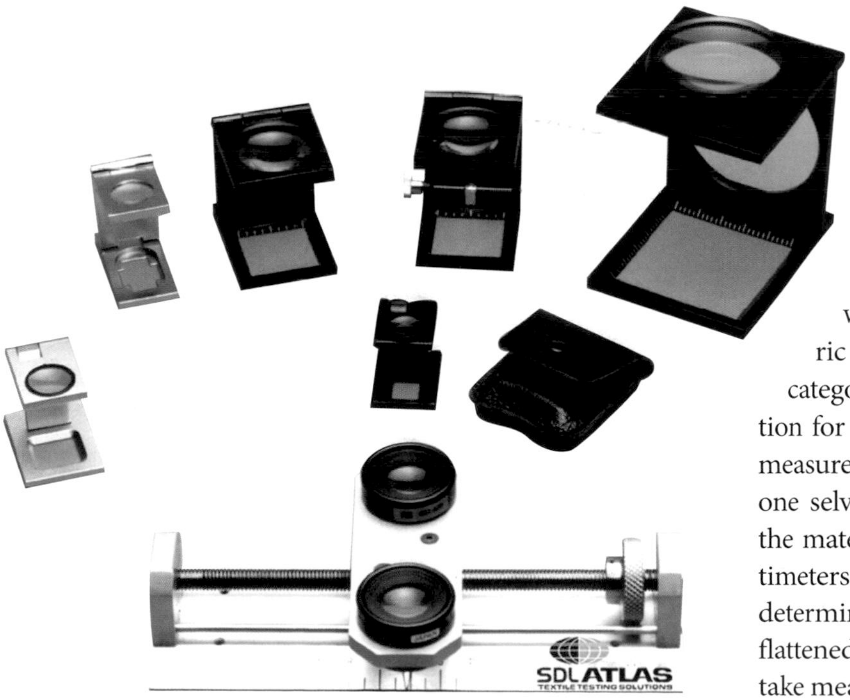

Fabric Thickness

Fabric thickness is defined as the dimension between the top/face and bottom/back surfaces of a material. The fabric's structure and yarn size contribute to its thickness. In the case of nonwoven materials that are not constructed from yarns, the diameter of the fibers as well as the fabric structure contributes to the thickness which is evaluated to determine a material's density rather than count. When measuring fabric thickness the pressure of the gauge tester must be specified in order to maintain consistency.[21] If the pressure applied by the tester is not consistent, the thickness readings will not be accurate. See Figure 11.12 for a variety of fabric thickness testers that can be used.

Fabric Weight

Fabric weight is the mass per unit area of a length of material that also plays a role in determining the density of a material. The fiber content, yarn size, and fabric count impact the weight of the material. Fabric weight is measured on a scale or balance and can be reported as mass per unit area, mass per linear yard or per linear meter, or linear yards per pound or linear meters per kilogram (see Figure 11.13). Refer to Table 11.6 for definitions of weight and method of reporting. Designers, product developers, manufacturers, and suppliers often refer to fabrics as top weight (6 oz/yd^2 or 203.43 g/m^2 or less) or bottom weight (8 oz/yd^2 or 271.25 g/m^2 or more). Fabric weights are further delineated within these two categories. Because fabric width is part of the calculation for linear weight it is important to note how it is measured. For flat goods, fabric width is measured from one selvedge to the other with no tension applied to the material. Width can be reported in inches or centimeters but is always reported in whole numbers. For determining width of tubular knits the diameter of the flattened, relaxed tube is measured. It is important to take measurements at various intervals along the length of the fabric to ensure accuracy. See Table 11.7 for fabric weight designations and common apparel uses.

Figure 11.11 Fabric pick counter device
Photo used by permission of SDL Atlas, LLC

(a)

Figure 11.13 Fabric scale/balance and specimen cutter for measuring weight
Photo used by permission of SDL Atlas, LLC

(b)

(c)

Figure 11.12 a–c Fabric thickness gauges (a) Fabric thickness gauge; (b) Digital material thickness gauge; (c) Hand-held thickness gauge
(a) Michael Zhang/Dreamstime.com; (b) Photo used by permission of SDL Atlas, LLC; (c) Image courtesy Long Island Indicator Service, Inc.

Table 11.6 Fabric Weight Definitions and Method of Reporting

Fabric Weight Term Defined	Reporting Method
Ounces per Square Yard Mass per unit area of a 36-inch by 36-inch piece of material	oz/yd^2
Grams per Square Meter Mass per unit area of a 100-centimeter by 100-centimeter piece of material	g/m^2
Ounces per Linear Yard Mass per unit area of a piece of material that measures 36 inches by the total fabric width in inches	oz/yd
Grams per Linear Meter Mass per unit area of a piece of material that measures 100 centimeters by the total fabric width in centimeters	g/m
Linear Yards per Pound The number of yards of fabric equal to 1 pound using the total width in inches	yd/lb
Linear Meters per Kilogram The number of meters of fabric equal to 1 kilogram using the total width in centimeters	g/kg

Source: ASTM International. *Online Standards 2014: D3776/3776M – 09a (2013) Standard Test Method for Mass Per Unit Area (Weight) of Fabric*

Table 11.7 Fabric Weight Designations and Common Uses for Apparel Products

Fabrics	Weight Range in oz/yd² & g/m²	Uses
Extra-light top weight	1 to 3 oz/yd² 33.91 to 101.72 g/m²	Sheer blouses Lingerie Tissue-weight knitted tops T-shirts
Light top weight	4 to 6 oz/yd² 135.62 to 203.43 g/m²	Blouses Casual skirts Dresses Dress shirts Knitted tops Pajamas Sweaters T-shirts Undergarments
Tropical weight	4.5 to 8.5 oz/yd² 152.58 to 288.20 g/m²	Dresses Jackets Knitted tops Suits[1] Trousers
Bottom or medium weight	7 to 9 oz/yd² 237.34 to 305.15 g/m²	Coats Dresses Jackets Jeans Knitted tops Pants Shorts Skirts Suits[2] Sweaters Sweatshirts Trousers
Heavy bottom weight	10 to 12 oz/yd² 339.06 to 406.87 g/m²	Coats Denim garments Jackets Jeans Pants Parkas Suits[3] Sweaters Sweat pants Sweatshirts
Extra-heavy bottom weight	14 to 16 oz/yd² 474.68 to 542.49 g/m²	Denim garments Jackets Jeans Pants Parkas Sweaters Sweat pants Sweatshirts Winter coats

Note: Suits[1] – Intended for wear in summer or hotter climates
Suits[2] – Intended for all-season wear
Suits[3] – Intended for winter or cold-weather climates
Source: Janace Bubonia. *Fashion Production Terms and Processes,* (New York: Fairchild Books, 2012)

See Table 11.8 for a listing of common international test methods used for determining characteristics of textile materials. The fiber content, yarn construction, fabric count, thickness, and weight all play important roles in materials selection for apparel items. They can affect aesthetic and functional characteristics of gar-ments such as drape, durability, abrasion, breathabil-ity, wicking ability, resiliency, strength, elongation and recovery, surface texture, ease of care, stability, shrink-age or growth during refurbishment, and safety. Each can contribute to the quality level, cost, and perfor-mance of the finished product.

Table 11.8 Common Standard International Test Methods for Fabric Characterization

Fiber Identification	
AATCC 20	Fiber Analysis: Qualitative
AATCC 20A	Fiber Analysis: Quantitative
ASTM D276	Standard Test Method for Identification of Fibers in Textiles
BS EN ISO 1833-10	Textiles Quantitative Chemical Analysis. Mixtures of Triacetate or Polylactide and Certain Other Fibers (Method Using Dichloromethane)
BS EN ISO 1833-11	Textiles Quantitative Chemical Analysis. Mixtures of Cellulose and Polyester Fibers (Method Using Sulfuric Acid)
BS EN ISO 1833-12	Textiles Quantitative Chemical Analysis. Mixtures of Acrylic, Certain Modacrylics, Certain Chlorofibers, Certain Elastanes and Certain Other Fibers (Method using Dimmethylformamide)
BS EN ISO 1833-13	Textiles Quantitative Chemical Analysis. Mixtures of Chlorofibres and Certain Other Fibers (Method Using Carbon Disulfide/acetone)
BS EN ISO 1833-14	Textiles Quantitative Chemical Analysis. Mixtures of Acetate and Certain Chlorofibers (Method Using Acetic Acid)
BS EN ISO 1833-15	Textiles Quantitative Chemical Analysis. Mixtures of Jute and Certain Animal Fibers (Method by Determining Nitrogen Content)
BS EN ISO 1833-16	Textiles Quantitative Chemical Analysis. Mixtures of Polypropylene Fibers and Certain Other Fibers (Method Using Xylene)
BS EN ISO 1833-17	Textiles Quantitative Chemical Analysis. Mixtures of Chlorofibers (Homopolymers of Vinyl Chloride) and Certain Other Fibers (Method Using Sulfuric Acid)
BS EN ISO 1833-18	Textiles Quantitative Chemical Analysis. Mixtures of Silk and Wool or Hair (Method Using Sulfuric Acid)
BS EN ISO 1833-20	Textiles Quantitative Chemical Analysis. Mixtures of Elastane and Certain Other Fibers (Method Using Dimethylacetamide)
BS EN ISO 1833-21	Textiles Quantitative Chemical Analysis. Mixtures of Chlorofibers, Certain Modacrylics, Certain Elastanes, Acetates, Triacetates and Certain Other Fibers (Method Using Cycloheanone)
BS EN ISO 1833-22	Textiles Quantitative Chemical Analysis. Mixtures of Viscose or Certain Types of Cupro or Modal or Lyocell and Flax Fibers (Method Using Formic Acid and Zinc Chloride)
BS EN ISO 1833-24	Textiles Quantitative Chemical Analysis. Mixtures of Polyester and Certain Fibers (Method Using Phenol and Tetraachloroethane)
BS EN ISO 1833-26	Textiles Quantitative Chemical Analysis. Mixtures of Melamine and Cotton or Aramide Fibers (Method Using Hot Formic Acid)
BS ISO 2076	Textiles – Man-made Fibers. Generic Names
BS ISO17751	Textiles – Quantitative Analysis of Animal Fibers by Microscopy – Cashmere, Wool, Specialty Fibers, and Their Blends
JIS L 1030-1	Test Methods for Quantitative Analysis of Fiber Mixtures of Textiles – Part 1: Testing Methods for Fiber Identification
JIS L 1030-2	Test Methods for Quantitative Analysis of Fiber Mixtures of Textiles – Part 2: Testing Methods for Quantitative Analysis of Fiber /Mixtures

Table 11.8 Continued	
Yarn Construction	
ASTM D861	Practice for Use of the Tex System to Designate Linear Density of Fibers, Yarn Intermediates, and Yarns
ASTM D1244	Standard Practice for Designation of Yarn Construction
BS EN ISO 2061	Textiles – Determination of Twist in Yarns – Direct Counting Method
ISO 2	Textiles – Designation of the Direction of Twist in Yarns and Related Products
ISO 1139	Designation of Yarns
ISO 1144	Textiles – Universal System for Designated Linear Density (Tex System)
JIS L 0101	Tex system to Designate Linear Density of Fibers, Yarn Intermediate Yarns and Other Textile Materials
Fabric Thickness	
ASTM 1777	Standard Test Method for Thickness of Textile Materials
BS EN ISO 5084	Textiles – Determination of Thickness of Textiles and Textile Products
Fabric Weight	
ASTM D3776/3776M	Standard Test Methods for Mass per Unit Area (Weight) of Fabric
ISO 3801	Textiles – Woven Fabrics – Determination of Mass per Unit Length and Mass Per Unit
Fabric Count	
ASTM D3775	Standard Test Method for Warp (End) and Filling (Pick) Count of Woven Fabrics
ISO 7211-1	Textiles – Woven Fabrics – Construction – Methods of Analysis Part 1: Methods for the Presentation of a Weave Diagram and Plans for Drafting, Denting, and Lifting
ISO 7211-2	Textiles – Woven Fabrics – Construction – Methods of Analysis Part 2: Determination of Number of Threads per Unit Length
ISO 7211-3	Textiles – Woven Fabrics – Construction – Methods of Analysis Part 3: Determination of Crimp of Yarn in Fabric
ISO 7211-4	Textiles – Woven Fabrics – Construction – Methods of Analysis Part 4: Determination of Twist in Yarn Removed from Fabric
ISO 7211-5	Textiles – Woven Fabrics – Construction – Methods of Analysis Part 5: Determination of the Linear Density of Yarn Removed from Fabric
ISO 7211-6	Textiles – Woven Fabrics – Construction – Methods of Analysis Part 6: Determination of the Mass of Warp and Weft per Unit Area of Fabric

INDUSTRY SCENARIO 11.1 Activewear Customer Complaint

In March 2013, Lululemon recalled close to 17 percent of their black luon yoga pants that retail for $98.00 due to customer complaints that the fabric was see-through. This quality problem has led to approximately $20 million in losses for the company.[22] The company's founder was interviewed November 7, 2013, by Bloomberg TV, and he made the statement that "Frankly, some women's bodies just don't actually work [for the yoga pants]... It's more really about the rubbing through the thighs, how much pressure is there over a period of time, how much they use it."[23] As you can imagine, this comment did not sit well with customers. Another common customer complaint is pilling that results after the yoga pants are worn several times.

■ What are your quality expectations for yoga pants that retail for around $100.00?
■ How could the company have better handled this problem?
■ What measures could have been taken to ensure these quality issues were not reaching consumers?
■ What would you recommend the company do to increase quality of their garments? How should they monitor the quality of the goods they produce?

SUMMARY

As previously stated, quality is measured through testing and evaluation during the development and manufacturing phases to ensure specifications and standards are being met, as well as complying with mandatory or voluntary regulations. This chapter focused on the importance of test methods that allow for companies to obtain reliable and reproducible results regarding the materials and garments they are producing and selling. Testing and evaluation allows for problems to be identified and corrected so they do not reach the customer. Brand image and perception can be significantly impacted by poor quality products. The basic components of test methods were discussed along with selection of samples and preparation of specimens for testing. Methods for evaluating fabric characterization were also identified to provide insight into how compliance with specification data is verified.

ACTIVITIES

1. Convert the following temperatures:

    85°F = _____ °C   25°C = _____ °F

    32°F = _____ °C   15°C = _____ °F

    70°F = _____ °C   30°C = _____ °F

2. Calculate the mean for the following individual test observations.

Number of Observations	Test Result _____ Mean
1	85
2	86
3	87
4	85
5	88

3. Select a woven and a knitted fabric, and complete fabric counts for each. Calculate the means, and report results as indicated in this chapter.

4. Using the woven fabric from activity 3, count the yarns per inch close to the selvedge, and compare your findings with the fabric count conducted properly on the fabric sample. How do the numbers differ?

5. Remove yarns from the materials used in activity 3. Identify the yarn construction for each specimen. Based on the fiber content of the fabric, what yarn number system would be used for determining yarn number for each of the specimens? Identify the twist direction of the yarn for each specimen.

APPAREL QUALITY LAB MANUAL

Please refer to Lab Activity 9.1 Test Methods for Evaluating Selected Garments; Lab Activity 9.2 Piece Goods Appearance and Performance Testing; Lab Activity 9.3 Comparison Garment Appearance and Performance Testing; and Lab Activity 9.4 Comparison Project Garment Results and Performance Specifications in the *Apparel Quality Lab Manual*. These activities will correspond to both Chapters 11 and 12 of this book.

ENDNOTES

1. ASTM International (2013). *ASTM International Standards 2013: ASTM D123-13a2 Standard Terminology Relating to Textiles*, Section 7 Textiles, p. 7.

2. ASTM International (2013). *ASTM International Standards 2013: ASTM D3181-10 Standard Guide for Conducting Wear Tests on Textiles*, Section 7 Textiles, pp. 1–6.

3. ASTM International (2013). *ASTM International Standards 2013: ASTM D123-13a Standard Terminology Relating to Textiles*, Section 7 Textiles, p. 40.

4. ASTM International (2013). *ASTM International Standards 2013: ASTM D123-13a Standard Terminology Relating to Textiles*, Section 7 Textiles, p. 27.

5. ASTM International (2013). *ASTM International Standards 2013: ASTM D5034-09 Standard Test Method for Breaking Strength and Elongation of Textile Fabrics (Grab Test)*, Section 7 Textiles, pp. 1–8.

6. ASTM International (2013). *ASTM International Standards 2013: ASTM D1776-08e1 Standard Practice for Conditioning and Testing Textiles*, Section 7 Textiles, pp. 1–4.

7. British Standards Institute. *BS EN ISO 139: 2005 + A1: 2011, Textiles Standard Atmosphere for Conditioning and Testing.*

8. McGraw-Hill (2003). *Dictionary of Scientific and Technology Terms,* 6th ed. New York: McGraw-Hill, p. 60.

9. ASTM International (2013). *ASTM International Standards 2013: ASTM D3181-10 Standard Guide for Conducting Wear Tests on Textiles,* Section 7 Textiles, Vol. 07.01. West Conshohocken, PA: ASTM International, pp. 1–6.

10. AATCC (2011). "AATCC Test Method 20-2010 Fiber Analysis: Qualitative." *Technical Manual of the American Association of Textile Chemists and Colorists,* Vol. 86. Research Triangle Park: American Association of Textile Chemists and Colorists, pp. 40–58.

11. ASTM International (2013). *ASTM International Standards 2013 ASTM D276-12 Standard Test Methods for Identification of Fibers in Textiles,* ASTM.org. Accessed November 8, 2013, pp. 1–14.

12. Olympus America, Inc. (2012). *Microscope Objectives Introduction.* Microscope Resource Center. Accessed April 8, 2013, http://www.olympusmicro.com/primer/anatomy/objectives.html.

13. Olympus America, Inc. (2012). *Polarized Light Microscopy.* Microscope Resource Center. Accessed April 8, 2013, http://www.olympusmicro.com/primer/techniques/polarized/polarizedhome.html.

14. McGraw-Hill (2003). *Dictionary of Scientific and Technology Terms,* 6th ed. New York: McGraw-Hill, p. 1076.

15. McGraw-Hill (2003). *Dictionary of Scientific and Technology Terms,* 6th ed. New York: McGraw-Hill, p. 299.

16. ASTM International (2013). *ASTM International Standards 2012: ASTM D276-OOa (2008) Standard Test Methods for Identification of Fibers in Textiles,* Section 7 Textiles, Vol. 07.01. West Conshohocken: ASTM International, p. 11.

17. ASTM International (2013). *ASTM International Standards 2013: D1244-98 (2011) Standard Practice for Designation of Yarn Construction,* Section 7 Textiles, pp. 1–5.

18. ASTM International (2013). *ASTM International Standards 2013: D3775-12 Standard Test Method for Warp (End) and Filling (pick) Count of Woven Fabrics,* Section 7 Textiles, pp. 1–4.

19. ISO. *International Standard 7211-2 :1984, Textiles — Woven Fabrics — construction — Methods of analysis — Part 2: Determination of number of threads per unit length, printed in Switzerland,* pp. 1–6.

20. ASTM International (2008). *ASTM International Standards 2013: D3887-96 (2008) Standard Specification for Tolerances for Knitted Fabrics,* Section 7 Textiles, pp. 1–5.

21. ASTM International (2011). *ASTM International Standards 2013: D1777-96 (2011)... Standard Test Method for Thickness of Textile Materials,* Section 7 Textiles, pp. 1–5.

22. Melissa Lustrin and Felicia Patinkin (November 7, 2013). "Lululemon Founder Chip Wilson Blames Women's Bodies for Yoga Pant Problems." Accessed November 8, 2013, http://abcnews.go.com/US/lululemon-founder-chip-wilson-blames-womens-bodies-yoga/story?id=20815278.

23. Bloomberg TV (November 5, 2013). Street Smart. "Lululemon Pants Don't Work for Some Women: Founder." Accessed November 8, 2013, http://www.bloomberg.com/video/lululemon-pants-don-t-work-for-some-women-founder-ATKjgs7jQduIr_ou1z8XYg.html.

CHAPTER TWELVE

Raw Materials and Sewn Products Testing

Objectives:

- To gain an understanding of common cleaning methods for apparel products
- To identify tests to evaluate product appearance and performance for evaluating quality
- To provide an overview of the contents of a standard specification

- To describe how test data is evaluated against standard specifications to determine if materials or products are performing at industry levels for acceptability or are failing
- To discuss corrective measures that can be taken to improve product quality

Garments need to look good as well as function properly for their intended use for the practical life of the product. An apparel item's appearance and performance plays a major role in customer satisfaction and perception of quality. If a garment pills, fades, or discolors after a few washes, the customer is likely to be dissatisfied with the product. Likewise, if a garment shrinks or grows and is no longer comfortable to wear, the customer will also be dissatisfied with the product. If the fabric of a garment shows early signs of wear such as holes or tears, this experience will negatively impact the customer's perception of quality and value the brand offers. Testing and evaluating materials and finished garments can allow for improvements to increase customer satisfaction and avoid unnecessary returns due to poor performance that can be corrected during the development and production stages. Testing also allows for verification of compliance with mandatory regulations for safety and labeling that must be met in order to deliver safe products to consumers and provide information to allow them to make informed purchasing decisions. Apparel products that are tested and analyzed for performance, function, safety, and appearance are generally better-quality garments and ultimately lead to higher customer satisfaction.

CLEANING METHODS

When customers purchase apparel products, they expect garments to maintain their shape and appearance during wear and after multiple cleanings. When designers are developing products, they must take into consideration the care methods required for all of the garment materials and components to ensure compatibility when cleaning occurs. Standards for care labeling, such as those created by ISO/GINITEX, ASTM International, and JIS, provide both manufacturers and consumers with consistent care symbols, terminology, and methods to minimize confusion when refurbishing apparel products (refer to Chapter 9, Figures 9.1–9.3 for care symbol guides). Apparel product developers and manufacturers are responsible for providing appropriate care instructions that will not cause damage to the product. To understand how care methods for sewn products are tested and evaluated, the various cleaning processes such as laundering, drycleaning, and wetcleaning will be discussed.

Laundering

The cleaning process most familiar to consumers is laundering. **Laundering** is a cleaning method that utilizes an aqueous (water) detergent solution and mechanical action such as agitation or tumbling to remove soils and stains, followed by rinsing, extracting (spinning), and drying to refurbish the garment. **Water-soluble soils** such as sugar, salt, syrup, perspiration, and other body fluids, are dissolved and removed with this cleaning process. During laundering, the surface tension of the water must be reduced in order to effectively wet the garments so they can be cleaned. **Wetting** is the process that allows material to be immersed in water or an aqueous solution and become moistened or wet. For example, in a tub of water the molecules are surrounded and attracted by other water molecules, therefore leaving tension at the surface. When garments are placed into water without detergent the surface tension causes beads of water to form on the fabric, which slows the wetting process and can prevent effective cleaning. **Surface active molecules**, also known as **surface active agents** or **surfactants**, are present in soaps and detergents and help facilitate the wetting process. Surfactant molecules are composed of two parts—a carboxylate head that is **hydrophilic**, having an affinity for water (water-loving), and a hydrocarbon chain tail that is **hydrophobic**, having an aversion to water (water-repelling; see Figure 12.1).[1]

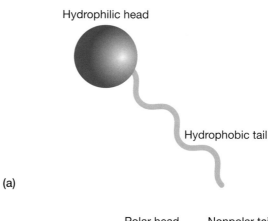

Hydrophilic head

Hydrophobic tail

(a)

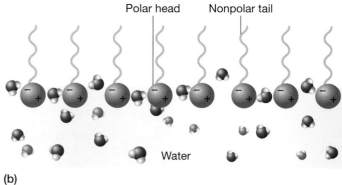

Polar head   Nonpolar tail

Water

(b)

Figure 12.1 a and b Surfactant molecules
Illustrations by Q2A Media Services Private Limited

Laundry Soap Versus Detergent

Laundry soaps and detergents both contain surfactant molecules and can be used for cleaning. **Soaps** are made from fats and oils or fatty acids from animal or plant sources that are treated with strong alkali, such as sodium or potassium. Although soaps are water soluble, they are less desirable for use in laundering because they are not as effective in cleaning due to their reaction with hard water. Soaps and hard water form **insoluble compound deposits**, known as soap scum, which build up on clothing and cleaning equipment. The calcium and magnesium ions present in hard water combined with soap are the primary catalysts for forming insoluble compounds that inhibit sudsing. Hard water minerals are still present in low concentrations in soft water and can also be found in soils on garments, so cleaning in soft water does not eliminate this problem.[1]

The more effective alternative to soap is detergent. **Synthetic detergents** are composed of alcohol, sulfate, and **petrochemicals** derived from petroleum or **oleochemicals** derived from fats and oils. Detergents are preferred for laundering because they do not react with hard water minerals like soap does. The hydrocarbon chains found in petrochemicals and oleochemicals make up the tail ends of the surfactant molecules. Whereas these hydrocarbon chains have an aversion to water, they possess an affinity for soils containing oil and grease (oil and grease loving). Trioxide, sulfuric acid, and ethylene oxide comprise the water-loving portion of the surfactant molecule in detergents.[1] During the laundering process, surfactants not only aid in wetting garments, they also assist with loosening, emulsifying, and suspending soils in the wash bath until they are rinsed away. The water-loving heads of the surfactant molecules are attracted to the water molecules in the wash bath, whereas the water-averting tails are attracted to the soils containing oil and grease. **Micelles** composed of surfactant molecules are formed to surround and loosen soils in the wash bath with the assistance of hand or machine agitation or tumbling action. Micelle formations hold soils in suspension until they are rinsed away to prevent them from re-depositing on garments during laundering (see Figure 12.2). See Table 12.1 for detergent ingredients and their cleaning functions.

Standard Reference Laundry Detergent is available in liquid or powder form and can be purchased with or without optical brighteners. These detergents are used for testing materials and garments in a laboratory setting to provide consistency and reproducibility of results. According to AATCC (American Association of Textile Chemists and Colorists), "powder detergents perform optimally at higher pHs

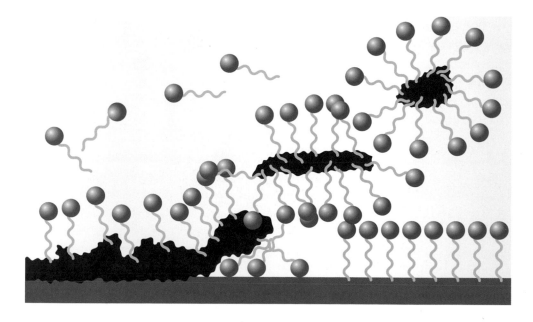

Figure 12.2 Micelle formation
Illustration by Q2A Media Services Private Limited

Table 12.1 Detergent Ingredients and Cleaning Functions

Ingredients	Cleaning Functions
Surfactants	Facilitate wetting of garments
	Loosening, emulsifying, and suspending soils in the wash bath until they are rinsed away
Builders	Control pH level of water
	Soften the water by holding hard water minerals in suspension until they are rinsed away
	Protect washing machines from corrosion
Enzymes*	Aid in removal of protein and starch based soils
Protease Enzymes	Lift protein soils
Amylase Enzymes	Lift starch soils
Optical Brighteners/ Fluorescent Whiteners	Make fabrics appear intensely white or colors more vibrant
Soluble Dyes	Serve no cleaning function. Enhance appearance of detergent only.
Perfumes	Serve no cleaning function. Enhance the scent of detergent and laundered items.

Note: Enzymes*are also commonly found in pre-treat laundry products to aid in stain removal.

(pH=~10). This higher pH is a relatively hostile environment for stains, making powdered detergents very effective at stain removal; however, the higher pH also tends to negatively impact fibers and dyes."[2] Furthermore, "liquid detergents perform optimally at lower pHs (pH=~8.5). Because this pH is closer to neutrality, liquid laundry detergents tend to be less harsh on fabrics and dyes."[2] The AATCC Standard Reference Laundry Detergents are considered comparable to the top five nationally marketed detergents in the United-States.[2] These detergents are used when conducting testing using AATCC home laundering and colorfastness methods. SDC (Society of Dyers and Colourists) Standard Reference Detergents IEC Non Phosphate Reference Detergent (without fluorescent brighteners) or ECE Phosphate Reference Detergent (contains fluorescent brighteners) are available in powder form and used when conducting testing using ISO, BS, and EN, home laundering, and colourfastness test methods.[3]

Laundering Equipment

ISO 6330 *Textiles – Domestic washing and drying Procedures for Textile Testing* standard designate three types of domestic washing machines used for testing: Type A – Horizontal axis front-loading, Type B – Vertical axis top-loading agitator, and Type C – Vertical axis top-loading pulsator.[4] AATCC M6 *Standardization of Home Laundering Test Conditions* designates three types of washing machines: Top-loading, high efficiency top-loading, and front-loading washing machines.[5] See Figure 12.3 for illustrations of washing machine styles. The high efficiency top-loading washing machines are similar to standard top-loading machine models except they are equipped with automatic temperature control settings that regulate the water temperature of the wash cycle.[5] Top-loading washing machines have either an oscillating washing action or a pulsating movement. For those having an agitator, the vertical axis moves in a back and forth motion to help clean the clothes. Pulsating machines utilize a multi-directional tornado-like action that pushes garments from the bottom of the wash tub up to the top in a whirling action. Front-loading washing machines use tumbling action. A wash tub having a horizontal axis is designed with **baffles** or paddles inside the tub to submerge the clothes into the wash water by means of a tumbling action to help with cleaning. See Figure 12.4 for types of washing action found in top-loading and front-loading washing machines.

ISO 6330 *Textiles – Domestic washing and drying Procedures for Textile Testing* standard and AATCC M6 *Standardization of Home Laundering Test Conditions* designates a tumble dryer as the equipment needed to machine dry materials and garments when testing.[4,5] The **dryer drum** is where the clothing items are placed for drying. There are baffles inside this drum that keep the garments tumbling through the

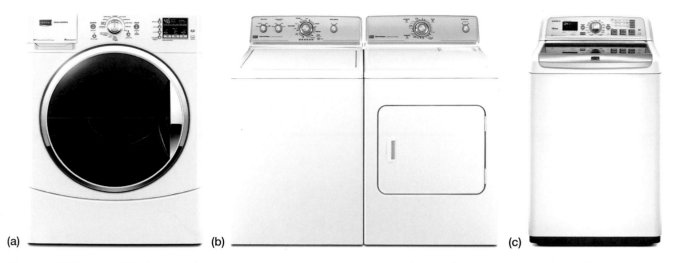

(a) (b) (c)

Figure 12.3 a–c Washing machine types (a) Front-loading washing machine with horizontal axis; (b) Top-loading washing machine with vertical axis agitator; (c) High-efficiency top-loading washing machine with vertical axis agitator © Whirlpool Corporation

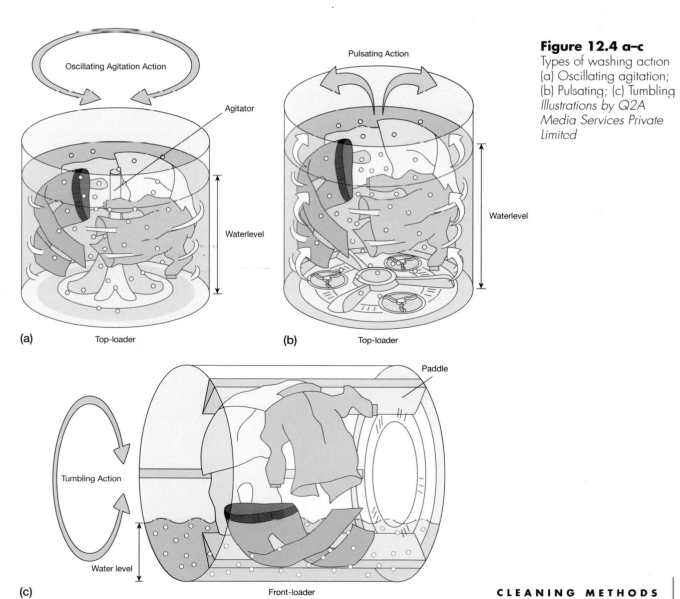

Oscillating Agitation Action

Agitator

Waterlevel

(a) Top-loader

Pulsating Action

Waterlevel

(b) Top-loader

Figure 12.4 a–c
Types of washing action
(a) Oscillating agitation;
(b) Pulsating; (c) Tumbling
Illustrations by Q2A Media Services Private Limited

Paddle

Tumbling Action

Water level

(c) Front-loader

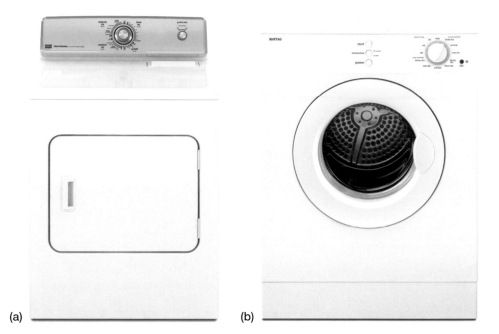

Figure 12.5 a and b
Tumble dryers
© Whirlpool Corporation   (a)   (b)

air to assist with moisture removal. See Figure 12.5 for tumble dryers appropriate for testing. Most consumer dryers are equipped with an automatic moisture-sensing cycle and have moisture-sensing bars or strips (see Figure 12.6). When the automatic moisture sensing drying cycle is selected, the moisture of the wash load in the drum is monitored by an electronic circuit board that communicates with the sensing bars to determine the electrical resistance. When the moist garments come in contact with the sensors, the electricity transferred between the strips is measured. Electricity is easily transferred when water is present. When moisture is no longer present in the drum, the electronic control board will signal the dryer timer to advance to the cool down cycle or shut off.[6] In a laboratory setting, timed drying is used rather than moisture-sensing controls to maintain consistency, reproducibility, and reliability of results. The wash water temperatures and cycle times as well as drying temperatures, heat output, and drying times vary according to the type of machines used and the particular type of test to be conducted, in addition to the test standard selected.

Bleach

The two categories of **oxidizing bleach** used in commercial and domestic/home laundering include chlorine and oxygen. **Chlorine bleach** used for laundering is available in a liquid form. Water is considered a solvent and acts as the basis for diluting the other

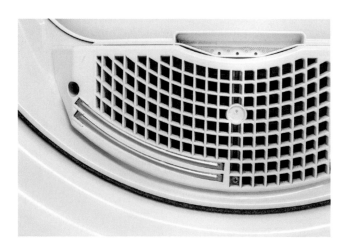

Figure 12.6 Dryer moisture sensor
© Ken Cavanagh Photo courtesy of KenCavanagh.com

Table 12.2 Bleach Ingredients and Functions

Bleach Type	Ingredients	Function
Chlorine Liquid Bleach	Water	Base for dilution
	Sodium Hypochlorite	Primary active ingredient that whitens Aids in cleaning and stain removal Kills certain organisms found on laundry items
Oxygen Liquid Bleach	Water	Base for dilution
	Hydrogen Peroxide	Primary active ingredient for stain removal Sanitizes the wash load
	Myristamine Oxide	Thickening agent
	Sodium C10-16	Surfactant used to remove oily and grease-based soils
	Alkylbenzenesulfonate	Acts as a sudsing agent
	Disodium Distyrylbiphenyl Disulfonate	Optical/fluorescent brightening and whitening agent
	Sodium Hydroxide	Adjusts pH level Aids in removal of grease, oil, and acid-based stains
Oxygen Powder Bleach	Sodium Chloride	Stabilizes and thickens the liquid solution
	Sodium Carbonate or	Builds alkalinity by neutralizing acids to improve cleaning efficiency
	Soda Ash	Aids in the removal of grease and alcohol-based stains
	Sodium Hydroxide or Caustic Soda	Adjusts pH level of chlorine bleach Aids in removal of grease, oil, and acid-based stains
	Sodium Polyacrylate	Prevents soils from re-depositing on the garments during laundering

Sources: The Clorox Company, (2013), accessed June 25, 2013, http://www.clorox.com/products/clorox-regular-bleach/#Doing Laundry Product-Clorox® Regular-Bleach ID-18-Whites; The Clorox Company, (2013), *What's in it anyway? Clorox Regular Bleach: Whites*, accessed June 25, 2013, http://www.clorox.com/products/clorox-regular-bleach/

ingredients found in chlorine bleach to reduce its corrosive nature. See Table 12.2 for bleach ingredients and their functions. The primary active ingredient whitens, aids in cleaning and stain removal, as well as killing certain organisms found on laundry items (see Table 12.3 for a list of germs found on laundry items). When consumers do laundry, the recommended amount of liquid chlorine bleach to add to a load of white items is 3/4 cup.[7]

The other form of oxidizing bleach used in laundering is **oxygen bleach**. This type is available in liquid or powder form and is considered a color-safe bleach. Water is the base for diluting the other ingredients found in liquid oxygen bleach (see Table 12.2). The primary active ingredient helps remove stains and sanitizes the wash load. Oxygen bleach is also available in powder form (see Table 12.2). When this

Table 12.3 Common Germs/Organisms Found on Laundry Items

Bacteria	Viruses
E. coli	Adenovirus Type 2
Salmonella	Cytomegalovirus
Pseudomonas aeruginosa	Flu
Shigella dysenteriae	Hepatitis A virus
Staphylococcus	Herpes simplex Type 2
Fungi	Respiratory Syncytial Virus (RSV)
Candida albicans (a yeast)	Rhinovirous
Trichophyon mentagrophytes (cause of athlete's foot)	Rotavirus
	Rubella virus

Source: The Clorox Company, (2013), accessed June 25, 2013, http://www.clorox.com/products/clorox-regular-bleach/#Doing Laundry Product-Clorox® Regular-Bleach ID-18-Whites

bleach agent is dissolved in water, hydrogen peroxide is released to aid in the removal of soils and help brighten colors or whiten white materials.

Drycleaning

Drycleaning is a refurbishment method that utilizes non-aqueous organic solvents and mechanical tumbling or rocking motion to remove soils, followed by extraction (spinning) and recovery (drying) to evaporate remaining solvent. Solvent soluble stains such as grease, oil, and wax are dissolved and removed during drycleaning. According to Dryclean USA International, drycleaning garments "avoids saturating the fabric with water. While clothes are immersed, the solvent does not penetrate the fibers of the fabric, thereby avoiding the possible swelling and shrinking that can occur with water saturation."[8]

Drycleaning Solvents

The most common drycleaning solvents used for refurbishing textiles and apparel products include **perchloroethylene (perc)**- and **petroleum**-based solvents. The Worldwatch Institute estimates that worldwide there are 180,000 drycleaners using perc.[9] Perc, also known as **tetrachloroethylene**, is a nonflammable synthetic liquid solvent composed of halogenated hydrocarbons. There are typically two tanks of perc solvent—**pure solvent** (perc only) and charged solvent. The **charged solvent** is used during the cleaning cycle and contains a minimal amount of detergent and moisture (water) to assist in the removal of water-soluble stains, and the load is rinsed in pure solvent. After cleaning, the used solvent is recycled and reused during the next cleaning cycle. The dirty solvent is first filtered and a portion is returned to the charged solvent tank. The remaining solvent is then distilled to remove water, detergent, and any **nonvolatile residue (NVR)** such as grease, oils, and particulate matter made up of **insoluble soils** (i.e., dust, sand, lint, hair, dandruff, and so on).[10] During distillation approximately 98 percent of the perc solvent can be recovered and reused.

Petroleum solvents used for drycleaning are highly flammable liquid hydrocarbon distillates similar to kerosene and are known as **Stoddard solvents**.[10, 11] This type of solvent is less expensive and more economical than perc. Petroleum solvents are filtered to clean the solvent between drycleaning loads so it can be reused and is typically not distilled due to its hazardous combustible nature and the dangers associated with accumulating petroleum vapors.[11]

Drycleaning Equipment

The three types of drycleaning machines commonly used today include **transfer machines, dry-to-dry vented machines**, and **dry-to-dry closed-loop machines**. In the past, drycleaning transfer machines (in which cleaning occurs in one machine and the load was then transferred to another machine where it was dried) were used with both perc and petroleum solvents. However, in recent years, significant improvements have been made to drycleaning equipment in an effort to reduce and control the release of perc solvent into the air. Transfer machines are now reserved for use with petroleum solvent due to environmental regulations established to control the release of perc into the environment as well as exposure to workers. Both of the dry-to-dry-style machines allow cleaning, extracting, and recovery (drying) to be self-contained within one machine. This significantly reduces workers' exposure to perc drycleaning solvent, because the wash load does not have to be moved from one machine to another to be dried. There are dry-to-dry machines that can also be used with petroleum solvent. Perc is a suspected carcinogen among other health hazards such as dizziness, loss of coordination, mild memory loss, and visual perception, related to prolonged inhalation and skin contact.[12] The dry-to-dry vented machines allow for residual solvent vapors to be exhausted outside the drycleaning establishment. Some of these systems direct the perc vapor through a recovery system before venting them into the environment. A better alternative is the dry-to-dry closed-loop machine that does not release perc vapor into the environment at all, but rather recirculates the perc through two recovery systems. This type of machine significantly reduces the amount of perc that workers are exposed to and minimizes the amount of perc released into the environment.[12] See Figure 12.7 for an example of a drycleaning machine.

Wetcleaning

Wetcleaning is an evolving alternative technology that is more eco-friendly than drycleaning because the water discharged from this process can be safely disposed into municipal sanitation systems.[13] This cleaning method has been around since the early 20th century and has been used around the world before

Figure 12.7 Drycleaning machine
Creative Commons

drycleaning solvents became available. Wetcleaning uses a specially formulated aqueous (water) detergent solution and mechanical action similar to hand washing to gently and effectively clean most garments normally recommended for dryclean care methods. Water soluble soils as well as oils, grease, and pigments are easily dissolved or broken up and removed with this cleaning process. Significant improvements have been made to wetcleaning detergents and equipment over the past 10 years to improve this green cleaning method.

Wetcleaning Detergents

Wetcleaning detergents are available in liquid form and are generally composed of alcohol ethoxylate, lauryl trimethyl ammonium chloride, protease enzyme, citric acid, and water.[14] **Alcohol ethoxylate** is a surfactant and is the primary ingredient found in wetcleaning detergents. During the wetcleaning process, this surfactant aids wetting garments, loosening, emulsifying, and suspending soils in the wash bath until they are rinsed away. **Lauryl trimethyl ammonium chloride** acts as a conditioner to protect against felting and shrinkage, and improves the stability of dyes. **Protease enzymes** are protein molecules added to wetcleaning detergents to help remove protein-based soils that are more difficult for surfactants to remove. **Citric acid** provides antimicrobial qualities to detergent to disinfect the wash load. This mild detergent is a very effective cleaning agent with minimal washing action required.

Wetcleaning Equipment

A wetcleaning system consists of a washer-extractor machine (specifically designed for wetcleaning) with horizontal axis that provides a reversing-rotating motion to simulate hand washing and a moisture-controlled dryer. The cylinder rotation speed of the machine for washing, rinsing, and extracting can be precisely controlled depending upon the contents of the wash load. The washing rotation speed is significantly slower than a standard washing machine

in color of a textile material or product after cleaning, storage, or exposure to heat, humidity, solvents, bleach, spotting chemicals, various light sources, the combination of perspiration and light, ozone, and atmospheric contaminants. A gray scale for evaluating color change is used for comparing the level of color loss or gain on the tested specimen to the numeric ratings on the standard scale for determining acceptability (see Figure 12.11). The structural characteristics of materials that influence colorfastness include fiber content, dye or pigment type/structure, amount, and application of the colorants to the fiber or material, and finish type if applicable.

Abrasion and Durability Testing

Abrasion impacts both the strength and appearance of sewn products and can occur during wear or refurbishment. **Abrasion** occurs when one material rubs against itself or another surface. Variables that affect abrasion include directionality (one direction versus multidirectional), moisture, pressure, and tension applied to the fabric or garment. The three types of abrasion materials or garments are commonly subjected to flat abrasion, flex abrasion, and edge abrasion. **Flat abrasion** happens when two smooth/plane surfaces rub against each other or against another object. When the fabric is repeatedly folded and unfolded, the yarns wear against each other and cause what is referred to as **flex abrasion**. **Edge abrasion** affects the edges of sewn products where the fabric edge rubs against another surface, causing wear. Yarn breakage, snagging, pile pullout, pilling, and color change are common effects resulting from these forms of abrasion. **Pilling** is when loose fibers on the surface of a fabric become entangled, forming small balls. Color change can be caused by rubbing (crocking) or **frosting**, which is the resulting white cast that appears on the surface of textile materials caused by loss of color due to abrasion and poor dye penetration. Some dye classes do not penetrate the fiber so dye remains on the exterior surface only; therefore, the overall aesthetic appearance is compromised.

It is important to evaluate the strength of garment components in relation to functionality and end use to avoid fabric or seam failure. A material's **tensile strength** refers to its ability to resist tension before rupturing or breaking. There are many aspects of strength that can be independently tested to determine if corrective measures need to be made so product performance is not compromised. Breaking strength and tearing strength tests are commonly used to evaluate the tensile strength of woven materials. **Breaking strength** is measured by the amount of force applied to a material before the yarns break and a tear occurs. **Tearing strength** is tested to determine the amount of force that can be applied to a material to continue a tear that already exists by breaking one or a couple yarns at a time. Materials are tested independently in both the warp and filling directions. Bursting strength and modulus tests are commonly used to evaluate the tensile strength of knitted materials. **Bursting strength** is measured by

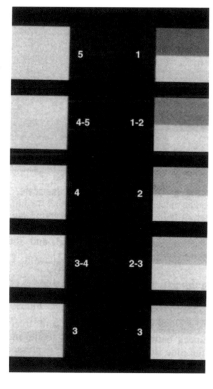

Figure 12.11
Gray scale for evaluating color change
Courtesy of AATCC

5	1
4-5	1-2
4	2
3-4	2-3
3	3

the amount of multidirectional force applied to a material to cause the yarns to rupture, creating a hole in the fabric. Woven and nonwoven materials can also be tested for bursting strength. For example, a men's dress shirt that has been treated with a wrinkle-free finish should be tested to evaluate bursting strength at the elbow. Whereas the finish enhances the appearance of the garment it often reduces the strength of the material and can cause it to tear more easily when force is applied to the elbow area of the sleeve. **Modulus** is measured by applying directional force at repeated intervals to stretch/elongate and relax (allow for recovery) a knitted material (both low and high power) to determine its resistance limit before permanent damage or distortion is caused.

Testing and evaluating seam construction is another critical aspect of garment performance and quality. When stitches and seams are selected for assembling garments the thread fiber content and construction as well as the fabric's properties and intended use of the product must be carefully considered. **Seam strength** refers to the amount of force that can be applied to a seam to rupture the stitching or bonding. During testing, **fabric failure** can occur when force is applied to a garment seam and the construction of the seam is stronger than the material of the product, causing the material to tear at the edge of the seam line. On the other hand, **seam slippage** can result when tension is applied to a seam of a garment, causing the yarns of the material to slide away from the seam.

Specimens are prepared, tested, and evaluated using standardized test methods that can provide valuable information regarding the strength and abrasion of fabrics, seam construction, and their combined effects in garments. See Table 12.7 for a list of commonly used abrasion and durability test methods for textile materials and apparel products. The structural characteristics of materials that influence abrasion and durability include fiber content, yarn construction, fabric count, construction and thickness, seam construction, dye or pigment type/structure, amount, and application of the colorants to the fiber or material, and finish type, if applicable.

Safety Testing

Safety of apparel items is a critical area of concern within the apparel industry, and testing must be conducted to ensure compliance with governmental regulations and to provide customers with products that will not cause them harm when the product is used as intended. The three main areas of concern include flammability, toxicity, and strangulation from drawstrings in children's apparel. Chapter 10 covered these wearing apparel safety regulations, guidelines, and the testing required for compliance in order for products to enter into commerce.

PERFORMANCE TEST SELECTION AND QUALITY EVALUATION

Fabrics and sewn products are analyzed to determine which tests should be conducted. Test selection considerations include the function and intended use of the sewn product, performance characteristics and requirements, aesthetic expectations, intended method of cleaning, seam construction, and required fabric characteristics and **subassemblies** (fasteners, closures, stitches, and seams incorporated into a finished product). There needs to be a means for measuring acceptability to determine conformance when products are developed and evaluated for appearance, performance, and safety. **Performance specifications** are standards used to determine requirements for acceptability of materials or sewn products based on results obtained through testing. These specifications are established by organizations that develop standardized test methods, but they can also be created by individual companies or agencies who want to set performance ratings above minimum industry expectations.

Table 12.7 Test Methods Commonly Used for Evaluating Abrasion and Durability of Textile Materials or Garments

Test Method Designation	Name
AATCC 93	Abrasion Resistance of Fabrics Accelerator Method
AATCC 136	Bond Strength of Bonded and Laminated Fabrics
ASTM D1336	Standard Test Method for Distortion of Yarn in Woven Fabrics
ASTM D1424	Standard Test Method for Tearing Strength of Fabrics by Falling-Pendulum (Elmendorf-Type) Apparatus
ASTM D1683	Standard Test Method for Failure of Sewn Seams of Woven Apparel Products
ASTM D2261	Standard Test Method for Tearing Strength of Fabrics by the Tongue (Single Rip) Procedure (Constant-Rate-of-Extension Tensile Testing Machine)
ASTM D2594	Standard Test Method for Stretch Properties of Knitted Fabrics Having Low Power
ASTM D2724	Standard Test Method for Bonded, Fused, and Laminated Apparel Fabrics
ASTM D3107	Standard Test Method for Stretch Properties of Fabrics Woven from Stretch Yarns
ASTM D3511	Standard Test Method for Pilling Resistance and Other Related Surface Changes of Textile Fabrics: Brush Pilling Tester
ASTM D3512	Standard Test Method for Pilling Resistance and Other Related Surface Changes of Textile Fabrics: Random Tumble Pilling Tester
ASTM D3514	Standard Test Method for Pilling Resistance and Other Related Surface Changes of Textile Fabrics: Elastomeric Pad
ASTM D3786	Standard Test Method for Bursting Strength of Textile Fabrics—Diaphragm Bursting Strength Tester Method
ASTM D3786M	Standard Test Method for Bursting Strength of Textile Fabrics—Constant-Rate-of-Transverse (CRT) Ball Burst Test
ASTM D3884	Standard Test Method for Abrasion Resistance of Textile Fabrics (Rotary Platform, Double-Head Method)
ASTM D3885	Standard Test Method for Abrasion Resistance of Textile Fabrics (Flexing and Abrasion Method)
ASTM D3886	Standard Test Method for Abrasion Resistance of Textile Fabrics (Inflated Diaphragm Apparatus)
ASTM D3939	Standard Test Method for Snagging Resistance of Fabrics (Mace)
ASTM D4157	Standard Test Method for Abrasion Resistance of Textile Fabrics (Oscillatory Cylinder Method)
ASTM D4685	Standard Test Method for Pile Fabric Abrasion
ASTM D4964	Standard Test Method for Tension and Elongation of Elastic Fabrics (Constant-Rate-of-Extension Type Tensile Testing Machine)
ASTM D4966	Standard Test Method for Abrasion Resistance of Textile Fabrics (Martindale Abrasion Tester Method)
ASTM D4970	Standard Test Method for Pilling Resistance and Other Related Surface Changes of Textile Fabrics: Martindale Tester
ASTM D5034	Standard Test Method for Breaking Strength and Elongation of Textile Fabrics (Grab Test)
ASTM D5035	Standard Test Method for Breaking Force and Elongation of Textile Fabrics (Strip Method)
ASTM D5278	Elongation of Narrow Elastic Fabrics (Static Load Testing)
ASTM D5362	Standard Test Method for Snagging Resistance of Fabrics (Bean Bag)
ASTM D5587	Standard Test Method for Tearing Strength by Trapezoid Procedure
ASTM D6614	Standard Test Method for Stretch Properties of Textile Fabrics – CRE Method
ASTM D6770	Standard Test Method for Abrasion Resistance of Textile Fabrics (Hex Bar Method)
ASTM D6775	Standard Test Method for Breaking Strength and Elongation of Textile Webbing, Tape, and Braided Material
ASTM D6797	Standard Test Method for Bursting Strength of Fabrics Constant-Rate-of-Extension (CRE) Ball Burst
EN ISO 9073-4	Textiles – Test Methods for Nonwovens – Part 4: Determination of Tear Resistance
EN ISO 9073-5	Textiles – Test Methods for Nonwovens – Part 5: Determination of Resistance to Mechanical Penetration (Ball Burst Procedure)
EN ISO 9073-18	Textiles – Test Methods for Nonwovens – Part 18: Determination of Breaking Strength and Elongation of Nonwoven Materials Using the Grab Tensile Test
EN ISO 12945-1	Textiles – Determination of Fabric Propensity to Surface Fuzzing and to Pilling – Part 1: Pilling Box Method
EN ISO 12945-2	Textiles – Determination of Fabric Propensity to Surface Fussing and to Pilling – Part 2: Modified Martindale Method
EN ISO 12947-1	Textiles – Determination of Abrasion Resistance of Fabrics by the Martindale Method – Part 1: Martindale Abrasion Testing Apparatus

Table 12.7 Continued

Test Method Designation	Name
EN ISO 12947-2	Textiles – Determination of the Abrasion Resistance of Fabrics by the Martindale Method – Part 2: Determination of Specimen Breakdown
EN ISO 12947-3	Textiles – Determination of Abrasion Resistance of Fabrics by the Martindale Method – Part 3: Determination of Mass Loss
EN ISO 12947-4	Textiles – Determination of the Abrasion Resistance of Fabrics by the Martindale Method – Part 4: Assessment of Appearance Change
EN ISO 13770	Textiles – Determination of Abrasion Resistance of Knitted Footwear Garments
EN ISO 13934-1	Textiles – Tensile Properties of Fabrics – Part 1: Determination of Maximum Force and Elongation at Maximum Force Using the Strip Method
EN ISO 13934-2	Textiles – Tensile Properties of Fabrics – Part 2: Determination of Maximum Force and Elongation Using the Grab Method
EN ISO 13935-1	Textiles – Seam Tensile Properties of Fabrics and Made-up Textile Articles – Part 1: Determination of Maximum Force to Seam Rupture Using the Strip Method
EN ISO 13935-2	Textiles – Seam Tensile Properties of Fabrics and Made-up Textile Articles – Part 2: Determination of Maximum Force to Seam Rupture Using the Grab Method
EN ISO 13936-1	Textiles – Determination of the Slippage Resistance of Yarns at a Seam in Woven Fabrics – Part 1: Fixed Seam Opening Method
EN ISO 13936-2	Textiles – Determination of the Slippage Resistance of Yarns at a Seam in Woven Fabrics – Part 3: Needle Clamp Method
EN ISO 13936-3	Textiles – Determination of the Slippage Resistance of Yarns at a Seam in Woven Fabrics – Part 1: Fixed Seam Opening Method
EN ISO 13937-1	Textiles – Tear Properties of Fabrics – Part 1: Determination of Tear Force Using Ballistic Pendulum Method
EN ISO 13937-2	Textiles – Tear Properties of Fabrics – Part 2: Determination of Tear Force of Trouser-Shaped Test Specimens (Single Tear Method)
EN ISO 13937-3	Textiles – Tear Properties of Fabrics – Part 3: Determination of Tear Force Of Wing-Shaped Test Specimens (Single Tear Method)
EN ISO 13937-4	Textiles – Tear Properties of Fabrics – Part 4: Determination of Tear Force of Tongue-Shaped Test Specimens (Double Tear Test)
EN ISO 13938-1	Textiles – Bursting Strength Properties of Fabrics – Part 1: Hydraulic Method of Determination of Bursting Strength and Bursting Distension
EN ISO 14704-1	Determination of Elasticity of Fabrics – Part 1: Strip Method
EN ISO 14704-2	Determination of Elasticity of Fabrics – Part 2: Multiaxial Tests
EN ISO 14704-3	Determination of Elasticity of Fabrics – Part 3: Narrow Fabrics
EN ISO 29073	Textiles – Test Methods for Nonwovens – Part 3: Determination of Tensile Strength and Elongation
JIS L 1061	Test Methods for Bagging of Woven and Knitted Fabrics
JIS L 1062	Test Methods for Distortion and Slippage of Yarn in Woven Fabrics
JIS L 1075	Testing Methods for Pile Retention of Woven and Knitted Fabrics
JIS L 1076	Test Methods for Pilling of Woven and Knitted Fabrics
JIS L 1093	Test Methods for Seam Strength of Textiles
JIS L 1901	Test Methods for Frosting Due to Yarn Reversing of Woven or Knitted Fabrics
JIS L 1905	Test Methods for Assessing Appearance of Seam Pucker on Textiles
JIS L 1910	Test Methods for Percentage of Breaking Strength and Bursting Strength Lowering of Textiles to Oxygen Bleaching

Sources: 2013 *Annual Book of ASTM Standards*, West Conshohocken, PA; AATCC, *2013 Technical Manual of the American Association of Textile Chemists and Colorists*, Vol. 88, Research Triangle Park: NC; ANSI eStandards store, accessed July 29, 2013, http://webstore.ansi.org/default.aspx; JSA Web Store accessed April 7, 2013, http://www.webstore.jsa.or.jp/webstore/JIS/FlowControl.jsp; CEN, European Committee for Standardization, Catalogue of Published Standards, accessed April 7, 2013, http://esearch.cen.eu/esearch/extendedsearch.aspx

Components of a Performance Specification Standard

The contents of performance specification standards follow similar formats regardless of the developing source such as ASTM International, although the heading for each topic covered within the specification may vary slightly. The basic framework of a performance specification will be explained to provide an understanding of the contents included. Each performance specification standard will indicate the developing source and be designated by a specification name and number. The specification name distinguishes the type of item covered, such as knit swimwear fabrics, and can also include the user (if applicable) such as men's and boys' knitted dress shirt fabrics.

The first section of a performance specification is the **scope**, which summarizes the type of material(s), garment(s), and intended user(s) covered by the standard. **Referenced documents**, also known as **normative references**, follow and present additional standards and test methods related to the selected performance specification. Important terms used within the specification are defined in the **terminology** section. **Specification requirements** indicate which fabric and garment properties should conform to the standard. Not all performance specifications will contain a section on **significance and use**, but for those that do, information regarding acceptability of test results data should be explained, if there is any deviation from the specification requirements outline that has been agreed upon by the supplier and the purchaser. The **sampling** or **test specimens** section contains information regarding acceptance testing and procedures for taking lot and lab samples, and test specimens. The **test methods** section lists and briefly summarizes the tests used to obtain data to meet the requirements of the performance specification. **Key words** may also be listed for important terms used within the performance specification.

Managing and Evaluating Test Results

Quality must be carefully controlled and continually monitored. **Quality control** is the process for ensuring specified quality levels are maintained through continually testing at different phases of production, performing frequent inspections, and making sure equipment is properly used, and established procedures are followed. Data gathered from testing is evaluated using performance specifications to determine acceptability.

When materials or products are not meeting quality standards, action must be taken to correct any problems affecting product appearance, performance, and safety in order to maintain customer satisfaction and protect the brand's reputation. There are many corrective measures that can be taken to prevent customer dissatisfaction or product recalls. Using the earlier example, when companies **overcut** garments, the customer wears and refurbishes the garment and the fit becomes better because the shrinkage restores the intended dimensions of the product. When a manufacturer pre-washes or pre-shrinks garments, although more expensive, it is typically worth the investment because the consumer does not experience a significant change in the products dimensions, which can negatively impact their perception of the brand. Pre-washing can also be used to remove loose dye from the surface of a garment to help minimize color rub off or staining. If staining is an issue, some dyes can be set/stabilized when drycleaned. Again, this is an added expense; however, if a manufacturer can avoid rejection of product by drycleaning the fabric or garments prior to shipment to minimize this problem, it is worth the additional effort. Recommended care is important information for consumers to avoid damaging the product during refurbishment. If a care method is tested on a garment and it is not compatible, other methods must be explored to maintain the appearance of the garment. See Table 12.8 for common recommended cleaning methods for garments by fiber type.

Flammability testing of children's sleepwear (covered extensively in Chapter 10) is an excellent way for manufacturers to be sure fabrics and garments are meeting compulsory regulations and are safe for sale and use. The application of flame retardant finishes may be required to bring sleepwear products into compliance with regulations. It is against the law for a

Table 12.8 Common Recommended Cleaning Methods by Garment and Fiber Type

Garment	Fiber Type	Recommended Care
Blouse or Shirt	Cotton, Synthetic fiber	Laundering
	Silk	Dryclean
Dress	Cotton	Laundering
	Linen, Rayon, Silk, Wool	Dryclean
Jacket (lined)	Fur, Leather, Silk, Suede, Wool	Dryclean
	Synthetic fiber	Laundering
Jacket (unlined)	Cotton, Synthetic fiber	Laundering
	Silk, Wool	Dryclean
Jeans	Cotton	Laundering
Lingerie	Cotton, Synthetic fiber	Laundering
	Silk	Dryclean
Overcoat	Fur, Leather, Suede, Wool	Dryclean
Pajamas or Robes	Cotton, Synthetic fiber	Laundering
	Silk	Dryclean
Shapewear	Synthetic fiber	Laundering
Skirt	Cotton	Laundering
	Linen, Rayon, Silk, Wool	Dryclean
Suit	Linen, Rayon, Silk, Wool	Dryclean
Sweater	Cotton, Wool, Silk	Laundering
Trouser or Pant	Cotton	Laundering
	Leather, Linen, Rayon, Silk, Wool	Dryclean
Undergarments	Cotton, Synthetic fiber	Laundering

manufacturer, importer, or retailer to promote or sell any sleepwear garment that does not meet flammability regulations. Additionally, they cannot legally label the sleepwear product to indicate this product "does not meet the requirements of the children's sleepwear flammability standards and is not intended or suitable for use as sleepwear."[20]

Manufacturers with a mission to provide quality products will invest in testing throughout design, development, and production to ensure the delivery of products that will meet or exceed customer expectations. The additional effort almost always leads to better quality garments and higher customer satisfaction. The key is to take corrective measures when necessary to improve the product so the customer is not disappointed with his or her purchase.

INDUSTRY SCENARIO 12.1 Dress Damaged When Drycleaned

A women's casual sheath dress with beading accents has a retail price of $138.00. The recommended method of cleaning on the garment label is dryclean only. The customer wore the garment and then took it to the drycleaner to be refurbished. When the dress was drycleaned the beads dissolved in the cleaning solvent, leaving loops of thread on the garment where the beads were attached. When the customer picked up the dress from the drycleaner she was very upset and blamed the drycleaner for ruining the garment. The drycleaner explained to her that the care method on the garment label was followed and they were not responsible for any damage to the garment.

- ■ Was it the drycleaners fault for the beads dissolving in the drycleaning solvent?
- ■ Was there any way for the drycleaner to know the beads would dissolve during cleaning?
- ■ What measures could have been taken to prevent this from happening?

SUMMARY

Testing is an important aspect of quality evaluation that can be conducted by testing labs of the developing brand, mills, manufacturers or by third-party laboratories such as Bureau Veritas, Intertek, and SGS, to name a few. Third-party testing labs can provide testing, inspecting, and certification of products for companies that do not have testing facilities or are seeking verification of in-house test results with data from an external source. This chapter focused on the standards used for testing and evaluating raw materials and products. Test methods and standard specifications for determining acceptability were introduced to increase understanding of quality assessment methods. Continual testing throughout the development and production processes allows products to be improved and for problems to be corrected in an effort to avoid customer dissatisfaction due to quality issues and build trust in brands. Visual inspection of goods is important and will be discussed in detail in Chapter 13, but it cannot determine the performance of a product's color permanence, durability, or dimensional stability, nor can it verify cleaning methods with certainty. Only testing can verify if products meet safety standards and regulations.

ACTIVITIES

1. Select a woven garment from your wardrobe, and make a list of the types of testing that would be important to conduct in order to evaluate the characteristics of the fabric, appearance, performance, and safety aspects of the product. Prepare a brief description of the garment and include at least one photo of the item. List the fabric properties that impact the performance of the product.

2. Repeat the same activity using a knit garment.

3. Make a list of the types of testing that would be important to evaluate for children's sleepwear.

4. Think about a garment that you were not satisfied with. Describe the item and what led to your dissatisfaction. Make a list of the types of testing that could be conducted to indicate problems during development or production. What corrective measures do you think could be taken to increase the quality of the garment?

APPAREL QUALITY LAB MANUAL

Please refer to Lab Activity 9.1 Test Methods for Evaluating Selected Garments; Lab Activity 9.2 Piece Goods Appearance and Performance Testing; Lab Activity 9.3 Comparison Garment Appearance and Performance Testing; and Lab Activity 9.4 Comparison Project Garment Results and Performance Specifications in the *Apparel Quality Lab Manual*. These activities will correspond to both Chapters 11 and 12 of this book.

ENDNOTES

1. Soap and Detergent Association of Canada. *Soaps and Detergents*. Accessed July 18, 2013, http://www.healthycleaning101.org/english /SDAC_soaps.html.
2. AATCC. "2003 AATCC Standard Reference Liquid Laundry Detergent." *2013 Technical Manual of the American Association of Textile Chemists and* Colorists, Vol. 88, p. 438.
3. SDC. *Standard Reference Detergents*. Accessed June 19, 2013, http://www.tuservices.com /detergent.pdf.
4. ISO (2012). *ISO 6330 Textiles—Domestic Washing and Drying Procedures for Textile Testing*, 3rd ed. April 15, 2012, pp. 1–33.
5. AATCC (2013). "AATCC Monograph M6 Standardization of Home Laundering Test Conditions." *2013 AATCC Technical Manual of the American Association of Textile Chemists and Colorists*, Vol. 88, pp. 444–446.
6. The Appliance Clinic. *Moisture Sensor*. Accessed June 23, 2013, http://www.the-appliance-clinic .com/moisture_sensor.html.
7. The Clorox Company (2013). *How to Use: Doing Laundry—Whites*. Accessed June 25, 2013, http://www.clorox.com/products/clorox-regular -bleach/.

8. DryClean USA International (2013). *Understanding Fabricare*. Accessed June 25, 2013, http://www.drycleanusa.com/pages/understanding fabricare.jsp.

9. Worldwatch Institute (2013). *Life-Cycle Studies: Drycleaning*. Accessed June 25, 2013, http://www.worldwatch.org/node/6380.

10. U.S. Environmental Protection Agency. *4.1 Drycleaning*. Accessed June 26, 2013, http://www.epa.gov/ttnchie1/ap42/ch04/final/c4s01.pdf.

11. ASTM (2013). "ASTM D235-02(2012) Standard Specification for Mineral Spirits (Petroleum Spirits) (Hydrocarbon Dry Cleaning Solvent)." *2013 Annual Book of Standards*, Section 6, Vol. 6.04.

12. U.S. Department of Labor Occupational Safety and Health Administration (2006). *Reducing Worker Exposure to Perchloroethylene (PERC) in Dry Cleaning*. Accessed June 26, 2013, http://www.osha.gov/dsg/guidance/perc.pdf.

13. eco-drycleaners.com (2010). "How the Wet Clean System Works." YouTube, uploaded May 3. Accessed June 27, 2013, http://www.youtube.com/watch?v=AgxR4GWthjk.

14. U.S. Patent Office (October 31, 2000). *Wet cleaning of delicate, non-structured garments with minimized wrinkling, shrinkage and color damage US 6139587 A*. Accessed June 27, 2013, http://www.google.com/patents/US6139587.

15. ISO. *International Standard ISO 6330 Textiles — Domestic Washing and Drying Procedures for Textile Testing*. Geneva, Switzerland, p. 21.

16. AATCC (2013). "AATCC Test Method 150-2012 Dimensional Changes of Garments after Home Laundering." Vol. 88, *AATCC 2013 Technical Manual of the American Association of Textile Chemists and Colorists*, Research Triangle Park, NC: American Association of Textile Chemists and Colorists, p. 279.

17. AATCC (2013). "AATCC Test Method 158-2011 Dimensional Changes on Drycleaning in Perchloroethylene: Machine Method." Vol. 88, *AATCC 2013 Technical Manual of the American Association of Textile Chemists and Colorists*, Research Triangle Park, NC: American Association of Textile Chemists and Colorists, p. 287.

18. AATCC (2013). "AATCC Test Method 143-2011 Appearance of Apparel and Other Textile End Products after Repeated Home Laundering." Vol. 88, *AATCC 2013 Technical Manual of the American Association of Textile Chemists and Colorists*, Research Triangle Park, NC: American Association of Textile Chemists and Colorists, p. 264.

19. ASTM (2013). "ASTM D123-2013 Standard Terminology Relating to Textiles." *2013 Annual Book of Standards*. Section 7, Vol. 7.01, p. 10.

20. U.S. Government Printing Office (GPO). *Code of Federal Regulations Annual Edition 2012: 16 CFR 1615-Standard for the Flammability of Children's Sleepwear: Sizes 0 through 6X (FF 3-71)*. Accessed January 7, 2013, http://www.gpo.gov/fdsys/pkg/CFR-2012-title16-vol2/pdf/CFR-2012-title16-vol2-part1615.pdf, p. 741.

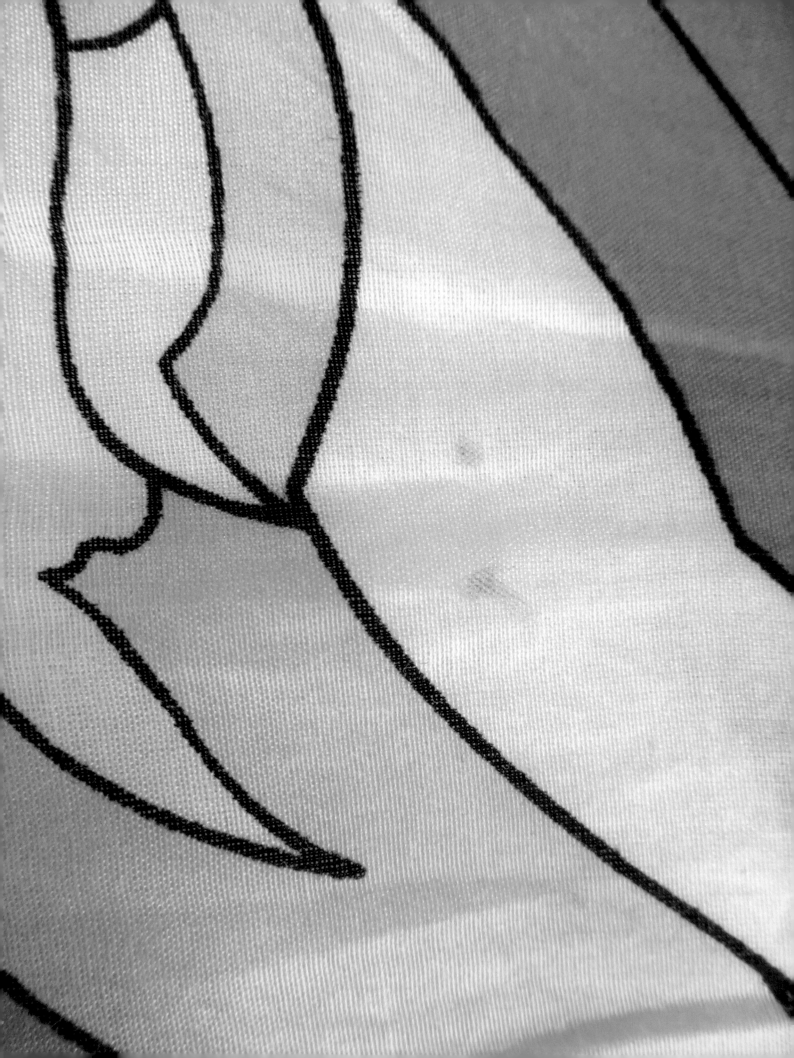

Quality Assurance Along the Supply Chain

CHAPTER THIRTEEN

Objectives:

- To gain an understanding of the importance of inspection related to apparel products
- To discuss the types of inspection and at which stages they occur

- To describe inspection procedures used in the apparel industry
- To identify common defects found in fabrics and garments

Controlling the quality of garments and protecting a brand's reputation takes a dedicated effort, careful planning, and fiscal responsibility. Better quality does not necessarily have to translate to higher costs and often reduces costs because problems can be identified early to avoid most costly repairs or loss of salable product later. Substandard quality is often a reflection of poor resource utilization, whereas quality that is up to standard conveys that resources are being appropriately managed, typically resulting in reduced costs.[1] Quality can also be impacted by price constraints. The cost of quality is impacted each time mistakes or defects are discovered because it can lead to reworking garments, retesting to evaluate performance, revising size specifications to improve shape and fit, modifying care methods to avoid damaging the product, and requiring additional processing to improve or correct appearance, colorfastness, shrinkage, or safety concerns. Then goods need to be re-inspected. In worst-case scenarios some product defects result in loss of revenue because the products cannot be sold. Ultimately, companies determine whether they want to invest in the development and production of good quality garments or provide consumers with subpar products. The purchase price and end use of the garment must always be taken into consideration along with customers' expectations for the quality of the item in relation to the price paid.

Quality control begins with materials selection and continues through to the delivery and sale of the finished product. Conscious efforts to maintain consistent quality levels, from initial fabric selection and inspection through production and final evaluation of the finished product, help to ensure consistent product quality, which leads to customer satisfaction. **Statistical process control (SPC)**, also referred to as **statistical quality control (SQC)**, focuses on improving processes and prevention of problems by controlling quality throughout all product producing phases. Two common SPC/SQC tools organizations use include histograms and Pareto charts. These tools are largely used for identifying the source or cause of defects on representative samples in order to make informed decisions regarding improvement of processes, thereby increasing product quality. Histograms provide data on process variations and frequency of defect occurrences that are displayed in a bar chart format. Normal distribution is shown as a bell curve. Vertical bars are used to indicate each type of variation, and their height illustrates the frequency in which each variation occurs.[2] This allows organizations to evaluate quality problems and the frequency in which they are occurring. Pareto charts go a step further to provide more detailed information, which allows organizations to hone in on the most significant factors leading to process problems where improvement is needed to avoid further defects from occurring. This bar graph vertically charts the occurrence of defects or customer complaints through measuring the frequency or cost and quantities of those defects. The most significant problem will have the tallest bar and be reported in the column farthest to the left, with each subsequent issue charted in descending order from left to right. The sum of all of the factors is typically equal to 100 percent. These percentages are indicated by a line graph overlaid on the bar graph that illustrates the cumulative percentage for each successive factor. This visual representation allows for organizations to easily identify areas for improvement of product quality.[2,3]

Inspection is defined by the American Society for Quality as "the process of measuring evaluating, testing, or otherwise comparing the unit of product with the requirements."[4] In the apparel industry this process includes testing and visually examining fabric, component parts, and sewn products at various stages of completion and measuring garment dimensions in relation to required specification standards. Diligent testing, inspecting, and evaluating fabrics and garments to monitor conformance with specifications, to detect defects, and take corrective action when possible, are all part of controlling product quality. Quality assurance (QA) plays a vital role in customer satisfaction and brand perception.

INSPECTION STANDARDS FOR APPAREL PRODUCTS

Inspection and evaluation involve the visual assessment and physical measurement to determine acceptability and ensure compliance with required specifications and allowed tolerances. **Inspectors** are individuals who are trained to conduct visual examinations of raw materials and sewn garments to effectively assess products and determine if they will meet brand or customer expectations in relation to appearance, size, performance, and function. Whereas testing provides hard data relating directly to product performance and function, visual inspection can also signal problem areas, such as missed or broken stitches that can lead to seam failure. Written specification standards are used by inspectors to compare materials and products to determine if they meet established requirements.

Inspection is critical because it allows for fabric or garment defects to be identified and traced (if necessary) so corrective measures can be taken. This lessens the incidence of the same types of faults from occurring repeatedly. **Product inspections** are conducted by inspectors to visually determine if garments comply with product specifications and dimension tolerances. When evaluating garment dimensions, measuring tapes, rulers, or templates are used. A **standard inspection procedure (SIP)** includes step-by-step instructions for evaluating garments that must be followed so that each garment is inspected the same way, to provide accurate and consistent results. Within these procedures, specific details pertaining to defects that may be present are well defined, and the classification of the flaw (critical, major, or minor) is also indicated. Defects will be discussed in the last section of this chapter. Standard inspection procedures are specific to a garment type (i.e., onesie, a trouser, a dress shirt, a jacket, and so on). Inspectors must draw on their experience and use good judgment to determine if a defect is something that will prevent a customer from purchasing the garment or cause them to return it.

SAMPLING AND LEVELS OF INSPECTION

The options for inspection range from no inspection to 100 percent inspection, and it is the sole prerogative of each individual company to decide which type is best suited for their brand(s). When product quality is not a concern, companies may opt for **no inspections** to be conducted at all. This decision can negatively impact the brand when defective merchandise is purchased and then returned, because customers may decide to never buy the brand again. Consumers need just one bad experience. The effects can also reach farther than just the customer that returned the merchandise. It is human nature for people to share both positive and negative experiences with their friends and family, and social media has become a favored outlet for people to voice their opinions based on their experiences. Research has shown that people are more likely to share negative experiences than positive ones. For a company to remain competitive and survive in a highly saturated apparel market, some level of inspection needs be conducted. **Inspection by spot check sampling** is another option that requires minimal evaluation and time. At this level, shipments are randomly selected for inspection and decisions for acceptance or rejection are based solely on the garments that have been evaluated. Therefore, many products may be accepted without inspection and defective garments can reach the customer. A better alternative is **inspection by random sampling**, which requires inspection of a specific percentage, typically 10 percent of a shipment regardless of the number of units, and acceptance or rejection of an entire shipment based solely on those evaluated garments. This method does have its drawbacks, such as the number of units being too large to effectively inspect or too small to be representative of the shipment.[5,6,7] A more practical method that is commonly used is **inspection by statistical sampling**, which is similar to random sampling except acceptance or rejection is based on statistics, reducing the risk of under-inspecting smaller shipments or over-inspecting larger ones.[5] ANSI/ASQ Z1.4 (formerly known as MIL-STD-105E) and ISO 2859 standards provide sampling procedures for inspection by attributes. In these standards a sample is described as one or more randomly selected units from an inspection lot. An inspection lot is defined as a group of units from which a sample is selected to determine the level of conformance based on criteria for acceptability. The tables in these methods provide ranges of designated lot sizes and sample sizes as well as the corresponding percentages for determining the **acceptable quality level (AQL)**. AQL is the maximum percent of defective products allowed for inspection sampling to be deemed satisfactory when using these standards. For example, a lot size of 500 units will have a sample size of 50 and an AQL of 4.0 percent. This means that the number of defective pieces found must be five or fewer for the lot to be accepted; if six or more defective pieces are found, the lot will be rejected.[8,9] Another level is **100 percent inspection**, where each unit of every shipment is inspected, and individual garments are accepted or rejected. Although this is the most thorough method, it is very time consuming and cost prohibitive unless the level and severity of defects requires every unit to be re-inspected. Most companies will opt for one of the routine inspection types that is somewhere in the middle between 100 percent and no inspection. See Figure 13.1 for the inspection options. The time generally allotted for the inspection of each garment (one-piece style) is 2 minutes. For multi-piece styles, each individual garment is allotted 2 minutes; therefore, 6 minutes would be allocated for the inspection of a three-piece style two minutes per piece.[4,5,6,10,11]

Acceptance quality limit is defined as the maximum percent of defects allowed for an acceptable inspection sample. The general levels of inspection defined in the *ANSI/ASQ Z 1.4 Sampling Procedures and Tables for Inspection by Attributes* standard include normal, tightened, and reduced. **Normal inspection** (level II) is used when the acceptance quality limit is consistently met. In general, if the percentage of defects exceeds the acceptance quality limit, having two out of five consecutive unacceptable shipments or lots, the level is raised to **tightened inspection** (level III) status. This heightened status will usually return to normal inspection (level II) once five consecutive shipments or lots are found to be acceptable. In the event that 10 shipments or lots are meeting acceptance quality limits under level II normal inspection, then **reduced inspection** (level I) status may be instituted.[11] "Under reduced inspection (level I), the sampling procedure may terminate without [the inspector] making a decision. In these circumstances, the lot or batch will be considered acceptable, but normal inspection (level II) will be reinstated starting with the next lot or batch."[11]

STAGES OF INSPECTION, TESTING, EVALUATION

Defects can arise at various stages of design and manufacturing; therefore, it is important to monitor the quality of materials, assembly, and finishing very carefully so flaws can be detected and corrected to minimize defective finished products from reaching consumers. See Figure 13.2 for the inspection cycle. Companies develop **inspection specifications** to indicate when assessment will occur along the stages from initial development through distribution and sale. These specifications for garments typically include raw materials inspection, receiving inspection, in-process inspection, and end-item or final product inspection. It is ideal for all of these inspections to occur in conjunction with testing to provide the highest quality products at the designated price point.

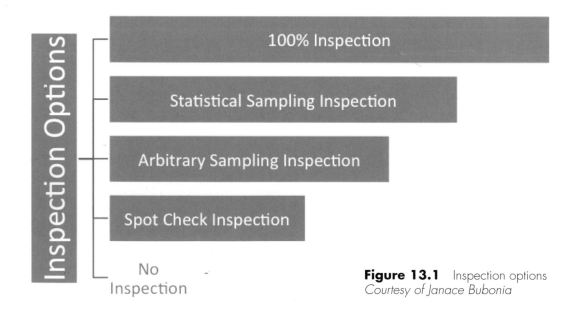

Figure 13.1 Inspection options
Courtesy of Janace Bubonia

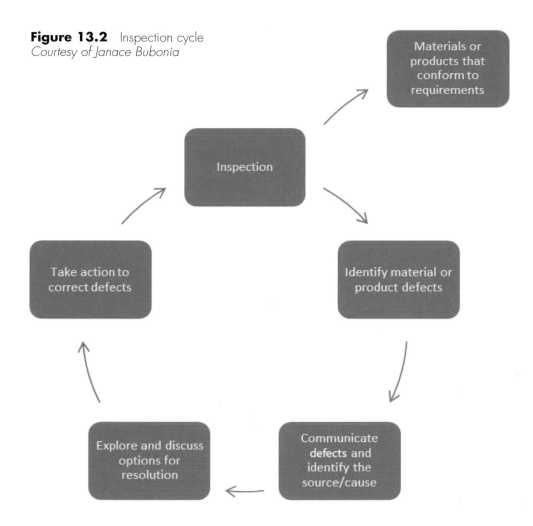

Figure 13.2 Inspection cycle
Courtesy of Janace Bubonia

Materials or products that conform to requirements

Inspection

Take action to correct defects

Identify material or product defects

Explore and discuss options for resolution

Communicate defects and identify the source/cause

Ultimately it is up to individual companies to determine the level of inspection and testing that will occur and at which production stages that will be conducted and when they will occur.

Product Development

The measure of quality begins with the design and development of apparel products. Accurate pattern development is critical to the entire manufacturing process because it serves as the guide for creating the size range as well as for cutting the pieces to make the garment. If there are problems with the pattern they will be carried through to the end product. When a patternmaker creates a pattern for a garment style, a first sample is assembled to test and perfect the fit, function, and proportions to ensure accurate design interpretation. This is followed by perfecting the final production pattern and sample. Production samples should be sent for testing to evaluate aesthetic appearance, fit, performance, function, and compliance with applicable safety regulations so that any problems can be corrected prior to production. Fabric selection is equally important to determine if the materials are appropriate for the design of the garment and must meet the aesthetic, function, and performance needs of the style. The materials selected for incorporation in an apparel item must be compatible with the intended care requirements and meet the customers' quality-level expectations of the brand. Material testing is conducted in the development stage before production begins. Fabrics and component parts are tested to determine if they meet required specifications for characterization, appearance, performance, and cleaning procedures in relation to the product's end use. If the materials are not acceptable, corrective measures are needed to prevent finished garments from being rejected or returned due to customer dissatisfaction.

Manufacturing

Mills will conduct raw materials inspections to evaluate the quality of each roll of fabric to document flaws and their specific locations. The 4-point grading system and the 10-point grading system are commonly used methods for inspecting piece goods. *ASTM D 5430 Standard Test Methods for Visually Inspecting and Grading Fabrics* defines these two systems as "numerical designations for grading of fabrics from a visual inspection."[12] Penalty points are assigned to defects based on their location and length within the fabric and if they occur in consecutive yards or linear meters within the fabric roll (see Table 13.1). The points are calculated to determine the number of demerits assigned per yard or linear meter. A criterion for acceptance or failure is determined by the purchaser based on negotiated specifications with the supplier. Visual inspections require a fabric inspection machine with a flat viewing area with the capacity to control the speed and rewind when flaws are detected so they can be marked accordingly (see Figure 13.3). Receiving inspections are important because they are used to verify shipments of piece goods and component parts through testing, visual evaluation, and measurement of raw materials at the onset of manufacturing. This ensures defective fabric and component flaws are not incorporated into the finished sewn product. When garment factories receive piece goods shipments, it is always best to conduct raw materials inspections to compare the number and locations of defects reported by the mill to verify compliance with specified standards. Some manufacturers will forego receiving inspections and require suppliers to provide a certificate of compliance (COC).

Table 13.1 Assignment of Penalty Points for 4-and 10-Point Inspection Systems

4-Point System		
Defect Length Greater than English Units	Defect Length Up To and Including SI Units	Demerit Point(s)
0–3 inches	0–75 mm	1
3–6 inches	75–150 mm	2
6–9 inches	150–230 mm	3
9 inches	230 mm	4
10-Point System		
Warp Defect Length Greater than English Units	Warp Defect Length Up To and Including SI Units	Demerit Point(s)
0–1 inch	0–25 mm	1
1–5 inches	25–125 mm	2
5–10 inches	125–250 mm	5
10–36 inches	25–900 mm	10
Filling Defect Length Greater than English Units	Filling Defect Length Up To and Including SI Units	Demerit Point(s)
0–1 inch	0–25 mm	1
1–5 inches	25–125 mm	3
5 inches to ½ fabric width	125 mm to ½ fabric width	5
½ fabric width to full width	½ fabric width to full width	10

Source: ASTM International, D 5430-13 Standard Test Methods for Visually Inspecting and Grading Fabrics, 2013, 2013 Annual Book of Standards, Section 7, Vol. 7.02

Figure 13.3 Fabric inspection machine
Courtesy of Paramount Instruments

This document certifies that goods from the supplier meet all of the required standards and specifications and provide information documenting the flaws and locations within each roll.

In-process inspection, also referred to as in-line inspection or du-pro inspection, occurs during production and is ongoing and continuous. Fabrics are spread and cut after inspection. It is important for workers to make sure the layup (total number of plies in a fabric spread) is relaxed, on-grain, and properly aligned with the correct nap direction, if applicable. Assembly, seam appearance, and garment shape can be affected if not cut properly. As garment pieces are offloaded from the cutting table, they need to be checked to make sure the placement of notches and drill holes are correct, shades from different dye lots are marked, and pieces are checked to ensure sizes are bundled properly. During garment assembly, inspection procedures need to be followed to ensure the correct stitching and seam constructions are used for each area of the garment, and the dimensions remain compliant with specifications. If patterns such as stripes or plaids need to be matched, this must also be monitored. Inspection should occur on the sewing line to allow for identification and correction of defective parts, thus preventing more costly repairs or failures during finished product inspection. Potential safety hazards must also be monitored, such as the attachment of buttons and snaps on children's garments. Garments are finished after they are sewn. During this stage products should be monitored for proper pressing, accurate labeling content and location, and packaging to avoid defects. In-line inspections can typically be conducted when a minimum of 20 percent of the garments in the production run is completed. There inspections are conducted to ensure that every product is assembled exactly the same as the approved production sample.

End-item inspection, also known as **finished product inspection**, generally takes place once the production run is 100 percent assembled and a minimum of 80 percent is packaged. When workmanship defects are detected, they are documented to indicate the problem, tagged, and sent back to the sewing floor to be reworked. Garments that cannot be repaired are discarded and referred to as **scrap**. During end-item inspection, stitching, seam construction, attachment of findings and trims, placement of pockets, matching of patterns, garment dimensions, appearance, coloration, and packaging are all evaluated to determine conformity with specification standards. See Figure 13.4 for an example of directions and diagrams used for end-item inspection of a shirt to verify garment size and dimensions. Samples of finished garments should also be sent for testing to verify the performance, function, fit, appearance, and compliance with product performance specifications and applicable safety regulations.

Inspections that take place in factories where the products are produced are called **in-plant inspections**. Inspections that occur in distribution centers are known as **DC inspections**. Most retailers do both types of inspections. The advantage to evaluating the product at the factories is that time is not wasted shipping merchandise back for repairs. The garments are simply sent back to the sewing or finishing floor for correction and re-inspection as scheduled. When inspections are conducted at distribution centers, the incoming shipments are held and a portion is inspected. Incoming shipments to distribution centers are not entered into the system as "received" until the goods have been accepted by the quality assurance department. At the conclusion of inspection, quality assurance can accept the shipment as is, reject the shipment and cancel the purchase order, or request the shipment be returned to the factory for correction and reinspection in the plant.[5]

In-plant audits can also be conducted during this production stage to monitor the conditions of the factory to make sure the facilities are clean and safe for workers, to ensure employees are properly trained and have access to standards and specifications as needed, and to assess management and quality control systems. These audits cover all aspects of the production facility such as the environment (i.e., lighting, cleanliness, ventilation, and machine/equipment

Measurement Instructions

1. Bust/Chest*
- With front of garment facing up, measure straight across bust/chest from side to side at armholes seam.
- On garments with pleats, fully extend pleats without stretching fabric.

2. Across Chest
- With front of garment facing up, measure 5 in. down from high shoulder point parallel to center front.
- Measure straight across 5 in. from armhole to armhole.
- On garments with pleats, fully extend pleats without stretching fabric.

3. Sweep* - Garments with Vents or Shirttail Hems
- Lay garment flat in closed position.
- Measure straight across from side to side at top of vent or shirttail hem.

4. Sweep* - Garments with Straight Hems
- Lay garment flat in closed position.
- Measure from side to side along bottom of garment.

Take measurements with:
- *a dressmaker's or fiberglass coated tape measure (checked periodically against a metal ruler to assure accuracy).*
- *garments laid on a flat surface in a relaxed position.*
- *all wrinkles gently smoothed out.*
- *buttons and/or zippers fully closed (unless otherwise stated).*

5. Front Length
- Measure from high shoulder point, down front body, to bottom of garment

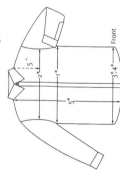

6. Across Shoulder
- With back of garment facing up, locate shoulder points (where shoulder seam meets top of armhole, or where natural fold of shoulder meets top of armhole) on each side of garment.
- Measure straight across shoulders from point to point.
- If garment is sleeveless, measure excluding any trim at armhole.

7. Across Back
- With back of garment facing up, measure 4 in. down from high shoulder point parallel to center back.
- Measure across at 4 in. mark from armhole to armhole.

8. Center Back Length
- Measure from center of back neck seam, down center of the back, to bottom of garment.

9. Shoulder Slope
- Draw an imaginary line parallel with hem from high shoulder point out to shoulder width.
- From that point, measure straight down to shoulder point.

10. Sleeve Length - Garments with Set-In-Sleeves
- With back of garment facing up, measure half of shoulder width starting at center back neck, to shoulder point at top of armhole, then along center fold of sleeve to cuff edge.

11. Vent Height
- Measure from bottom edge of garment to top of vent opening.

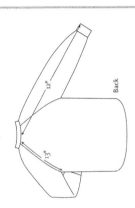

(a)

12. Sleeve Length - Garments with Raglan Sleeves
- Lay garment with back facing up.
- Measure from center back neck at base of neck, in a straight line down sleeve, to sleeve edge.

13. Armseye - Raglan Back
- Lay back of garment facing up, with body panel lying flat (without wrinkles at armhole seam).
- Measure from base of neck following contour of seam to armhole/side seam intersection point.

14. Armseye - Raglan Front
- Lay garment with front facing up and body panel lying flat (without wrinkles at armhole seam).
- Measure from base of neck following contour of seam to armhole/side seam intersection point.

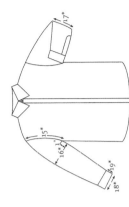

17. Elbow*
- Fold sleeve in half, so edge of cuff is positioned at bottom of armhole.
- Measure straight across this fold from underarm to center fold.

18. Cuff Opening*
- Measure straight across bottom of sleeve from underarm side of cuff to center fold side of cuff.
- For button cuff, cuff should be measured closed and buttoned on first button.

19. Cuff Height
- Measure from cuff/sleeve seam down to edge of cuff.

15. Armseye - Sleeved & Sleeveless*
- Lay front of garment facing up with body panel lying flat (without wrinkles at armhole seam).
- Following armhole seam contour, measure from bottom of armhole to top of armhole keeping tape on body side of seam.
- Care must be taken to rotate tape measure so that measuring edge is absolutely flat along armhole seam.

16. Upper Arm*
- Measure 1 in. down from underarm, then from that point measure straight across sleeve perpendicular to center fold of sleeve.

(b)

20. Neck Width
- Lay garment flat.
- Measure straight across from high shoulder point to high shoulder point at base of ribbing or collar.
- If there is no collar or trim, measure from edge to edge at high shoulder point.

21. Front Neck Depth
- Lay garment flat with front facing up.
- Draw an imaginary line at base of neck from high shoulder point to high shoulder point.
- From that center point, measure straight down to base of ribbing or collar at center front.

22. Back Neck Depth
- Lay garment flat with back facing up.
- Draw an imaginary line at base of neck from high shoulder point to high shoulder point.
- From that center point, measure straight down to base of ribbing or collar at center back.

23. Collar Height
- Measure at center back from base of collar to top outer edge of collar.

24. Collar Length at Outer Edge
- Undo all the buttons and lay collar flat so that inside of garment is facing up.
- Measure along collar edge from collar point to collar point.

25. Collar Point
- Lay collar flat.
- Measure from base of collar to outer edge of collar point.
- If there is no collar band, measure from neck seam to collar point.

26. Collar Band Height
- Measure at center back from neck line seam to top of band.

27. Collar Base Edge - With or Without Band
- Undo all buttons and lay collar flat with inside of garment facing up.
- Measure along collar base from edge to edge.
- If garment has a zipper exclude the zipper from the measurement.

(c)

28. Neck Circumference
- Undo all buttons and lay collar flat so that inside of garment is facing up.
- Measure from center of button to farthest end of buttonhole along inside of collar band.

29. Placket Width
- Measure placket on exterior of garment from seam or stitched edge to finished edge.

30. Placket Length
- Measure placket on exterior of garment from top edge to bottom seam or stitched edge.

31. Pocket Width - Exterior
- Measure the pocket across the top opening edge to edge.

32. Pocket Length - Exterior
- Measure at longest point from top opening edge to bottom finished edge.

(d)

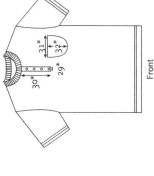

Figure 13.4 Directions for inspecting a shirt to verify garment size and dimensions *Courtesy of Fairchild Books*

maintenance), materials storage, workflow, production rates, product evaluation, and quality inspection procedures.

There are approved and certified suppliers that are used by companies to manufacture their products. **Approved suppliers** are vendors that have been selected to manufacture products based on their reputation and negotiated quality level and price. A **certified supplier** "is a source that through previous experience and qualification can provide material of such quality that it needs little, if any, receiving inspection or test before becoming approved stock or being released into the production process."[10] To be considered a certified supplier, they must be an established approved vendor; have a consistent track record of producing quality products free of defects or below the **acceptable quality limit (AQL)**, and void of product recalls; and have an established quality assurance program with documented procedures and a record for consistently meeting garment specifications, standards, and requirements.[5,13]

Retail

Customer satisfaction is vital for retailers and manufacturers of apparel products to sustain their business in this highly competitive industry. It should be taken seriously when a customer is dissatisfied with a purchase and returns it to the store it. Customer service personnel or management should inquire as to the reason for return. This information can be very useful in determining how to resolve the problem. When customers are dissatisfied with apparel products due to defects in appearance or those impacting the function and performance of the garment, retailers will return the merchandise to the supplier. Some vendors will require an evaluation of the product to determine the cause of product dissatisfaction or failure in an effort to prevent the problem from reoccurring.

Any product that has been introduced into commerce that is found to cause harm to consumers must be recalled. A **product recall** is prompted when defective merchandise is known to pose a serious safe-

ty hazard. This process calls for quickly retrieving defective merchandise from the distribution chain and possession of consumers to avoid risk to human health and safety.[14,15]

Manufacturers and regulatory agencies are the ones who typically initiate product recalls, but retailers may also if they discover a problem with one of the products they sell. Retailers are responsible for communicating product recalls to their customers so they understand the importance of immediately discontinuing use and returning the merchandise for a refund or replacement product. Common methods for communicating product recalls include in-store signage, online postings, email, and paid-for notices in media outlets.[16]

TYPES OF DEFECTS

A **defect** is a flaw that deviates from the level of quality planned for materials and garments. When a product has a number of flaws it can be deemed **defective** because it may no longer satisfy the intended appearance or functional characteristics desired for the product's use. It is important to understand the difference between **nonconformance** of a product and one that is defective. When a material or garment characteristic is noted during inspection as nonconforming, it means it does not meet the quality requirements defined in the specification. When a product has a number of flaws, it can be deemed **defective** because it may no longer satisfy the intended appearance or functional characteristics desired for the products use.

According to *ANSI/ASQ Z 1.4 Sampling Procedures and Tables for Inspection by Attributes*, apparel defects can be classified by three rating categories: critical defects, major defects, and minor defects. **Critical defects** are severe flaws that can cause minor to fatal injuries or unsafe conditions during use and maintenance of the product. Injuries can range from a cut on the skin caused by a broken needle or straight pin that has been stitched into the garment, to a scrape from a prong cap of a no-sew snap or metal eyelet that has not been completely secured/attached, to severe injury or death caused by burns from a flammable children's garment in which the required garment label was missing. This type of defect typically involves legislative requirements for safety, as well as other labeling requirements that must be adhered to for legal sale of the merchandise (i.e., accurate disclosure of fiber content or country of origin). The entire shipment fails inspection when a critical defect is found, even if only one defect is discovered. If the critical defect can be remedied, the entire shipment must be re-inspected and approved in order for goods to be sold to consumers. **Major defects** impact the functional performance of a product, meaning it is highly likely the defect will cause product failure at some point during usage, typically sooner than later. Major defects can include a faulty zipper or an open seam. Flaws that only impact the aesthetic appearance of a garment are rated as **minor defects**. These defects include color differences of component materials (mismatched dye lots) or a stain on the fabric.[4,3,5] Even though class 3 defects are aesthetic in nature, they are still undesirable and should be avoided in order to maintain brand integrity and the customer's perception of quality the brand offers. The three major classifications of defects are further divided into subcategories: a) material defects, b) production defects, and c) packaging defects.[4,5]

Material Defects

Defects commonly found in woven and knitted fabrics used for apparel will be defined in this section. Fabric defects are divided into three groups: woven fabric defects, knitted fabric defects, and fabric finishing defects.

Defects in Woven Fabrics

Woven fabric defects affect the visual appearance and the structure of the textile materials. Flaws can occur in the warp or filling directions and are typically a re-

sult from a yarn defect or formed due to a malfunction of the loom during weaving.

Broken pick is a severed filling yarn that creates a space in the fabric caused by the yarn breaking (see Figure 13.5).[17]

Figure 13.5 Broken pick
Photo courtesy of Janace Bubonia

Coarse yarn or **thick yarn** is significantly larger in size (linear density) than the other yarns in the fabric that are next to it (see Figure 13.6).

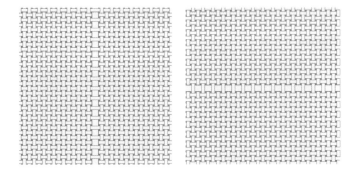

Figure 13.6 Course/thick yarn
Illustration by Q2A Media Services Private Limited

Double pick is when two filling yarns are placed into the same shed (temporary space between the upper and lower warp yarns during weaving; see Figure 13.7).

is severed when the buttonhole opening is cut, causing the thread to pull out (see Figure 13.42).

Figure 13.42 Unraveling buttonhole
Photo courtesy of Janace Bubonia

Unrelated seam is an area of a garment that, due to operator error, is inadvertently caught in the seam.

Visible stay stitching is stitching used to stabilize the fabric to prevent stretching or distortion from occurring when sewing a particular garment part that has not been removed or concealed within the garment (see Figure 13.43).

Figure 13.43 Visible stay stitching
Photo courtesy of Janace Bubonia

Wavy seam is a seam that does not lay flat as a result of the fabric being stretched during sewing (see Figure 13.44).

Figure 13.44 Wavy seam
Photo courtesy of Janace Bubonia

Wrong thread color is mismatched thread colors that do not meet specifications.

Wrong thread type and size is the use of a thread construction that was not specified (see Figure 13.45).

Figure 13.45 Wrong thread type and size
Photo courtesy of Janace Bubonia

INDUSTRY SCENARIO 13.1 Radioactive Belts Recalled

In January, 2013, the online retailer Asos, based in the UK, voluntarily recalled a batch of leather belts embellished with brass studs that were found to contain radioactive material in the metal. U.S. Border Control tested a shipment of the belts and found that it contained the radioactive isotope Cobalt-60. Forty-nine belts sold in 14 countries around the world were recalled.[20,21] The recalled belts have been contained in a radioactive storage facility. *The Guardian* news source reviewed the retailer's internal report that stated, "None of these belts are suitable for public use or possession." Furthermore, *The Guardian* reported the belts "could cause injury to the wearer if worn for more than 500 hours."[20] The internal company report also stated, "Unfortunately, this incident is quite a common occurrence. India and the Far East are large consumers of scrap metal for their home and foreign markets. During the refining process of these metals, orphaned radioactive sources are sometimes accidentally melted at the same time. This in turn [contaminates the process] and traps the radioactivity in the metal as an alloy or in suspension."[21] It is unknown how many of the recalled belts were actually returned.

- Did the retailer act responsibly in initiating a recall of this item?
- Do you think the retailer's reputation has been hurt by this recall?
- What could this retailer have done to prevent the belts from being sold and then recalled?
- At what stages could testing have been conducted?
- What additional measures could have been taken to provide customers with safe product?

SUMMARY

This chapter focused on the importance of quality control tools and inspection of apparel products. Carefully monitoring, testing, and inspecting raw materials and garments from selection through production are important steps to ensure consistent quality is maintained. Common defects were featured in this chapter along with images to assist the reader with identifying flaws. The establishment of QA programs can save money in the long run and increase profits by minimizing scrap and customer returns. When companies focus on producing quality garments, they have higher rates of customer satisfaction and brand loyalty.

ACTIVITIES

1. Look at a wide variety of apparel items and document a minimum of 10 defects.

2. For each defect found in activity 1, indicate at which stage it may have occurred and explain how the brand could have prevented the garment defect from reaching the consumer.

APPAREL QUALITY LAB MANUAL

Please refer to Lab Activity 10.1 Inspection of Randomly Selected Garments; Lab Activity 10.2 Comparison Project Garment Inspection; and Lab Activity 10.3 Comparison Garment Customer Satisfaction Survey in the *Apparel Quality Lab Manual.*

ENDNOTES

1. Armand V. Feigenbaum (1991). *Total Quality Control*, 3rd ed. revised. New York: McGraw-Hill Inc.

2. Encyclopedia of Business (2013). "Statistical Process Control." *Encyclopedia of Business*, 2nd ed. Accessed November 29, 2013, http://www.referenceforbusiness.com/encyclopedia/Sel-Str/Statistical-Process-Control.html.

3. ASQ. *Pareto Chart & Diagram*. Accessed November 29, 2013, http://asq.org/learn-about-quality/cause-analysis-tools/overview/pareto.html.

4. American Society for Quality. *ANSI/ASQ Z 1.4-2008 Sampling Procedures and Tables for Inspection by Attributes*. Milwaukee: Quality Press, p. 1.

5. Pradip V. Mehta (2004). *An Introduction to Quality Assurance for Retailers*. New York: iUniverse, Inc.

6. Bon Ton Stores Inc. *Quality Inspections: Requirements and Procedures 2011/2012*. Accessed July 4, 2013, http://logistics.bonton.com/Documents/BON-TON%20QA%20INSPECTION%20MANUAL.pdf.

7. Tween Brands, Inc. *Garment Inspection Procedures*, revised February 26, 2010. Accessed July 4, 2013, http://www.globalbrandpartners.com/agreements/Documents/TWEEN%20BRANDS%20INC%20SOP%20022610.pdf.

8. American Society for Quality. *ANSI/ASQ Z 1.4-2008 Sampling Procedures and Tables for Inspection by Attributes*. Milwaukee: Quality Press.

9. ISO (2011). *ISO 2859 Sampling Procedures for Inspection by Attributes Package*. November 29, 2013.

10. Fashion Manufacturers Ltd. *Quality Assurance Program*. Accessed July 4, 2013, http://www.garmento.org/mg311/simple_qa_program.pdf.

11. American Society for Quality. *ANSI/ASQ Z 1.4-2008 Sampling Procedures and Tables for Inspection by Attributes*. Milwaukee: Quality Press, p. 6.

12. ASTM International (2013). *D 5430-13 Standard Test Methods for Visually Inspecting and Grading Fabrics, 2013 Annual Book of Standards*, Section 7, Vol. 7.02.

13. Richard Maass, John Brown, and James Bossert (1990). *Supplier Certification: A Continuous Improvement Strategy*. Milwaukee: American Society for Quality, p. xiii.

14. Richard Maass, John Brown, and James Bossert (1990). *Supplier Certification: A Continuous Improvement Strategy*. Milwaukee: American Society for Quality.

15. Sara J. Kadolph (2007). *Quality Assurance for Textiles and Apparel*, 2nd ed. New York: Fairchild Publications, Inc.

16. U.S. Consumer Product Safety Commission (March, 2012). *Product Recall Manual.* Accessed July 6, 2013, http://www.cpsc.gov//PageFiles/106141/8002.pdf.

17. ASTM International (2013). *D 5430-13 Standard Test Methods for Visually Inspecting and Grading Fabrics, 2013 Annual Book of Standards,* Section 7, Vol. 7.02.

18. ISO (2003). *International Standard ISO 8499 Knitted Fabrics – Discrimination of Defects – Vocabulary.* December 1, 2013.

19. Simon Neville (2013). "Asos Pulls Belts in Radioactive Scare." *The Guardian,* May 27. Accessed November 29, 2013, http://www.theguardian.com/business/2013/may/27/asos-withdraws-belts-radioactive-scare?INTCMP=SRCH.

20. MSN News (2013). "Radioactive Belts Recalled by UK Fashion Retailer." *MSN News,* May 28. Accessed November 30, 2013, http://news.msn.com/world/radioactive-belts-recalled-by-uk-fashion-retailer.

GLOSSARY

100 Class Stitches. A category of chain stitches designated by ISO and ASTM in which stitches are formed by the intralooping or interloping of one needle thread passing through the fabric and held in place by subsequent loops. (Chapter 6)

100% Inspection. Each individual garment within a lot is inspected, and acceptance or rejection is based only the unit inspected. (Chapter 13)

10-Point Grading System. Standardized method used for inspecting piece goods that assigns penalty points to fabric flaws on a scale of 1 to 10 to determine if the roll will be accepted or rejected. (Chapter 13)

200 Class Stiches. A category of hand stitches designated by ISO and ASTM in which stitches are formed by hand or are machine simulations of hand stitches. (Chapter 6)

300 Class Stiches. A category of lockstitches designated by ISO and ASTM in which stitches are formed with a bobbin thread and one or more needle threads that pass through the fabric and interlace to secure each stitch. (Chapter 6)

400 Class Stitches. A category of chain stitches designated by ISO and ASTM in which stitches are formed with a looper thread and one or more needle threads that pass through the fabric and interlace with loops that interloop on the underside of the material. (Chapter 6)

4-Point Grading System. Standardized method used for inspecting piece goods that assigns penalty points to fabric flaws on a scale of 1 to 4 to determine if the roll will be accepted or rejected. (Chapter 13)

500 Class Stitches. A category of overedge stitches designated by ISO and ASTM in which stitches are formed by one group of threads penetrating through the fabric and held in place by intralooping (ISO term) or interloping (ASTM term) to cover the edge of the material where subsequent loops pass through the fabric to form the stitch. The threads can also be secured by one group of threads interlooping with loops formed by one or more interlooped groups before subsequent loops from the first group are passed back through the fabric to cover the edge and form the stitch. (Chapter 6)

600 Class Stitches. A category of cover stitches designated by ISO and ASTM in which stitches are formed by two or more groups of threads that enclose the raw edges of both surfaces of the fabric plies by covering them. The threads are cast on the surface of the fabric and then interlooped with loops of thread formed on the underside of the fabric. (Chapter 6)

AATCC (American Association of Textile Chemists and Colorists). A nonprofit organization that develops and publishes voluntary standardized test methods for international use. (Chapter 1)

Abrasion. Rubbing of a material against itself or another surface. (Chapter 12)

Acceptance Quality Limit (AQL). The total amount of defects allowed for an inspection sample to be accepted. (Chapter 13)

Acceptance Testing. Evaluation conducted to determine if a material or product meets the specified criteria for approval. (Chapter 11)

Aesthetic Characteristics. The overall attractiveness of the materials, styling, and design of the garment in relation to its intended use. (Chapter 1)

Aesthetics. The appearance, comfort, sound, and smell of a garment; any portion of a garment that engages the senses. (Chapter 1)

Agile Manufacturing. Manufacturing with focus on speed and flexibility to decrease lead time and meet market demands for continuous style change. (Chapter 8)

Air Entangled Thread. A twisted thread that is formed when continuous filament fibers are passed through high-pressure air jets that cause them to become entwined. (Chapter 6)

Air Temperature. The degree of coolness or hotness of air. (Chapter 11)

Alcohol Ethoxylate. The primary active ingredient (surfactant) in wetcleaning detergent. (Chapter 12)

All-in-one Facing (Combination Facing). A facing that accommodates more than one garment area (i.e., neckline and armhole). (Chapter 4)

Amorphous Regions. The unorganized regions of a fiber. (Chapter 11)

Analyzer. Second or additional polarizer. (Chapter 11)

ANSI (American National Standards Institute). A private non-profit organization that administrates and coordinates the voluntary standardization system in the United States. (Chapter 1)

Anthropometric Data. Information gathered from measuring human populations to determine variations and commonalities in body dimension and shape for use in standardizing sizes of apparel and accessories. (Chapter 5)

Apparatus. Machine or equipment used for conducting a test. (Chapter 11)

Appearance. The overall visual aesthetic of a textile or garment. (Chapter 12)

Appearance Retention. Ability of a material or garment to maintain its aesthetic look during use, refurbishment, and storage. (Chapter 12)

Approved Suppliers. Vendors selected by a company to manufacture products based on reputation and negotiated quality level and price. (Chapter 13)

Aqueous Solution. Water and detergent mixture that acts as the solvent to dissolve water soluble soils during laundering and wetcleaning. (Chapter 12)

ASTM International. Formerly known as the American Society of Testing and Materials, develops and publishes voluntary standards for international use. (Chapter 1)

Asymmetric (Informal Balance). A garment that is not the same on both sides of the center; design details vary from one side to the opposite side of the garment. (Chapter 2)

Atom. The smallest unit of an element. (Chapter 11)

Azo Dyes. A group of synthetic dyestuffs based on nitrogen used in textile and leather products. (Chapter 10)

Baffles. Paddles found inside a horizontal-axis washing machine, drycleaning machine, or dryer to keep garments moving by means of tumbling action. (Chapter 12)

Balance. When the right and left side of the garment appear to be even. (Chapter 2)

Balanced Plain Weave. Woven fabric constructed having the same size, type, and number of yarns in both the warp and filling directions. (Chapter 3)

Balanced Thread Tension. When the stitching threads interlock at the mid-point of the fabric layers, providing a smooth, flat appearance. (Chapter 6)

Balanced Twist. The single yarns within a ply yarn typically possess an S-twist, whereas the overall yarn containing the plies is twisted in the Z direction. Each of the yarns contains a specified number of turns per inch, per centimeter, or per meter to balance the twist. A ply yarn having balanced twist will not kink or twist back on itself when folded in half. (Chapter 6)

Ballast. Pieces of white or light color plain weave fabric that are added to a wash load during testing to maintain the specified weight required for the load. (Chapter 12)

Band Hem. An edge finish that utilizes a strip of material that is stitched to conceal the fabric raw edge along the hem. (Chapter 4)

Band Placket. Two finished strips of fabric are used to form a lapped closure and finish the raw edge. (Chapter 4)

Barre. A knit fabric defect that gives the visual appearance of streaks across the width of the fabric. (Chapter 13)

Base Burn or **Base Fabric Ignition.** When a fabric with a raised surface is ignited and continues to burn the foundation yarns of the material. (Chapter 10)

Better Price Point. The price category that includes above-average prices for mass-produced apparel products with consumer expectations of better quality fabrics and more advanced construction details. (Chapter 1)

Bias Facing. A narrow strip of fabric cut on the bias is stitched along the opening to finish and stabilize the edge. (Chapter 4)

Bias-faced Waistline. A facing cut on the bias is used to contour and shape the waistline area. (Chapter 4)

Bias Grain. A diagonal line that usually runs at a 45 degree angle from the perpendicular lengthwise and crosswise grainlines. (Chapter 2, 4)

Bill of Materials (BOM). Part of a technical package that details component material specifications such as interlinings, trim, and findings for the production of a garment. (Chapter 5)

Birdseye Defect. The occurrence of two consecutive tuck stitches in a knitted fabric that are not intended. (Chapter 13)

Birefringence or **Double Refraction.** Direction and transmittance of polarized light used to determine the reflective index of a fiber's optical property. (Chapter 11)

Blind Hem. A hem finish where the raw edges are folded or covered with seam tape and sewn with a blind stitch so the stitches are not visible on the face of the garment. (Chapter 4)

Blind Tucks. A series of repeating parallel folds that are designed to have the fold meet at the stitch line of the next tuck. (Chapter 4)

Blistering or **Bubbling.** Visible pebbled appearance on the surface of the garment due to improper fusing. (Chapter 13)

Block. A tag board or digital pattern developed to a brand's specifications for a sample size that is used to develop first patterns of new designs or modifications of existing styles. (Chapter 2)

Bound Buttonhole (Welt Bound Buttonhole). Two separate strips of fabric are stitched to form the lips where the button will pass through. (Chapter 4)

Bound Hem (Welt Finished Edge or **Hong Kong Finish).** A bias strip of material used to cover the raw edges of the material at the hemline of a garment. (Chapter 4)

Bound Placket. Two bindings are used to cover the raw edges of the opening without creating a lap. (Chapter 4)

Bow. The visual appearance of arcs across the width of woven or knitted fabric resulting from displaced yarns. (Chapter 13)

Brand. The reputation of a product or company conveyed through brand image, word mark, logo, product design, quality, marketing and promotion, distribution of goods, and customer service. (Chapter 1)

Break. Folds in the pant legs of trousers near the hem where it hits the instep of the foot. (Chapter 5)

Breaking Strength. Amount of force applied to a material before the yarns break and a tear occurs. (Chapter 12)

Bridge Price Point. The price category for mass-produced apparel products priced between the better and designer price categories with customer perceptions and expectations of high-quality fabrics and elements of designer apparel at a price point lower than designer products. (Chapter 1)

Broken Pick. A severed filling yarn in a fabric. (Chapter 13)

Broken Stitch. A severed stitch thread in a garment. (Chapter 13)

BS Bound Seam Class. ASTM International designation for assembling seams constructed with the raw edges of the seam allowance of one or more plies of fabric covered with a binding, and stitched with one or more rows of stitches. (Chapter 7)

BSI (British Standards Institution). A non-profit organization that develops and publishes standards used in the United Kingdom. (Chapter 1)

Budget Price Point. The lowest price category for mass-produced apparel products, geared toward a wide range of market segments. (Chapter 1)

Builder. Detergent additive that softens and controls the pH level of the water while protecting washing machines from corrosion. (Chapter 12)

Bundle Coupons. Used to track and compensate sewing operators for completed operations. (Chapter 8)

Bundle Ticket. A master list of operations for a bundle that includes bundle coupons, routing information, piece rate, style number, size, and shade number. (Chapter 8)

Buoyant Force. The force applied from beneath a submerged specimen by a lower density liquid than the specimen. (Chapter 11)

Burn Time or **Flame Spread Time.** The time measured on the flammability testing apparatus from the point of ignition to when the stop thread is severed through. (Chapter 10)

Burst Seam. Broken stitches within a seam due to improperly joined materials or tension on the garment. (Chapter 13)

Bursting Strength. Amount of multidirectional force applied to a material to cause the yarns to rupture, creating a hole in the fabric. (Chapter 12)

Button. A form of closure or decoration made from a variety of materials (plastics, wood, metals, natural products) in various shapes and sizes and attached to a garment by sewing through the center of the button or a button shank, or is secured by a prong. (Chapter 4)

Buttonhole. A finished opening made to accommodate a button to pass through and remain secured. (Chapter 4)

Button Loop. A chain of thread, braid, cord, or fabric is folded to form a U-shape that is stitched into the seam to accommodate a button to pass through and remain secured. (Chapter 4)

CA Number. A number issued by the Competition Bureau for the purpose of identifying Canadian manufacturers, importers, or distributers of apparel products. (Chapter 9)

Calculation. The formula used for computing test results data. (Chapter 11)

Calibration. Process of controlling the output from equipment or a testing standard to ensure accuracy of performance and results. (Chapter 11)

Care Labeling of Textile Wearing Apparel and Certain Piece Goods. U.S. labeling regulation 16 CFR 423 for disclosure of care instructions on garment labels. (Chapter 9)

CAS. Chemical Abstract Service. (Chapter 10)

CAS Number. The registration designation assigned to individual chemical substances located in the CAS database to provide information specific to a wide range of substances. CAS numbers are assigned by the American Chemical Society. (Chapter 10)

Casing. Fabric that is folded over and stitched at the edge of the garment or a separate strip of material that is applied to the garment to accommodate a drawstring or elastic. (Chapter 4)

CEN (European Committee for Standardization). An international non-profit organization developing voluntary national standards for European countries. (Chapter 1)

Center Zipper Insertion (Slot Zipper). The seam edges of the opening are abutted over the center of the zipper chain to conceal it. (Chapter 4)

Certificate of Compliance (COC). Document provided by a supplier that certifies that goods comply with all of the required standards and specifications. (Chapter 13)

Certified Supplier. An established vendor that has been approved to produce products that require minimal inspection due to their strong quality control program and consistent record for manufacturing products that meet or exceed required specifications. (Chapter 13)

Charged Solvent. Drycleaning solvent that contains detergent and moisture to aid in stain removal. (Chapter 12)

Char Length. The area of a flammability test specimen that is burned, charred, or damaged after exposure to an ignition source. (Chapter 10)

Chemical Bonding. A chemical reaction between the fabric of the garment and the adhesive used to glue the seam. (Chapter 7)

Chlorine Bleach. A bleach used to whiten garments. (Chapter 12)

Citric Acid. Disinfectant used in wetcleaning detergents. (Chapter 12)

Class 1, Normal Flammability. A U.S. distinction for fabric flammability of plain or raised fiber surface fabrics. Plain surface fabrics must have a minimum burn time of 3.5 seconds, and raised fiber surface fabrics must possess a minimum burn time of 7 seconds or cannot exceed a surface flash of 7 seconds without causing a base burn when tested. Class 1 fabrics can be sold in the U.S. (Chapter 10)

Class 2, Intermediate Flammability. A U.S. distinction for fabric flammability for raised surface fabrics only. Raised fiber surface fabrics possessing a burn time between 4 to 7 seconds and result in a base burn. Class 2 fabrics can be sold in the U.S. (Chapter 10)

Class 3, Rapid and Intense Burning. A U.S. distinction for fabric flammability. Highly flammable fabrics possessing a burn time less than 4 seconds and result in a base burn. Class 3 fabrics cannot be sold in the U.S. (Chapter 10)

Class A Children's Nightwear. The EU classification system for designating flammability of children's nightwear by age group or garment type, and provides requirements for minimum flammability standards. Children's nightwear (excluding pyjamas) for children over 6 months old up to 14 years of age, having a height of 68 cm (26.77 inches) up to 176 cm (69.29 inches) for girls and up to 182 cm (71.65 inches) for boys. Class A exhibits a flame spread of less than 15 seconds, having a char length less than 520 mm (20.47 inches) and not breaking the 3rd marker thread when tested and cannot exhibit surface flash. (Chapter 10)

Class B Children's Nightwear. The EU classification system for designating flammability of children's nightwear by age group or garment type, and provides requirements for minimum flammability standards. Children's pyjamas for children over 6 months old up to 14 years of age, having a height of 68 cm (26.77 inches) up to 176 cm (69.29 inches) for girls and up to 182 cm (71.65 inches) for boys. Class B exhibits a flame spread of less than 10 seconds having a char length less than 520 mm (20.47 inches), not breaking the 3rd marker thread when tested. (Chapter 10)

Class C Children's Nightwear. The EU classification system for designating flammability of children's nightwear by age group or garment type, and provides requirements for minimum flammability standards. Babies' nightwear produced for infants up to 6 months old and up to 68 cm (26.77 inches) in height. Class C products do not require testing; therefore, there are no minimum flammability requirements. (Chapter 10)

Closure. Finding used to secure a garment opening. (Chapter 4)

CNIS (China National Institute of Standardization). A non-profit organization that develops standards to be implemented by the government within China. (Chapter 1)

Coarse Yarn or **Thick Yarn.** A yarn within a fabric that has a larger linear density than the other yarns it is adjacent to. (Chapter 13)

Color. Created through the absorption and reflectance of light. The seven color classifications in the visual spectrum include red, orange, yellow, green, blue, indigo, and violet. (Chapter 2)

Colorants. Dyes, pigments, and optical brighteners used to apply color to fibers, yarns, fabrics, and garments. (Chapter 3)

Color Change. Loss or change in color. (Chapter 12)

Color Evaluation. Assessing color against standards throughout the design development and production processes. (Chapter 2)

Colorfastness. Resistance to change color characteristics or transfer colorant(s) to adjacent materials. (Chapter 12)

Color Management. The monitoring of color throughout the development, manufacturing, and distribution processes. (Chapter 2)

Color Match. When the spectral data of a color sample and the color standard are the same or near identical. (Chapter 2)

Color Out. Missing color within a print design. (Chapter 13)

Color Permanence. Ability of dyes, pigments, and brighteners used for coloring textile materials to remain vibrant, stable, durable, and unchanged. (Chapter 12)

Color Production Standards. Approved reproducible hues that are consistent during manufacturing across a variety of materials and dye formulations. (Chapter 2)

Color Smear. Smudged color on a printed fabric. (Chapter 13)

Color Specifications. Requirements for matching color standards that include the dye or pigment formulations for reproducing color on designated materials in order to match color standards. (Chapter 2)

Color Staining. Transfer of color from one material to another. (Chapter 12)

Color Standards. Color samples by which product materials (fabrics, thread, findings, and trims) are used to match to ensure color consistency between materials. (Chapter 2)

Colorimeter (Spectrophotometer). An instrument used to digitally measure color in a numeric representation. (Chapter 2)

Colour Index. An online publication that provides the chemical formulations for dyes and pigments. (Chapter 2)

Compliance. The ability of a material, finding, or apparel product to conform to established standards and specifications. (Chapter 1)

Concave Darts. The legs of the dart curve toward the body from the fullest point converging to a diminishing point. (Chapter 4)

Conditioning Room, Chamber, or **Cabinet.** Contained place used to bring samples or specimens up to the designated standard atmospheric conditions for testing. (Chapter 11)

Conditioning. Exposure of specimens and materials to standard atmospheric conditions to prepare them for testing. (Chapter 11)

Conformance. The degree to which the design and performance of a product meets established standards. (Chapter 1)

Conformity Assessment. The process for monitoring whether products, materials, and processes are meeting required standards and specifications. (Chapter 1)

Construction Details Sheet. Part of a technical package that includes detailed information for assembling a garment for production. Product details such as trims and decorative stitching are also identified. (Chapter 5)

Contemporary Price Point. The price category that is between better and bridge and offers very trendy fashion forward apparel items for the junior and misses markets. (Chapter 1)

Continuous Placket. One uninterrupted binding used to finish the edges. (Chapter 4)

Contoured Waistband. A shaped band and facing created to contour the waistline of the garment and finish the edge. (Chapter 4)

Control Measurements. A sizing system's body measurements that are used for designating the appropriate garment size for the customer. (Chapter 5)

Control. Fabric sample or a garment used as a standard for drawing comparisons. (Chapter 11)

Convex Darts. The legs of the dart curve away from the body from the fullest point converging to a diminishing point. (Chapter 4)

Core Spun Thread. A continuous filament fiber core that is wrapped with spun yarn and twisted. (Chapter 6)

Cost Per Wear. A calculation used to determine the value of a product by dividing the purchase price of a garment by the number of times it has been worn. (Chapter 1)

Cotton Count (cc or Nec). Linear density in length per unit mass of cotton and cotton blended yarns measured in 840 yard lengths per pound. (Chapter 3)

Courses. Rows of knit stitches or horizontal loops that run in the crosswise direction of knitted fabrics. (Chapter 3)

Covalent Bond. The result of a chemical reaction that causes pairs of electrons to be shared between atoms. (Chapter 7)

Cracked Seam or **Cracked Stitches.** Broken stitch or seam in garments made from knitted fabrics that have been stretched beyond capacity. (Chapter 13)

Crease Mark. A fabric portion that has inadvertently been folded and set/pressed or not removed properly during finishing and cannot be pressed out. (Chapter 13)

Crease Retention. Ability to maintain a crease intentionally set into the fabric. (Chapter 12)

Critical Defects. Garment flaws having the potential to cause minor to fatal injuries or unsafe conditions during use and maintenance of the product. (Chapter 13)

Crocking. Color rub-off caused by loose dye on the surface of an item. (Chapter 12)

Cross Tucks. A series of parallel and perpendicular folds created in a grid pattern and stitched down. (Chapter 4)

Cross-grain. Runs in the filling or courses direction of a fabric and is perpendicular to the selvedge. (Chapter 4)

Crystalline Regions. Organized regions of a fiber. (Chapter 11)

Cut-Make-Trim (CMT). Method of sourcing using vendors contracted to spread and cut fabric and then assemble the component parts (garment pieces, findings and trim) into garments according to specifications provided by the contracting firm. (Chapter 8)

Dart. A triangular fold created to take up excess fabric in a garment in an effort to shape a garment section around a body contour. (Chapter 4)

Dart Equivalent. Integrates the dart into a shaped seam to fit a body contour. (Chapter 4)

Dart Slash. One leg of the dart is gathered to shape around a body contour or add fullness. (Chapter 4)

Dart Tucks. Fabric is folded back on itself to form a dart that is stitched to a designated length and the remaining fabric is released rather than converging into a point. (Chapter 4)

DC Inspections. Evaluations of apparel product shipments that are conducted at distribution centers. (Chapter 13)

Decitex (dtex). Mass per unit length of fine filament yarns from silk or manufactured fibers measured in grams per 10,000 meters. (Chapter 3)

Decorative Dart. The triangular folded portion of a dart that is formed/exposed on the exterior of the garment. (Chapter 4)

Deep Notch. A visible hole in the garment due to a notch that was cut too long. (Chapter 13)

Defect. A flaw in material or sewn product that is not acceptable for the planned quality level. (Chapter 13)

Defective. A product having one or more flaws that prevent it from satisfying the appearance or performance functions for its intended use. (Chapter 13)

Delamination. The breakdown of the adhesive bond between an interlining and a shell fabric. (Chapter 13)

Demographic Data. Statistical information about a population that includes age, gender, income, education, geographic area, family size, housing type, nationality/ethnicity/race, marital status, occupation, spending patterns, and religious affiliations. (Chapter 1)

Demonstrated Capacity. The total quantity of goods produced at a particular quality level within a specific amount of time. (Chapter 8)

Denier (den). Mass per unit length of filament yarns from silk or manufactured fibers measured in grams per 9,000 meters. (Chapter 3)

Design Detail. An element of a garment that creates visual interest within a silhouette. (Chapter 2)

Design Ease (Style Ease). Functional ease plus any additional fullness required to create the desired style or silhouette. (Chapter 4, 5)

Designer Price Point. The highest price category for mass-produced apparel products with customer expectations of exclusive design, high-quality fabrics, and construction details for a narrowly defined niche target market. (Chapter 1)

Design Specifications. Standards for styling details, design features, and characteristics of an apparel item in relation to its aesthetic appeal. (Chapter 1)

Destructive Tests. Testing directly on a sample or specimen that requires it to be cut or damaged in order for testing and evaluation to occur. (Chapter 11)

Digital Print. Fabric patterns applied to the surface of fabrics with a digital inkjet printer containing disperse dyes or pigment inks. (Chapter 3)

Dimensional Change. Change in the physical length or width of a material or apparel; shrinkage or growth. (Chapter 12)

Dimensional Pleats. Creased-ridge fabric folds that are permanently set into a pattern. (Chapter 4)

Dimensional Stability. Ability of textile materials and garments to retain their shape in the length and width directions when subjected to specific conditions relating to temperature and humidity. (Chapter 12)

Direct Yarn Number System. System for measuring the mass/weight per unit length of filament yarn. (Chapter 3, 11)

Disodium Distyrylbiphenyl Disulfonate. Optical brightener. (Chapter 12)

Dobby Weave. Woven geometric patterned created during the weaving process. (Chapter 3)

Domestic Sourcing. Manufacturing sourced within the country goods will be sold. (Chapter 8)

Donning and Doffing. The ease of putting a garment on and taking it off again. (Chapter 4)

Double Cloth. Two fabrics woven on the same loom where the two layers are interlocked by another set of yarns that is interlaced to attach the layers together. (Chapter 3)

Double-ended Dart ("Fish-eye" Dart or Double Pointed Dart). The dart originates at the apex level, extends to the hip level, and contours the fabric to the curves of the body from the bust to the waist to the hips. (Chapter 4)

Double-folded Hem. A hem finish that is created by folding the materials edge two times then it is stitched. (Chapter 4)

Double Pick. Two filling yarns in a woven fabric located within the same shed. (Chapter 13)

Drag Lines. Horizontal or vertical folds in a garment that are not planned as part of the design, indicating fitting problems that need to be resolved. (Chapter 5)

Drill Hole Defect. A visible puncture in the fabric due to a misplaced drill mark. (Chapter 13)

Dry Finish. Chemical application in the form of a liquid or foam used to change the physical performance characteristics of the fabric. (Chapter 3)

Dry Prints. Dry pigment adhered to fabric by means of a resin binder that must be heat cured to form a pattern on the surface of a fabric. (Chapter 3)

Drycleaning. A method of refurbishment that uses a non-aqueous organic solvent for cleaning. (Chapter 12)

Dryer Drum. The chamber in which clothes are dried. (Chapter 12)

Dry-to-dry Closed Loop Machines. Drycleaning machines where both the washing and drying takes place in one machine and the residual solvent vapors are recirculated to recover it. (Chapter 12)

Dry-to-dry Vented Machines. Drycleaning machines where both the washing and drying takes place in one machine and the residual solvent vapors are vented outside the building. (Chapter 12)

Durability. Resistance to physical and mechanical deterioration. (Chapter 1)

Dyes. Complex water soluble organic molecules used to add color to fibers, yarns, fabrics, or garments. (Chapter 3)

Ease. The amount of material in a garment designed to accommodate body movement. (Chapter 4)

EDANA (European Disposables and Nonwovens Association). A non-profit organization that develops and publishes standards primarily for the nonwovens industries in Europe, the Middle East, and Africa. (Chapter 1)

Edge Abrasion. Caused by the edge of a garment rubbing against another surface. (Chapter 12)

EF Edge Finish Seam Class. ASTM International designation for assembling seams constructed with one or two plies of fabric used to cleanly finish the unfinished or raw edge of a garment. (Chapter 7)

Elasticized Waistline. Elastic applied directly to the waistline opening or inserted into a casing to provide stretch. (Chapter 4)

Element. The simplest chemical substance that is the basis for building molecular structures and cannot be further broken down using chemical means. (Chapter 11)

Emphasis. Focal point of a garment. (Chapter 2)

End Out. A missing warp yarn within a fabric. (Chapter 13)

End-item Inspection or **Finished Product Inspection.** An evaluation of garment quality that occurs once the production run is 100 percent assembled and a minimum of 80 percent is packaged. (Chapter 13)

Engineered Print. A fabric print that is strategically placed and created to fit into a garment's shape/design. (Chapter 2)

Environmental Trend Research (Market and Global Trends Research). Gathering, evaluating, and tracking economic, political, cultural, and social trends and technology influences that have occurred over the past 12 months to provide insight for projections for the coming year(s) relating to factors that impact consumer spending. (Chapter 2)

Enzymes. A detergent or pre-treat laundry product additive that aids in the removal of protein and starch based soils. (Chapter 12)

Evaluation. Rating using photographic standards, visual standards, or gray scales. (Chapter 11)

Even Twill. A balanced twill weave having the same number of yarns passing over and under in the warp and filling directions. (Chapter 3)

Exposed Zipper Insertion. Zipper stitched into the garment to show the teeth and part of the zipper tape. (Chapter 4)

Extended Facing. The facing cut as part of the shell garment and folded back on itself to provide a soft draped edge. (Chapter 4)

Extracting. The process of spinning to remove excess moisture during the cleaning processes. (Chapter 12)

Extrinsic Quality Cues. External influences that contribute to the consumer's perception of quality such as price, image, and reputation of the brand and retailer, country of origin, advertising and marketing, and visual presentation. (Chapter 1)

Fabric. Substrate composed of fiber or fiber made into yarns that have been woven, knitted, or chemically, thermally, or mechanically bonded. (Chapter 3)

Fabric Construction. Structure of a material. (Chapter 3)

Fabric Count. The number of threads per 1 inch or per 25 mm in both the warp and fill directions or the number of wale loops and course loops per inch or per 2.5 cm. (Chapter 3, 11)

Fabric Failure. Force applied to a garment seam where the construction of the seam is stronger than the material of the product, causing the material to tear. (Chapter 12)

Fabric Failure. The rupture of yarns within a fabric. (Chapter 7)

Fabric Fallout. Wasted fabric after garment parts have been cut. (Chapter 8)

Fabric Sheet. Part of a technical package that details fabric specification information for the production of a garment, such as fabric name, construction, weight, width, fiber content, color, finish (if applicable), and placement on the garment. (Chapter 5)

Fabric Specifications. Detailed information about fiber content, yarn composition, fabric structure, construction, weight, finishes, defect tolerances, color standards, and performance requirements for materials used in apparel production. (Chapter 5)

Fabric Thickness. The dimension between the top/face and bottom/back surfaces of a material. (Chapter 3, 11)

Fabric Weight. Mass per unit area of a length of material. (Chapter 3, 11)

Faced Hem. A piece of material (facing) shaped the same as the garment edge, stitched to the garment to conceal the raw edges and stabilize the hem. (Chapter 4)

Faced-slashed Placket. Used to conceal the edges and provide stability to the opening when a vent or seam is not planned and no overlap is desired. (Chapter 4)

Facing. A piece of fabric that contours the edge of the outer portion of the garment to finish and stabilize the garment opening. (Chapter 4)

Factory Layout. Physical arrangement of the space within a manufacturing plant that contains areas for production, administration, raw materials storage, inspection and quality control, and employee service. (Chapter 8)

Faulty Zipper. A broken zipper or one that does not function properly. (Chapter 13)

Features. Physical characteristics or special components that enhance and support product performance. (Chapter 1)

Fiber. The smallest unit within the structure of a textile material. (Chapter 3)

Fiber Density. Mass per unit volume of a fiber. (Chapter 11)

Fiber Identification. Verification of fiber content. (Chapter 11)

Filament Fibers. Long continuous strands of fiber. (Chapter 3)

Findings. Any materials other than the shell fabric used to construct an apparel item such as support materials, shaping devices, trims, and surface embellishments. (Chapter 3)

Fine Yarn or **Thin Yarn.** A yarn within a fabric that has a smaller linear density than the other yarns it is adjacent to. (Chapter 13)

Finishing Specifications. Detailed information for completing the garment's final appearance, such as pressing, tagging, folding, or hanging. (Chapter 5)

First Pattern. The initial pattern developed for a sample garment that includes seam and hem allowances. (Chapter 2)

First Sample. The initial prototype constructed to provide a means for evaluating the garment for fit, function, and overall aesthetic appearance. (Chapter 5)

Fit. The relationship between the body and the size and styling of the garment. (Chapter 4)

Fit History. Documentation of changes made to measurements of the garment during the patternmaking and sampling process. (Chapter 5)

Flame Retardant. A chemical finish applied to give textiles flame resistance to prevent the spread of fire when a material is exposed to a flame. (Chapter 10)

Flammability. The ability of a material to ignite and burn. (Chapter 10)

Flange Dart. A pleat that is formed in the fabric, stitched down to a specified length then released at the opposite end to fit the contours of the body or add fullness to an area. (Chapter 4)

Flaring. When the horizontal balance of a garment is not level causing the garment to hang improperly. (Chapter 5)

Flat Abrasion. Caused by two plane surfaces rubbing together. (Chapter 12)

Flat Pleats. Folds of fabric creased, stitched to a desired length, or left unpressed that singly, in groups, or in an evenly spaced repeating pattern. (Chapter 4)

Flex Abrasion. Repeated folding that causes the yarns to wear against each other. (Chapter 12)

Float Defect. Yarn that passes over several other yarns rather than interlacing with each yarn. (Chapter 13)

Fluorinated Organic Compounds. Man-made chemical compounds used in apparel products to provide water, oil, or grease resistance. (Chapter 10)

Fly-front Concealed Zipper Application. A lap formed when one side of a zipper is stitched to a facing that extends slightly beyond the closure; can accommodate two fasteners such as a zipper and snaps. (Chapter 4)

Formaldehyde. A chemical composed of hydrogen, oxygen, and carbon used as a binder for dyes and pigments when combined with other compounds or applied as a finish for some wrinkle free apparel items. (Chapter 10)

Frayed Edge Defect. Garment panel edges with displaced yarns. (Chapter 13)

French Dart. A diagonal dart that extends from the bust to the side seam at any point between the waist area and the hip. (Chapter 4)

FS Flat Seam Class. ASTM International designation for assembling seams constructed with the raw edges of the material plies abutted or slightly overlapped and joined together with stitching that covers the joint. (Chapter 7)

Full-fashioned. Two-dimensional garment panels that are shaped as they are knitted and emerge from the knitting machine ready to assemble. (Chapter 4)

Functional Characteristics. The physical features of a garment related to fit, durability, effectiveness, and ease of care. (Chapter 1)

Functional Ease (Wearing Ease). The appropriate amount of fullness added to a garment to allow for body movement. (Chapter 4)

Functional Ease. Fullness added to a garment pattern to allow for body movement. (Chapter 5)

Fur Products Labeling Act (FPLA). U.S. labeling regulation 16 CFR 301 for labeling garments containing animal fur outlining disclosing of fiber content, registered identification number or identity of manufacturer, or importer, distributor or retailer, and country of origin. (Chapter 9)

Fused Edges. Edges of a garment panel that have melted and bonded with other layers in the fabric spread during cutting. (Chapter 13)

Garment Opening. An area of a garment that allows access for the body to enter it. (Chapter 4)

Gathers. Even distribution of fullness in a garment that is created by drawing in one or more parallel rows of machine gathering stitches. (Chapter 4)

Gauge. The fineness of the knit; the number of needles per inch, per 2.5 centimeters, or 25 millimeters used in a machine to create knit fabrics; the size of the knit stitch. (Chapter 3)

Gauntlet Button. A button and buttonhole positioned in the sleeve placket to secure the opening and eliminate gaping. (Chapter 4)

Godet. Triangular or rounded panel that is inserted and sewn into a seam to provide fullness. (Chapter 4)

Golden Ratio (Divine Proportion). The irrational mathematical constant equal to approximately 1.618 that is used for aesthetically dividing or sectioning in design. (Chapter 2)

Gore. Vertical panels that are shaped to taper to the waist and are seamed together to provide fit. (Chapter 4)

Grade Rules. Directions for proportionately increasing and decreasing a garment pattern at specified points and designated amounts to produce all sizes in the range for mass production. (Chapter 5)

Grading. The measurements of the production pattern (created in the sample size) are re-adjusted (increased or decreased) in designated areas in an effort to create all the sizes in the range. (Chapter 2)

Growth. An increase in the dimension of a garment after cleaning. (Chapter 12)

Gusset. Diamond-shaped inset stitched into garment areas to provide fullness where additional ease is needed. (Chapter 4)

Harmony. When all of the design elements of a garment work together to create a unified overall pleasing aesthetic. (Chapter 2)

Harness. Rectangular loom frames that hold the heddles threaded with yarns. (Chapter 3)

Heddles. Needle-like wires in the harness of a loom threaded with yarns. (Chapter 3)

Hem. A finish used to provide stability and cover fabric raw edges along the bottom edge of a garment or sleeves. (Chapter 4)

Hemline. The area of a garment where the hem is to be folded, faced, or finished. (Chapter 4)

Hemmed-edge Placket. A band applied to finish the edges at the sleeve hem; a soft pleat is formed when folded back. (Chapter 4)

Hole. An unwanted opening in fabric due to damaged yarns. (Chapter 13)

Hook and Eye and Bar. A metal fastener that can be paired with an eye or bar to secure a garment closed. Hooks can also be paired with a fabric loop to form a closure. (Chapter 4)

Hue. The purest form of color. (Chapter 2)

Hydrogen Peroxide. The primary active ingredient in oxygen bleach. (Chapter 12)

Hydrophilic. Water-loving; having an affinity for water. (Chapter 12)

Hydrophobic. Water-repelling; having an aversion to water. (Chapter 12)

Hygrometer. A psychrometer having a wet-bulb thermometer that is kept moist through ventilation by aspiration and a dry-bulb thermometer. (Chapter 11)

Incorrect Ply Tension. Fabric layup that is spread too tight or too loose. (Chapter 13)

Incorrect SPI or SPC. The wrong number of stitches per inch or per centimeter. (Chapter 13)

INDA (Association of the Nonwoven Fabrics Industry). A non-profit organization that develops and publishes international standards for the nonwoven materials industry. (Chapter 1)

Indirect Yarn Number System. System for measuring the length per unit of mass/weight of spun yarn made from staple fibers. (Chapter 11)

Infrared Spectrophotometer. Apparatus used for measuring the electromagnetic radiation to determine the chemical compounds within a specimen. (Chapter 11)

Infrared Spectroscopy (IR Spectroscopy). Method for chemically analyzing fiber specimens through measurement using infrared radiation. (Chapter 11)

Infrared Spectrum. The portion of wavelengths with the electromagnetic spectrum that emit infrared radiation. (Chapter 11)

In-plant Audits. Evaluation of a factory to monitor the management, efficiency, quality control, and working conditions of a manufacturing plant. (Chapter 13)

In-plant Inspections. Evaluations that occur in the factory where the products are produced. (Chapter 13)

In-process Inspection, In-line Inspection, or **Dupro Inspection.** Evaluation of garments during production. (Chapter 13)

Insoluble Compound Deposits. Greasy film or soap scum that results from a reaction between soap and hard water minerals. (Chapter 12)

Inspection. The process for evaluating factories in relation to capacity and quality control, function and appearance of materials and components, random selection of production garments to identify defects and deviations from contracted specifications to ensure that quality standards are being met. (Chapter 1)

Inspection. The process of testing and visually examining fabric, component parts, and sewn products at various stages of completion and checking garment dimensions to determine if they comply with required specification standards. (Chapter 13)

Inspection by Random Sampling. A method of inspection where a specific percentage of a shipment is inspected to determine acceptance or rejection of an entire shipment and is based solely on those garments evaluated. (Chapter 13)

Inspection by Spot Check Sampling. A method of inspection where products are arbitrarily selected for evaluation and decisions for acceptance or rejection are based solely on the garments evaluated. (Chapter 13)

Inspection by Statistical Sampling. A method of inspection where a specific percentage of a shipment is inspected to determine acceptance or rejection of an entire shipment based on statistics. (Chapter 13)

Inspection Specifications. Standards developed by a company that are used to indicate the stages in which inspection will occur. (Chapter 13)

Inspectors. Individuals trained to conduct visual examinations of raw materials and sewn garments to determine if they will meet brand or customer expectations in relation to appearance, size, performance, and function. (Chapter 13)

Interlacing. A stitch formed by two or more sewing threads passing through fabric, forming a loop that intertwines around a different loop of thread. (Chapter 6)

Interlooping. The stitch formation created with two or more threads passing through one or more loops formed by different threads. (Chapter 6)

Intralooping. A term used by ISO to indicate the stitch formation of a single sewing thread when it creates a loop that is then looped back through it. (Chapter 6)

Intrinsic Quality Cues. The physical features, performance characteristics, and product benefits consumers use to make determinations about quality. (Chapter 1)

Invisible Zipper Insertion. The chain of the zipper is completely concealed when closed and appears like a seam. (Chapter 4)

Irregular stitching. Garment stitching that has not been sewn straight. (Chapter 13)

ISO (International Organization for Standardization). The largest organization for developing and publishing standards worldwide. (Chapter 1)

Jacquard Weave. Woven figured pattern or motif woven into the structure of the fabric. (Chapter 3)

Jerk-in. An extra filling yarn that has been inadvertently pulled into the fabric and does not extend across the width of the woven material. (Chapter 13)

JISC (Japanese Industrial Standards Committee). Japanese committee that develops and administers the JIS regulatory standards for use in Japan. (Chapter 1)

JSA (Japanese Standards Association). Publishes the JIS regulatory standards for use in Japan. (Chapter 1)

Key Words. Important terms used within a testing standard. (Chapter 11)

Kilotex (ktex). Mass per unit length of filament yarns of thick spun yarns from silk or manufactured fibers measured in kilograms per 1,000 meters. (Chapter 3)

Knit-and-wear or **Seamless Apparel.** Three-dimensional pre-shaped garments knitted to fit the shape of the body and do not require any additional operations for assembly; they emerge from the knitting machine ready to wear. Some garments require minimal operations or finishing. (Chapter 4)

Lab Dip. Physical or digital representations of dyed fabric that are evaluated against color standards for accuracy of color matching. (Chapter 2)

Label Sheet. Part of a technical package; details label specification information for the production of a garment. (Chapter 5)

Lab Samples. Materials or garments obtained from the lot sample to supply specimens for testing. (Chapter 11)

Ladder or **Run.** A vertical line of unraveled stitches in a knitted fabric or garment. (Chapter 13)

Landed Duty Paid Supplier (LDP). A supplier responsible for the landed value of a product plus any import duties such as shipping, duty, delivery, insurance, and customs clearance costs. (Chapter 8)

Lap Zipper Insertion. The zipper is stitched to the back folded opening while the other garment opening is folded and stitched along the zipper tap to form a tuck to conceal the zipper. (Chapter 4)

Laser Welding. Infrared laser technology transmitted through materials to melt a specified portion of the fabric's surface to bond it together. (Chapter 7)

Laundering. Cleaning process that utilizes aqueous detergent solution and mechanical action to remove soils, followed by rinsing, extracting, and drying to refurbish the garment. (Chapter 12)

Lauryl Trimethyl Ammonium Chloride. A conditioner added to wetcleaning detergent to prevent shrinkage and felting. (Chapter 12)

Layup. Total number of plies in a fabric spread. (Chapter 13)

Lead Time. The amount of time between when an order is released to start production to when it is shipped. (Chapter 8)

Lead. A highly toxic naturally occurring chemical element found in the crust of the earth and used in some garment findings made from metal or plastic or in textiles treated with surface coatings or printing. (Chapter 10)

Lean Manufacturing. Production of small quantities of merchandise close to the time needed. (Chapter 8)

Left-hand Twill. Woven twill fabric having diagonal lines that extend from the lower right to the upper left. (Chapter 3)

Letter Code Sizing. Garment size designation reported by one or more letters such as XS or M. (Chapter 5)

Lifestyle Data. The social and psychological factors that motivate consumers to buy such as life stage, reference groups/peers, social class, personality, attitudes and values, generation group, and cultural preferences based on ethnic or cultural influences. (Chapter 1)

Line. A continuous stroke or contour used to create a silhouette or form shapes within a garment. (Chapter 2)

Linen Lea (lea). Linear density in length per unit mass of linen and linen-like yarns measured in 300 yard lengths per pound. (Chapter 3)

Linking (Looping). Attaching knit trim components to the body of the garment by matching each stitch and joining them together. (Chapter 4)

Logistics. Distribution process. (Chapter 8)

Loose Buttons. Buttons that have not been properly secured to the garment. (Chapter 13)

Loose-fitting Sleepwear. A Canadian designation for children's night garments and sleepwear up to size 14X that is designed to fit looser around the body. (Chapter 10)

Loose Thread End. Thread end on a garment that has not been properly trimmed. (Chapter 13)

Lot Samples. Randomly selected garments or materials taken from one or more main stock or production lot shipments used for conducting acceptance testing. (Chapter 11)

LS Lapped Seam Class. ASTM International designation for assembling two or more plies of material that are overlapped with the raw edges exposed or the seam allowance folded under and joined with one or more rows of stitching. (Chapter 7)

Maintenance. Care and repair of a garment. (Chapter 1)

Major Defects. Flaws that impact the functional performance of a product; will lead to failure at some point during usage. (Chapter 13)

Make-through or **Whole Garment Production System.** A production processes where one individual assembles a garment from start to finish. (Chapter 8)

Mandatory/Regulatory Standards. Test methods and specifications required by law that are enforced by government. (Chapter 1)

Manity Sizing. Vanity sizing used in the menswear industry. (Chapter 5)

Manufacturer-defined Quality. The level of excellence of a product that is determined by its ability to conform to production standards and specifications. (Chapter 1)

Marker. The planned layout of pattern pieces used for cutting fabric for garment assembly. (Chapter 8)

Material Specifications. The designated performance expectations required for all materials used to complete a garment style. (Chapter 1)

Mean (x-bar or $\bar{x}$). Average of the data obtained from a specified number of observations. (Chapter 11)

Mechanical Bond. The penetration of adhesive into the fabric caused by applied pressure and temperature to glue the seam. (Chapter 7)

Melting Point. The temperature at which deformation or liquefaction of a specimen begins. (Chapter 11)

Metamerism. When colors match under certain lighting conditions and not in others. (Chapter 2)

Metric Count (mc or Nm). Linear density in length per unit mass of all spun yarns measured in 1,000 meter lengths per gram. (Chapter 3)

Micelle. A formation consisting of surfactant molecules that surround and loosen soils in the wash bath. (Chapter 12)

Microscope Objectives. Forms the image and determines the level of image quality produced by the microscope. (Chapter 11)

Microscopic Observation. Method for observing magnified specimens for purposes of identification. (Chapter 11)

Minor Defects. Flaws that impact the aesthetic appearance of a garment. (Chapter 13)

Misaligned Plies. Each layer of fabric within a layup with edges that are not lined up properly. (Chapter 13)

Mismatched Fabric Design. The misaligned fabric pattern on garment panels within a finished product. (Chapter 13)

Misregister. Incorrect alignment of colors within a print. (Chapter 13)

Missing Component. A required garment element or piece that was inadvertently omitted during assembly. (Chapter 13)

Moderate Price Point. The price category that includes average prices for mass-produced apparel products geared toward meeting the needs of middle-income families and individuals. (Chapter 1)

Modular Production System. A production process involving small teams of sewing operators that work together to assemble garments. (Chapter 8)

Modulus. Application of directional force at repeated intervals to elongate and relax a knitted material to determine its resistance limit before permanent damage or distortion is caused. (Chapter 12)

Moiré Effect. The appearance of water spotting or wavy striping on a garment fabric due to the alignment of the adhesive pattern on the interlining or the shell fabric. (Chapter 13)

Moisture Equilibrium. Material that has reached the maximum level of moisture absorption. (Chapter 11)

Moisture Sensing Bars. Metal bars that communicate electrical resistance to the circuit board in dryers equipped with moisture sensing cycle. (Chapter 12)

Molecules. Bonded atoms. (Chapter 11)

Monofilament Thread. One single continuous filament fiber that requires no twist. (Chapter 6)

Myristamine Oxide. A type of surfactant. (Chapter 12)

National Standards Body (NSB). Part of the British Standards Institute that oversees the development of standards for use in the United Kingdom and represents the UK in European and International standards forums. (Chapter 1)

National Standards System (NSS). Develop voluntary standards and adapt international standards for use in Canada. (Chapter 1)

Nearshore. Manufacturing sourced in a country located in close proximity to the one goods will be sold in. (Chapter 8)

Needle Damage. Hole in the fabric caused by the sewing needle during assembly. (Chapter 13)

Needle Line. A vertical line of distorted stitches in a knitted fabric resulting from a bent needle. (Chapter 13)

Needle Size. The diameter of a needle measured in hundredths of a millimeter. (Chapter 6)

Nickel. A toxic naturally occurring chemical substance found in the crust of the earth and used in some metal garment findings such as buttons, rivets, snaps, and zippers. (Chapter 10)

Nightwear. Any garments intended to be sold and worn as sleepwear or bathrobes. (Chapter 10)

No Inspections. No evaluation or assessment is conducted on piece goods, component parts, or finished products. (Chapter 13)

Nonconformance. When material or garment characteristics do not meet specified quality standards. (Chapter 13)

Nondestructive Test. Testing directly on a lab sample without causing aesthetic or physical damage. (Chapter 11)

Nonvolatile Residue (NVR). Particulate matter, grease, and oils that remain in the bottom of the distillation tank after solvent is cleaned. (Chapter 12)

Nonwoven Fabrics. Materials constructed as fiber web structures by mechanical entanglement, chemical bonding agents, or by fusing thermoplastic fibers together with heat. (Chapter 3)

Normal Inspection (Level II). Standard level of inspection used when products are consistently meeting the acceptance quality limit. (Chapter 13)

Numeric Sizing. Garment size designation reported as a number that is based off of specific body dimensions. (Chapter 5)

Off-grain. The warp and filling yarns in a fabric are skewed and do not meet at right angles at the points of intersection. (Chapter 4)

Offshore. Manufacturing sourced in a different country than they will be sold in. (Chapter 8)

Oleochemicals. Substances derived from fats and oils used as primary components of synthetic detergents for laundering that are. (Chapter 12)

On-grain. The warp and filling yarns in a fabric meet at right angles at the points of intersection. (Chapter 4)

Onshore or **Domestic Sourcing.** Sourcing manufacturing domestically. (Chapter 8)

Open Seam. An area of a garment where all the fabric plies are not caught in the seam. (Chapter 13)

Optical Brightener/Fluorescent Brightener/ Whitener. A detergent additive that makes fabrics appear intensely white or more vibrant. (Chapter 12)

Optical Brighteners (Fluorescent Dyes, or **Whiteners).** Chemical solutions applied to fabrics to enhance the color appearance to create an intense white. (Chapter 3)

Original Design Manufacturing (ODM) or **Full Package Contractor.** This type of contractor handles the design of the product, assembly, finishing, packaging, and carries the financial burden for procurement of materials and production costs. When an ODM supplier is responsible for the distribution of goods they are referred to as a landed duty paid supplier. (Chapter 8)

Original Equipment Manufacturing (OEM) or Package Contractor. This type of contractor finances and sources fabrics and component garment parts needed to assemble garments based on contracted specifications and assembles, finishes, and packages the products for delivery to the retail destination. (Chapter 8)

OS Ornamental Seam Class. ASTM International designation for adding decoration to one or more plies of material by means of a series of stitches expressed in a straight, curved, or designated design for the purpose of adding decoration to a garment. (Chapter 7)

Overcut. Creating a garment pattern that is larger to accommodate the initial shrinkage that occurs during cleaning. (Chapter 12)

Over-edge Hem. Stitching is formed over the fabric's raw edge to create a garment finish at the hem. (Chapter 4)

Over-fusing. Weak bond between the interlining and shell materials due to excessive heat, time, or pressure during fusing causing the resin to transfer completely into the garment fabric. (Chapter 13)

Oxidizing Bleach. Chlorine and oxygen bleach used for cleaning textiles and apparel items. (Chapter 12)

Oxygen Bleach. Color-safe bleach. (Chapter 12)

Packaging Sheet. Part of a technical package that details packaging specifications for the production and shipment of a garment. (Chapter 5)

Packaging Specifications. Detailed instructions for how garments should be packaged for shipping. (Chapter 5)

Pajamas or **Pyjamas.** One or more garments intended for sleepwear or nightwear and can be designed with or without feet. (Chapter 10)

Parallax Error. When the pointer on a dial is read from a slight angle rather than directly in front. (Chapter 11)

Pattern. A repetitive design that is created by weaving, knitting, felting, dyeing, or printing to add aesthetic interest to apparel products. (Chapter 2)

Perceived Quality. The consumer's opinion of the level of superiority of a product based on brand reputation, value, and the ability of the product to meet the expectations of the wearer. (Chapter 1)

Perchloroethylene/Perc/Tetrachloroethylene. Drycleaning solvent composed of halogenated hydrocarbons. (Chapter 12)

Performance. The ability of a product to function as it is intended. (Chapter 1, 5)

Performance Features. The functional characteristics related to the intended use of a garment. (Chapter 1)

Performance Specification. Standards used to determine requirements for acceptability of materials or sewn products based on results obtained through testing. (Chapter 12)

Petrochemicals. Substance derived from petroleum used as primary components of synthetic detergents for laundering. (Chapter 12)

Petroleum. Drycleaning solvent composed of hydrocarbon distillates. (Chapter 12)

Physical Attributes. The design, material selection, construction, and finishing of a product. (Chapter 1)

Pictogram. Illustrations of body forms marked to indicate where specific body measurements (POM) should be taken. (Chapter 5)

Pigments. Add color to the surface of fibers and materials with the assistance of binding agents. (Chapter 3)

Pile Weave. Fabric woven with an additional set of yarns (warp or filling) in the base and loops on the surface of the fabric that can be cut or remain intact. (Chapter 3)

Pin Holes. Punctures along the selvedge of the fabric. (Chapter 13)

Pin Tucks. A single narrow fold or series of repeating parallel folds that are evenly spaced and stitched down from seam line to seam line or within a garment section. (Chapter 4)

Piped Tucks. Tucks that have cording inserted into the tuck. (Chapter 4)

Placket. A finished opening within a garment area that allows for the wearer to easily put the garment on or remove it. (Chapter 4)

Plain Surface Materials. Smooth surface fabrics that do not have a raised surface from fibers or yarns or fancy knit or woven structures. (Chapter 10)

Plain Weave. Woven fabric created using two harnesses with a shuttle passing the filling yarns over and under the warp yarns, alternating with each row. (Chapter 3)

Pleats. Fabric folded back on itself along the grain line to provide a means for fitting contours of the body and for design interest. (Chapter 4)

Ply Adhesion or **Ply Security.** The ability of a thread to maintain its structure without unraveling during sewing. (Chapter 6)

Ply Yarns. Two or more yarns twisted, wrapped, entangled, or chemically bound together. (Chapter 3)

Points of Measurement (POM). The measurement points indicated on a technical flat sketch of a garment. (Chapter 5)

Polarizer. Part of a microscope that allows the maximum amount of light to be transmitted through a specimen. (Chapter 11)

Precision. The agreement of data obtained from observations collected during testing. (Chapter 11)

Precision and Bias. Statistical data used for determining if a significant difference exists and if other factors may influence test results. (Chapter 11)

Price. The amount designated by the seller to be paid by the consumer in exchange for a product or service. (Chapter 1)

Price Point Classification. The range of prices, lowest to highest, upon which competitive products are offered in the marketplace. (Chapter 1)

Primary Dimension. The most important body or product dimension used to define the size of the item. (Chapter 5)

Primary Quality Indicators. The intrinsic attributes that comprise the physical structure of a product. (Chapter 1)

Princess Line Seam. A vertical seam that intersects the bust apex and extends to the shoulder or armhole. (Chapter 4)

Procedure. Instructions for how to perform a standard test. (Chapter 11)

Process Layout or **Skill Center.** A factory layout with equipment organized into pods of work areas. (Chapter 8)

Product Benefits. The physical attributes and performance features consumers desire to meet their needs and expectations. (Chapter 1)

Product Data Management. Software that is integrated with PLM to allow digital files for apparel products to be shared along the supply chain. (Chapter 8)

Product-defined Quality. The inherent measurable physical features and attributes of an apparel item that determined its level of excellence. (Chapter 1)

Production Pattern. The final pattern for a style that has been tested and perfected; includes seam and hem allowances, notches, grainlines, perforations, and pattern identifications. (Chapter 2)

Production Samples. Final sewn garment prototypes constructed with the exact same materials and methods that will be used for mass production of the garment. (Chapter 5)

Production System. Resources and sequencing of workflow in a factory needed to assemble a garment from beginning to end. (Chapter 8)

Product Layout or **Line Layout.** Factory layout of equipment arranged in assembly lines. (Chapter 8)

Product Lead Sheet/Design Sheet. The cover sheet for a technical package that provides preliminary information about the garment style. (Chapter 5)

Product Lifecycle Management (PLM). Software systems for managing and communicating information along the supply chain from start to finish. (Chapter 8)

Product Market Research. Gathering and analyzing information regarding competing products, innovative products being developed or introduced, and trend forecasts to provide insight for ways to improve existing products or to provide new opportunities in the marketplace for expanding business. (Chapter 2)

Product Recall. The action of removing defective products from the distribution chain and retrieving them from consumers to avoid harm to the customer due to a serious safety hazard. (Chapter 13)

Product Specifications. Standards for intrinsic components of a completed product such as size and fit, garment assembly, finishing, labeling, packaging, quality, and performance. (Chapter 1, 5)

Product Value. The customer's perception of quality in relation to the price paid. (Chapter 1)

Progressive Bundle System. A production process that utilizes assembly line methods and garment bundles that are moved manually according to the sequen-

tial order of machines used to complete the garment. (Chapter 8)

Proportion. The harmonious interrelationships of the position and scale between silhouette, design, details, style lines, and fabric grain within a given design. (Chapter 2)

Protease Enzymes. Protein molecules that help remove protein-based stains. (Chapter 12)

Prototype. A sample of a garment design developed in a physical form or virtual environment to provide a means for testing fit, function, and overall aesthetic appeal. (Chapter 5)

Psychrometer. Device that measures the temperature and relative humidity of the air. (Chapter 11)

Quality. An individual's perception of a garment's inherent characteristics and performance; the level of excellence or superiority of a product in relation to others in the marketplace; the ability of a product to function for its intended use and be free of defects. (Chapter 1)

Quality Assurance. The method for managing and controlling the processes for development and manufacturing of apparel to ensure product quality and compliance with safety regulations. (Chapter 1)

Quality Control. The process for ensuring specified standards for quality are maintained through continual testing at different phases of production, performing frequent inspections, and ensuring proper use of equipment and established procedures. (Chapter 1)

Quick Response Manufacturing (QRM). A strategy for manufacturing and delivering goods to the consumer faster by eliminating or reducing any handling that does not add value in an effort to improve product quality, reduce costs, and provide the brand with a competitive edge. (Chapter 8)

Raised Fiber Surface Materials. Fabrics made with a raised surface from fibers or yarns or fancy knit or woven structures having a pile, nap, tuft, or flocked surface. (Chapter 10)

RAPEX. The European Union's raid alert system for consumer product safety. (Chapter 10)

Raw Edges. Unfinished frayed ends of fabric at hemlines or seams in a garment where the material is not stitched properly. (Chapter 13)

Raw Materials. Fibers, yarns, and unfinished fabrics. (Chapter 3)

Raw Materials Inspection. The act of assessing fabric to document flaws and their specific locations within a roll to determine if the quality level meets required standards. (Chapter 13)

REACH. European Community Regulation that stands for Registration, Evaluation, Authorization, and restriction of CHemical substances that regulates the safe use of chemicals and publishes a directive for restricted substances. (Chapter 10)

Reagent. Substance or compound used for producing a chemical reaction. (Chapter 11)

Receiving Inspections. The act of evaluating shipments of piece goods and component parts through testing, visual evaluation, and measurement of raw materials. (Chapter 13)

Reduced Inspection (Level I). A lowered level of inspection that can be instated when 10 consecutive shipments or lots are meeting acceptance quality limits under level II normal inspection. (Chapter 13)

Referenced Documents or **Normative References.** Additional standards that are related to the selected test method. (Chapter 11)

Refractive Index. Speed in which polarized light travels through a specimen when compared to the speed of light in a vacuum. (Chapter 11)

Refurbishment. The process of cleaning and restoring the appearance of a garment. (Chapter 1)

Registration Number (RN). A number issued and registered by the U.S. Federal Trade Commission for the purpose of identifying U.S. manufacturers, importers, or distributors of apparel products. (Chapter 9)

Relative Humidity (RH). The amount of water vapor present in the air that is represented as a percentage of the maximum volume that the air can support at any specified temperature. (Chapter 11)

Release Tucks. A single fold or series of repeating parallel folds that are evenly spaced and stitched down for a designated length then released to direct fullness to a particular area of a garment. (Chapter 4)

Reliability. Consist, dependable, and reproducible test procedures and results obtained during testing. (Chapter 11)

Report. Documentation of procedures used for testing and calculation of data or standards used for rating, accompanied by a statement of results. (Chapter 11)

Reproducible. When testing is performed on the same material or garment, and the data collected is consistent. (Chapter 11)

Retail Price. The amount designated by the retailer to be paid by the consumer in exchange for a product or service. (Chapter 1)

Rhythm. The movement of the viewer's eyes through each part of a garment that is carefully planned. (Chapter 2)

Right-hand Twill. Woven twill fabric having diagonal lines that extend from the lower left to the upper right. (Chapter 3)

Rolled Hem. A narrow hem finish where the raw edge of the material is fed through an attachment where it is folded and stitched. (Chapter 4)

Ropy Hem. Skewed or twisted fabric within the hem of a garment. (Chapter 13)

Ruching. A controlled predetermined amount of fullness that is gathered and released to correspond to parallel a seam in a repeating pattern. (Chapter 4)

Run-off or Over-run Stitching. Top or edge stitching that was continued beyond the point where it was supposed to end. (Chapter 13)

Safety Precautions or **Hazards.** Precautions to be taken to ensure the lab technician's safety when conducting test procedures. (Chapter 11)

Sample Plan. Arrangement and procedure for obtaining test specimens from a sample. (Chapter 11)

Samples. Materials or garments selected for testing. (Chapter 11)

Sample Size. A size designated by a manufacturer that typically falls in the middle of its size range offerings, such as a size 8 or 10 for missy. (Chapter 5)

Sampling or **Test Specimens.** Section of a test method containing detailed procedures for taking and preparing specimens such as dimensions, the number required, and the methods for preparing them prior to testing. (Chapter 11)

Satin Weave. A woven fabric created with 5 to 12 harnesses having four or more yarns passing over before passing under one yarn. (Chapter 3)

Saturation. The sharpness or dullness of a color's intensity. (Chapter 2, 4)

Scalloped Tucks. Tucks that are formed by drawing in the folded edge at evenly spaced intervals and catching it at the stitch line to create a shell shaped edge. (Chapter 4)

SCC (Standards Council of Canada). The organization that administers the National Standards System in Canada. (Chapter 1)

Scope. Summary of the purpose of the test and the materials covered by the standard. (Chapter 11)

Scrimp. An undyed portion of a fabric print caused by the formation of a crease during printing. (Chapter 13)

Seam. Two or more layers of material joined together by means of stitching, ultrasonic sealing, laser welding, or thermal bonding. (Chapter 7)

Seam. Two or more plies of fabric are sewn together. (Chapter 4)

Seam Allowance. Measured distance between the stitchline of the seam and the raw edge of the fabric of a garment panel. (Chapter 7)

Seam Class 1. ISO designation for assembling two or more plies of fabric of which two are limited in width on the side where the seam is constructed. (Chapter 7)

Seam Class 2. ISO designation for assembling two or more plies of material that are limited in the width on opposite sides from each other, where they join into the seam. One of the plies of fabric is positioned below the other; then they are overlapped. (Chapter 7)

Seam Class 3. ISO designation for assembling seams are constructed with a minimum of one ply of fabric that is limited in width on one side and a binding that is limited in width on two sides that wraps over the raw edge of the other ply of material to finish the edge. (Chapter 7)

Seam Class 4. ISO designation for seams are constructed with a minimum of two pieces of material that are limited in width having the raw edges abutted and stitched to cover over the joint. (Chapter 7)

Seam Class 5. ISO designation for assembling seams constructed with a minimum of one ply of fabric that is unlimited on two sides and any other material integrated into the seam can be limited on one or two sides. (Chapter 7)

Seam Class 6. ISO designation for assembling seams constructed with one ply of fabric that is limited in width on either the right or left side. (Chapter 7)

Seam Class 7. ISO designation for assembling seams constructed with at least two pieces of material having one limited in width on one side and the other pieces being limited on two of the sides. (Chapter 7)

Seam Class 8. ISO designation for assembling seams constructed with a minimum of one ply of fabric that is limited in width on two sides and any additional components are equally limited in width on two sides. (Chapter 7)

Seam Efficiency. The relationship between the strength of a fabric and the strength of the seam construction. (Chapter 7)

Seam Failure. Rupture of the stitching and thread or separation of a sealed, welded, or thermal bond where fabrics are joined in a garment. (Chapter 7)

Seam Grin. The result of stitch balance being too loose which causes the seam to gap when stress is applied. (Chapter 7)

Seam Grin. Unwanted visible stitching within a seam on the exterior of the garment that is caused by unbalanced thread tension. (Chapter 13)

Seamless Garments. Three-dimensional pre-shaped garments that utilize knit-and-wear construction and do not contain seams. (Chapter 7)

Seam Pucker. Wrinkling of fabric in the stitching line. (Chapter 13)

Seam Repair. Re-stitching to correct broken stitches that are part of a seam. (Chapter 13)

Seam Slippage. The displacement of warp yarns within a material which causes them to slide and eventually pull out of the seam. (Chapter 7)

Seam Slippage. Tension applied to a garment seam causing the yarns of the material to slide away from the seam. (Chapter 12)

Seam Strength. Amount of force that can be applied to a seam to rupture the stitching or bonding. (Chapter 12)

Secondary Dimension. An ancillary body mass dimension that is used in conjunction with the primary dimension to distinguish the size of the item. (Chapter 5)

Secondary Quality Indicators. Extrinsic attributes that are not part of the physical makeup of a product that influence a consumer's perception of quality. (Chapter 1)

Separate Facing. A facing that finishes the edges of one garment area (i.e., a neckline or armhole). (Chapter 4)

Serviceability. The ease of care for a garment; ability of an apparel item to retain its shape and appearance. (Chapter 1)

Sewing Thread. A thin strand or ply of flexible yarn made from staple fibers, single monofilament, multiple filaments, or cords that are bonded together. (Chapter 6)

Sew-through Button. A button having two or four holes that are used for attaching them to a garment. (Chapter 4)

Shaded. The difference in color across the fabric width. (Chapter 13)

Shading. Mismatched dye lots of garment components and subassemblies that affect the appearance of the finished product. (Chapter 13)

Shank Button. A button containing a protruding loop or hole that is used for stitching it to a garment. The point of attachment is concealed from the face of the garment. (Chapter 4)

Shaped Facing. A separate piece of material ranging from 1½ to 2 inches (3.8 cm to 5.08 cm) in width that is stitched and folded back to hide the raw edges. (Chapter 4)

Shaping Devices. Structured pads, wires, boning, tapes, stays, and elastic used to provide architectural support for garments. (Chapter 3)

Shaping Methods (Shaping Strategies). Darts and dart equivalents used to fit a garment around the contours of the body. (Chapter 4)

Shrinkage. A decrease in the dimension of a garment after cleaning. (Chapter 12)

Side Panel. A vertical panel that extends to the armhole used in place of a side seam to provide more fit. (Chapter 4)

Significance and Use. Information regarding acceptance testing procedures and how to describe the data gathered. (Chapter 11)

Significant Figures. The number of decimal places needed when reporting test data to provide accuracy. (Chapter 11)

Silhouette. The overall shape or outline of a garment. (Chapter 2)

Singles Yarn. One continuous filament or staple fibers twisted together to form a spun yarn. (Chapter 3)

Size Defects. Problems with the gradation of sizes or differences in the measurement of one garment part to another. (Chapter 13)

Size Designations. Body size indicator for apparel items identified on a garment label as a letter code or number. (Chapter 5)

Size Specifications. Detailed information regarding specific dimensions and tolerances for a garment that are taken at designated measurement points based on the garment styling, fit, manufacturer size requirements, grade rules, size range, and production needs. (Chapter 5)

Sizing System. Body measurements classified by gender, age, and sometimes garment type to provide size classifications for mass produced apparel. (Chapter 5)

Skew. Displaced yarns within a knitted or woven fabric. (Chapter 13)

Skipped Stitch. When a stitch is not formed along the seam line. (Chapter 13)

Slot Buttonhole. A finished opening in a seam that allows a button to pass through and remain secured. (Chapter 4)

Slub. A yarn defect where one section is visibly thicker than the rest. (Chapter 13)

Smart Cards or **Electronic Bundle Tickets.** A card with a magnetic strip that can be swiped and read by a card reader that essentially contains the same information as bundle tickets and serves the same purpose as the bundle coupon to monitor work completed. (Chapter 8)

Snap. A fastener with a ball and socket that joined together to close. (Chapter 4)

Soaps. Water soluble cleaning agents made from fats and oils or fatty acids from animal or plant sources that are treated with strong alkali such as sodium or potassium. (Chapter 12)

Sodium C_{10-16} Alkylbenzenesulfonate. A type of surfactant. (Chapter 12)

Sodium Carbonate/Soda Ash. Alkalinity-builder in chlorine bleach. (Chapter 12)

Sodium Carbonate Peroxide. Primary active ingredient in powder oxygen bleach. (Chapter 12)

Sodium Chloride. Salt that is added to thicken and stabilize liquid bleach. (Chapter 12)

Sodium Hydroxide/Caustic Soda. Adjusts pH level of bleach and aids in removal of grease and alcohol based stains. (Chapter 12)

Sodium Hypochlorite. The primary active ingredient found in chlorine bleach. (Chapter 12)

Sodium Polyacrylate. Additive to chlorine bleach that prevents re-deposition of soils. (Chapter 12)

Soil. Chalk, ink, dirt, oil, or grease that creates a stain. (Chapter 13)

Soiled Yarn. A dirty yarn. (Chapter 13)

Solubility. Dissolving fibers in chemical substances or reagents to identify the fibers present in a material. (Chapter 11)

Sourcing Agent. The liaison between a manufacturer, factory, and retailer who helps oversee production and monitor quality based on product specifications. (Chapter 8)

Sourcing. The location and assessment of resources to acquire materials or manufacturing needed for apparel products that meet the quality standards required; procuring resources to acquire materials or manufactured apparel products. (Chapter 8)

Spaced Tucks. A single fold or series of repeating parallel folds that are evenly spaced and stitched down from seam line to seam line or within a garment section. (Chapter 4)

Spec Sheets. Part of a technical package that details size specification information for the production of a garment. (Chapter 5)

Specification Requirements. List of fabric and garment properties that should conform to the performance standard. (Chapter 12)

Specifications. Established requirements for determining whether a material or product satisfies quality standards related to performance criteria, safety, or physical, mechanical, or chemical properties. (Chapter 1)

Specimen. Fibers, yarns, sewing thread, material, garment sections, or component parts. (Chapter 11)

Spectral Data. The percentage of light reflected at each wavelength along the visual spectrum that is digitally measured using a colorimeter or spectrophotometer. (Chapter 2)

Speed-to-Market. The ability of a brand to quickly design, manufacture, and distribute products by means of reducing lead times so products enter the marketplace sooner for consumer consumption. (Chapter 8)

Split Yoke. A horizontal panel with a seam down the center front or center back that is used to shape a garment at the seams where it is joined. (Chapter 4)

Spun Thread. Single yarns comprised of staple fibers that are twisted together. (Chapter 6)

SS Superimposed Seam Class. ASTM International designation for assembling two or more plies of fabric that are overlaid, one on top of another, with their raw edges aligned and stitched together at a specified distance from the raw edge, with one or more rows of stitching. (Chapter 7)

Standard Atmosphere for Pre-conditioning Textiles. 122°F ± 2 degrees (50°C ± 1 degree) with relative humidity between 5 and 25 percent having a tolerance of ± 2 percent. (Chapter 11)

Standard Atmospheric Conditions. 70° Fahrenheit (±) 2 degrees (21° Celsius ± 1 degree) and 65 percent relative humidity ± 2 percent. (Chapter 11)

Standard Inspection Procedure (SIP). The guidelines for evaluating garments during inspection. (Chapter 13)

Standard Reference Laundry Detergent. A basic detergent formulation used in a laboratory setting for testing materials and garments. (Chapter 12)

Standardized Color Matching System. Systems used to specify and manage color throughout the design and manufacturing processes. (Chapter 2)

Standardized Test Methods. Procedures for conducting experiments, examining, and evaluating textile materials and apparel products. (Chapter 11)

Standards. Technical documents for test methods and specifications developed and established within the consensus of international, national, federal organizations and agencies, consortiums, or individual companies as a method for producing repeatable results to increase product quality and safety. (Chapter 1)

Staple Fibers. Short fibers ranging in length from ⅜ inch (5 mm) to 19.5 inches (500 mm). (Chapter 3)

Statistical Process Control (SPC) or **Statistical Quality Control (SQC).** A system for measuring and controlling quality that focuses on improving processes and prevention of problems throughout all product producing phases. (Chapter 13)

Stitch. The loop formation created by hand or machine to interlock one or more threads for the purpose of creating surface decoration or seams. (Chapter 6)

Stitching. A series of repeating stitches. (Chapter 6)

Stitch Length. The length of a stitch in measured in millimeters (mm). (Chapter 6)

Stitchless. Seams joined by means of thermal bonding, laser welding, and ultrasonic sealing rather than with thread and stitches. (Chapter 7)

Stitches Per Centimeter (SPC). The number of stitches measured within 1 centimeter. (Chapter 6)

Stitches Per Inch (SPI). The number of stitches measured within 1 inch. (Chapter 6)

Stoddard Solvent. Petroleum based drycleaning solvents. (Chapter 12)

Straight Buttonhole. A zigzag rectangular shaped opening that can accommodate a button to pass through and remain secured. (Chapter 4)

Straight Darts. The legs of the dart converge to a diminishing point creating line segments that are not curved. (Chapter 4)

Straight Grain. Runs in the warp or wale direction of a fabric and is parallel to the selvedge. (Chapter 4)

Straight Seam. Two or more plies of fabric sewn together from one point to another without any curves. (Chapter 4)

Straight Waistband. A straight band of material that is attached at the waistline of a garment to finish the top edge. (Chapter 4)

Stretch Waistband. Elastic is inserted into the waistband to provide elasticity. (Chapter 4)

Strike Back or **Back-bleed.** The appearance of adhesive on the surface of the interlining inside the garment due to over-liquefied resin during fusing. (Chapter 13)

Strike-off. Physical representations of printed fabric that are evaluated against color standards for accuracy of color matching. (Chapter 2)

Strike Through or **Bleed-through.** The appearance of adhesive on the surface of the garment due to over-liquefied resin during fusing. (Chapter 13)

S-twist. Yarn turned or twisted in the right direction, creating diagonal lines that extend from the upper left to the lower right duplicating the same line direction as the middle of the letter S. (Chapter 3)

Subassemblies. Fasteners, closures, stitches, and seams incorporated into a finished product. (Chapter 12)

Substrate. Fibers, yarns, and fabrics. (Chapter 2)

Summary of Test Method, Summary of Practice, or **Principle.** Portion of a test standard providing a concise explanation of the procedure to be performed. (Chapter 11)

Supply Chain. A network of suppliers, manufacturers, and retailers responsible for producing, handling, and distributing products. (Chapter 8)

Supply Chain Management. The integration of business functions combined with the expertise, resources, and organized efforts from suppliers, manufacturers, and retailers to manage the flow of raw materials through production, distribution, and sale to the end user. (Chapter 8)

Support Materials. Separate plies of fabrics used to reinforce portions of a garment to achieve desired silhouettes or shaping. (Chapter 3)

Surface Active Molecules/Surface Active Agents/Surfactants. Molecules found in soaps and detergents that aid in wetting and cleaning. They are composed of two parts—a carboxylate head that is hydrophilic (water-loving) and a hydrocarbon chain tail that is hydrophobic (water-repelling). (Chapter 12)

Surface Embellishments. Materials applied to the surface of a garment to add decoration such as applique, beads, embossing, embroidery, foiling, rhinestones, screen printing, sequins, and trapunto. (Chapter 3)

Surface Flash. When a flame quickly spreads across the surface of the fabric but ignition of the base materials does not occur. (Chapter 10)

Symmetric (Formal Balance). When a garment is vertically divided into two equal sides that appear identical. (Chapter 2)

Synthetic Detergents. Cleaning substances composed of petrochemicals or oleochemicals, alcohol, and sulfate used for laundering many apparel products. (Chapter 12)

Tack Buttons. A metal button containing a shank that attaches to the garment by means of a tack with a prong. (Chapter 4)

Tailored Placket. Two strips of unequal lengths of fabric are stitched to encase the raw edges of the opening. The narrower strip is hidden while the wider strip shows on the face of the garment when closed. (Chapter 4)

Target Market Research (Consumer Trend Research). Demographic and lifestyle-data gathered and analyzed based on a brand's customer. (Chapter 2)

Target Market Research. The examination of demographic and lifestyle data for both existing and potential customers within specific market segments. (Chapter 1)

Tearing Strength. Amount of force that can be applied to a material to continue a tear. (Chapter 12)

Technical Advisory Group (TAG). The organization that represents the United States (U.S.) in all ISO TC 38 Textile Committee actions. (Chapter 1)

Technical Packages/Production Package/Tech Pack. Detailed documents that include important information pertaining to the development, assembly, and packaging of a garment. (Chapter 5)

Technician Error or **Observer Error.** When a scale is misread. (Chapter 11)

Tensile Strength. Ability to resist tension before rupturing or breaking. (Chapter 12)

Terminology. Important terms used within the test standard. (Chapter 11)

Testing. Procedures for evaluating materials, component parts, and completed garments. (Chapter 11)

Test Method Name. Title of the test standard that distinguishes the type of test covered within the standard. (Chapter 11)

Test Method Number. Numeric configuration that identifies the test standard. (Chapter 11)

Test Methods. Specific technical procedures for conducting and gathering test results for identification, measurement, and evaluation purposes. (Chapter 1)

Tex (tex). Mass per unit length of spun yarns from silk or manufactured fibers measured in grams per 1,000 meters. (Chapter 3)

Textile Fiber Products Identification Act (TFPIA). U.S. labeling regulation 16 CFR 303 for disclosing fiber content, registered identification number or identity of manufacturer, or importer, distributor, or retailer, and country of origin on garment labels. (Chapter 9)

Textile Finishes. Mechanical or chemical treatments to fabrics to change their aesthetic or performance properties to produce a desired effect for the end product. (Chapter 3)

Textile Goods Quality Labeling Regulations. Japanese labeling regulation requiring garment labels to accurately disclose fiber content, country of origin, water repellency, manufacturer identification information, and care. (Chapter 9)

Textile Labelling and Advertising Regulations (TLAR). Canadian labeling regulation C.R.C., c.1551 for listing required accurate disclosure of fiber content and identification of the manufacturer, importer, or distributer on garment labels. (Chapter 9)

Textile Products (Labelling and Fibre Composition) Regulations. Regulation enacted for the United Kingdom (UK) and all member states as well as the European Union (EU) for accurate disclosure of fiber content on garment labels. (Chapter 9)

Texture. The surface contour or visual interest that influences the aesthetic appearance of textile products. (Chapter 2)

Textured Thread. Continuous filament fibers that have been heat set to create texture and add bulk. (Chapter 6)

Thermal Bonded Seams. Seam components are glued together using thermoplastic film adhesives. (Chapter 7)

The Rule of Thirds. Dividing a design into three unequal portions in an effort to control where the viewer's eyes are drawn. (Chapter 2)

Thin Place. Fabric defect in which the yarns are thinner and more loosely spaced in comparison to the rest of the fabric. (Chapter 13)

Thread Discoloration. Change in the thread color of garment stitching caused by the pickup of excess dye from the fabric during wet processing. (Chapter 13)

Thread Size. The linear density or mass per unit length of thread; thickness or diameter of thread. (Chapter 6)

Thread Specifications. Detailed information describing thread size and composition for each sewing operation of a garment, performance requirements, and color standards for manufacturing. (Chapter 5)

Thread Tension. The relationship among sewing threads that comprise stitching. (Chapter 6)

Ticket Number. The amount of raw fiber contained in an unfinished sewing thread. (Chapter 6)

Ties. Opposing pairs of ribbon or strips of fabric used to secure a garment. (Chapter 4)

Tightened Inspection (Level III). A heightened level that requires more shipments to be inspected due to the number of defects that exceed the acceptance quality limit. (Chapter 13)

Tight-fitting Sleepwear. Children's sleepwear that fits very closely to the body that is designed and produced based on maximum garment measurements to reduce the risk of the garment catching fire. (Chapter 10)

Tow. Filament fiber that has been cut into staple lengths. (Chapter 3)

Toxicity. A safety hazard resulting from chemical substances used in some apparel products that come in contact with the wearer's skin and cause skin sensitivity and some substances are carcinogenic. (Chapter 10)

Transfer Machines. Drycleaning equipment composed of a machine where the clothes were cleaned and then moved to another machine to be dried. (Chapter 12)

Trend Forecasting Services. Companies that predict and provide seasonal color, materials, and style direction based on research of global mega trends, political, social, and cultural trends, as well as consumer behavior, lifestyle changes, and stimuli from various types of media outlets. (Chapter 2)

Trim. Decorative linear materials attached to the surface of the garment or inserted and sewn into a seam to enhance the design such as braid, cording, fringe, lace, passementerie, piping (cordedge), and ribbon. (Chapter 3)

Trim Sheet. Part of a technical package that details trim specification information for the production of a garment. (Chapter 5)

Trouser Fly Zipper Insertion. A facing is stitched to the zipper and extends beyond the center to hide the other side of the zipper that is stitched to a fabric underlay. (Chapter 4)

Trouser Waistband (Curtain Waistband). A commercially prepared waistband material containing a reinforced bias strip is stitched to the top edge of the waistband and allowed to hang free at the bottom edge. (Chapter 4)

True Bias. Grain that runs at a 45° angle from the intersection of straight and cross-grains. (Chapter 4)

Tucks. Fabric that is folded back on itself along the grainline and stitched down completely or partially then released. (Chapter 4)

Turns Per Centimeter (tpcm). The amount of twist applied to a yarn measured in centimeters. (Chapter 3)

Turns Per Inch (tpi). The amount of twist applied to a yarn measured in inches. (Chapter 3)

Turns Per Meter. The amount of twist applied to a yarn measured in meters. (Chapter 3)

Twill Weave. Woven structure formed using three or more harnesses whereas the shuttle carrying the filling yarn crosses over two or more warp yarns then passes under one or more yarns, creating a diagonal line to the right or left in subsequent rows. (Chapter 3)

Twisted Garment. Side seams of a garment that wrap to the front or back and distort the appearance. (Chapter 13)

Ultrasonic Sealing. High-frequency sound waves used to create friction between thermoplastic fibers of a fabric that produces enough heat to melt the material to fuse it together. (Chapter 7)

Ultrasonic Slitting. High-frequency sound waves used to cut and seal fabric edges of thermoplastic fiber fabrics. (Chapter 7)

Unbalanced Plain Weave. Plain weave structure having different warp yarns than filling yarns in size, type, and amount. (Chapter 3)

Unbalanced Stitch Tension. Stitching that is too tight causing puckers along the stitch line or seam, or too loose causing seam grin. (Chapter 13)

Unbalanced Thread Tension. When the thread tension for stitching is too tight or too loose, impacting the appearance, smoothness, and performance of stitching or seam construction. (Chapter 6)

Under-fusing. Weak bond between the interlining and shell materials due to insufficient heat, time, or pressure during fusing. (Chapter 13)

Uneven Seams. The measured difference in the length of seams that should be identical. (Chapter 13)

Uneven Twill. Unbalanced twill weave having more yarns on the face (known as **warp-faced twill**) or more on the back (known as **weft-faced twill**). (Chapter 3)

Unit Production System. A production method that utilizes assembly line production methods but individual garments are loaded into carriers that are electronically transported from operation to operation until the garment is completely assembled. (Chapter 8)

Unraveling Buttonhole. Buttonhole stitching that has not been secured at the end or that has been severed. (Chapter 13)

Unrelated Seam. An unintended seam in a garment caused by an area that is caught in the seam. (Chapter 13)

User-defined Quality. The ability of a product to meet individual customers' needs and wants in relation to their personal preferences for garment attributes and value. (Chapter 1)

Value (Luminance). The tints, midtones, and shade variations of a color. (Chapter 2)

Vanity Sizing. A method for sizing garments that appeals to an individual's ego by labeling a garment as a smaller size than its measured dimensions. (Chapter 5)

Virtual Prototype. Digital simulation of a garment developed using specialized software programs to convert two-dimensional pattern pieces into three-dimensional garments. (Chapter 5)

Visible Stay Stitching. Temporary stitching used to stabilize the fabric to prevent stretching or distortion from occurring during sewing that has not been removed or concealed within the garment. (Chapter 13)

Voluntary Standards. Test methods and specifications that are not enforced by law but are utilized to maintain quality standards that are developed by retailers, manufacturers, importers, government agencies, and consumers through consensus between all parties. (Chapter 1)

Wales. The vertical rows of knit stitches or loops that run in the lengthwise direction in knitted fabrics. (Chapter 3)

Warp-faced Satin. Woven fabric containing warp yarns that float on the surface before passing under one filling yarn. (Chapter 3)

Water Soluble Soils. Substances capable of dissolving in water. Examples include sugar, salt, syrup, dust, clay, and perspiration. (Chapter 12)

Water Spots. Discolorations on fabric caused by improper drying or contaminated water during dyeing. (Chapter 13)

Wavy Seam. A seam that does not lie flat. (Chapter 13)

Wear Testing or **Wear-service Conditions.** Garment samples are worn and evaluated to determine performance and appearance characteristic of the item in use. (Chapter 11)

Weft-faced Satin. Woven fabric containing filling yarns that float on the surface before passing under one warp yarn. (Chapter 3)

Wetcleaning/Organic Drycleaning. Cleaning process similar to laundering that can be used for cleaning fabrics typically intended for drycleaning. (Chapter 12)

Wet Prints. Liquid dyes mixed with thickening agents to form a paste that is printed onto fabric to form a pattern on the surface. (Chapter 3)

Wetting. The process allows material to be immersed in water or an aqueous solution and become moistened or wet. (Chapter 12)

Wool Products Labeling (WPL) Number. A number issued and registered by the U.S. Federal Trade Commission for the purpose of identifying the manufacturer, importer, or distributor of apparel products. The FTC no longer issues WPL numbers. (Chapter 9)

Wool Products Labeling Act of 1939. U.S. labeling regulation 16 CFR 300 for labeling garments containing wool, outlining disclosing of fiber content, registered identification number or identity of manufacturer, or importer, distributor or retailer, and country of origin. (Chapter 9)

Woolen Run (wr or **Nwe).** Linear density in length per unit mass of coarse woolen and woolen blended yarns measured in 1,600 yard lengths per pound. (Chapter 3)

Work Flow. The planned sequence for the movement of a garment through the production process. (Chapter 8)

Work in Process or **Work in Progress.** The amount of raw materials or number of garments that are not yet complete at any given time during manufacturing. (Chapter 8)

Working Pattern. A pattern that is in the process of being evaluated for design, fit, and modified for production. (Chapter 2)

Worsted Count (wc or Nww). Linear density in length per unit mass of fine worsted wool and worsted wool blends, and acrylic yarns measured in 560 yard lengths per pound. (Chapter 3)

Wrinkle Recovery. Elasticity to bounce back after being subjected to compression or deformation. (Chapter 12)

Wrinkle Resistant. Material's ability to oppose deformations resulting from folding or bending. (Chapter 12)

Wrong Grain. Garment panels are not cut on the designated grain. (Chapter 13)

Wrong Thread Color. Mismatched thread color. (Chapter 13)

Wrong Thread Type and Size. Improper thread construction. (Chapter 13)

Yarn Construction. Structure of the yarn including yarn number, twist direction, and number of turns per inch, per centimeter, or per meter. (Chapter 11)

Yarn Construction. The structure of the yarn. (Chapter 3)

Yarn Number. Method for measuring a yarn's fineness. (Chapter 3)

Yarn Number. Measurement of a yarn's fineness. (Chapter 11)

Yoke. A horizontal panel used to shape a garment at the seam where it is joined; used in lieu of darts. (Chapter 4)

Zipper. A fastener with molded plastic or metal teeth or coils that is used to open and close a garment. (Chapter 4)

Z-twist. Yarn turned or twisted in the left direction, creating diagonal lines that extend from the upper right to the lower left, duplicating the same line direction as the middle of the letter Z. (Chapter 3)

APPENDIX

Measurement Units	
U.S. Customary Units	SI Units
Length	
Inch (in)	Centimeter (cm)
Feet (ft)	Millimeters (mm)
Yard (yd)	Meter (m)
Area	
Square inch (in^2)	Square centimeter (cm^2)
Square foot (ft^2)	Square millimeter (mm^2)
Square yard (yd^2)	Square meter (m^2)
Mass	
Ounces (oz)	Grams (g)
Ounces per square yard (oz/yd^2)	Grams per square meter (g/m^2)

Note: SI = International System of Units; U.S. Customary Units = English System.

Convert U.S. Customary Units to SI Units		
U.S. Customary Unit	Multiply By	To Get SI Unit
Length Conversions		
in	2.54	cm
in	25.4	mm
ft	304.8	mm
ft	0.3048	m
yd	0.9144	m
Area		
in^2	6.4516	cm^2
in^2	645	mm^2
yd^2	0.83612736	m^2
Mass		
oz	28.35	g
oz/yd^2	33.90575	g/m^2

Convert SI Units to U.S. Customary Units		
SI Unit	Multiply By	To Get U.S. Customary Unit
Length Conversions		
cm	0.3937	in
mm	0.03937	in
mm	0.00328	ft
m	3.28084	ft
m	1.09361	yd
Area		
cm^2	0.1550	in^2
mm^2	0.00155	in^2
m^2	1.19599	yd^2
Mass		
g	0.0353	oz
g/m^2	0.0294935	oz/yd^2

U.S. Customary Units to SI Units					
	in	ft	yd	cm	mm
⅛	0.125			0.317	3.175
³⁄₁₆	0.188			0.477	4.775
¼	0.250			0.635	6.350
⅜	0.375			0.952	9.525
½	0.500			1.270	12.700
⅝	0.625			1.587	15.875
¾	0.750			1.905	19.050
1	1.000			2.540	25.400
1¼			1.250	3.175	31.750
1½			1.500	3.810	38.100
1¾			1.750	4.445	44.450
2	2.000			5.080	50.800
2¼			2.250	5.715	57.150
2½			2.500	6.350	63.500
2¾			2.750	6.985	69.850
3	3.000			7.620	76.200
3¼			3.250	8.255	82.550
3½			3.500	8.890	88.900
3¾			3.750	9.525	95.250
4	4.000			10.160	101.600
4¼			4.250	10.795	107.950
4½			4.500	11.430	114.300
4¾			4.750	12.065	120.650
5	5.000			12.700	127.000
5¼			5.250	13.335	133.350
5½			5.500	13.970	139.700
5¾			5.750	14.605	146.050
6	6.000	½ foot		15.240	152.400
6¼			6.250	15.875	158.750
6½			6.500	16.510	165.100

U.S. Customary Units to SI Units					
	in	ft	yd	cm	mm
6¾			6.750	17.145	171.450
7	7.000		17.780	17.780	177.800
7¼			7.250	18.415	184.150
7½			7.500	19.050	190.500
7¾			7.750	19.685	196.850
8	8.000			20.320	203.200
8¼			8.250	20.955	209.550
8½			8.500	21.590	215.900
8¾			8.750	22.225	222.500
9	9.000			22.860	228.600
9¼			9.250	23.495	234.950
9½			9.500	24.130	241.300
9¾			9.750	24.765	247.650
10	10.000		25.400	254.000	
10¼			10.250	26.035	260.350
10½			10.500	26.670	266.700
10¾			10.750	27.305	273.050
11	11.000		27.940	279.400	
11¼			11.250	28.575	285.750
11½			11.500	29.210	292.100
11¾			11.750	29.845	298.450
12	12.000	1 foot		30.480	304.800
24	24.000	2 feet		60.960	609.600
36	36.000	3 feet	1 yard	91.440	914.400
48	48.000	4 feet		121.920	1,219.200
60	60.000	5 feet		152.400	1,524.000
96	96.000	8 feet		243.840	2,438.400
108	108.000	9 feet	3 yards	274.320	2,743.200
120	120.000	10 feet		304.800	3,048.000

INDEX

lingerie hooks, 81, 82f
linking, 69
lock stitch machines, 125, 125f
lockstitches, 123–24, 123f, 124f
logistics, 174
looms, 45
looping, 69
loose buttons, 310, 310f
loose thread ends, 310, 310f
loose-fitting sleepwear, 226–27
lot samples, 242
LS lapped seam class, 146–50, 151f, 152f, 153f
Lululemon, 260b

M

maintenance, cost of, 5
major defects, 303
make-through production systems, 184–85, 185t
mandatory standards, defined, 12
manity sizing, 92
manufactured fibers, 40, 41t, 249, 251
manufacturer-defined quality approach, 4, 5
manufacturing. *See also* production processes
  in apparel industry structure, 174
  factory layouts, 178
  offshore *vs.* domestic, 175–76
  production capacity, 176
  production systems, 180–86, 182–84t, 185t
  production-related defects, 308–14
  quality compliance, 15–16
  quality inspections, 298–302
  time-based strategies, 176–77
markers, 178–79, 179f
market and global trends research, 24
materials. *See* fabrics, selection and performance of; raw materials, selection and performance of
Me-Ality, 93
mean, calculating, 241
mechanical bonds, 163
melting point, 253, 253t
men's wear, sizing of, 92
metamerism, 26, 26f
metric count, 112
micelles, 267, 267f
microscope objectives, 250
microscopic observation, 250, 250f, 251f

Minister of Economy, Japan, 207
minor defects, 303
misaligned plies, 307
mismatched fabric design, 307, 308f
misregister defects, 306
Mitford, Kathleen, 175
moderate price point, 7
modular production systems, 185, 185f, 185t
modulus, 283
moiré effect, 308
moisture equilibrium, 245–46, 246t
moisture sensing, 270
molecules, 246
monofilament thread, 110, 110f

N

National Retail Federation, 92
National Standard of Canada—Care Labelling of Textiles, 202
National Standards Body (NSB), 13
National Standards System (NSS), 14
natural fibers, 40–42, 41t, 249–50
nearshore production, 175
needle damage, 310, 310f
needle line defects, 306
needle size, 112
Nickel Directive, UK, 216–17
nickel toxicity, 216–17
nightwear, 227
The Nightwear (Safety) Regulations (1985), UK, 228–29
Nike, 189b
no inspections, 295
nondestructive tests, 248
non-slip backed waistbands, 78f
nonvolatile residue (NVR), 272
nonwoven fabrics, 48
Normal Flammability (Class 1), 222
normal inspection, 296
normative references, 241, 286
NSB (National Standards Body), 13
NSS (National Standards System), 14
numeric sizing, 90
NVR (nonvolatile residue), 272

O

observer error, 241
ODM (original design manufacturing), 177
OEKO-TEX Association, 231
OEM (original equipment manufacturing), 177

off-grain fabrics, 63, 63f
Office of Textiles and Apparel (OTEXA), 196, 218
offloading, pre-assembly, 180, 181f
offshore production, 175–76
oleochemicals, 267
100 class chain stitches, 119–21, 119f, 120f
100 percent inspection, 295
on-grain fabrics, 63, 63f
onshore production, 175
open seams, 310, 310f
openings, 71, 76–77
optical brighteners, 49, 50t, 51t
organizational structure, apparel industry, 174–75
original design manufacturing (ODM), 177
original equipment manufacturing (OEM), 177
ornamental-class seams, 154–55, 156f
ornamentation, 198, 203
OS ornamental seam class, 154–55, 156f
oscillating action, 268, 269f
OTEXA (International Trade Associations Office of Textiles), 196, 218
overcutting, 275–76, 286
overedge chain stitches, 125, 129f, 130f, 131f, 132f
over-edge hems, 82, 83f
over-fusing, 308
overlock machines, 125, 133f
over-run stitching, 311, 311f
oxidizing bleach, 270
oxygen bleach, 271–72

P

package contractors, 177
pajamas, 227
parallax error, 241, 241f
Pareto charts, 294
patterns
  in design development process, 25, 27, 28t, 29f
  grading, 25, 60
  quality inspections, 297
PBB (flame retardants), 221
PBDEs (flame retardants), 221
PCBs (flame retardants), 221
PDM (product data management), 174–75
penalty points, 298, 298t
perc (perchloroethylene)-based solvents, 272–73